QUANTUM AND WOODY
BY PRIEST & BRIGHT

AND SO...

CHRISTOPHER PRIEST | MD BRIGHT | GREG ADAMS

CONTENTS

Quantum & Woody created by MD Bright & Priest

Collection Cover Art: MD Bright

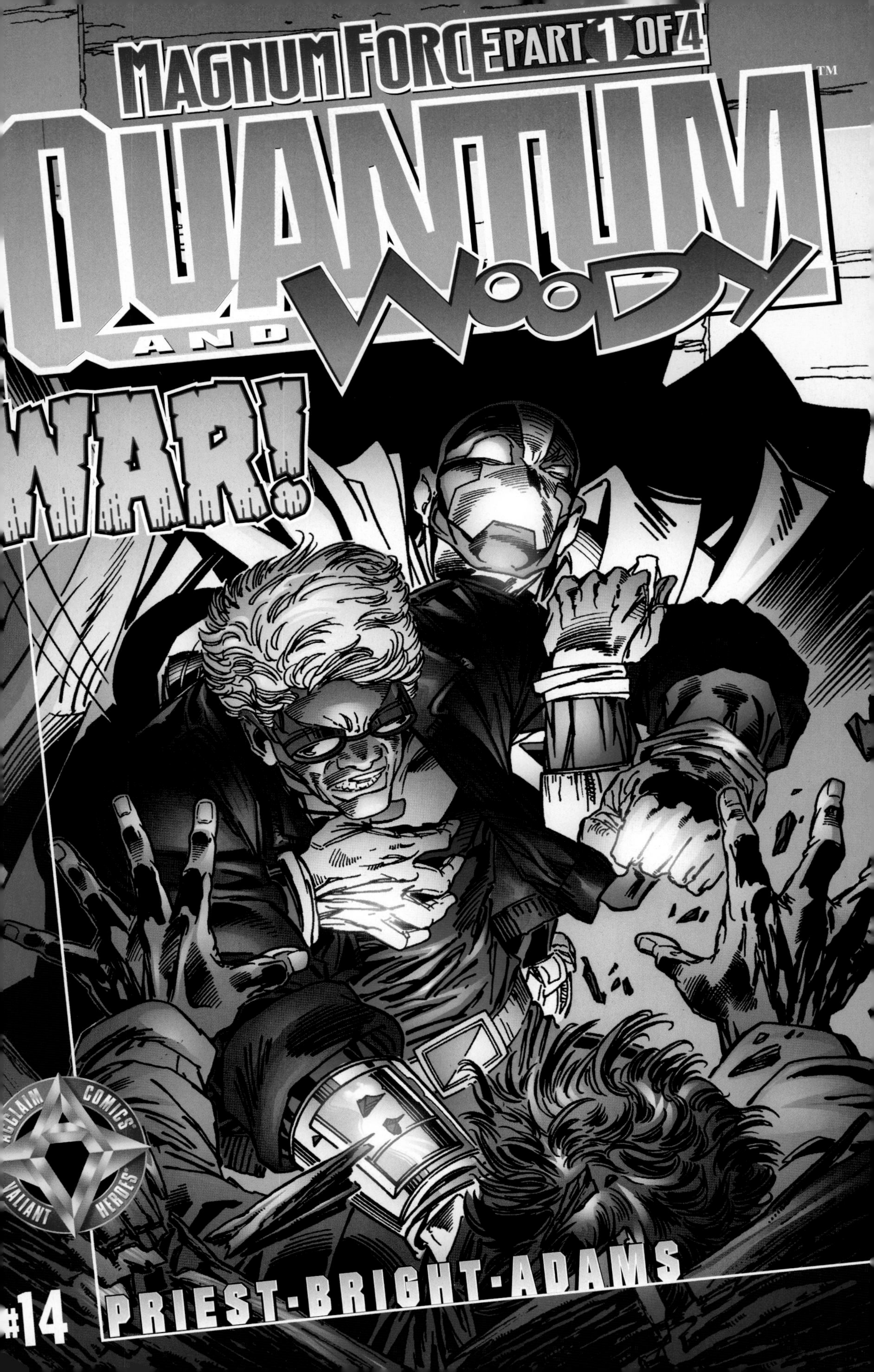
MAGNUM FORCE PART 1 OF 4
QUANTUM AND WOODY
WAR!
ACCLAIM COMICS VALIANT HEROES
#14
PRIEST-BRIGHT-ADAMS

"Retread City"

MAGNUM!!!

GUILTY AS CHARGED.

WHAMMM

COME ON *IN,* GENTLEMEN. I OBVIOUSLY CAN'T *STOP* YOU. I CONFESS AND SURRENDER.

EVERY MAN *MUST* KNOW HIS LIMITATIONS.

GO ON -- TAKE IT. IT'S ON THE DESK.

"IT'S ON THE DESK?"

NOW-- WHY POUR TEA--

--WHEN YOU'VE GOT A *COLA*--?

"MAGNUM HAD PART OF A *CIRCUIT BOARD*--

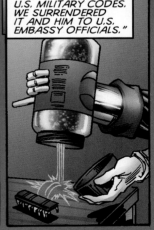

"--A PIECE OF A *DECRYPTION DEVICE* THAT COULD READ *U.S. MILITARY CODES.* WE SURRENDERED IT AND HIM TO U.S. EMBASSY OFFICIALS."

"The Plan"

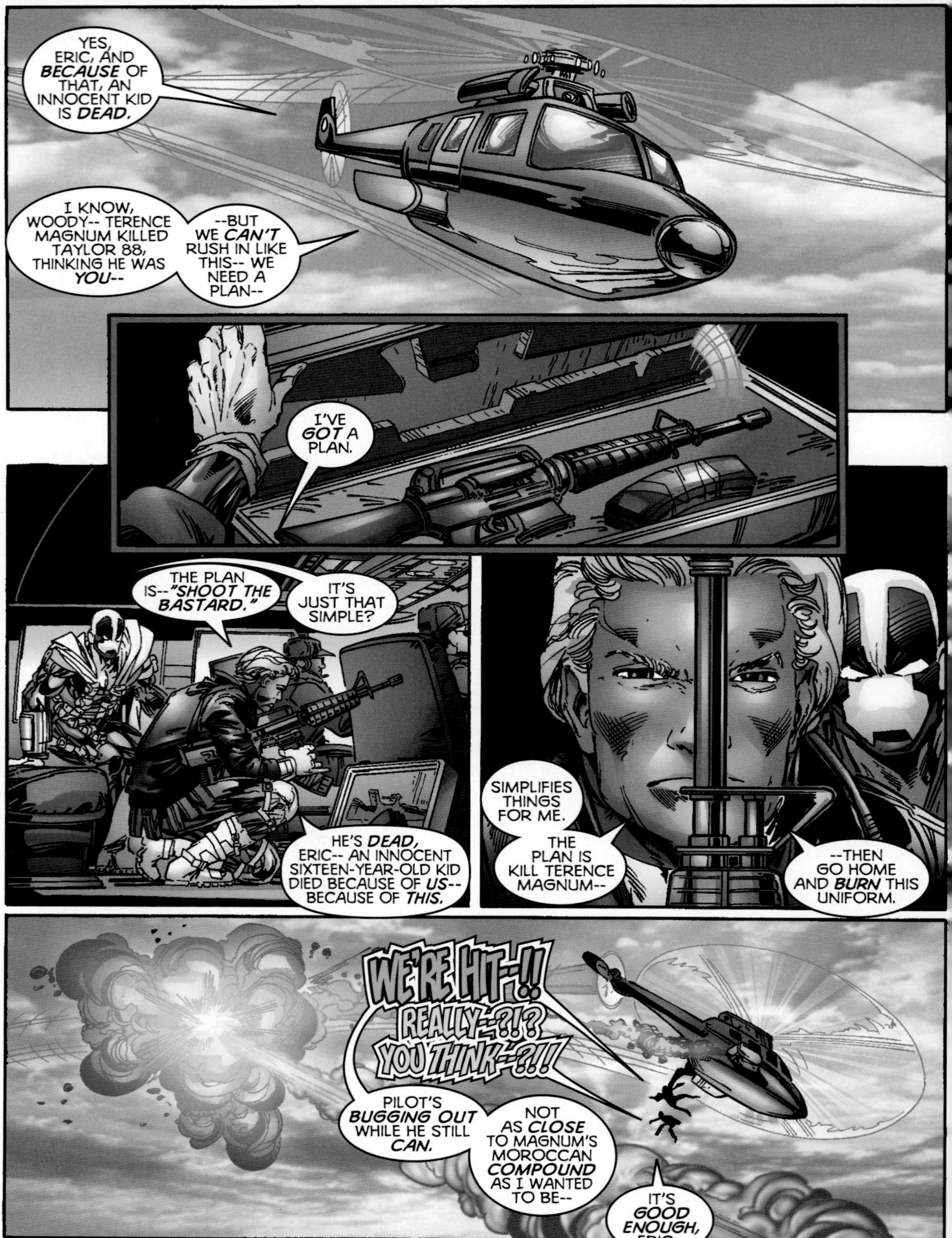

YES, ERIC, AND BECAUSE OF THAT, AN INNOCENT KID IS DEAD.
I KNOW, WOODY-- TERENCE MAGNUM KILLED TAYLOR 88, THINKING HE WAS YOU--
--BUT WE CAN'T RUSH IN LIKE THIS-- WE NEED A PLAN--
I'VE GOT A PLAN.
THE PLAN IS--"SHOOT THE BASTARD."
IT'S JUST THAT SIMPLE?
HE'S DEAD, ERIC-- AN INNOCENT SIXTEEN-YEAR-OLD KID DIED BECAUSE OF US-- BECAUSE OF THIS.
SIMPLIFIES THINGS FOR ME.
THE PLAN IS KILL TERENCE MAGNUM--
--THEN GO HOME AND BURN THIS UNIFORM.
WE'RE HIT--!!
REALLY--?!?
YOU THINK--?!!
PILOT'S BUGGING OUT WHILE HE STILL CAN.
NOT AS CLOSE TO MAGNUM'S MOROCCAN COMPOUND AS I WANTED TO BE--
IT'S GOOD ENOUGH, ERIC--

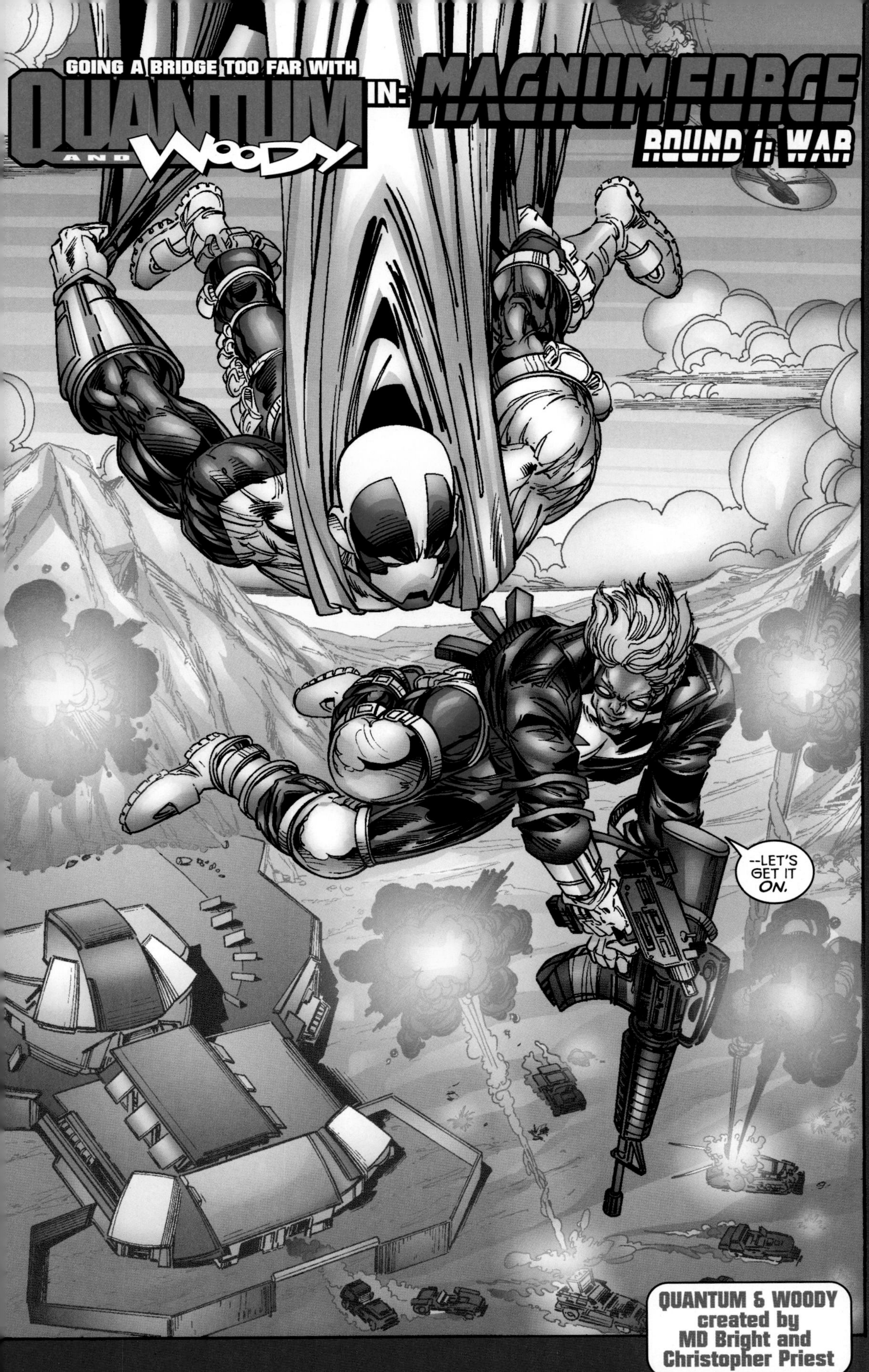
GOING A BRIDGE TOO FAR WITH
QUANTUM AND WOODY
IN: MAGNUM FORCE
ROUND 1: WAR
--LET'S GET IT ON.
QUANTUM & WOODY created by MD Bright and Christopher Priest

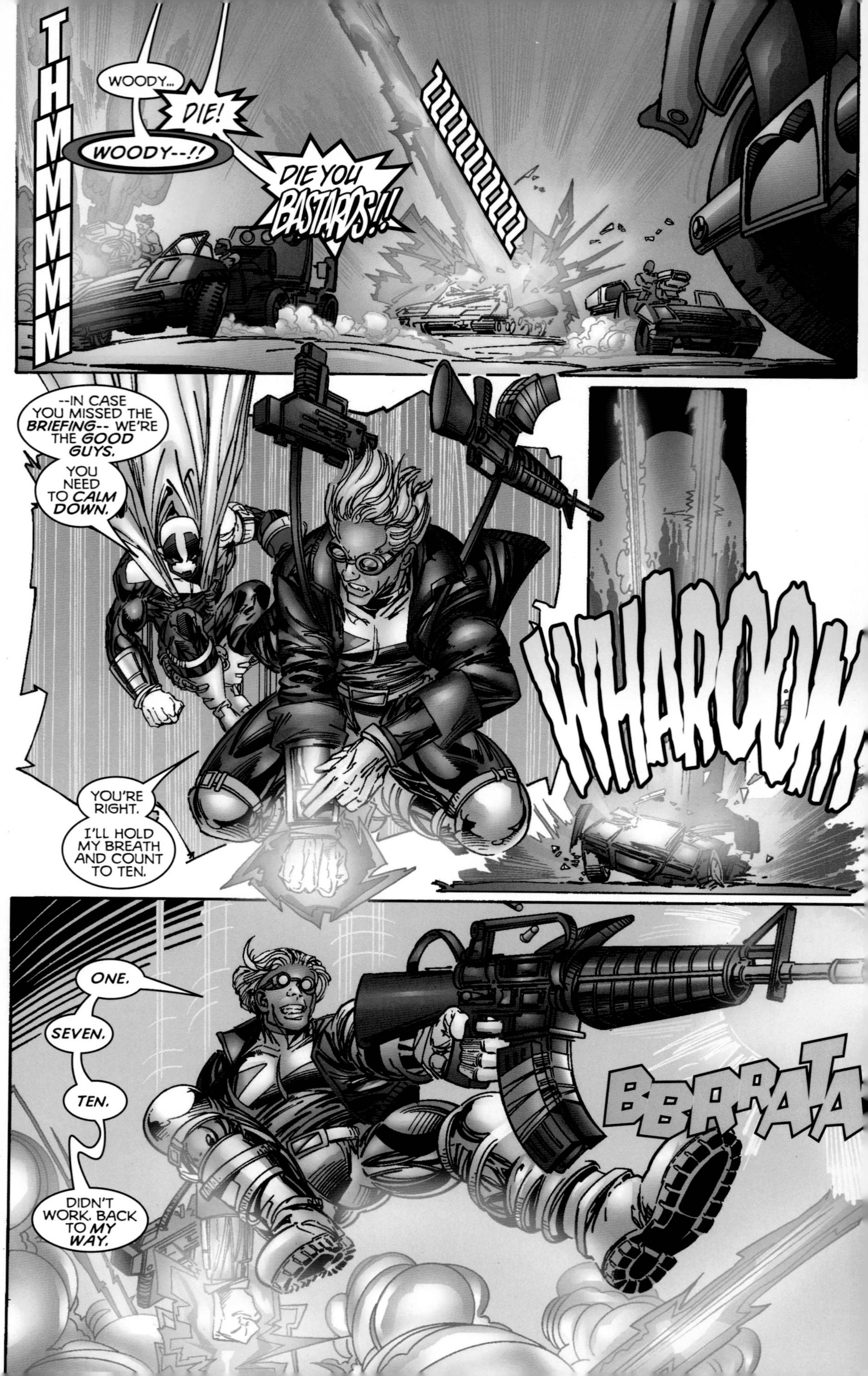
THMMMMM
WOODY...
DIE!
WOODY--!!
DIE YOU BASTARDS!!
--IN CASE YOU MISSED THE BRIEFING-- WE'RE THE GOOD GUYS.
YOU NEED TO CALM DOWN.
WHAROOM
YOU'RE RIGHT.
I'LL HOLD MY BREATH AND COUNT TO TEN.
ONE.
SEVEN.
TEN.
DIDN'T WORK. BACK TO MY WAY.
BBRRATAT

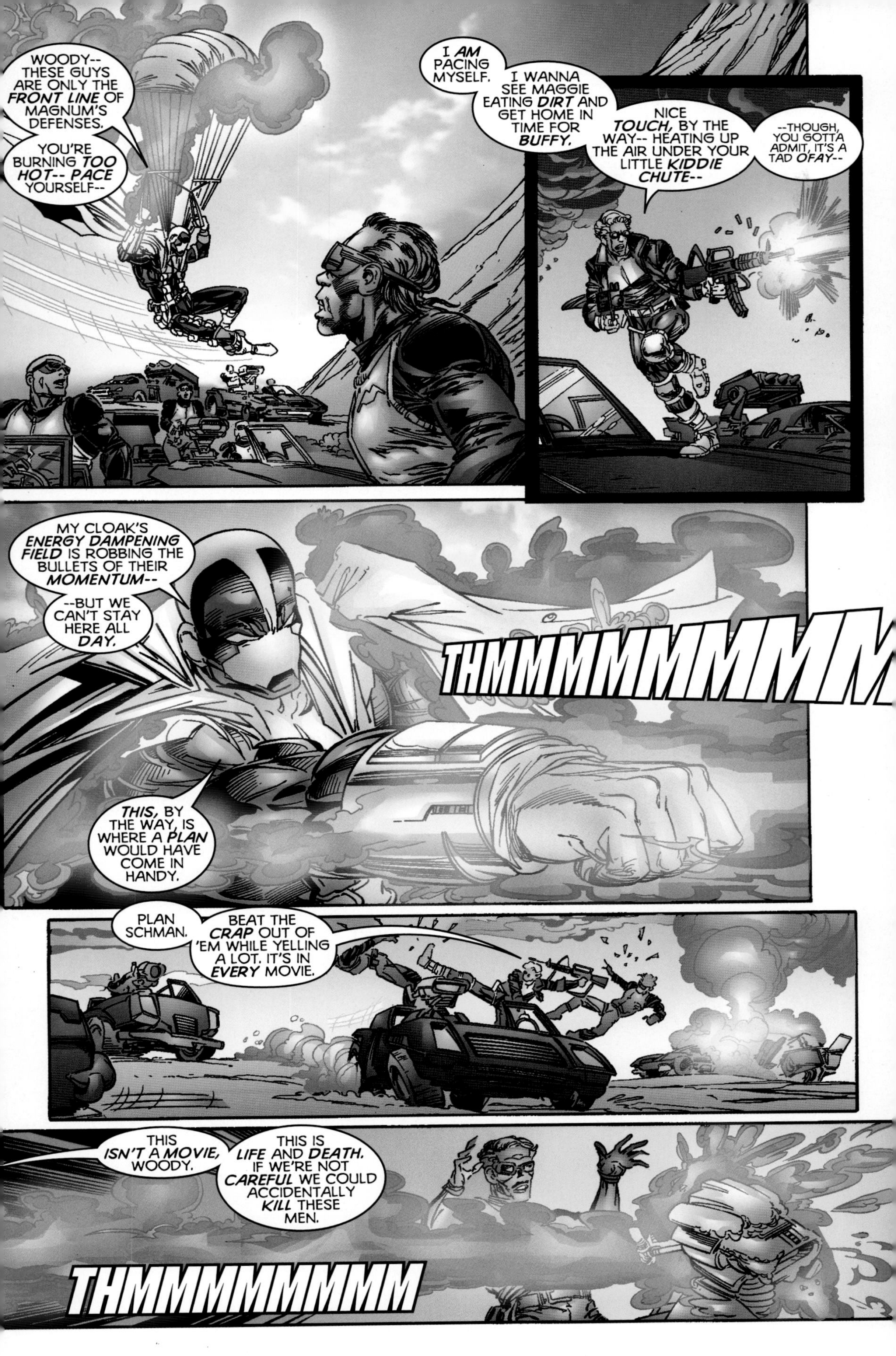
WOODY-- THESE GUYS ARE ONLY THE FRONT LINE OF MAGNUM'S DEFENSES.
YOU'RE BURNING TOO HOT-- PACE YOURSELF--
I AM PACING MYSELF.
I WANNA SEE MAGGIE EATING DIRT AND GET HOME IN TIME FOR BUFFY.
NICE TOUCH, BY THE WAY-- HEATING UP THE AIR UNDER YOUR LITTLE KIDDIE CHUTE--
--THOUGH, YOU GOTTA ADMIT, IT'S A TAD OFAY--
MY CLOAK'S ENERGY DAMPENING FIELD IS ROBBING THE BULLETS OF THEIR MOMENTUM--
--BUT WE CAN'T STAY HERE ALL DAY.
THMMMMMMMMMM
THIS, BY THE WAY, IS WHERE A PLAN WOULD HAVE COME IN HANDY.
PLAN SCHMAN.
BEAT THE CRAP OUT OF 'EM WHILE YELLING A LOT. IT'S IN EVERY MOVIE.
THIS ISN'T A MOVIE, WOODY.
THIS IS LIFE AND DEATH. IF WE'RE NOT CAREFUL WE COULD ACCIDENTALLY KILL THESE MEN.
THMMMMMMMMMM

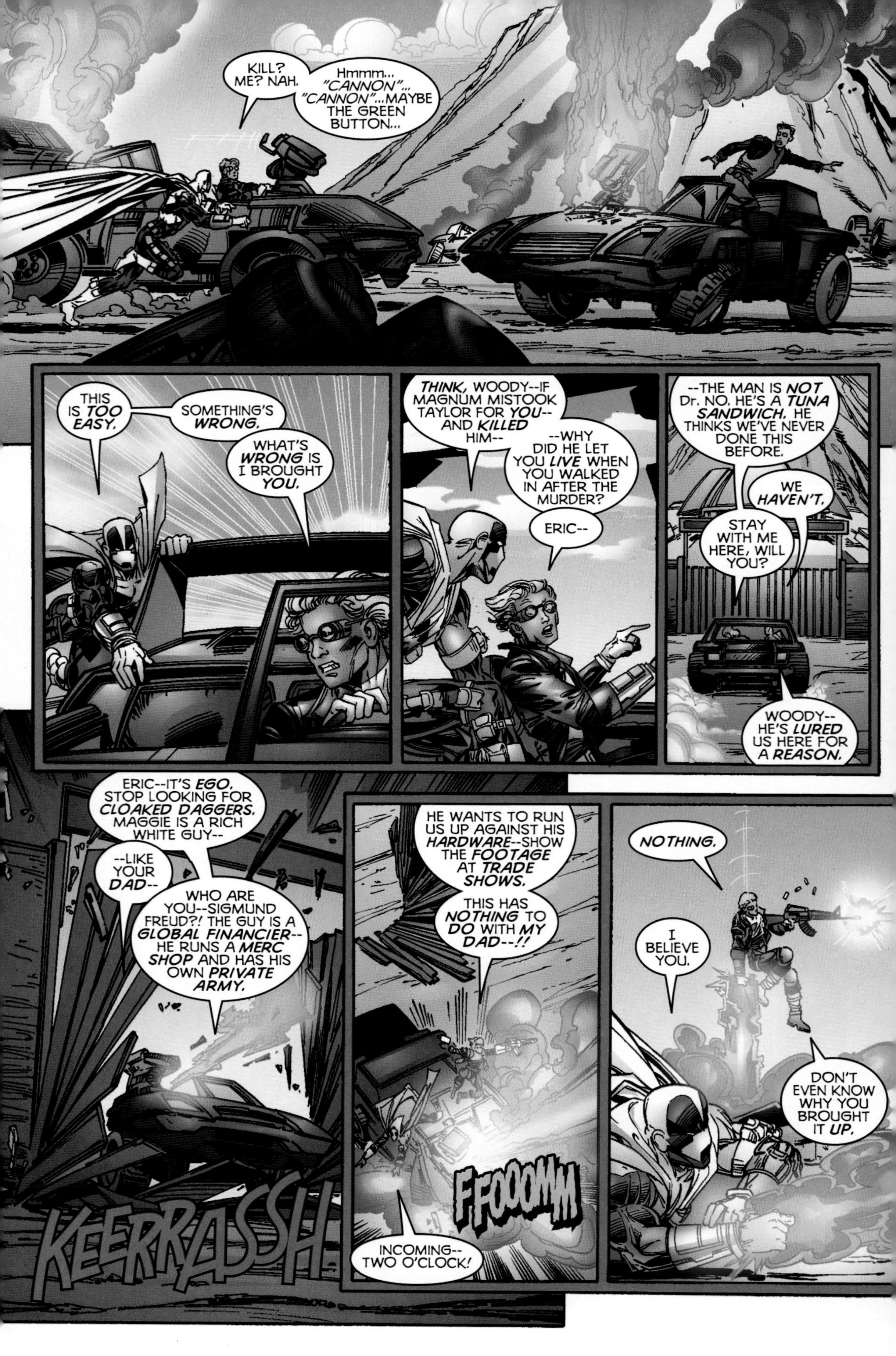
KILL? ME? NAH.
Hmmm... "CANNON"... "CANNON"...MAYBE THE GREEN BUTTON...
THIS IS TOO EASY.
SOMETHING'S WRONG.
WHAT'S WRONG IS I BROUGHT YOU.
THINK, WOODY--IF MAGNUM MISTOOK TAYLOR FOR YOU--AND KILLED HIM--
--WHY DID HE LET YOU LIVE WHEN YOU WALKED IN AFTER THE MURDER?
ERIC--
--THE MAN IS NOT Dr. NO. HE'S A TUNA SANDWICH. HE THINKS WE'VE NEVER DONE THIS BEFORE.
WE HAVEN'T.
STAY WITH ME HERE, WILL YOU?
WOODY--HE'S LURED US HERE FOR A REASON.
ERIC--IT'S EGO. STOP LOOKING FOR CLOAKED DAGGERS. MAGGIE IS A RICH WHITE GUY--
--LIKE YOUR DAD--
WHO ARE YOU--SIGMUND FREUD?! THE GUY IS A GLOBAL FINANCIER--HE RUNS A MERC SHOP AND HAS HIS OWN PRIVATE ARMY.
KEERRASSH
HE WANTS TO RUN US UP AGAINST HIS HARDWARE--SHOW THE FOOTAGE AT TRADE SHOWS.
THIS HAS NOTHING TO DO WITH MY DAD--!!
FFOOOMM
INCOMING--TWO O'CLOCK!
NOTHING.
I BELIEVE YOU.
DON'T EVEN KNOW WHY YOU BROUGHT IT UP.

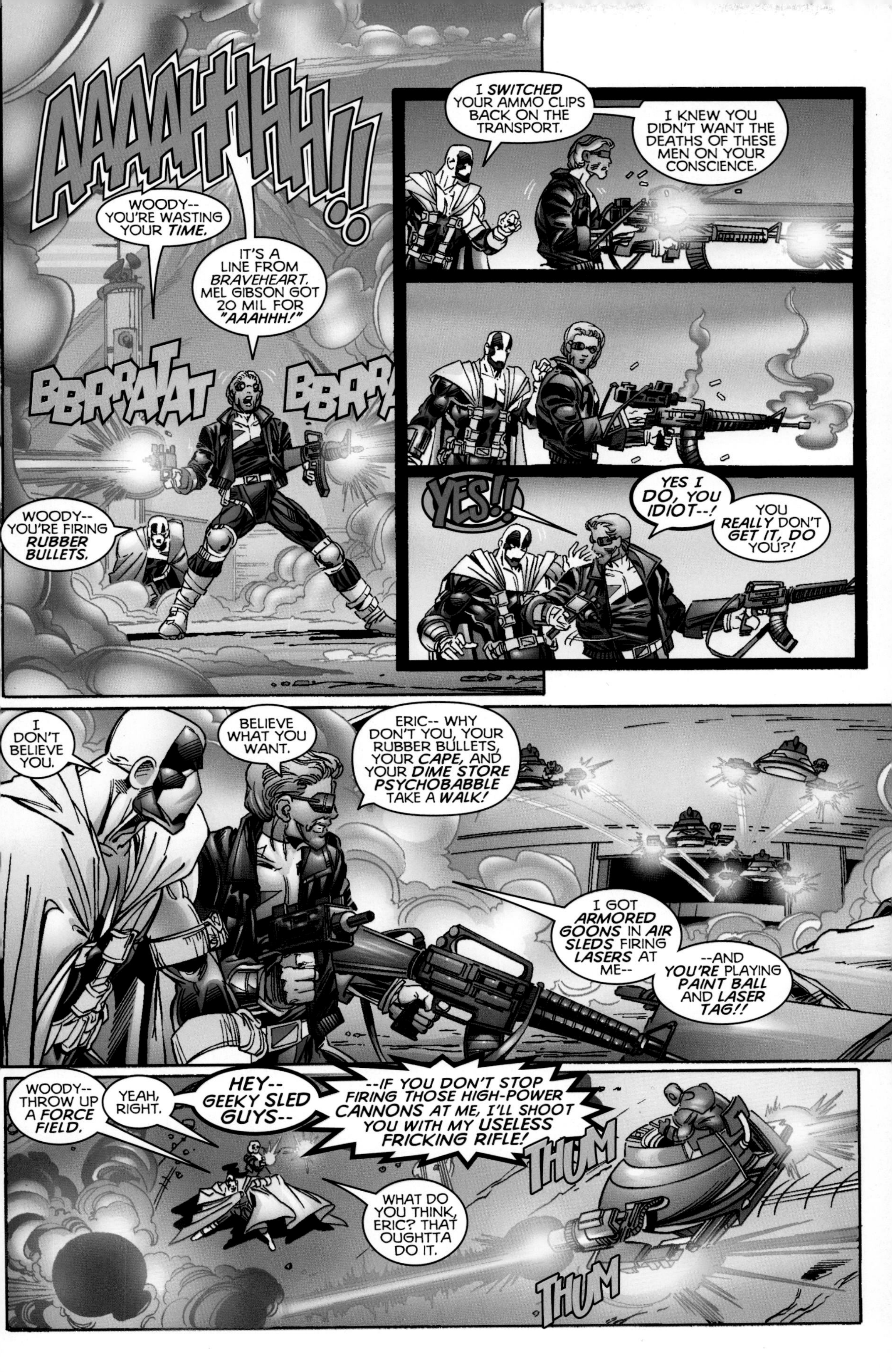
AAAAHHHH!!
WOODY-- YOU'RE WASTING YOUR TIME.
IT'S A LINE FROM BRAVEHEART. MEL GIBSON GOT 20 MIL FOR "AAAHHH!"
BBRRATAT
BBRRA
WOODY-- YOU'RE FIRING RUBBER BULLETS.
I SWITCHED YOUR AMMO CLIPS BACK ON THE TRANSPORT.
I KNEW YOU DIDN'T WANT THE DEATHS OF THESE MEN ON YOUR CONSCIENCE.
YES!!
YES I DO, YOU IDIOT--!
YOU REALLY DON'T GET IT, DO YOU?!
I DON'T BELIEVE YOU.
BELIEVE WHAT YOU WANT.
ERIC-- WHY DON'T YOU, YOUR RUBBER BULLETS, YOUR CAPE, AND YOUR DIME STORE PSYCHOBABBLE TAKE A WALK!
I GOT ARMORED GOONS IN AIR SLEDS FIRING LASERS AT ME--
--AND YOU'RE PLAYING PAINT BALL AND LASER TAG!!
WOODY-- THROW UP A FORCE FIELD.
YEAH, RIGHT.
HEY-- GEEKY SLED GUYS--
--IF YOU DON'T STOP FIRING THOSE HIGH-POWER CANNONS AT ME, I'LL SHOOT YOU WITH MY USELESS FRICKING RIFLE!
THUM
WHAT DO YOU THINK, ERIC? THAT OUGHTTA DO IT.
THUM

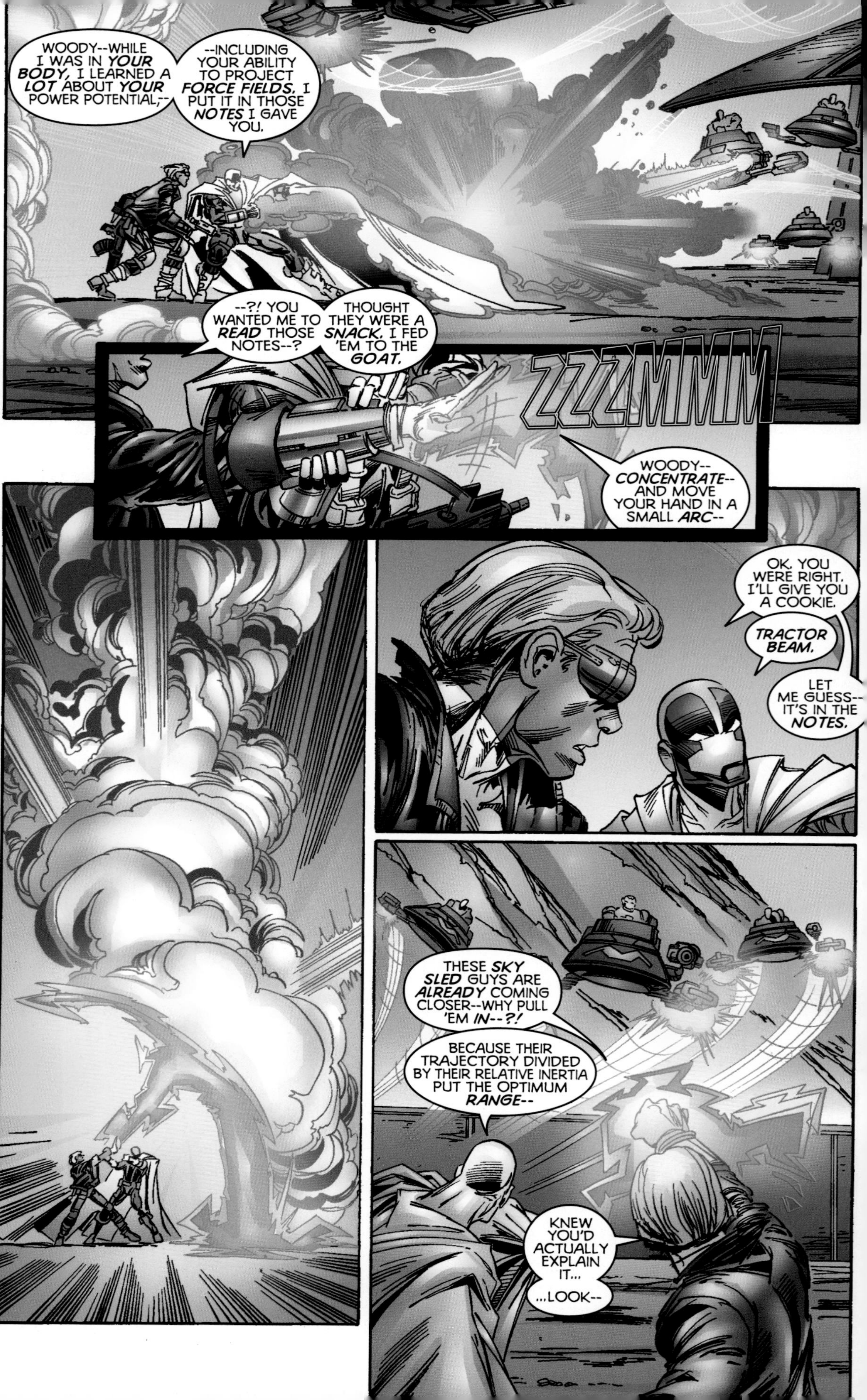
WOODY--WHILE I WAS IN YOUR BODY, I LEARNED A LOT ABOUT YOUR POWER POTENTIAL,--
--INCLUDING YOUR ABILITY TO PROJECT FORCE FIELDS. I PUT IT IN THOSE NOTES I GAVE YOU.
--?! YOU WANTED ME TO READ THOSE NOTES--?
THOUGHT THEY WERE A SNACK. I FED 'EM TO THE GOAT.
ZZZMMMM
WOODY--CONCENTRATE--AND MOVE YOUR HAND IN A SMALL ARC--
OK. YOU WERE RIGHT. I'LL GIVE YOU A COOKIE.
TRACTOR BEAM.
LET ME GUESS--IT'S IN THE NOTES.
THESE SKY SLED GUYS ARE ALREADY COMING CLOSER--WHY PULL 'EM IN--?!
BECAUSE THEIR TRAJECTORY DIVIDED BY THEIR RELATIVE INERTIA PUT THE OPTIMUM RANGE--
KNEW YOU'D ACTUALLY EXPLAIN IT...
...LOOK--

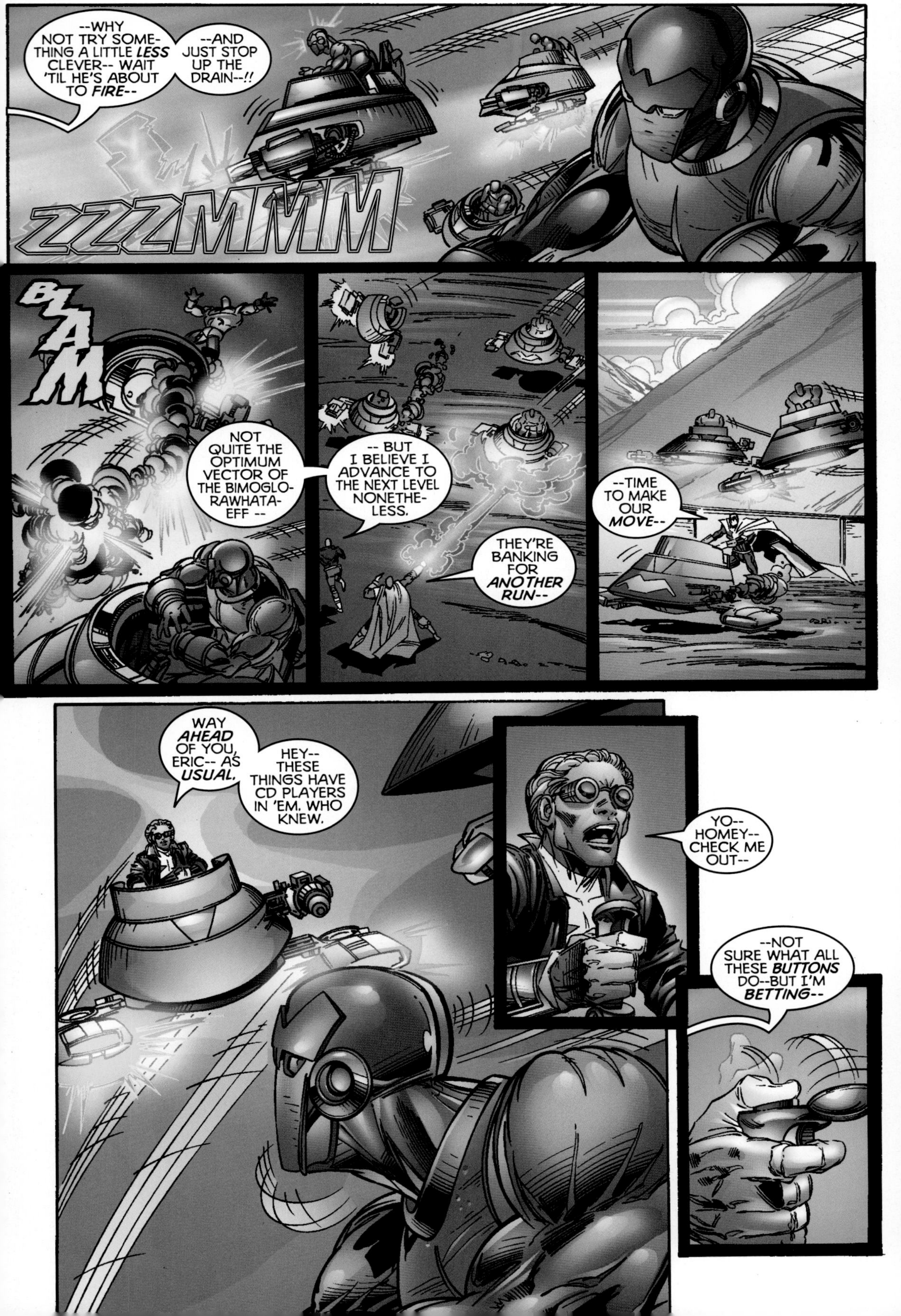
--WHY NOT TRY SOME-THING A LITTLE LESS CLEVER-- WAIT 'TIL HE'S ABOUT TO FIRE--
--AND JUST STOP UP THE DRAIN--!!
ZZZMMM
BLAM
NOT QUITE THE OPTIMUM VECTOR OF THE BIMOGLO-RAWHATA-EFF --
-- BUT I BELIEVE I ADVANCE TO THE NEXT LEVEL NONETHE-LESS.
THEY'RE BANKING FOR ANOTHER RUN--
--TIME TO MAKE OUR MOVE--
WAY AHEAD OF YOU, ERIC-- AS USUAL.
HEY-- THESE THINGS HAVE CD PLAYERS IN 'EM. WHO KNEW.
YO-- HOMEY-- CHECK ME OUT--
--NOT SURE WHAT ALL THESE BUTTONS DO--BUT I'M BETTING--

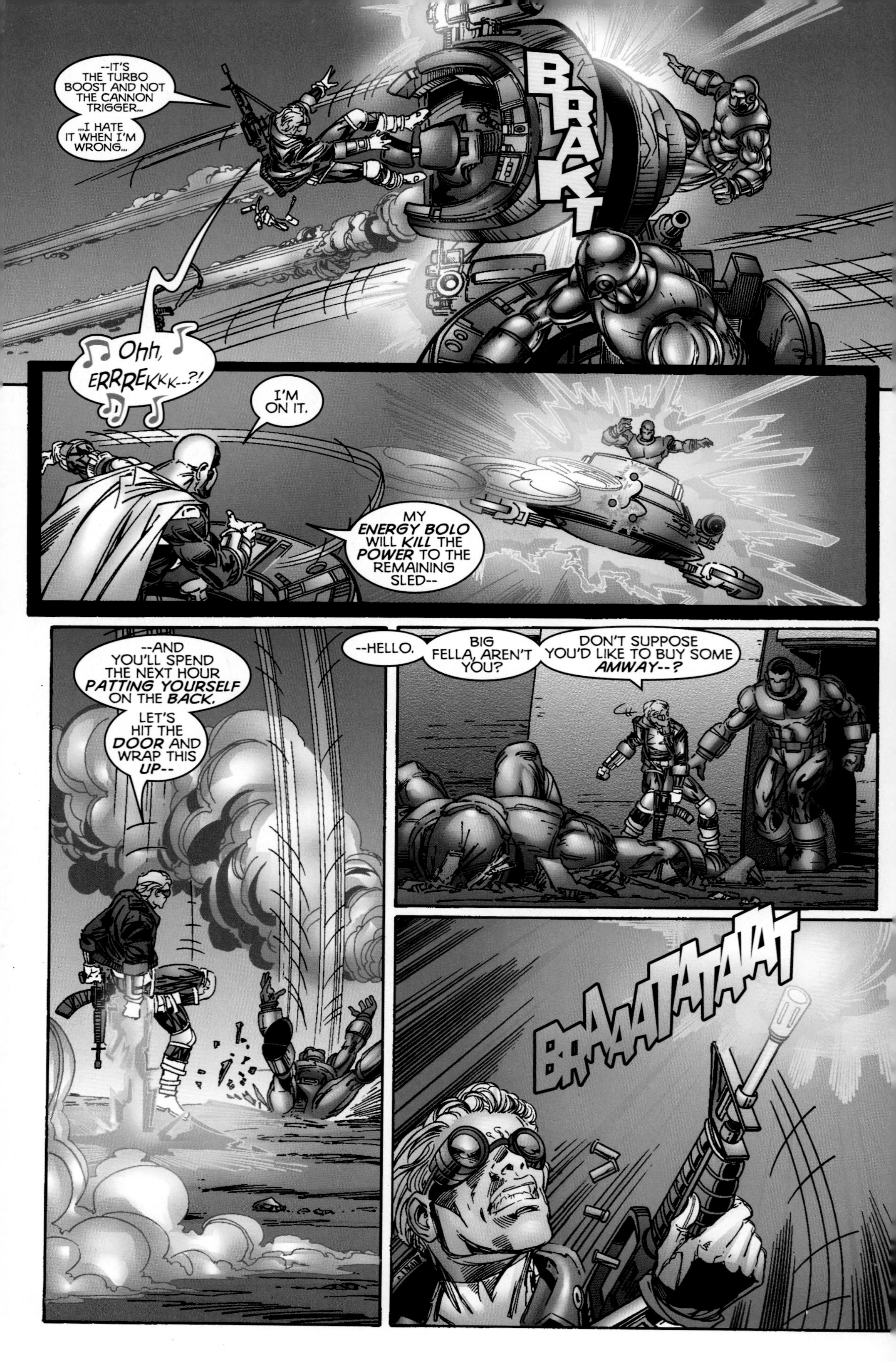
--IT'S THE TURBO BOOST AND NOT THE CANNON TRIGGER...
...I HATE IT WHEN I'M WRONG...
BRAKT
Ohh, ERRREKKK--?!
I'M ON IT.
MY ENERGY BOLO WILL KILL THE POWER TO THE REMAINING SLED--
--AND YOU'LL SPEND THE NEXT HOUR PATTING YOURSELF ON THE BACK.
LET'S HIT THE DOOR AND WRAP THIS UP--
--HELLO.
BIG FELLA, AREN'T YOU?
DON'T SUPPOSE YOU'D LIKE TO BUY SOME AMWAY--?
BRAAATATATAT

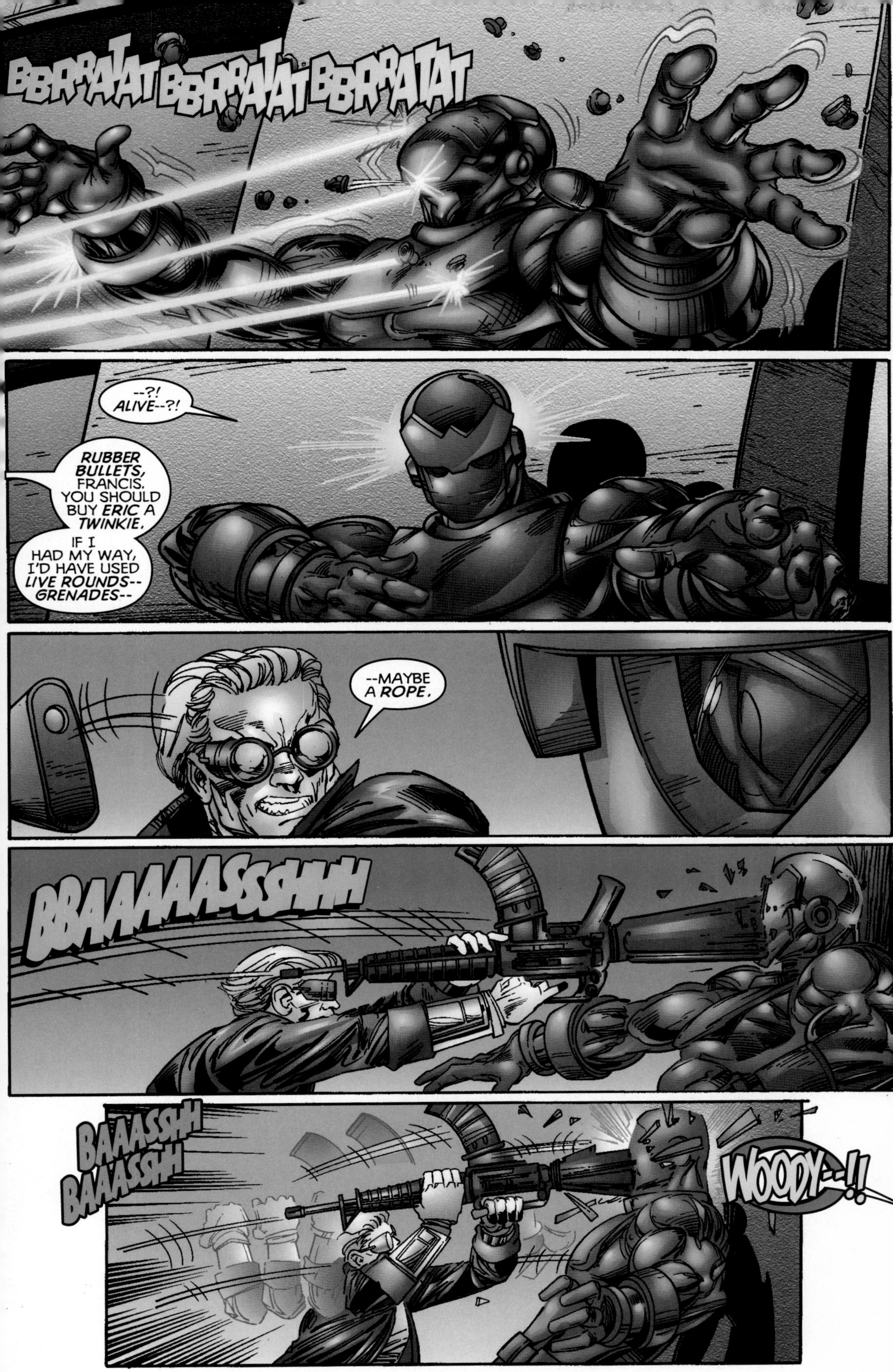
BBRRRATAT BBRRRATAT BBRRRATAT
--?! ALIVE--?!
RUBBER BULLETS, FRANCIS. YOU SHOULD BUY ERIC A TWINKIE.
IF I HAD MY WAY, I'D HAVE USED LIVE ROUNDS--GRENADES--
--MAYBE A ROPE.
BBAAAAASSSHHH
BAAASSHH BAAASSHH
WOODY--!!

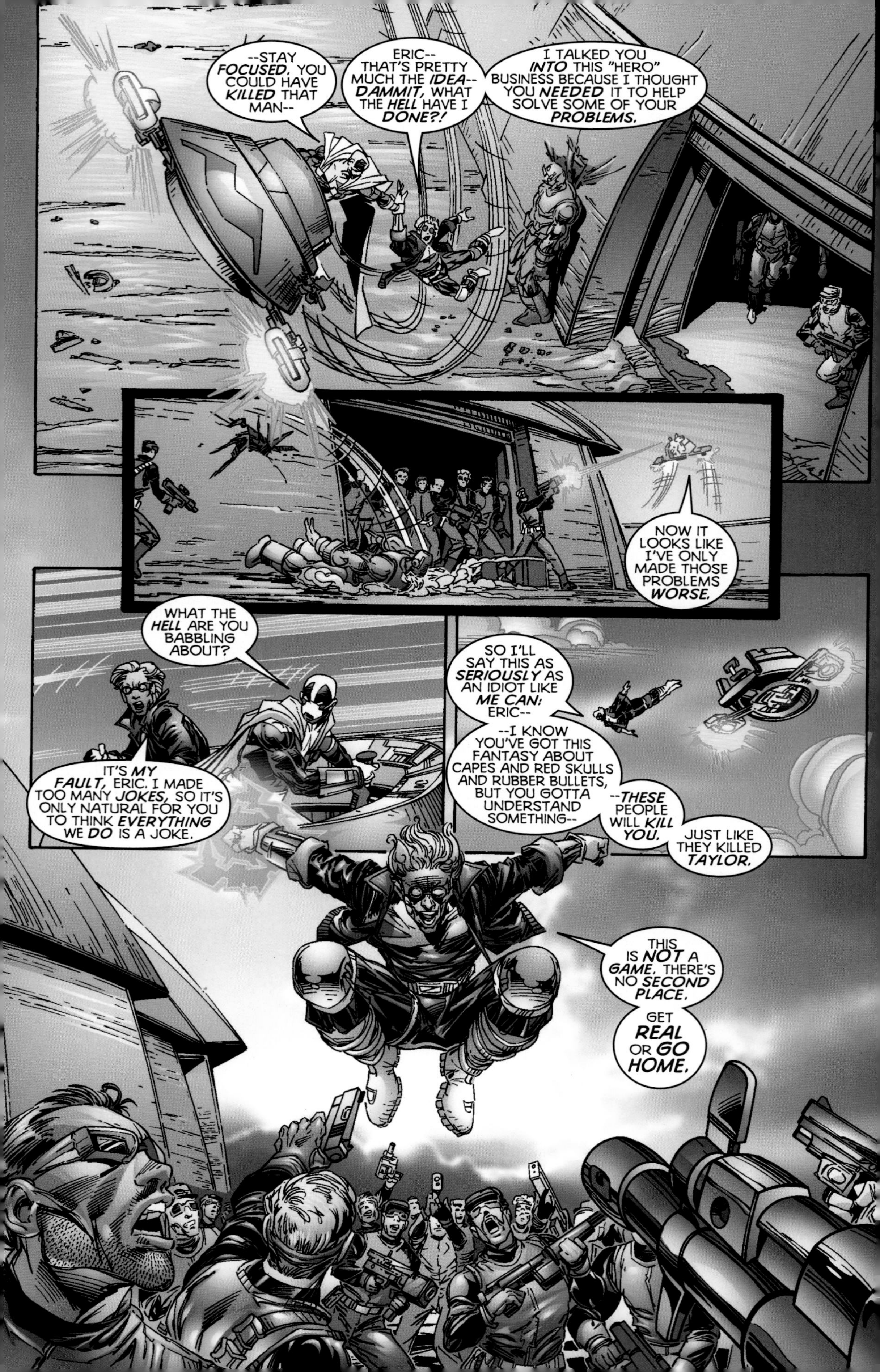
--STAY FOCUSED. YOU COULD HAVE KILLED THAT MAN--
ERIC-- THAT'S PRETTY MUCH THE IDEA-- DAMMIT, WHAT THE HELL HAVE I DONE?!
I TALKED YOU INTO THIS "HERO" BUSINESS BECAUSE I THOUGHT YOU NEEDED IT TO HELP SOLVE SOME OF YOUR PROBLEMS.
NOW IT LOOKS LIKE I'VE ONLY MADE THOSE PROBLEMS WORSE.
WHAT THE HELL ARE YOU BABBLING ABOUT?
IT'S MY FAULT, ERIC. I MADE TOO MANY JOKES, SO IT'S ONLY NATURAL FOR YOU TO THINK EVERYTHING WE DO IS A JOKE.
SO I'LL SAY THIS AS SERIOUSLY AS AN IDIOT LIKE ME CAN: ERIC--
--I KNOW YOU'VE GOT THIS FANTASY ABOUT CAPES AND RED SKULLS AND RUBBER BULLETS, BUT YOU GOTTA UNDERSTAND SOMETHING--
--THESE PEOPLE WILL KILL YOU.
JUST LIKE THEY KILLED TAYLOR.
THIS IS NOT A GAME. THERE'S NO SECOND PLACE.
GET REAL OR GO HOME.

"Pow Whack K-Blam Blam Pow"

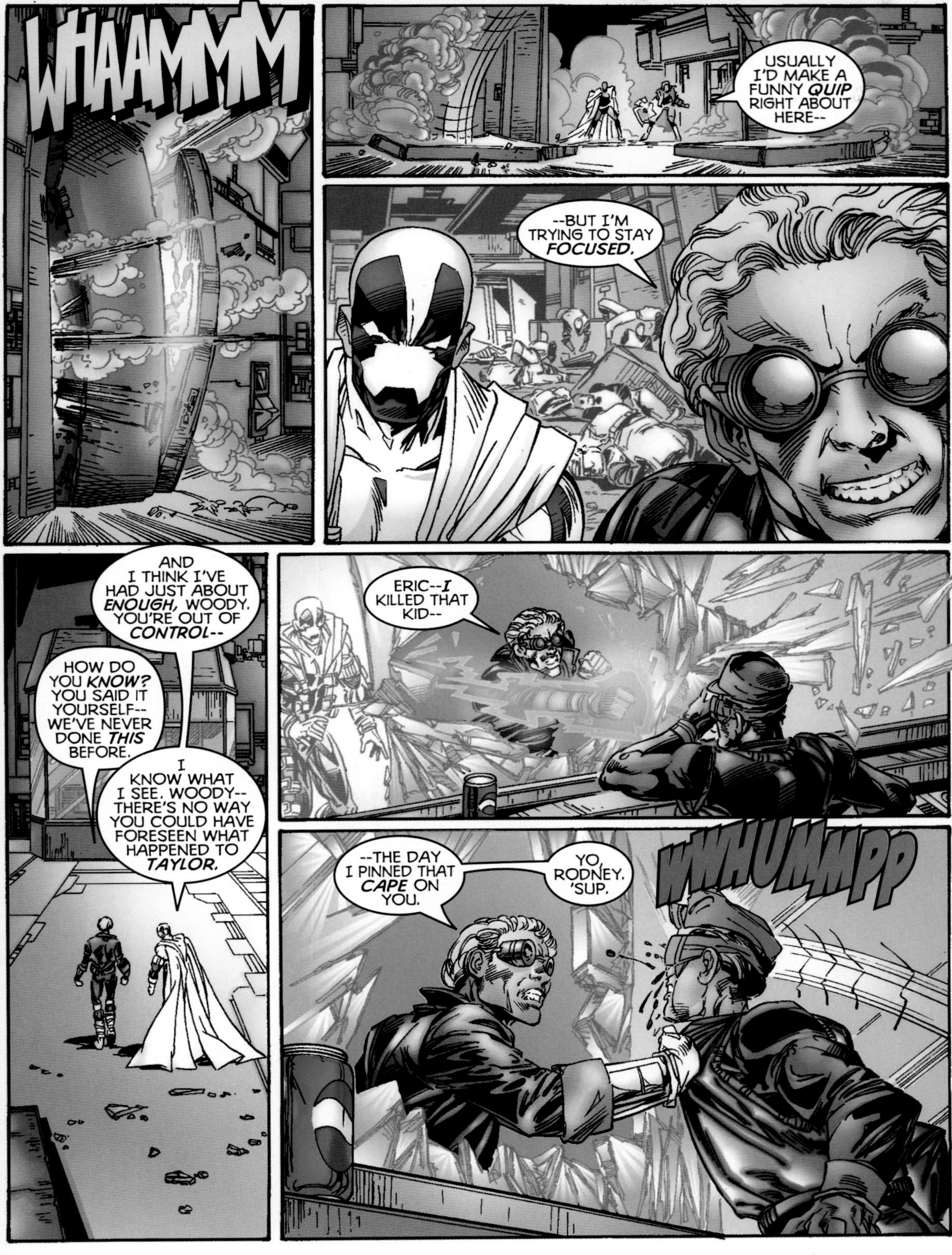
WHAAMMM
USUALLY I'D MAKE A FUNNY QUIP RIGHT ABOUT HERE--
--BUT I'M TRYING TO STAY FOCUSED.
AND I THINK I'VE HAD JUST ABOUT ENOUGH, WOODY. YOU'RE OUT OF CONTROL--
HOW DO YOU KNOW? YOU SAID IT YOURSELF-- WE'VE NEVER DONE THIS BEFORE.
I KNOW WHAT I SEE. WOODY-- THERE'S NO WAY YOU COULD HAVE FORESEEN WHAT HAPPENED TO TAYLOR.
ERIC--I KILLED THAT KID--
--THE DAY I PINNED THAT CAPE ON YOU.
YO, RODNEY. 'SUP.
WWHUMMPP

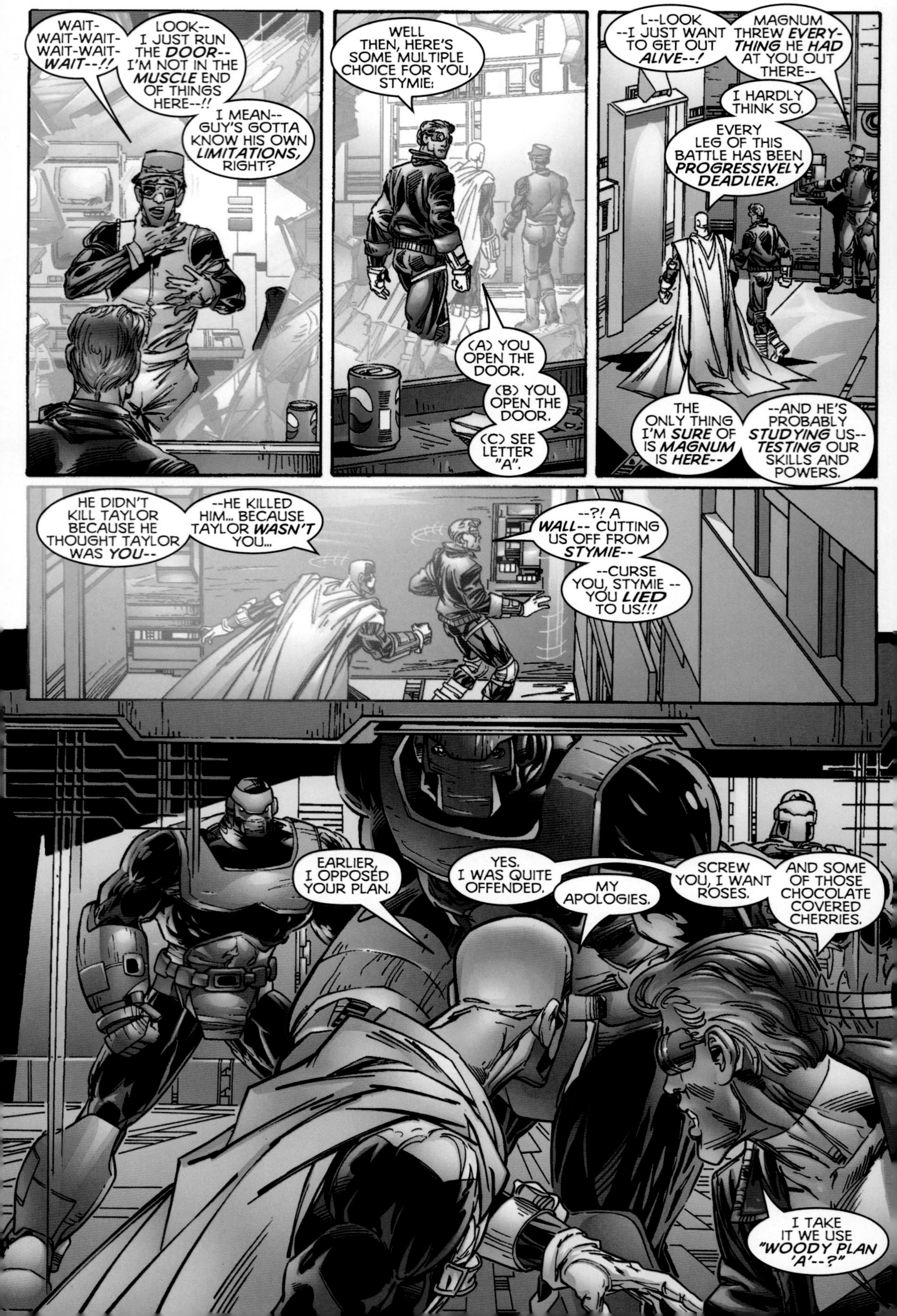
WAIT-WAIT-WAIT-WAIT-WAIT-WAIT--!!
LOOK-- I JUST RUN THE DOOR-- I'M NOT IN THE MUSCLE END OF THINGS HERE--!!
I MEAN-- GUY'S GOTTA KNOW HIS OWN LIMITATIONS, RIGHT?
WELL THEN, HERE'S SOME MULTIPLE CHOICE FOR YOU, STYMIE:
(A) YOU OPEN THE DOOR.
(B) YOU OPEN THE DOOR.
(C) SEE LETTER "A".
L--LOOK --I JUST WANT TO GET OUT ALIVE--!
MAGNUM THREW EVERYTHING HE HAD AT YOU OUT THERE--
I HARDLY THINK SO.
EVERY LEG OF THIS BATTLE HAS BEEN PROGRESSIVELY DEADLIER.
THE ONLY THING I'M SURE OF IS MAGNUM IS HERE--
--AND HE'S PROBABLY STUDYING US-- TESTING OUR SKILLS AND POWERS.
HE DIDN'T KILL TAYLOR BECAUSE HE THOUGHT TAYLOR WAS YOU--
--HE KILLED HIM... BECAUSE TAYLOR WASN'T YOU...
--?! A WALL-- CUTTING US OFF FROM STYMIE--
--CURSE YOU, STYMIE -- YOU LIED TO US!!!
EARLIER, I OPPOSED YOUR PLAN.
YES. I WAS QUITE OFFENDED.
MY APOLOGIES.
SCREW YOU, I WANT ROSES.
AND SOME OF THOSE CHOCOLATE COVERED CHERRIES.
I TAKE IT WE USE "WOODY PLAN 'A'--?"

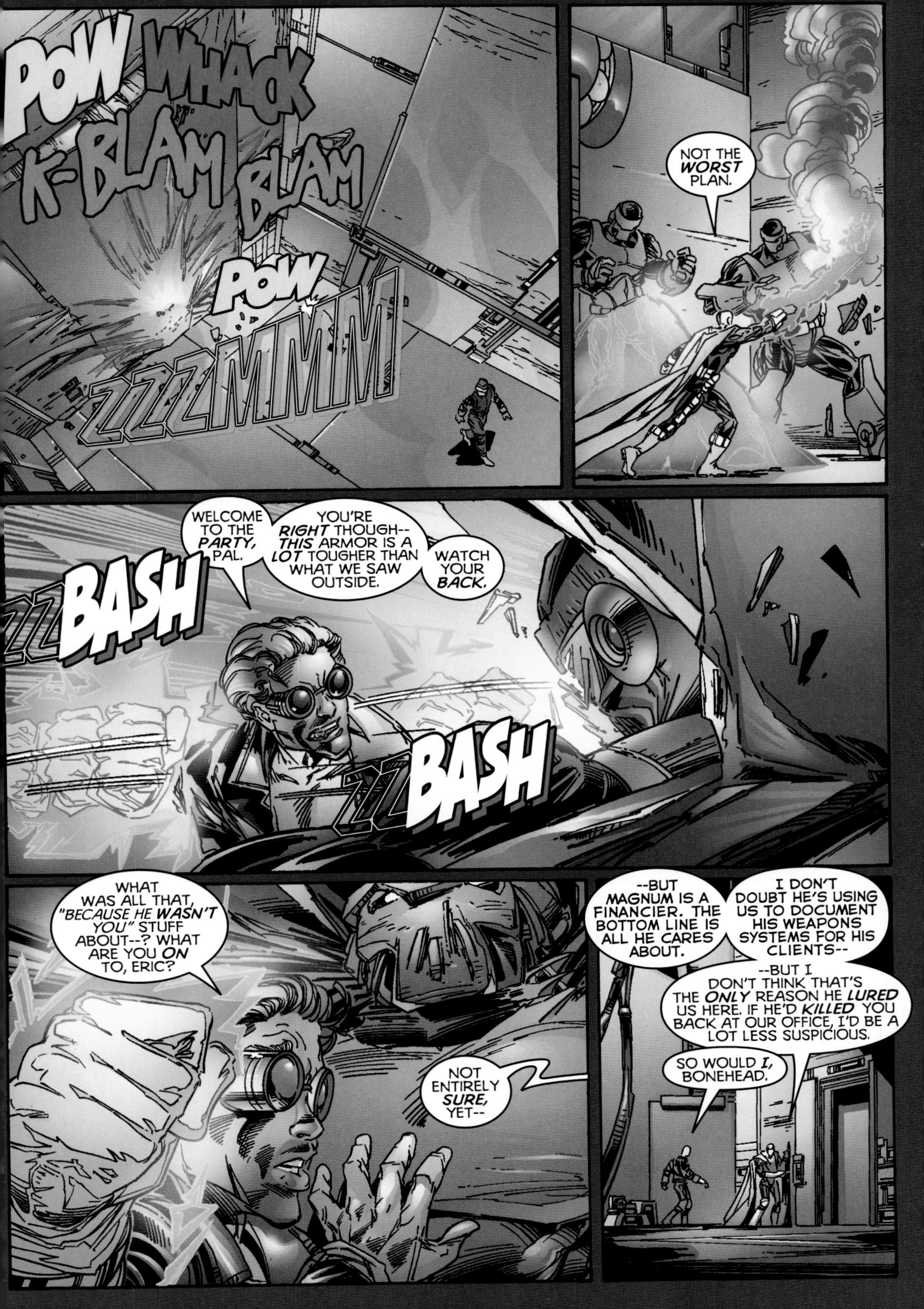
POW WHACK
K-BLAM BLAM
POW
ZZZMMMM
NOT THE WORST PLAN.
ZZBASH
WELCOME TO THE PARTY, PAL.
YOU'RE RIGHT THOUGH-- THIS ARMOR IS A LOT TOUGHER THAN WHAT WE SAW OUTSIDE.
WATCH YOUR BACK.
ZZBASH
WHAT WAS ALL THAT, "BECAUSE HE WASN'T YOU" STUFF ABOUT--? WHAT ARE YOU ON TO, ERIC?
NOT ENTIRELY SURE, YET--
--BUT MAGNUM IS A FINANCIER. THE BOTTOM LINE IS ALL HE CARES ABOUT.
I DON'T DOUBT HE'S USING US TO DOCUMENT HIS WEAPONS SYSTEMS FOR HIS CLIENTS--
--BUT I DON'T THINK THAT'S THE ONLY REASON HE LURED US HERE. IF HE'D KILLED YOU BACK AT OUR OFFICE, I'D BE A LOT LESS SUSPICIOUS.
SO WOULD I, BONEHEAD.

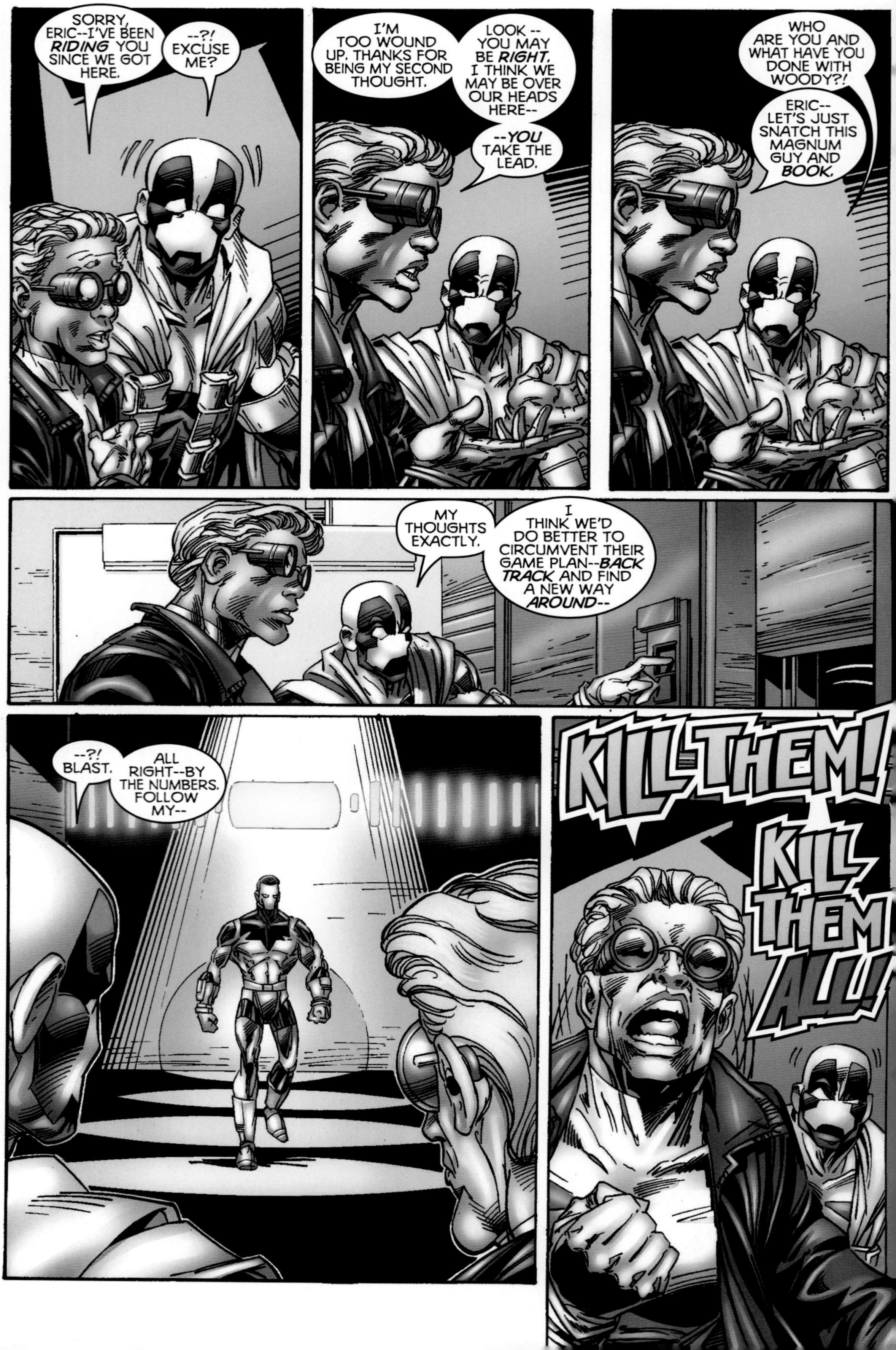
SORRY, ERIC--I'VE BEEN *RIDING* YOU SINCE WE GOT HERE.
--?! EXCUSE ME?
I'M TOO WOUND UP. THANKS FOR BEING MY SECOND THOUGHT.
LOOK -- YOU MAY BE *RIGHT*. I THINK WE MAY BE OVER OUR HEADS HERE--
--*YOU* TAKE THE LEAD.
WHO ARE YOU AND WHAT HAVE YOU DONE WITH WOODY?!
ERIC-- LET'S JUST SNATCH THIS MAGNUM GUY AND *BOOK*.
MY THOUGHTS EXACTLY.
I THINK WE'D DO BETTER TO CIRCUMVENT THEIR GAME PLAN--*BACK TRACK* AND FIND A NEW WAY *AROUND*--
--?! BLAST.
ALL RIGHT--BY THE NUMBERS. FOLLOW MY--
KILL THEM!
KILL THEM ALL!

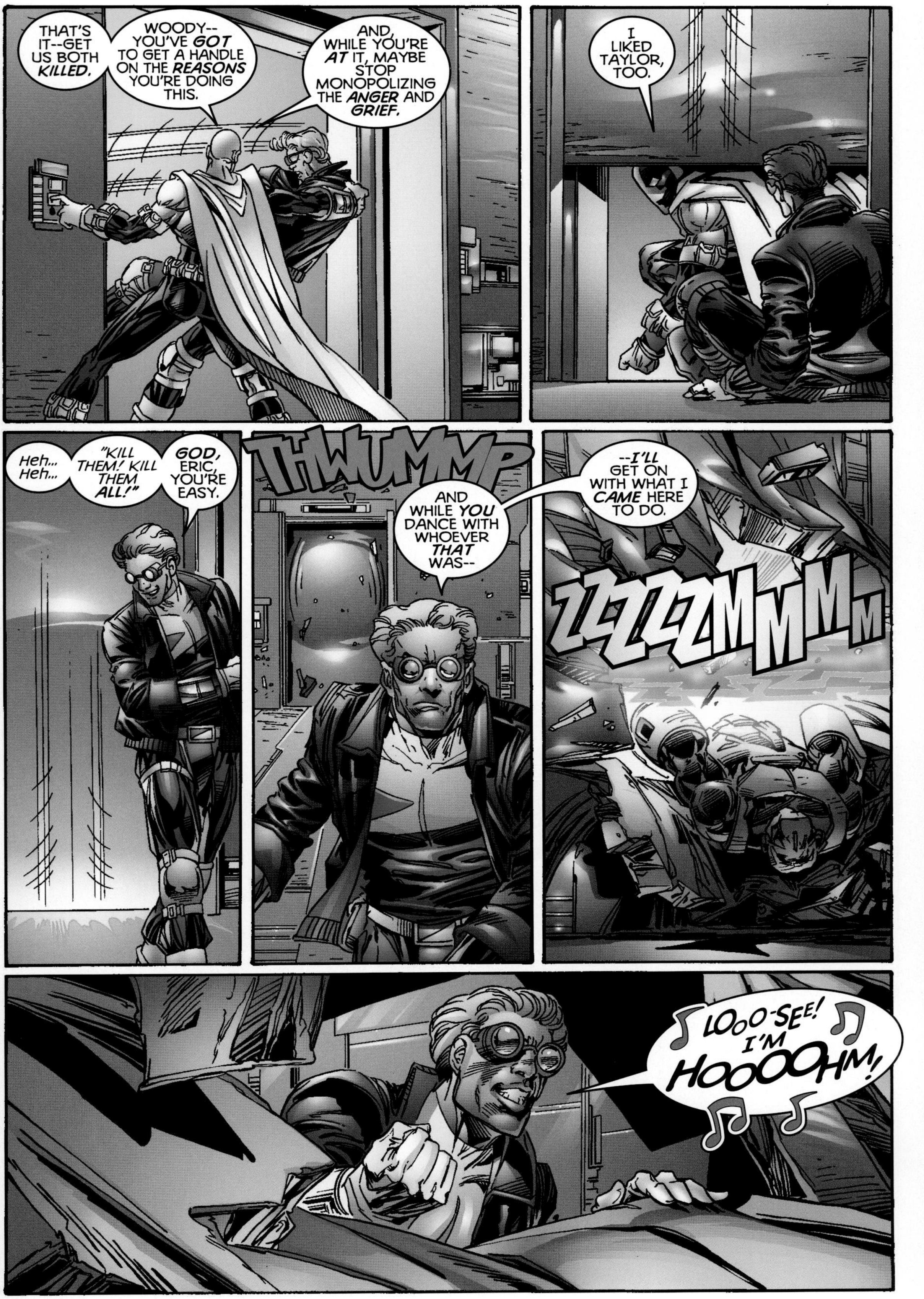
THAT'S IT--GET US BOTH KILLED.
WOODY-- YOU'VE GOT TO GET A HANDLE ON THE REASONS YOU'RE DOING THIS.
AND, WHILE YOU'RE AT IT, MAYBE STOP MONOPOLIZING THE ANGER AND GRIEF.
I LIKED TAYLOR, TOO.
Heh... Heh...
"KILL THEM! KILL THEM ALL!"
GOD, ERIC, YOU'RE EASY.
THWUMMP
AND WHILE YOU DANCE WITH WHOEVER THAT WAS--
--I'LL GET ON WITH WHAT I CAME HERE TO DO.
ZZZZZMMMMM
LOOO-SEE! I'M HOOOOHM!

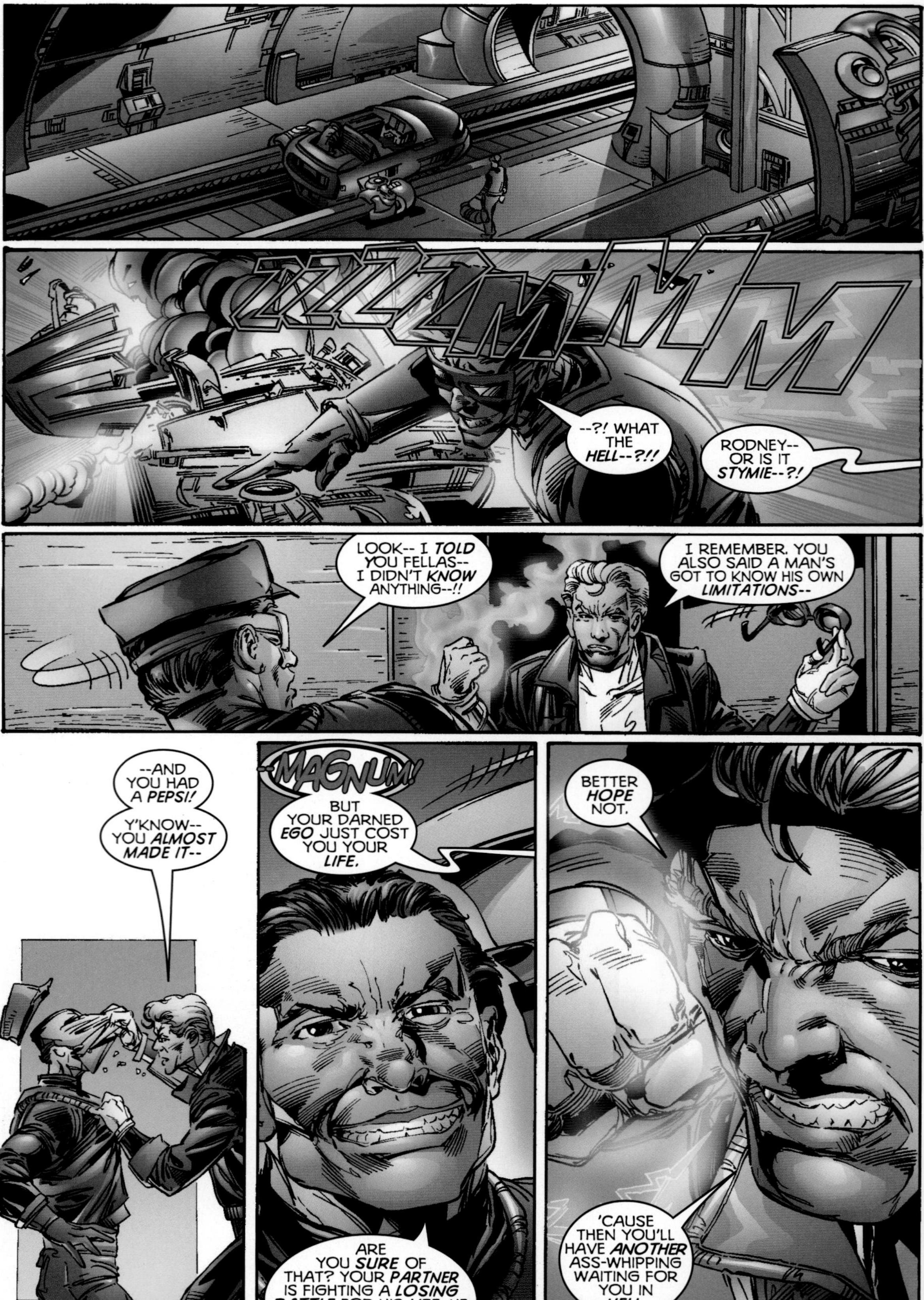
VRRMMMM
--?! WHAT THE HELL--?!!
RODNEY-- OR IS IT STYMIE--?!
LOOK-- I TOLD YOU FELLAS-- I DIDN'T KNOW ANYTHING--!!
I REMEMBER. YOU ALSO SAID A MAN'S GOT TO KNOW HIS OWN LIMITATIONS--
--AND YOU HAD A PEPSI!
Y'KNOW-- YOU ALMOST MADE IT--
MAGNUM!
BUT YOUR DARNED EGO JUST COST YOU YOUR LIFE.
ARE YOU SURE OF THAT? YOUR PARTNER IS FIGHTING A LOSING BATTLE FOR HIS LIFE. HE MAY BE DEAD ALREADY!
BETTER HOPE NOT.
'CAUSE THEN YOU'LL HAVE ANOTHER ASS-WHIPPING WAITING FOR YOU IN HELL.

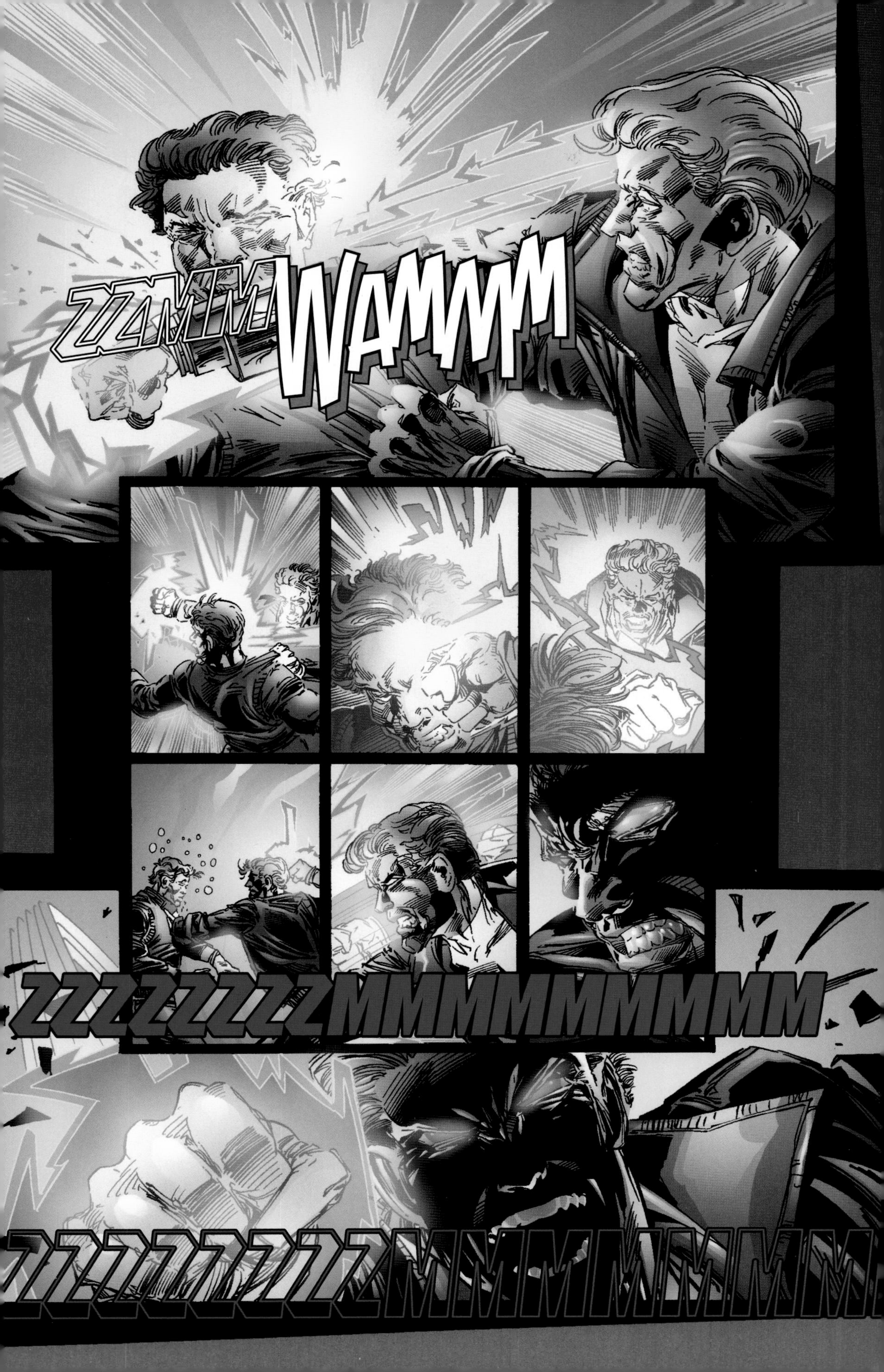
ZZMMM WAMMM
ZZZZZZZZZMMMMMMMMMMM
ZZZZZZZZZZZZMMMMMMMMM

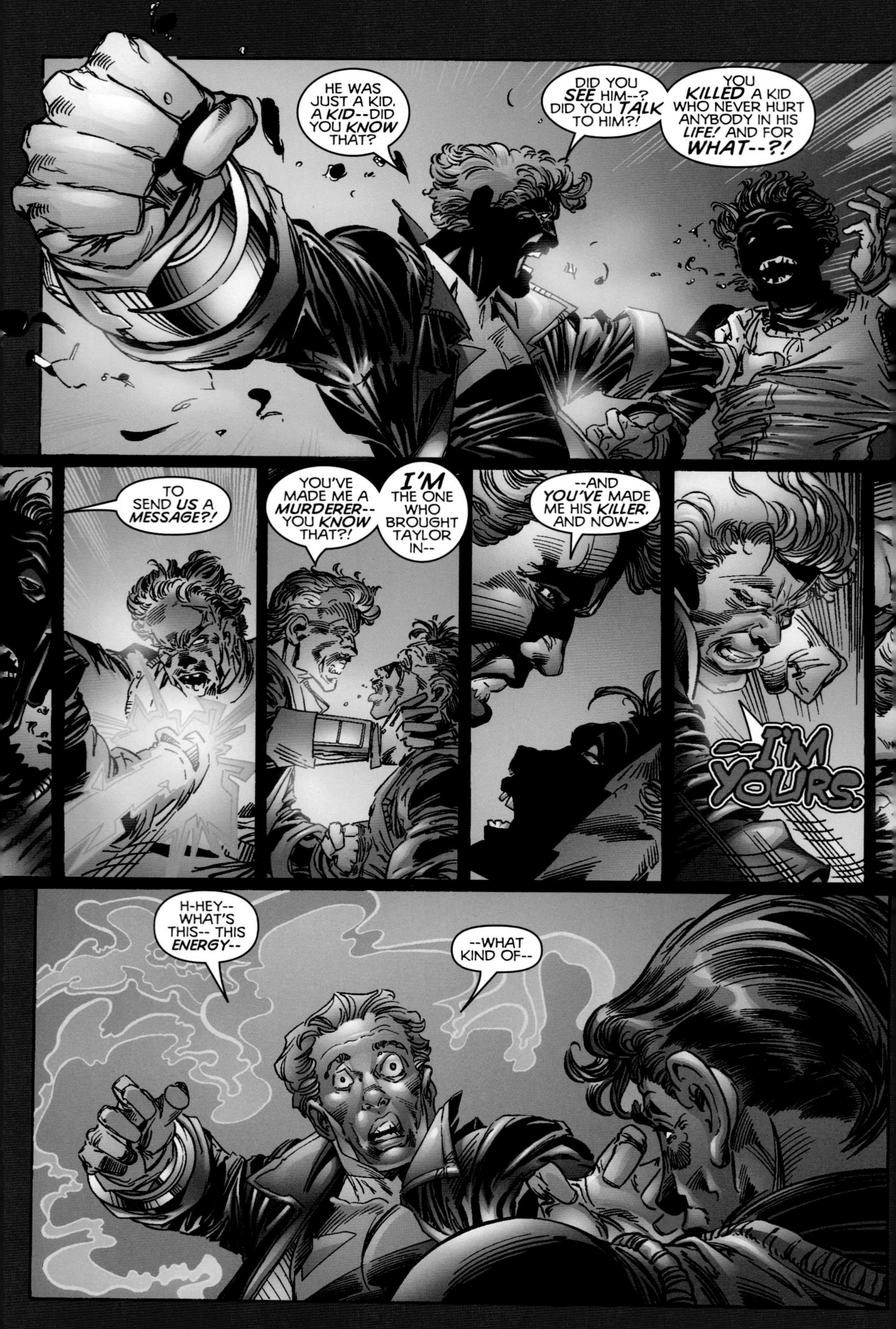
HE WAS JUST A KID. A KID--DID YOU KNOW THAT?
DID YOU SEE HIM--? DID YOU TALK TO HIM?!
YOU KILLED A KID WHO NEVER HURT ANYBODY IN HIS LIFE! AND FOR WHAT--?!
TO SEND US A MESSAGE?!
YOU'VE MADE ME A MURDERER-- YOU KNOW THAT?!
I'M THE ONE WHO BROUGHT TAYLOR IN--
--AND YOU'VE MADE ME HIS KILLER. AND NOW--
--I'M YOURS.
H-HEY-- WHAT'S THIS-- THIS ENERGY--
--WHAT KIND OF--

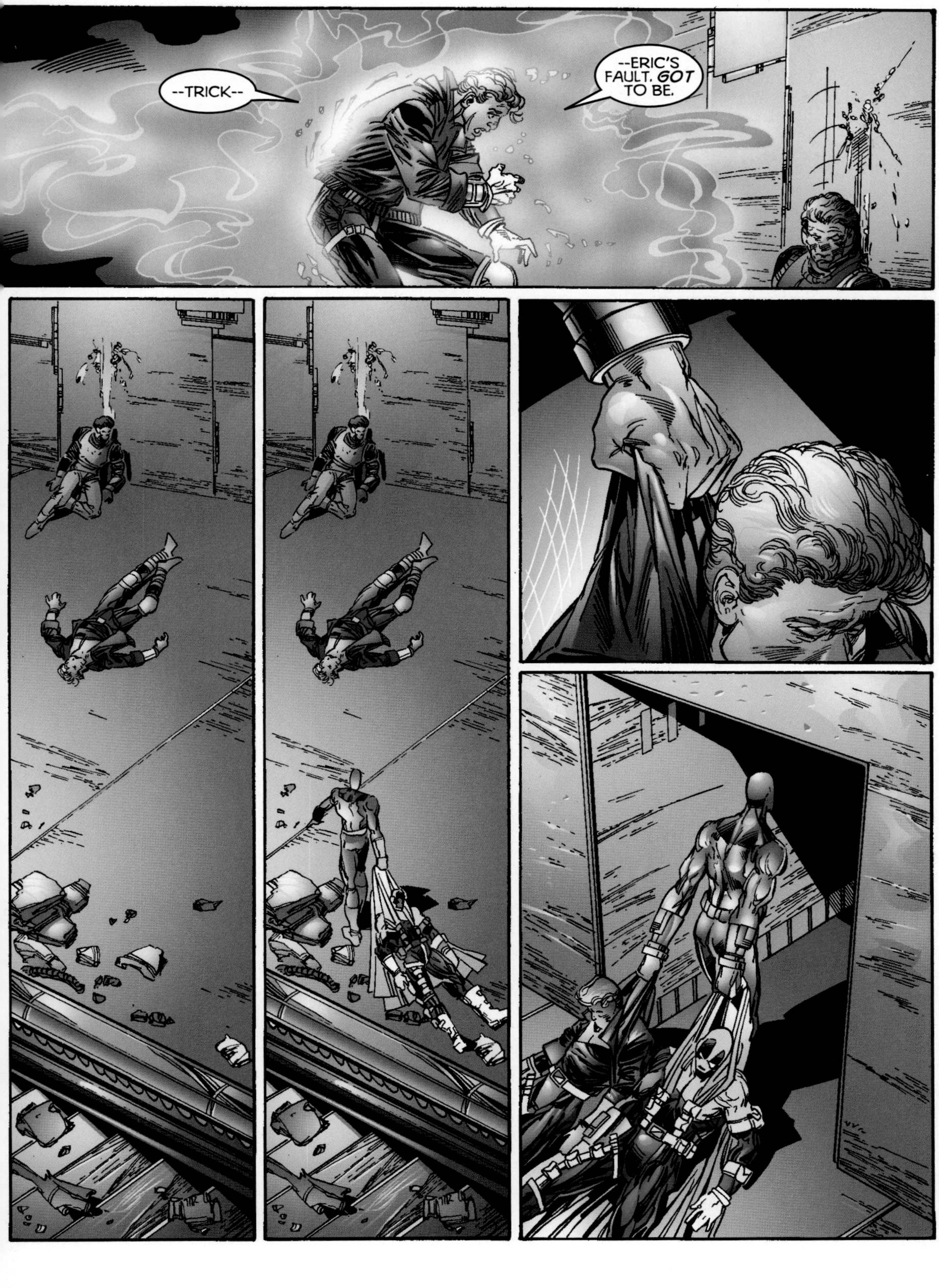
--TRICK--
--ERIC'S FAULT. GOT TO BE.

JABBA AND THE WET THONG

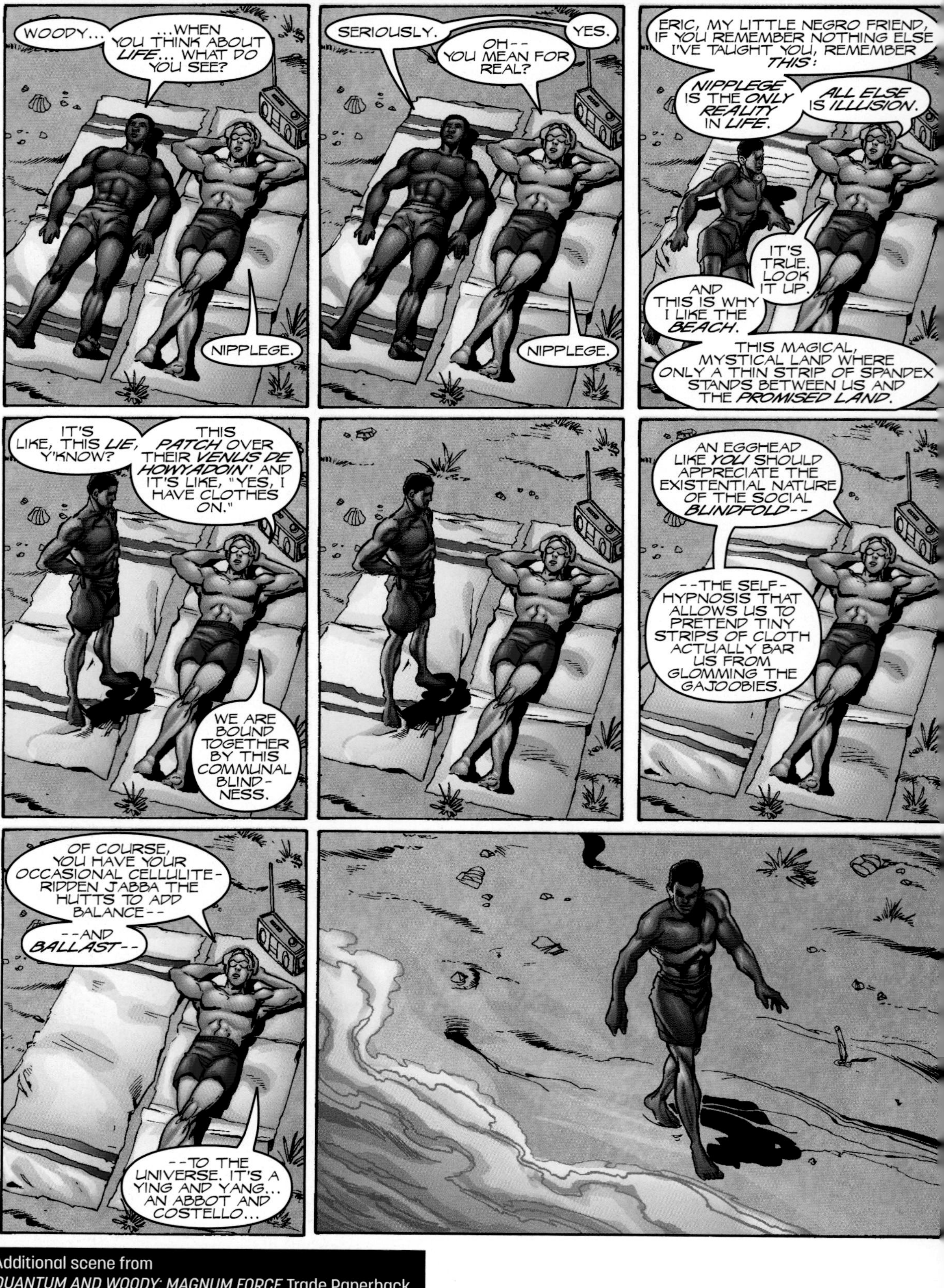

WOODY...
...WHEN YOU THINK ABOUT *LIFE*... WHAT DO YOU SEE?
NIPPLEGE.
SERIOUSLY.
YES.
OH-- YOU MEAN FOR REAL?
NIPPLEGE.
ERIC, MY LITTLE NEGRO FRIEND, IF YOU REMEMBER NOTHING ELSE I'VE TAUGHT YOU, REMEMBER *THIS*:
NIPPLEGE IS THE *ONLY REALITY* IN *LIFE*.
ALL ELSE IS *ILLLUSION*.
IT'S TRUE. LOOK IT UP.
AND THIS IS WHY I LIKE THE *BEACH*.
THIS MAGICAL, MYSTICAL LAND WHERE ONLY A THIN STRIP OF SPANDEX STANDS BETWEEN US AND THE *PROMISED LAND*.
IT'S LIKE, THIS *LIE*, Y'KNOW?
THIS *PATCH* OVER THEIR *VENUS DE HOWYADOIN'* AND IT'S LIKE, "YES, I HAVE CLOTHES ON."
WE ARE BOUND TOGETHER BY THIS COMMUNAL BLIND-NESS.
AN EGGHEAD LIKE *YOU* SHOULD APPRECIATE THE EXISTENTIAL NATURE OF THE SOCIAL *BLINDFOLD*--
--THE SELF-HYPNOSIS THAT ALLOWS US TO PRETEND TINY STRIPS OF CLOTH ACTUALLY BAR US FROM GLOMMING THE GAJOOBIES.
OF COURSE, YOU HAVE YOUR OCCASIONAL CELLULITE-RIDDEN JABBA THE HUTTS TO ADD BALANCE--
--AND *BALLAST*--
--TO THE UNIVERSE. IT'S A YING AND YANG... AN ABBOT AND COSTELLO...

Additional scene from
QUANTUM AND WOODY: MAGNUM FORCE Trade Paperback

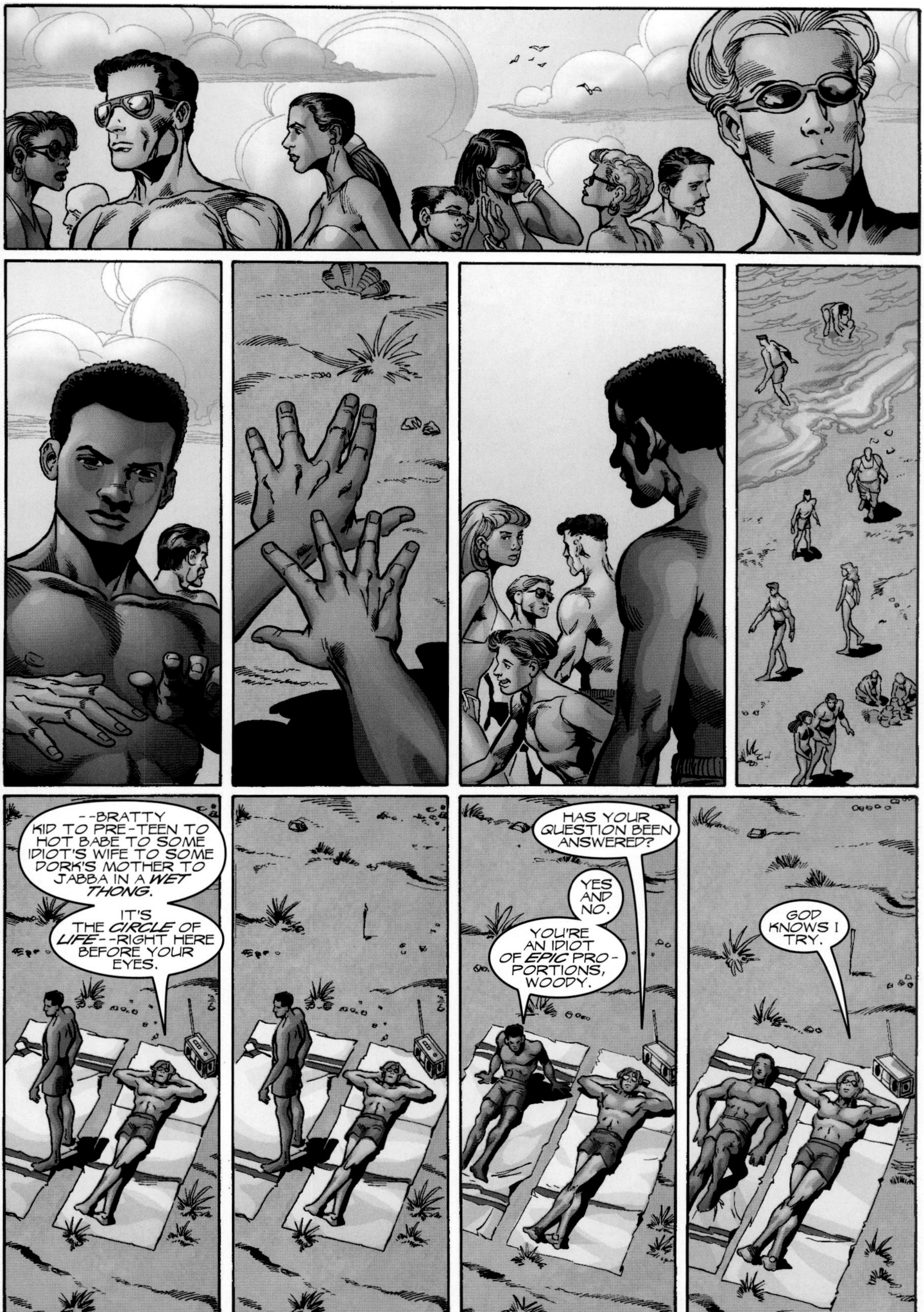
--BRATTY KID TO PRE-TEEN TO HOT BABE TO SOME IDIOT'S WIFE TO SOME DORK'S MOTHER TO JABBA IN A WET THONG.
IT'S THE CIRCLE OF LIFE--RIGHT HERE BEFORE YOUR EYES.
HAS YOUR QUESTION BEEN ANSWERED?
YES AND NO.
YOU'RE AN IDIOT OF EPIC PRO-PORTIONS, WOODY.
GOD KNOWS I TRY.

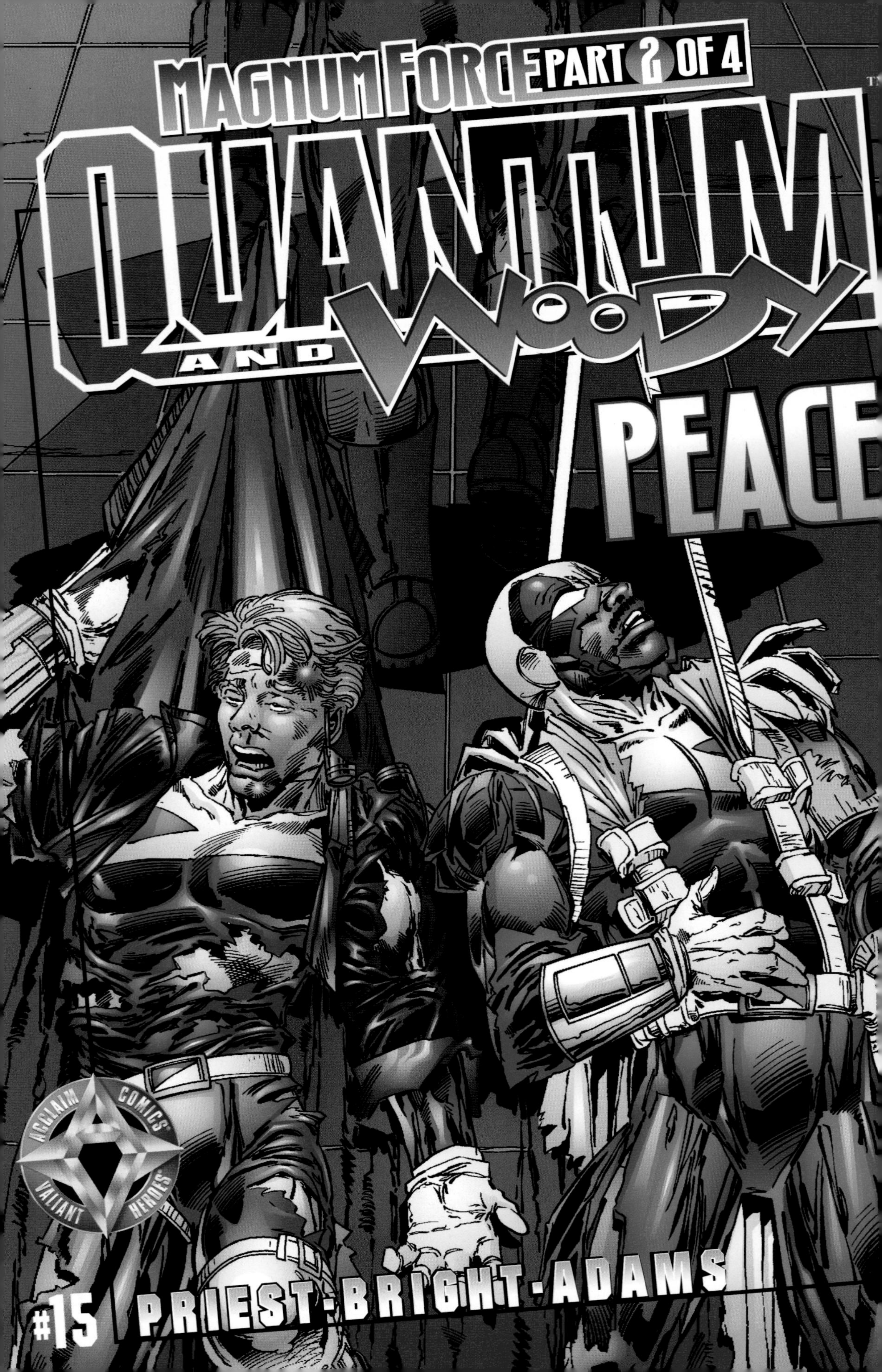
MAGNUM FORCE PART 2 OF 4
QUANTUM AND WOODY
PEACE
ACCLAIM COMICS
VALIANT HEROES
#15
PRIEST · BRIGHT · ADAMS

"Telephone For Mr. Locke"

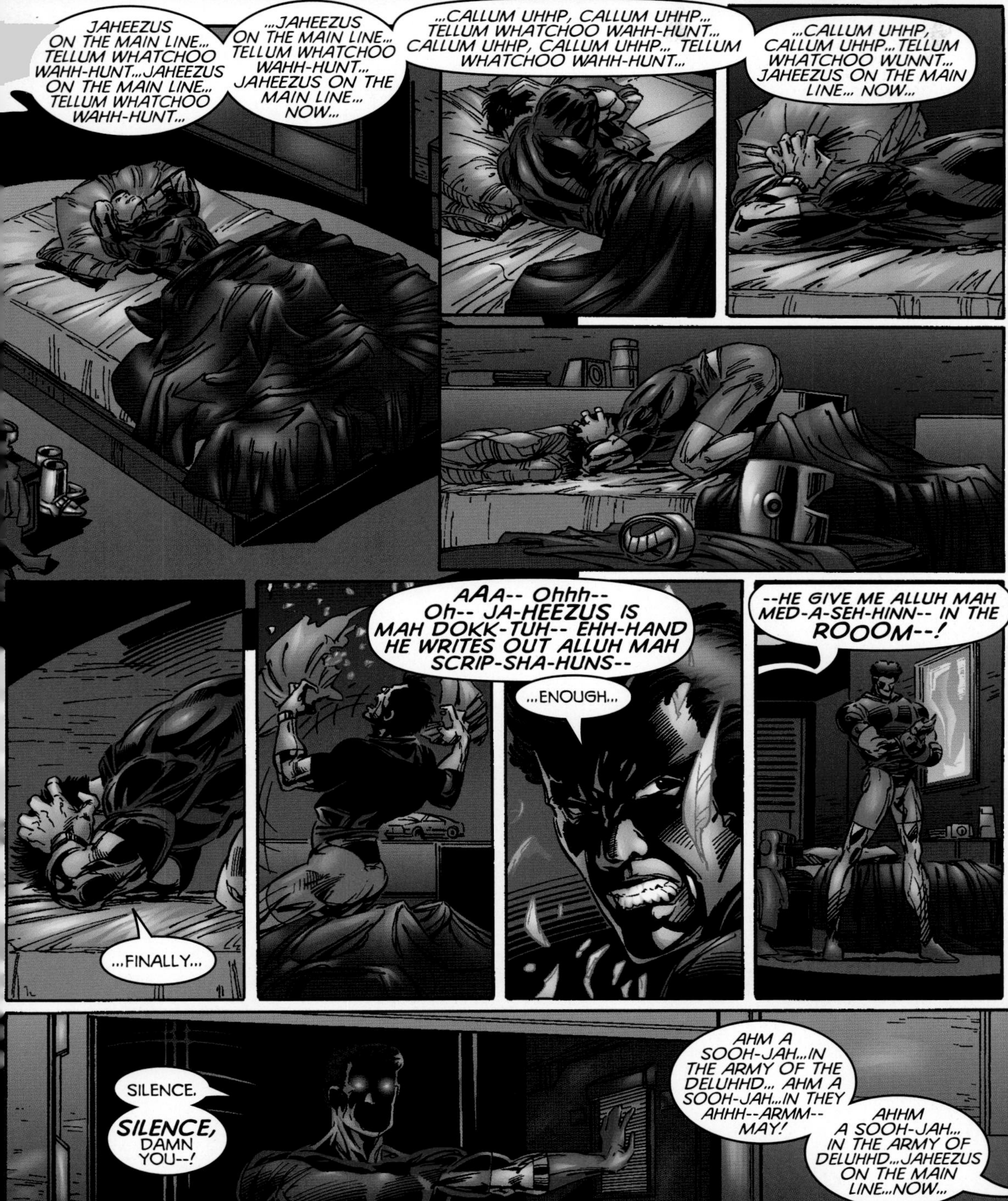

JAHEEZUS ON THE MAIN LINE... TELLUM WHATCHOO WAHH-HUNT...JAHEEZUS ON THE MAIN LINE... TELLUM WHATCHOO WAHH-HUNT...
...JAHEEZUS ON THE MAIN LINE... TELLUM WHATCHOO WAHH-HUNT... JAHEEZUS ON THE MAIN LINE... NOW...
...CALLUM UHHP, CALLUM UHHP... TELLUM WHATCHOO WAHH-HUNT... CALLUM UHHP, CALLUM UHHP... TELLUM WHATCHOO WAHH-HUNT...
...CALLUM UHHP, CALLUM UHHP...TELLUM WHATCHOO WUNNT... JAHEEZUS ON THE MAIN LINE... NOW...
...FINALLY...
AAA-- Ohhh-- Oh-- JA-HEEZUS IS MAH DOKK-TUH-- EHH-HAND HE WRITES OUT ALLUH MAH SCRIP-SHA-HUNS--
...ENOUGH...
--HE GIVE ME ALLUH MAH MED-A-SEH-HINN-- IN THE ROOOM--!
SILENCE.
SILENCE, DAMN YOU--!
AHM A SOOH-JAH...IN THE ARMY OF THE DELUHHD... AHM A SOOH-JAH...IN THEY AHHH--ARMM--MAY!
AHHM A SOOH-JAH... IN THE ARMY OF DELUHHD...JAHEEZUS ON THE MAIN LINE...NOW...

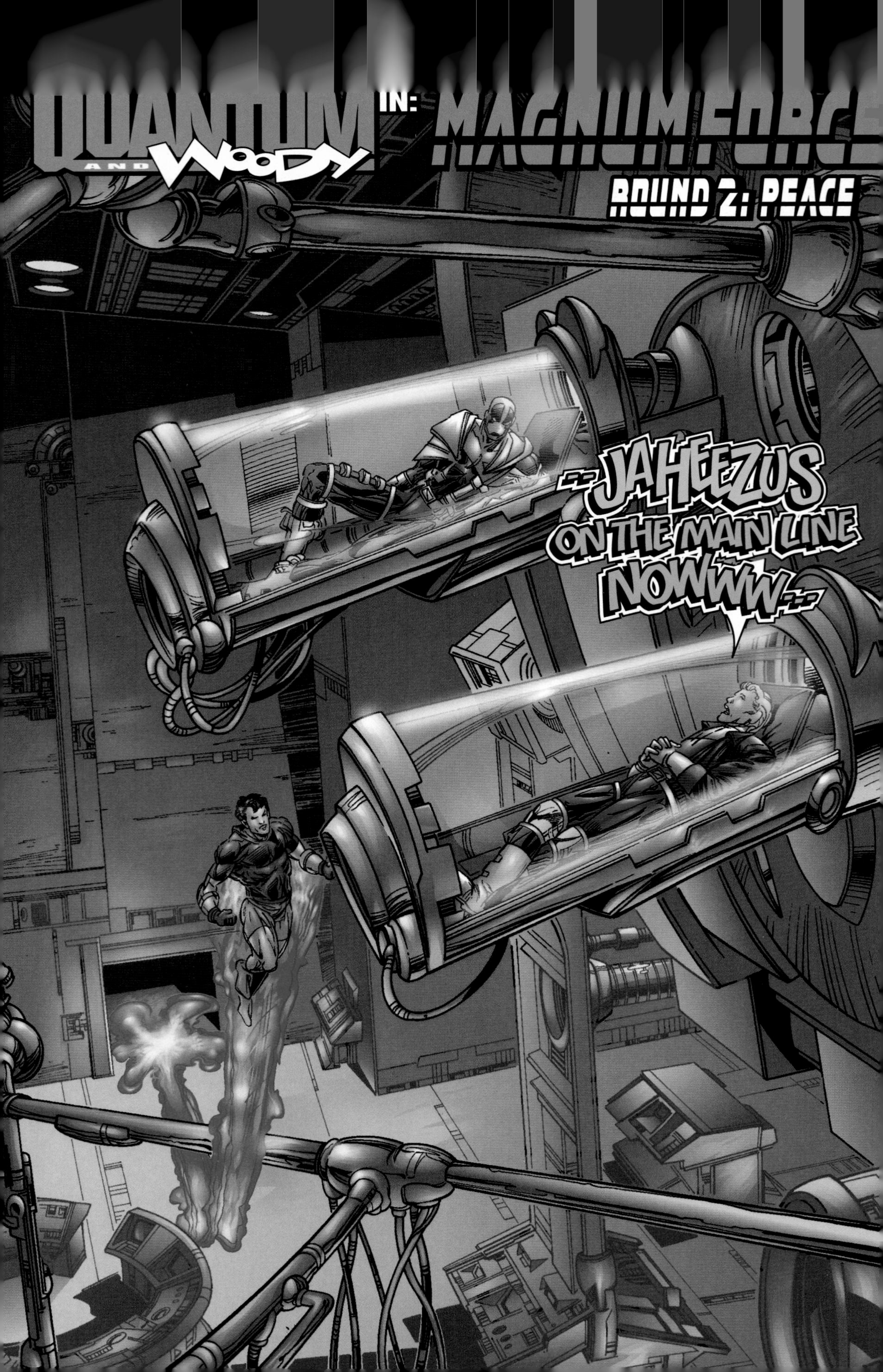
QUANTUM AND WOODY IN: MAGNUM FORCE
ROUND 2: PEACE
--JAHEEZUS ON THE MAIN LINE NOWWW--

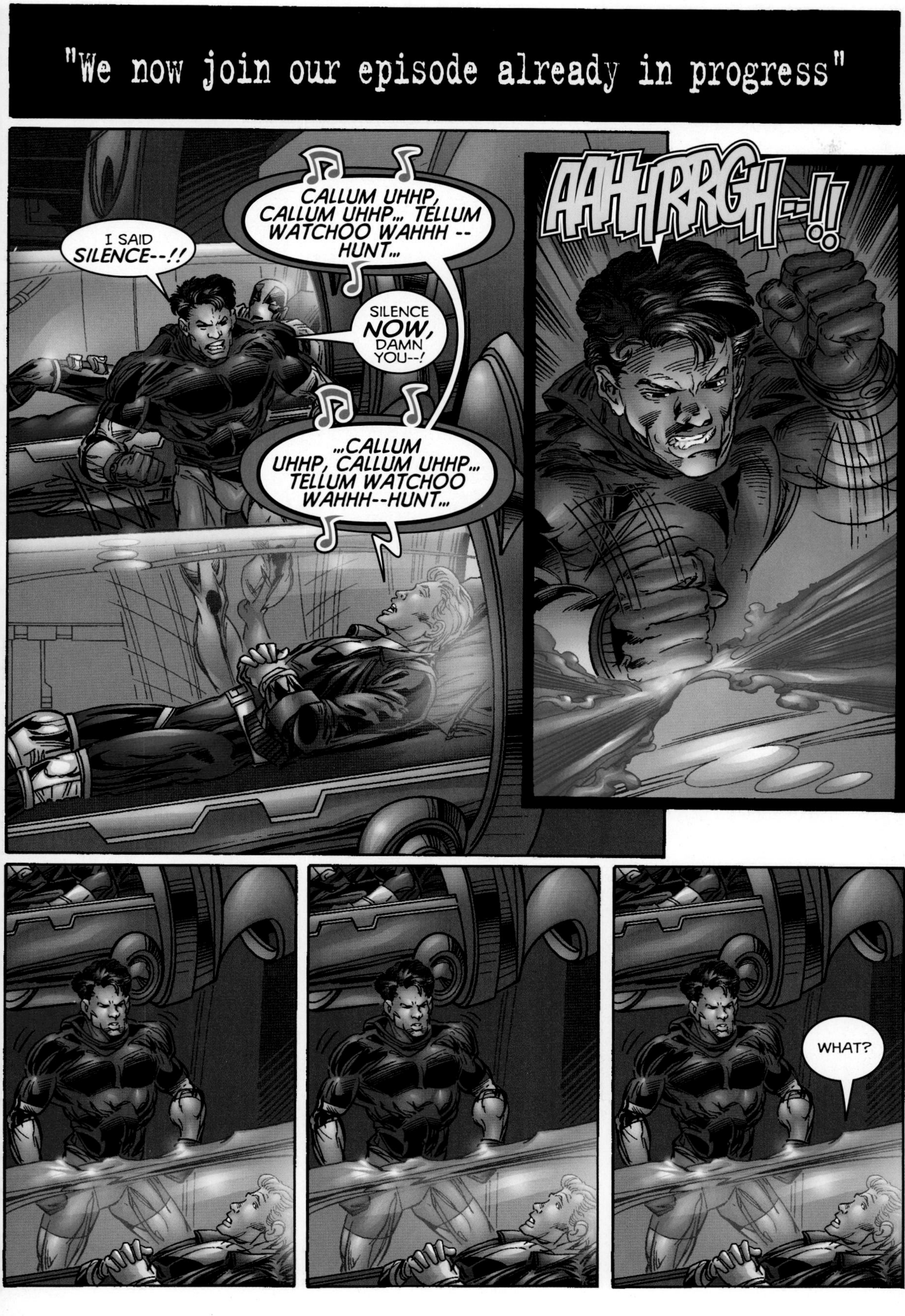
"We now join our episode already in progress"
I SAID SILENCE--!!
CALLUM UHHP, CALLUM UHHP... TELLUM WATCHOO WAHHH -- HUNT...
SILENCE NOW, DAMN YOU--!
...CALLUM UHHP, CALLUM UHHP... TELLUM WATCHOO WAHHH--HUNT...
AAHHRRGH--!!
WHAT?

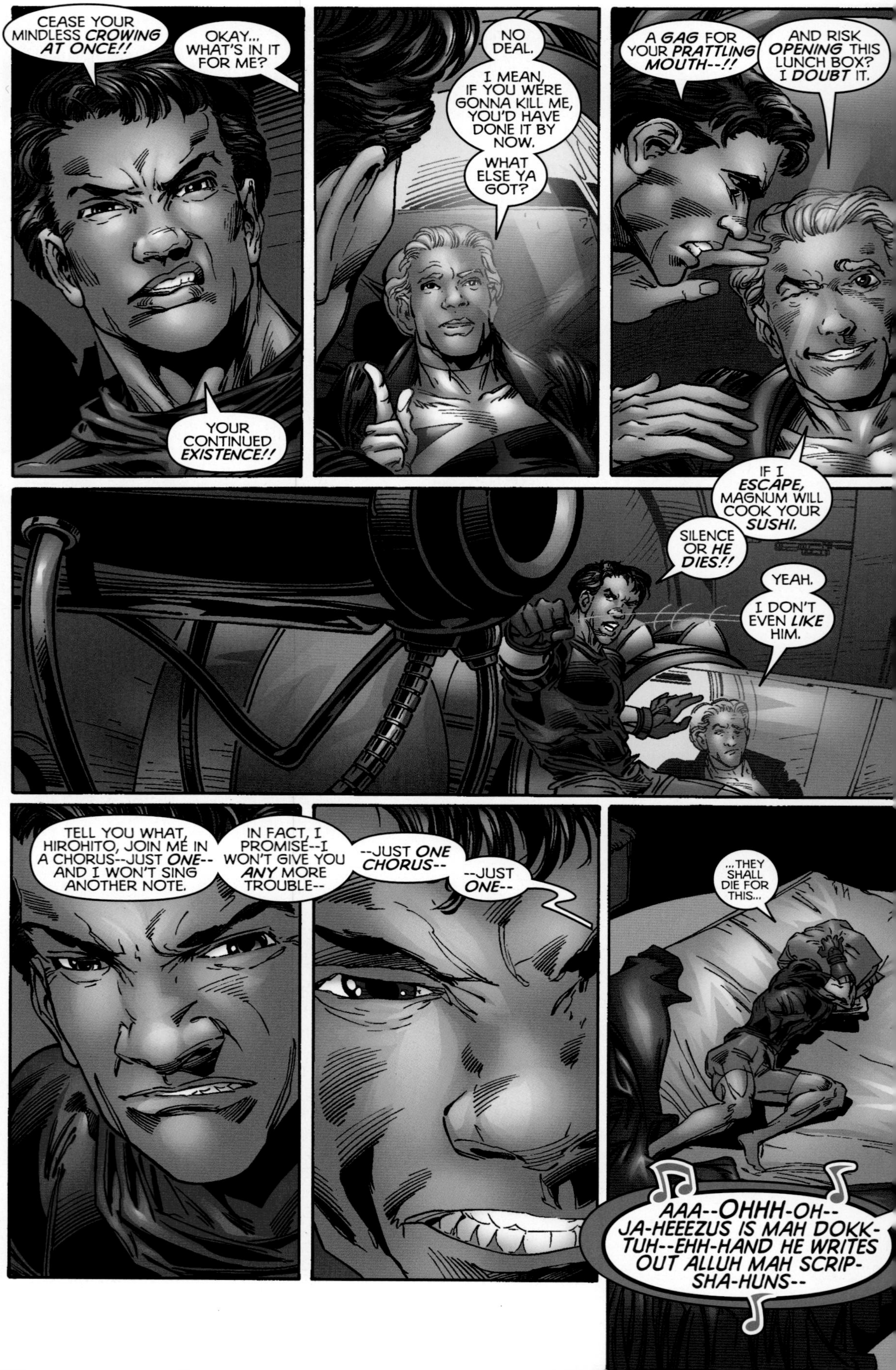
CEASE YOUR MINDLESS *CROWING AT ONCE!!*
OKAY... WHAT'S IN IT FOR ME?
YOUR CONTINUED *EXISTENCE!!*
NO DEAL.
I MEAN, IF YOU WERE GONNA KILL ME, YOU'D HAVE DONE IT BY NOW.
WHAT ELSE YA GOT?
A *GAG* FOR YOUR *PRATTLING MOUTH--!!*
AND RISK *OPENING* THIS LUNCH BOX? I *DOUBT* IT.
IF I *ESCAPE,* MAGNUM WILL COOK YOUR *SUSHI.*
SILENCE OR *HE DIES!!*
YEAH.
I DON'T EVEN *LIKE* HIM.
TELL YOU WHAT, HIROHITO, JOIN ME IN A CHORUS--JUST *ONE*-- AND I WON'T SING ANOTHER NOTE.
IN FACT, I PROMISE--I WON'T GIVE YOU *ANY* MORE TROUBLE--
--JUST *ONE CHORUS*--
--JUST *ONE*--
...THEY SHALL DIE FOR THIS...
AAA--OHHH-OH-- JA-HEEEZUS IS MAH DOKK-TUH--EHH-HAND HE WRITES OUT ALLUH MAH SCRIP-SHA-HUNS--

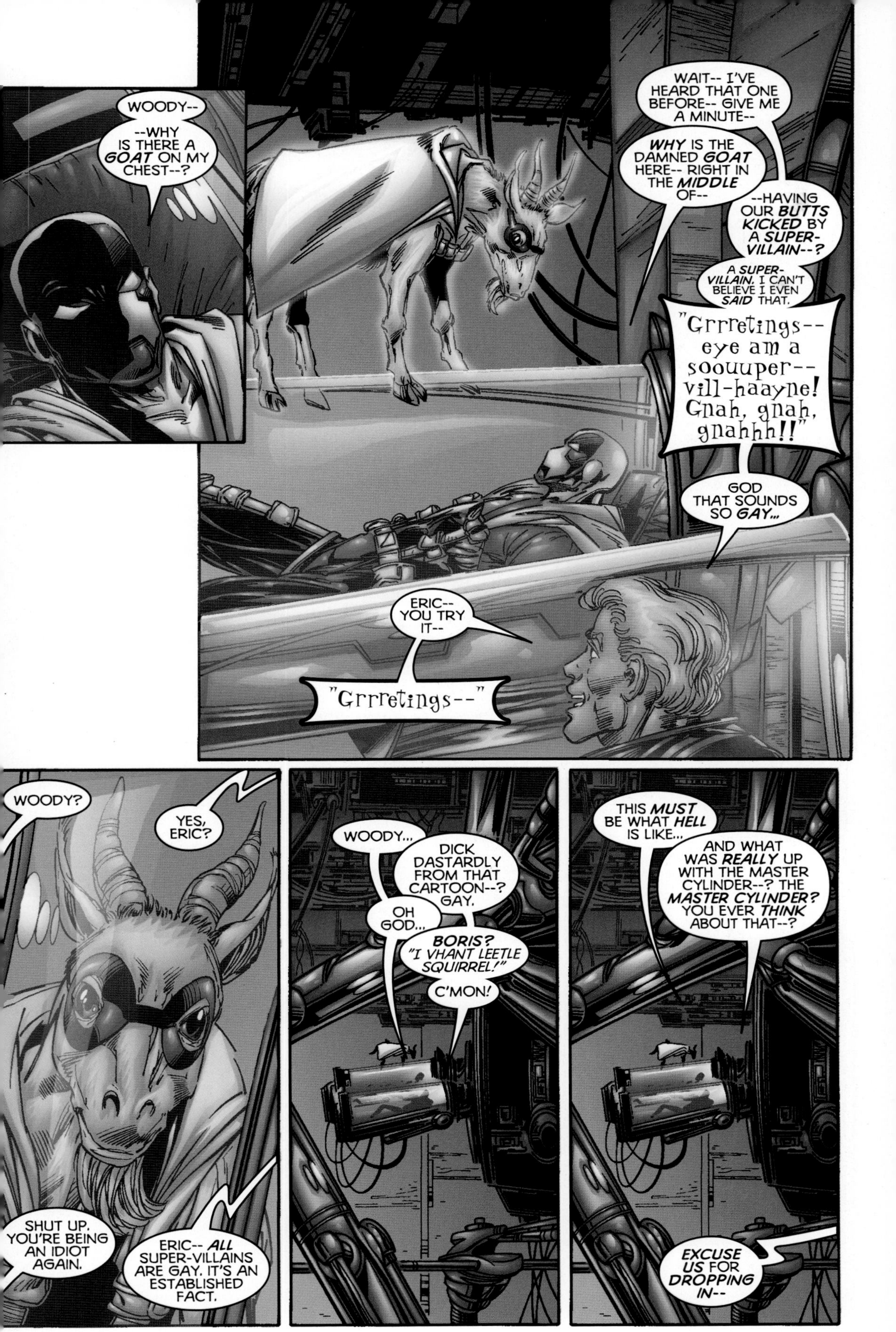
WOODY--
--WHY IS THERE A GOAT ON MY CHEST--?
WAIT-- I'VE HEARD THAT ONE BEFORE-- GIVE ME A MINUTE--
WHY IS THE DAMNED GOAT HERE-- RIGHT IN THE MIDDLE OF--
--HAVING OUR BUTTS KICKED BY A SUPER-VILLAIN--?
A SUPER-VILLAIN. I CAN'T BELIEVE I EVEN SAID THAT.
"Grrretings--eye am a soouuper--vill-haayne! Gnah, gnah, gnahhh!!"
GOD THAT SOUNDS SO GAY...
ERIC-- YOU TRY IT--
"Grrretings--"
WOODY?
YES, ERIC?
SHUT UP. YOU'RE BEING AN IDIOT AGAIN.
ERIC-- ALL SUPER-VILLAINS ARE GAY. IT'S AN ESTABLISHED FACT.
WOODY...
DICK DASTARDLY FROM THAT CARTOON--? GAY.
OH GOD...
BORIS? "I VHANT LEETLE SQUIRREL!"
C'MON!
THIS MUST BE WHAT HELL IS LIKE...
AND WHAT WAS REALLY UP WITH THE MASTER CYLINDER--? THE MASTER CYLINDER? YOU EVER THINK ABOUT THAT--?
EXCUSE US FOR DROPPING IN--

--BUT WE NEED TO *BORROW* YOUR *PET*. CITADEL HERE TRACED YOUR *COMM SIGNALS* IN YOUR UNIFORMS.

TEMPEST--! HEY--GREAT TO *SEE* YOU AGAIN--

--AND I MEAN THAT IN THE MOST *SINCERE* WAY--

WOODY-- WHERE DID YOU GUYS *GET* THE *GOAT*--? WHERE IS THE GOAT'S *HOME*?

Ah-- SOME CHINESE GUY--MAYBE TOKYO--?

FROM *MALAYSIA*-- A VILLAGE ON THE SOUTH-WEST MALAY PENINSULA.

WHAT IS YOUR *INTEREST* IN WOODY'S *GOAT*--?

LONG STORY.

AND WE'RE RUNNING OUT OF *TIME*--

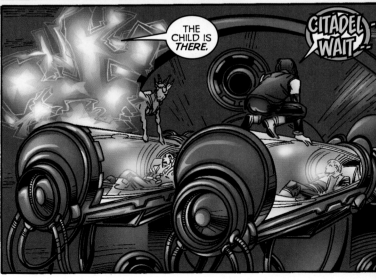

THE CHILD IS *THERE*.

CITADEL WAIT

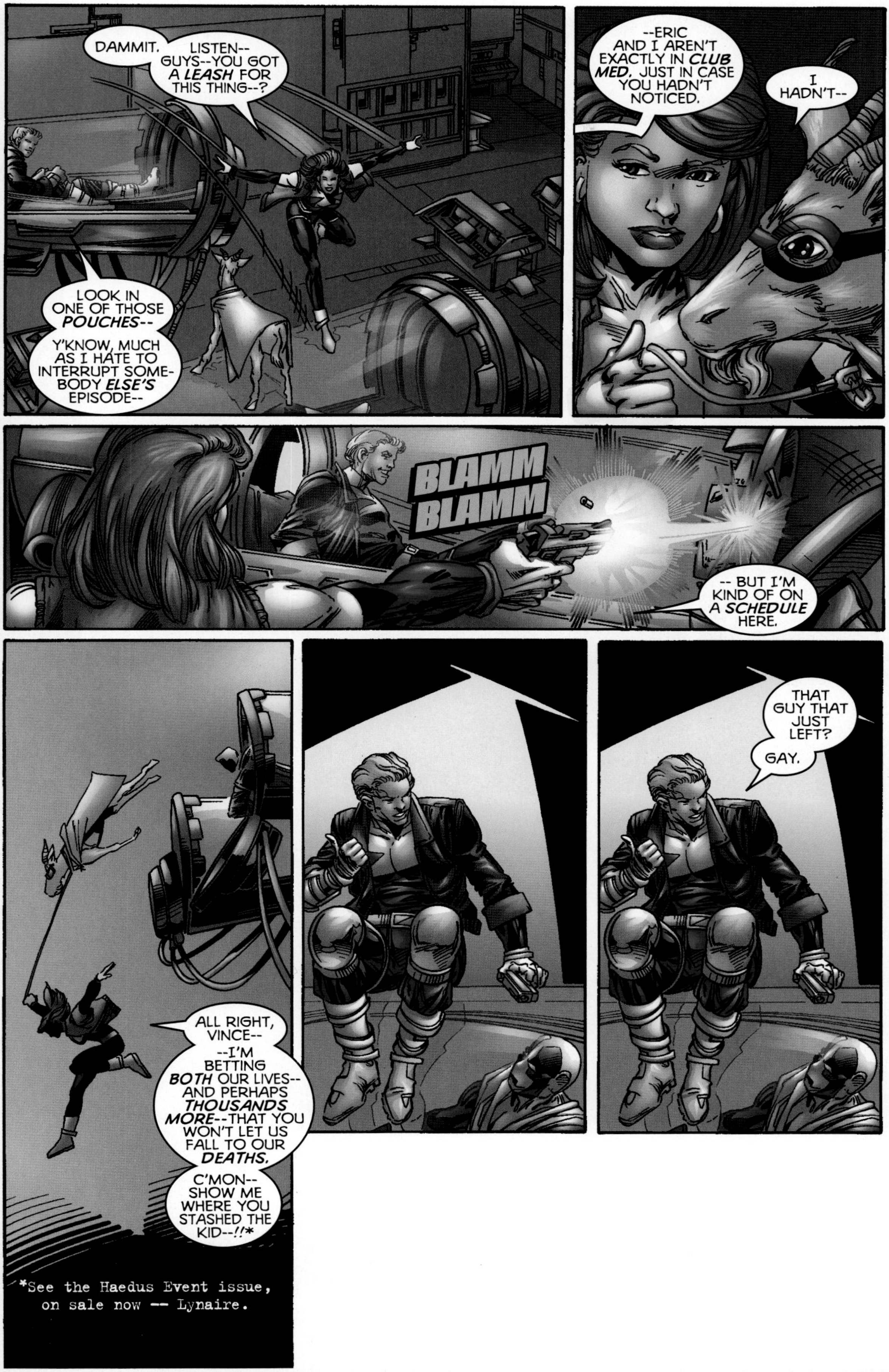
DAMMIT.
LISTEN-- GUYS--YOU GOT A *LEASH* FOR THIS THING--?
LOOK IN ONE OF THOSE *POUCHES*--
Y'KNOW, MUCH AS I HATE TO INTERRUPT SOME-BODY *ELSE'S* EPISODE--
--ERIC AND I AREN'T EXACTLY IN *CLUB MED*, JUST IN CASE YOU HADN'T NOTICED.
I HADN'T--
BLAMM
BLAMM
-- BUT I'M KIND OF ON A *SCHEDULE* HERE.
ALL RIGHT, VINCE--
--I'M BETTING *BOTH* OUR LIVES--AND PERHAPS *THOUSANDS MORE*--THAT YOU WON'T LET US FALL TO OUR *DEATHS*.
C'MON--SHOW ME WHERE YOU STASHED THE KID--!!*
*See the Haedus Event issue, on sale now -- Lynaire.
THAT GUY THAT JUST LEFT?
GAY.

"Oh...That"

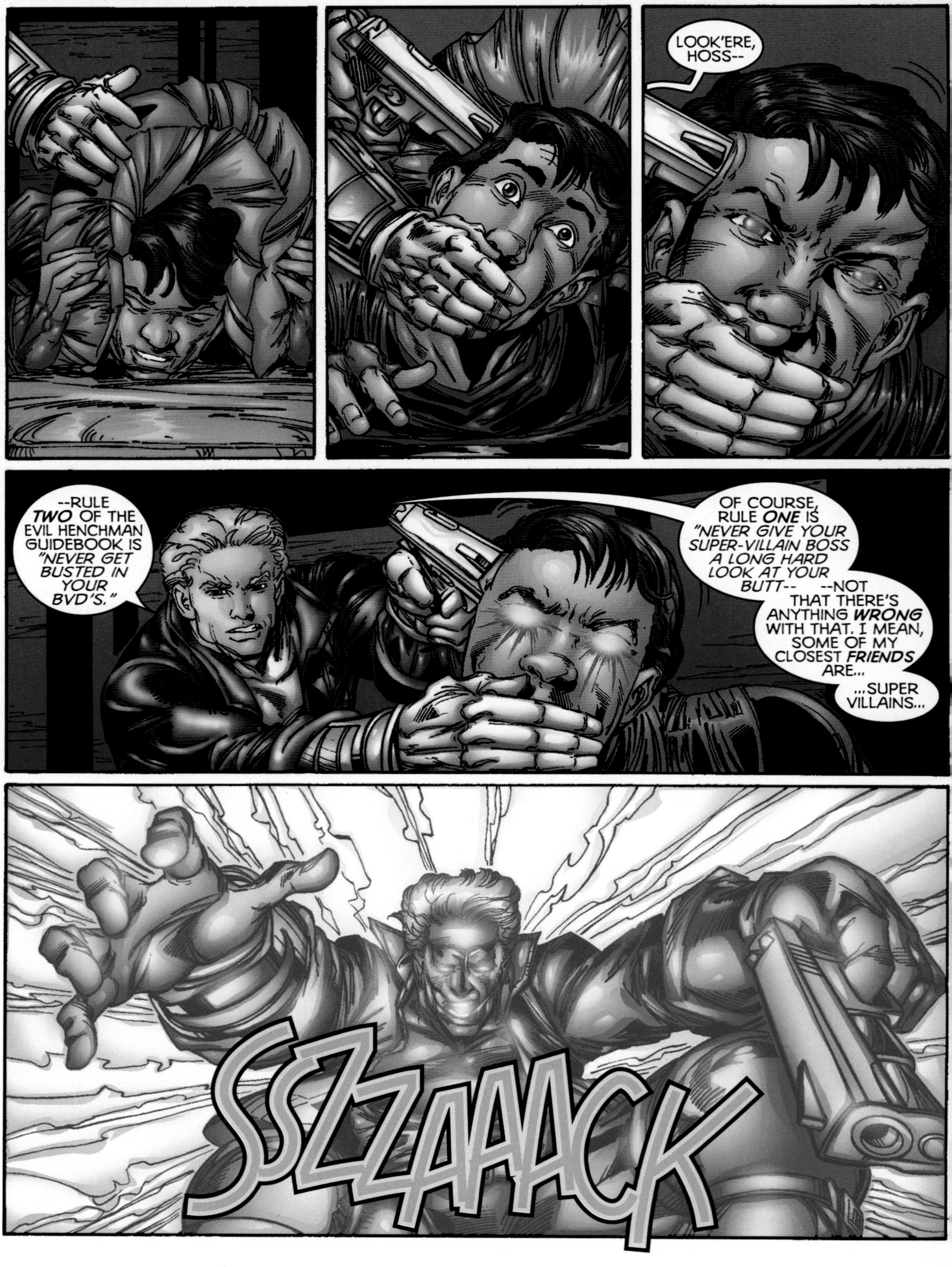
LOOK'ERE, HOSS--
--RULE TWO OF THE EVIL HENCHMAN GUIDEBOOK IS "NEVER GET BUSTED IN YOUR BVD'S."
OF COURSE, RULE ONE IS "NEVER GIVE YOUR SUPER-VILLAIN BOSS A LONG HARD LOOK AT YOUR BUTT--
--NOT THAT THERE'S ANYTHING WRONG WITH THAT. I MEAN, SOME OF MY CLOSEST FRIENDS ARE...
...SUPER VILLAINS...
SSZAAACK

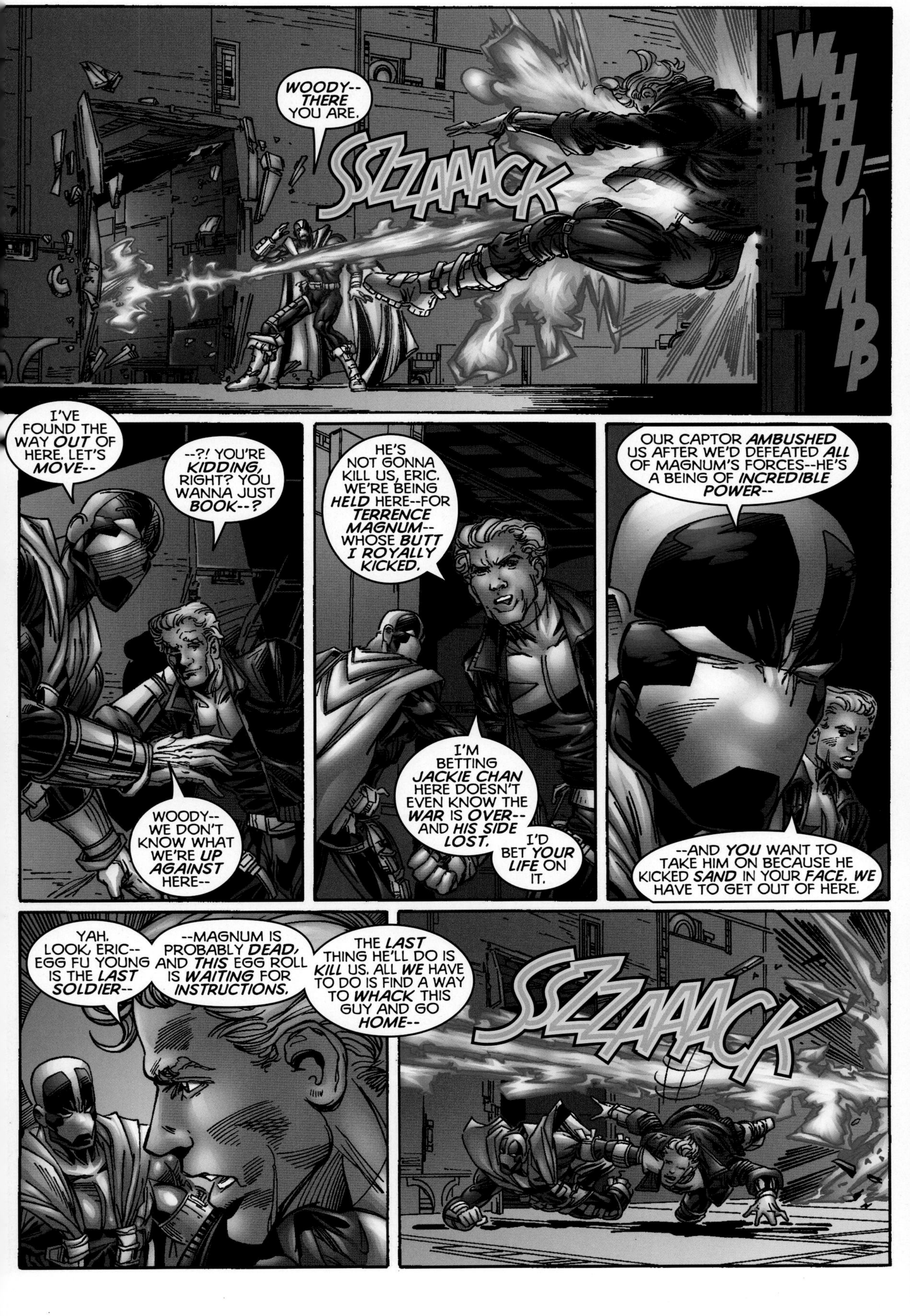
WOODY--
THERE
YOU ARE.
SSZAAACK
WHHUMMP
I'VE FOUND THE WAY OUT OF HERE. LET'S MOVE--
--?! YOU'RE KIDDING, RIGHT? YOU WANNA JUST BOOK--?
WOODY-- WE DON'T KNOW WHAT WE'RE UP AGAINST HERE--
HE'S NOT GONNA KILL US, ERIC. WE'RE BEING HELD HERE--FOR TERRENCE MAGNUM-- WHOSE BUTT I ROYALLY KICKED.
I'M BETTING JACKIE CHAN HERE DOESN'T EVEN KNOW THE WAR IS OVER-- AND HIS SIDE LOST.
I'D BET YOUR LIFE ON IT.
OUR CAPTOR AMBUSHED US AFTER WE'D DEFEATED ALL OF MAGNUM'S FORCES--HE'S A BEING OF INCREDIBLE POWER--
--AND YOU WANT TO TAKE HIM ON BECAUSE HE KICKED SAND IN YOUR FACE. WE HAVE TO GET OUT OF HERE.
YAH. LOOK, ERIC-- EGG FU YOUNG IS THE LAST SOLDIER--
--MAGNUM IS PROBABLY DEAD, AND THIS EGG ROLL IS WAITING FOR INSTRUCTIONS.
THE LAST THING HE'LL DO IS KILL US. ALL WE HAVE TO DO IS FIND A WAY TO WHACK THIS GUY AND GO HOME--
SSZAAACK

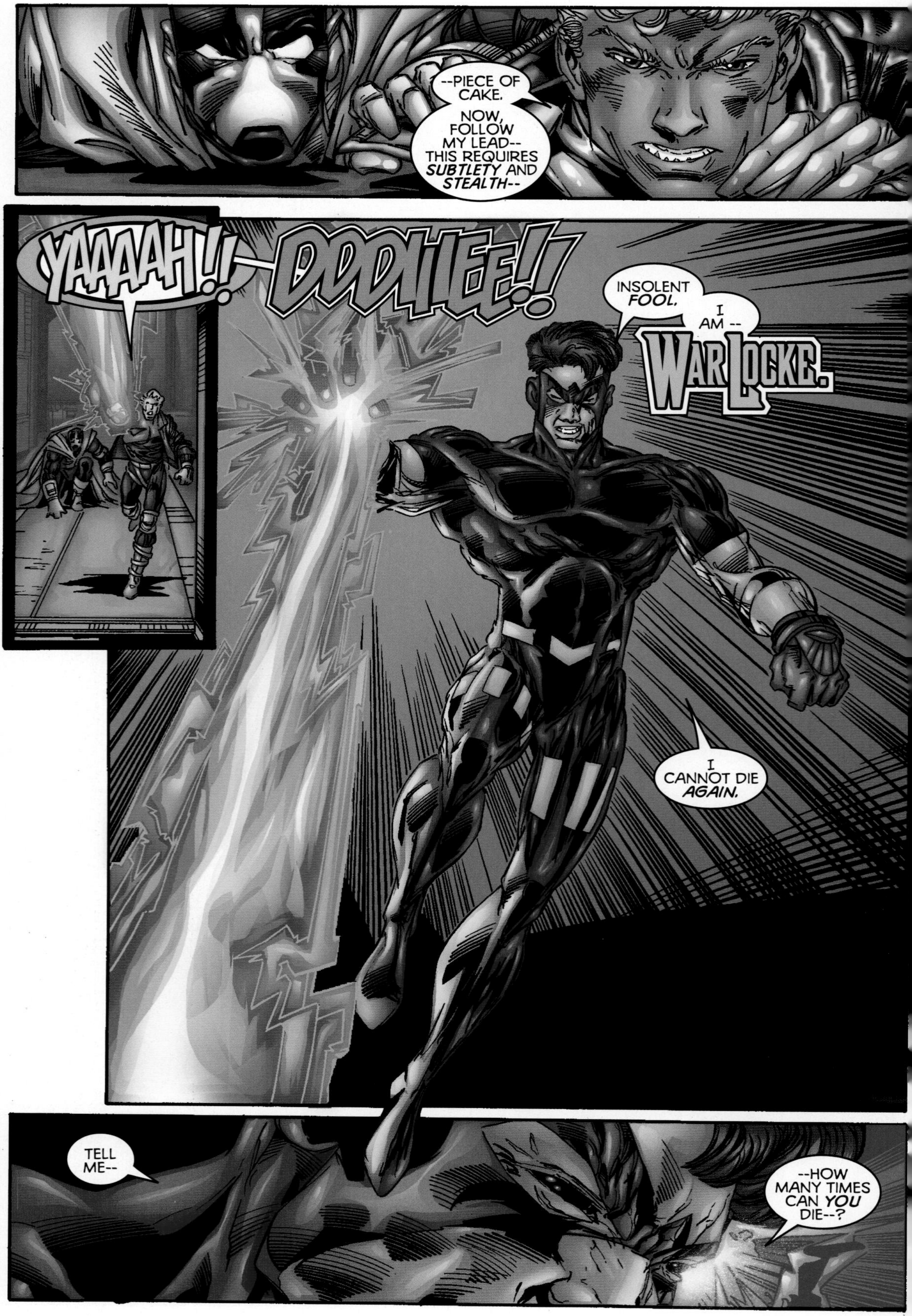
--PIECE OF CAKE.
NOW, FOLLOW MY LEAD-- THIS REQUIRES SUBTLETY AND STEALTH--
YAAAAH!!
DDDIIEE!!
INSOLENT FOOL.
I AM --
WARLOCKE.
I CANNOT DIE AGAIN.
TELL ME--
--HOW MANY TIMES CAN YOU DIE--?

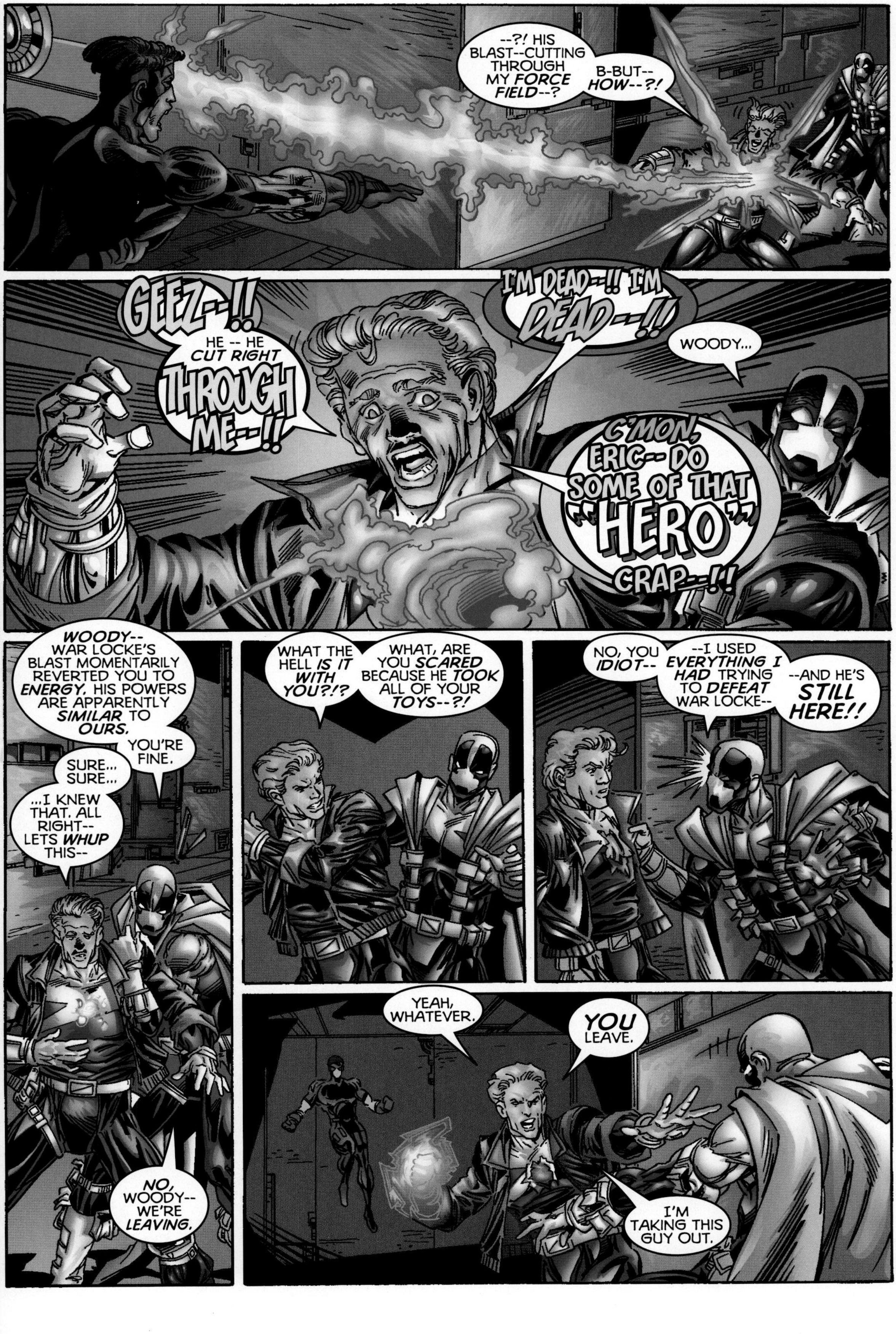
--?! HIS BLAST--CUTTING THROUGH MY FORCE FIELD--?
B-BUT-- HOW--?!
GEEZ--!!
HE -- HE CUT RIGHT THROUGH ME--!!
I'M DEAD--!! I'M DEAD--!!
WOODY...
C'MON, ERIC-- DO SOME OF THAT "HERO" CRAP--!!
WOODY-- WAR LOCKE'S BLAST MOMENTARILY REVERTED YOU TO ENERGY. HIS POWERS ARE APPARENTLY SIMILAR TO OURS.
YOU'RE FINE.
SURE... SURE...
...I KNEW THAT. ALL RIGHT-- LETS WHUP THIS--
NO, WOODY-- WE'RE LEAVING.
WHAT THE HELL IS IT WITH YOU?!?
WHAT, ARE YOU SCARED BECAUSE HE TOOK ALL OF YOUR TOYS--?!
NO, YOU IDIOT--
--I USED EVERYTHING I HAD TRYING TO DEFEAT WAR LOCKE--
--AND HE'S STILL HERE!!
YEAH, WHATEVER.
YOU LEAVE.
I'M TAKING THIS GUY OUT.

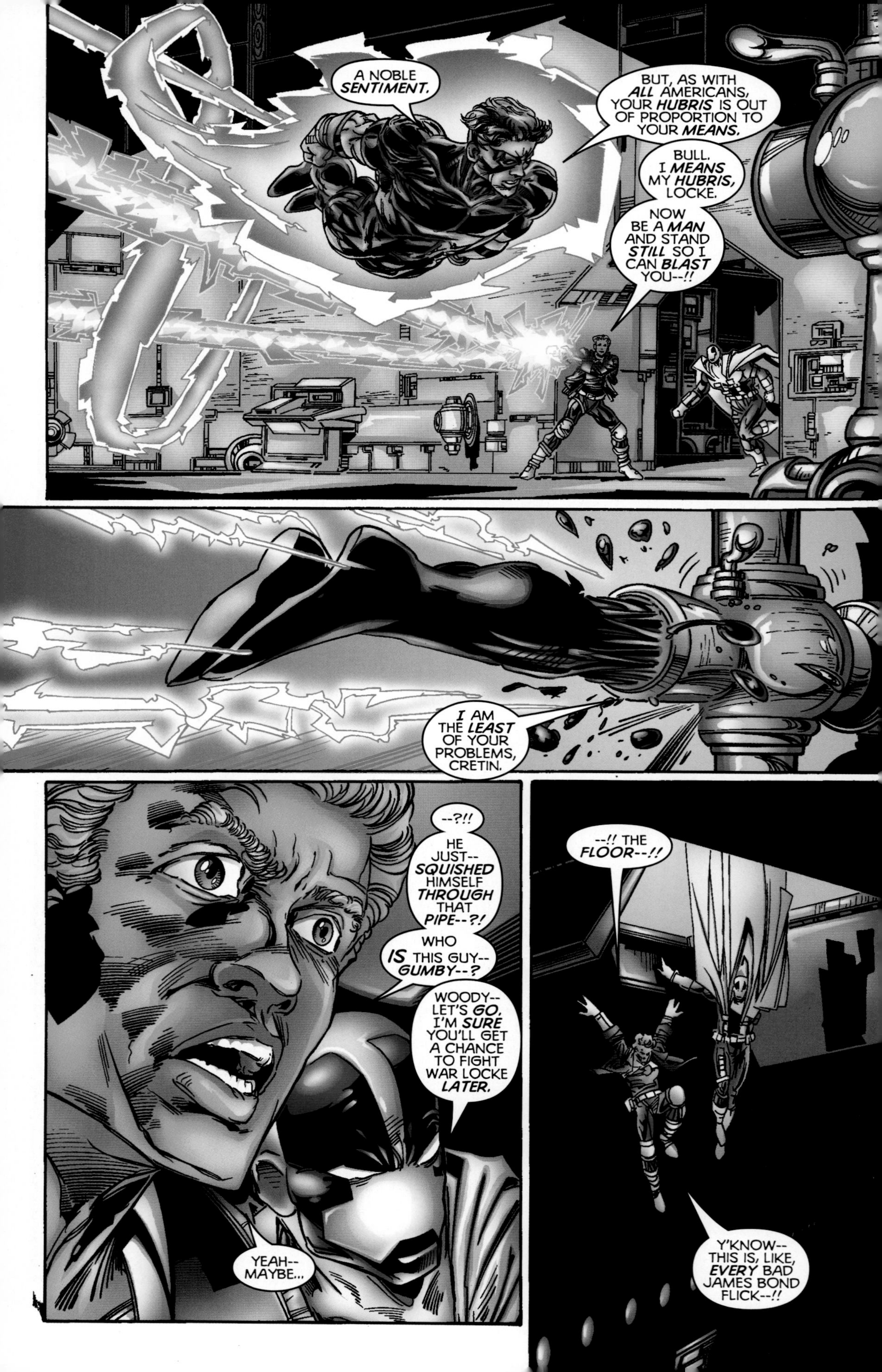
A NOBLE SENTIMENT.
BUT, AS WITH ALL AMERICANS, YOUR HUBRIS IS OUT OF PROPORTION TO YOUR MEANS.
BULL. I MEANS MY HUBRIS, LOCKE.
NOW BE A MAN AND STAND STILL SO I CAN BLAST YOU--!!
I AM THE LEAST OF YOUR PROBLEMS, CRETIN.
--?!!
HE JUST-- SQUISHED HIMSELF THROUGH THAT PIPE--?!
WHO IS THIS GUY-- GUMBY--?
WOODY-- LET'S GO. I'M SURE YOU'LL GET A CHANCE TO FIGHT WAR LOCKE LATER.
YEAH-- MAYBE...
--!! THE FLOOR--!!
Y'KNOW-- THIS IS, LIKE, EVERY BAD JAMES BOND FLICK--!!

Assistant Editor: Omar Banmally (#14-15)
Editors: Lynaire Thompson (#14-17)
and Omar Banmally (#16-21, 32)
Editor-in-Chief: Warren Simons

Peter Cuneo
Chairman

Dinesh Shamdasani
CEO & Chief Creative Officer

Gavin Cuneo
Chief Operating Officer & CFO

Fred Pierce
Publisher

Warren Simons
VP Editor-in-Chief

Walter Black
VP Operations

Hunter Gorinson
Director of Marketing,
Communications & Digital Media

Atom! Freeman
Matthew Klein
Andy Liegl
John Petrie
Sales Managers

Josh Johns
Digital Sales & Special Projects Manager

Travis Escarfullery
Jeff Walker
Production & Design Managers

Alejandro Arbona
Editor

Kyle Andrukiewicz
Tom Brennan
Associate Editors

Peter Stern
Publishing & Operations Manager

Andrew Steinbeiser
Marketing & Communications Manager

Danny Khazem
Operations Coordinator

Ivan Cohen
Collection Editor

Steve Blackwell
Collection Designer

Rian Hughes/Device
Trade Dress & Book Design

Russell Brown
President, Consumer Products,
Promotions and Ad Sales

Jason Kothari
Vice Chairman

WOODY-- WE ARE FIGHTING THE UNKNOWN, WHICH IS NEVER A GOOD IDEA. MAKING ME BE THE HUMORLESS SCHOOL TEACHER MIGHT BE FUN--
--WHICH IT IS--
--BUT YOU ARE THE ONE WHO'S GOING TO GET US BOTH KILLED.
ERIC-- LOOK, YOU'RE JUST SCARED.
THERE'S NOTHING WRONG WITH THAT. HELL, I'M SCARED, TOO.
BUT STOP BENDING YOURSELF INTO A PRETZEL RATIONALIZING IT--
--?! WHAT THE--?
WHAHOOM
click
"CLICK?"
LIGHTS--?
JUMP.
JUMP LIGHTS? WHAT THE HELL ARE "JUMP LIGHTS"--?
NO, YOU IDIOT--
--JUMP--!!

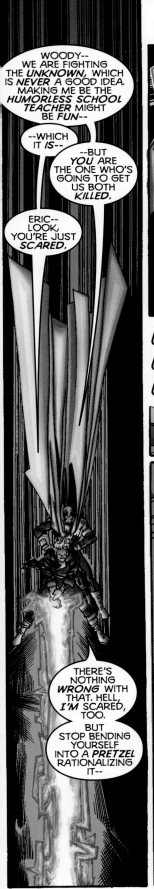

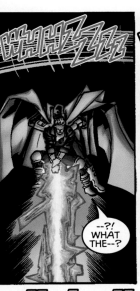

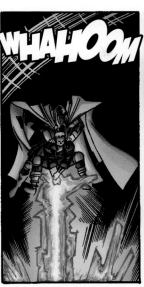

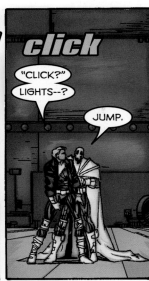

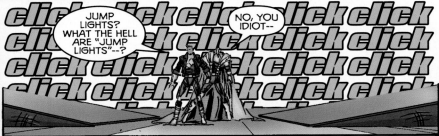

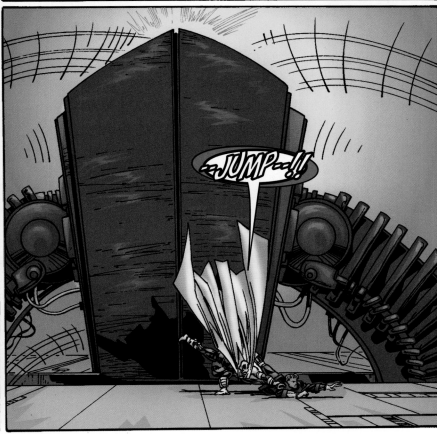

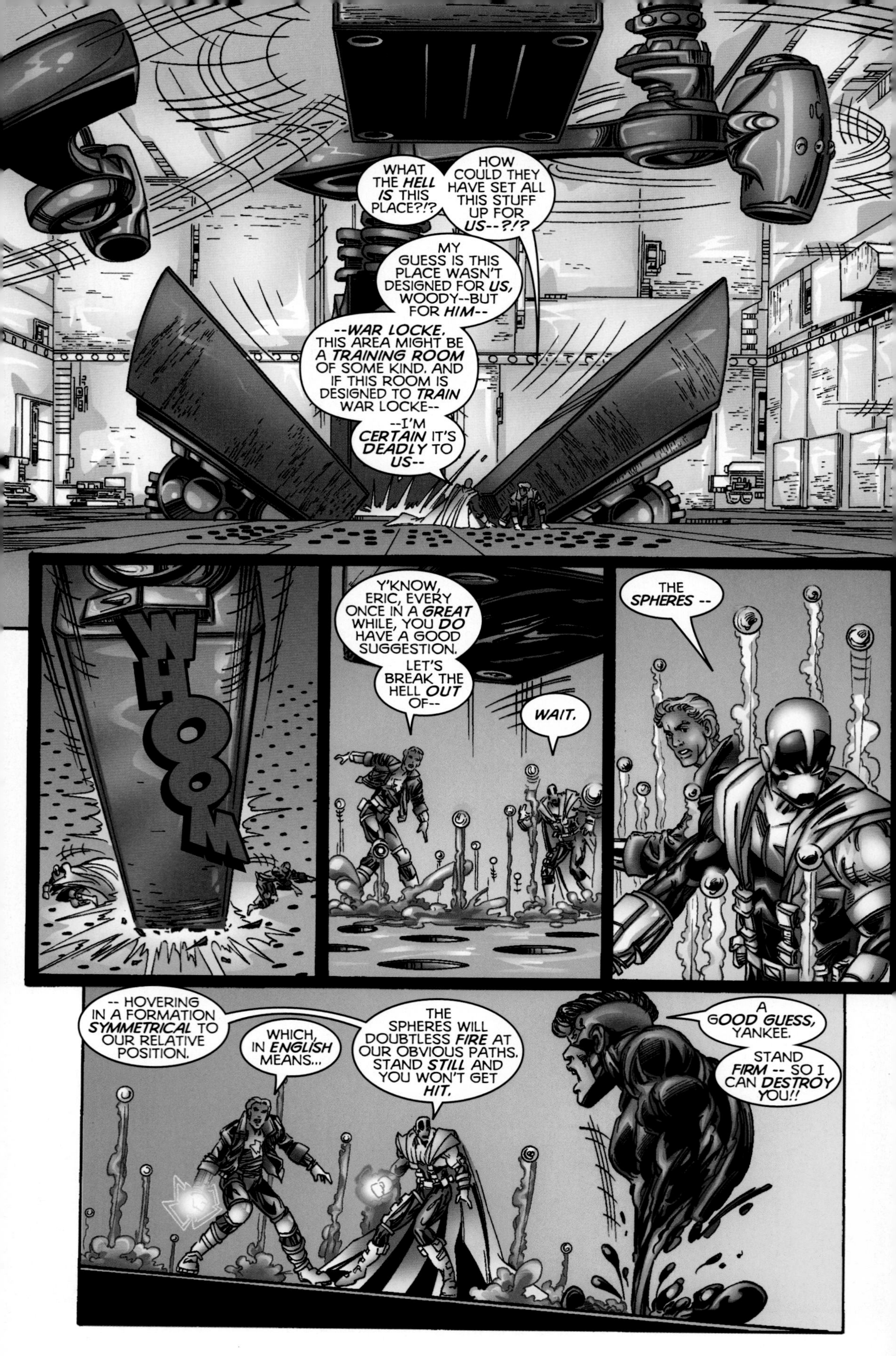
WHAT THE HELL IS THIS PLACE?!?
HOW COULD THEY HAVE SET ALL THIS STUFF UP FOR US--?!?
MY GUESS IS THIS PLACE WASN'T DESIGNED FOR US, WOODY--BUT FOR HIM--
--WAR LOCKE. THIS AREA MIGHT BE A TRAINING ROOM OF SOME KIND. AND IF THIS ROOM IS DESIGNED TO TRAIN WAR LOCKE--
--I'M CERTAIN IT'S DEADLY TO US--
WHOOM
Y'KNOW, ERIC, EVERY ONCE IN A GREAT WHILE, YOU DO HAVE A GOOD SUGGESTION.
LET'S BREAK THE HELL OUT OF--
WAIT.
THE SPHERES --
-- HOVERING IN A FORMATION SYMMETRICAL TO OUR RELATIVE POSITION.
WHICH, IN ENGLISH MEANS...
THE SPHERES WILL DOUBTLESS FIRE AT OUR OBVIOUS PATHS. STAND STILL AND YOU WON'T GET HIT.
A GOOD GUESS, YANKEE.
STAND FIRM -- SO I CAN DESTROY YOU!!

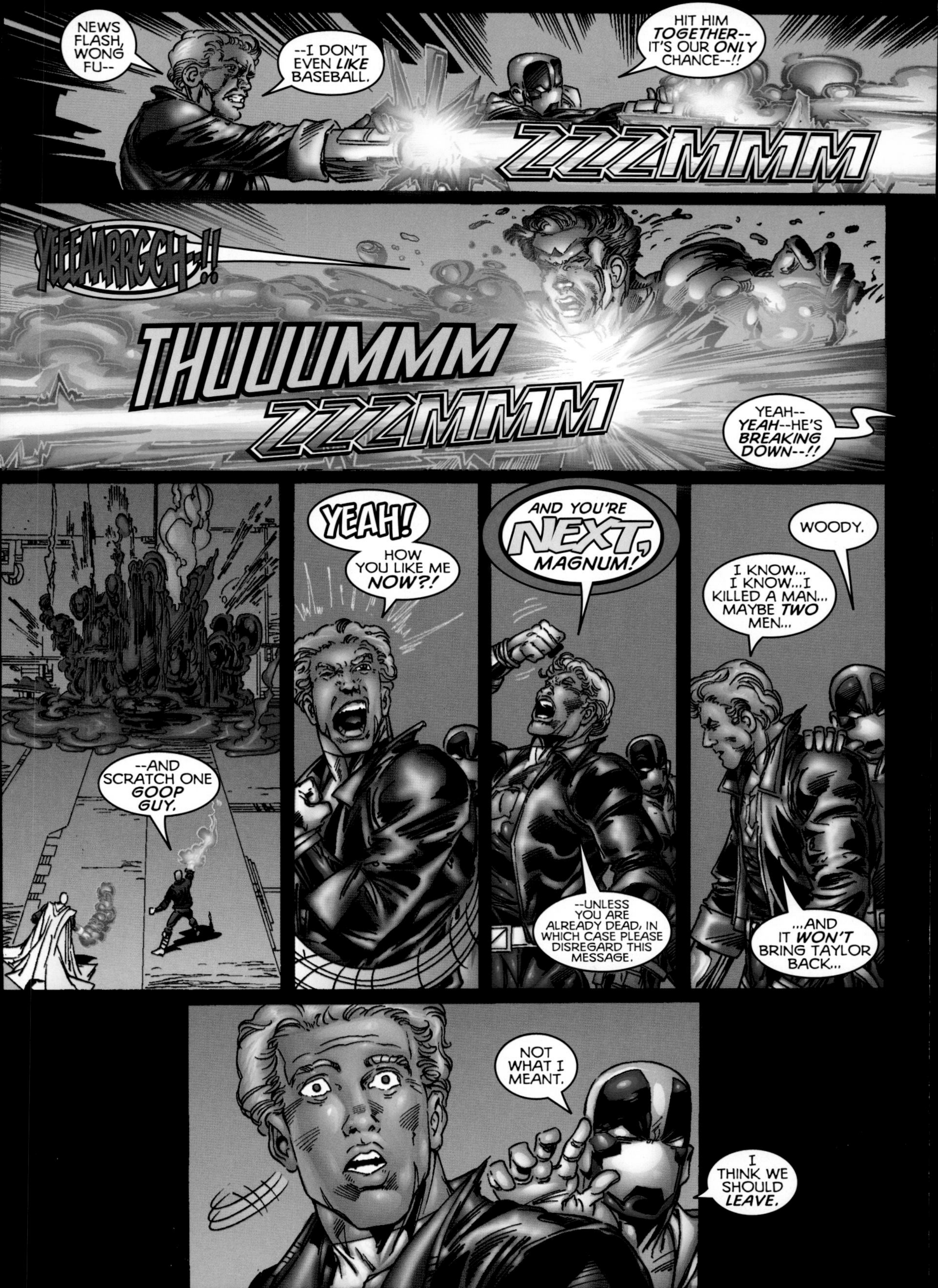
NEWS FLASH, WONG FU--
--I DON'T EVEN LIKE BASEBALL.
HIT HIM TOGETHER-- IT'S OUR ONLY CHANCE--!!
ZZZMMM
YEEEAARRGGH--!!
THUUUMMM
ZZZMMM
YEAH-- YEAH--HE'S BREAKING DOWN--!!
--AND SCRATCH ONE GOOP GUY.
YEAH!
HOW YOU LIKE ME NOW?!
AND YOU'RE NEXT, MAGNUM!
--UNLESS YOU ARE ALREADY DEAD, IN WHICH CASE PLEASE DISREGARD THIS MESSAGE.
WOODY.
I KNOW... I KNOW...I KILLED A MAN... MAYBE TWO MEN...
...AND IT WON'T BRING TAYLOR BACK...
NOT WHAT I MEANT.
I THINK WE SHOULD LEAVE.

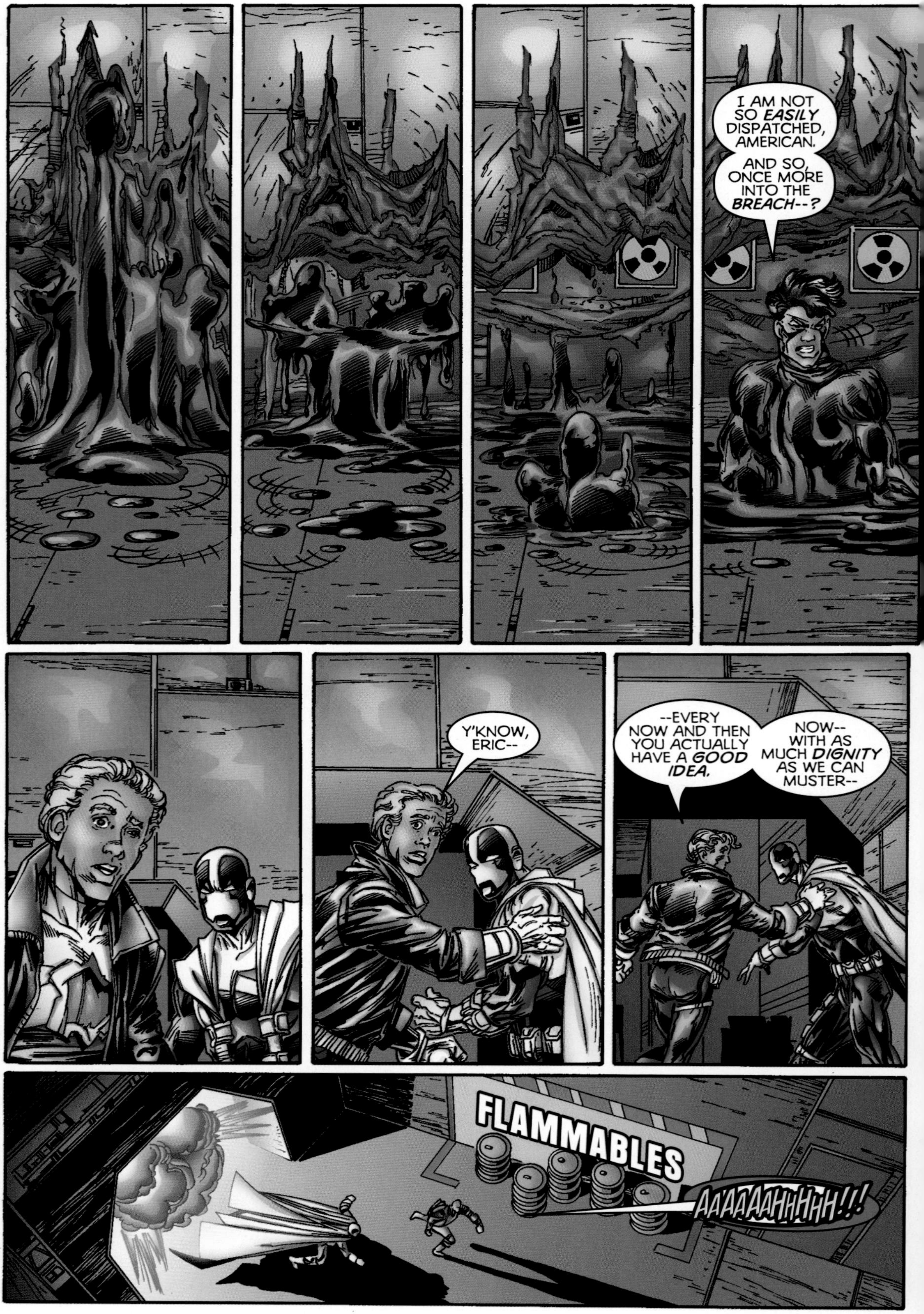
I AM NOT SO EASILY DISPATCHED, AMERICAN.
AND SO, ONCE MORE INTO THE BREACH--?
Y'KNOW, ERIC--
--EVERY NOW AND THEN YOU ACTUALLY HAVE A GOOD IDEA.
NOW-- WITH AS MUCH DIGNITY AS WE CAN MUSTER--
FLAMMABLES
AAAAAAHHHHH!!!

"I KNEW We Should Have Made That Right At The Men's Room"

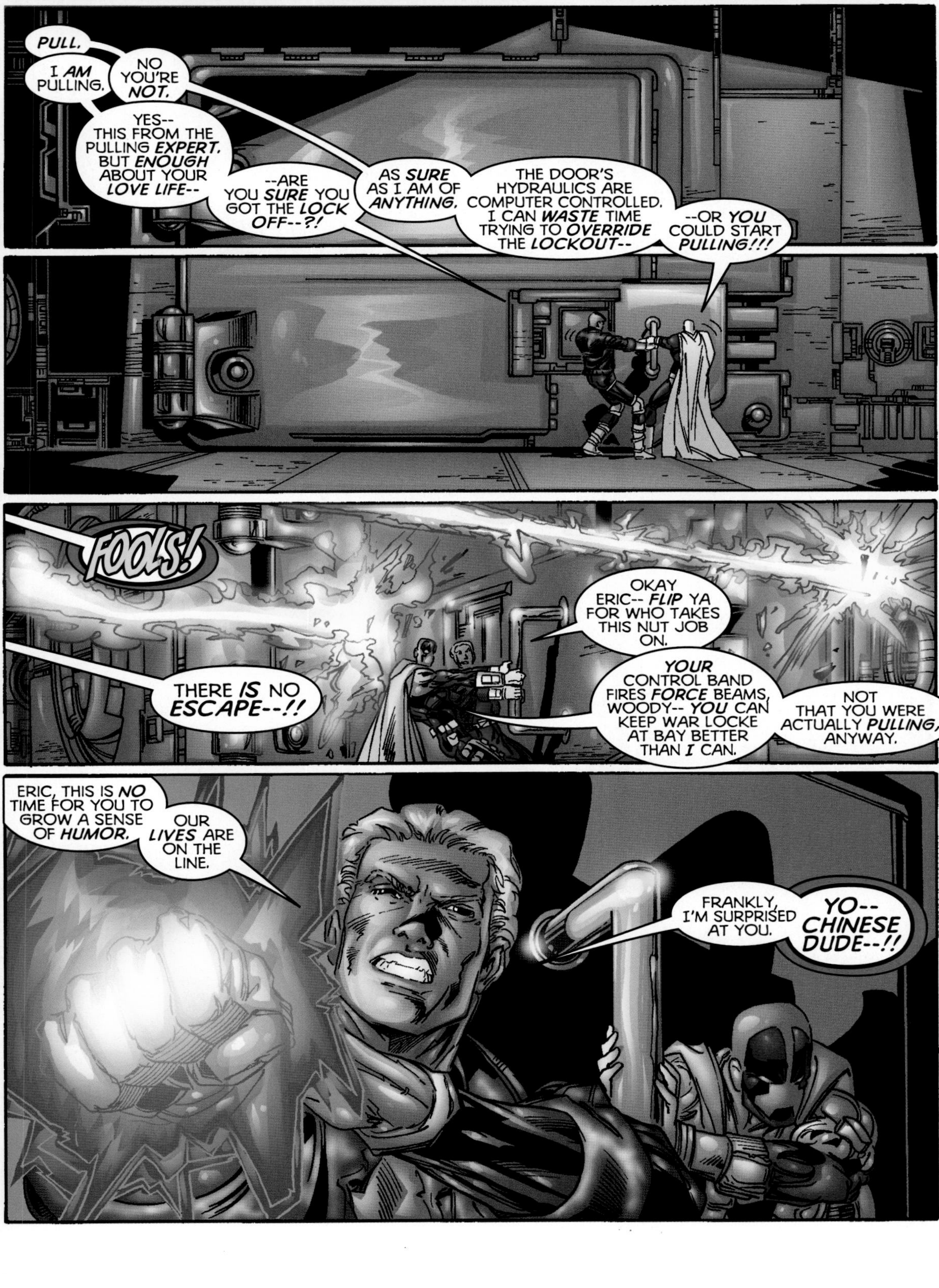

PULL.
I AM PULLING.
NO YOU'RE NOT.
YES-- THIS FROM THE PULLING EXPERT. BUT ENOUGH ABOUT YOUR LOVE LIFE--
--ARE YOU SURE YOU GOT THE LOCK OFF--?!
AS SURE AS I AM OF ANYTHING.
THE DOOR'S HYDRAULICS ARE COMPUTER CONTROLLED. I CAN WASTE TIME TRYING TO OVERRIDE THE LOCKOUT--
--OR YOU COULD START PULLING!!!
FOOLS!
THERE IS NO ESCAPE--!!
OKAY ERIC-- FLIP YA FOR WHO TAKES THIS NUT JOB ON.
YOUR CONTROL BAND FIRES FORCE BEAMS, WOODY-- YOU CAN KEEP WAR LOCKE AT BAY BETTER THAN I CAN.
NOT THAT YOU WERE ACTUALLY PULLING, ANYWAY.
ERIC, THIS IS NO TIME FOR YOU TO GROW A SENSE OF HUMOR.
OUR LIVES ARE ON THE LINE.
FRANKLY, I'M SURPRISED AT YOU.
YO-- CHINESE DUDE--!!

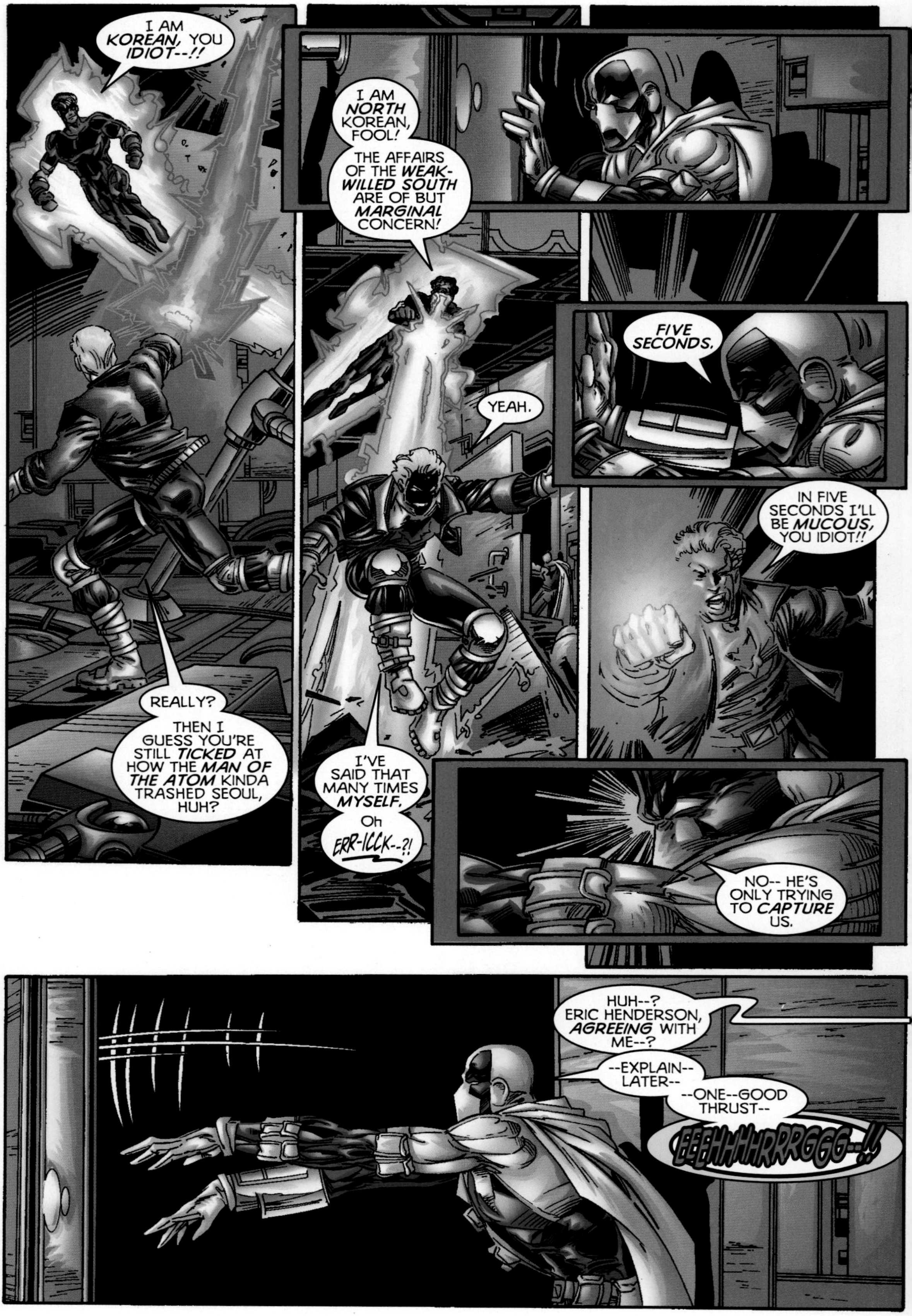
I AM KOREAN, YOU IDIOT--!!
REALLY? THEN I GUESS YOU'RE STILL TICKED AT HOW THE MAN OF THE ATOM KINDA TRASHED SEOUL, HUH?
I AM NORTH KOREAN, FOOL!
THE AFFAIRS OF THE WEAK-WILLED SOUTH ARE OF BUT MARGINAL CONCERN!
YEAH.
I'VE SAID THAT MANY TIMES MYSELF,
Oh ERR-ICCK--?!
FIVE SECONDS.
IN FIVE SECONDS I'LL BE MUCOUS, YOU IDIOT!!
NO-- HE'S ONLY TRYING TO CAPTURE US.
HUH--? ERIC HENDERSON, AGREEING WITH ME--?
--EXPLAIN-- LATER--
--ONE--GOOD THRUST--
EEEHHHHRRRGGG--!!

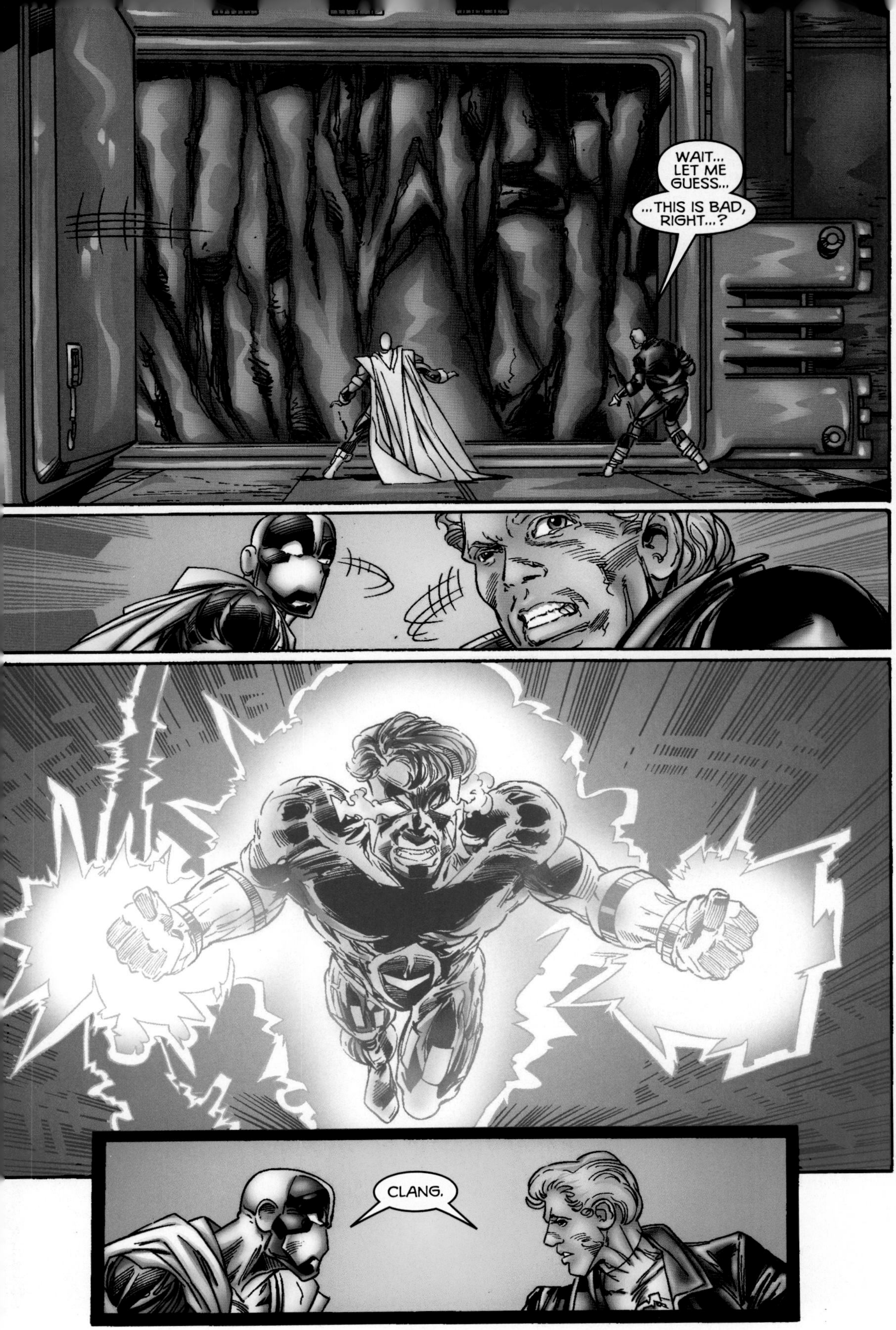
WAIT... LET ME GUESS...
...THIS IS BAD, RIGHT...?
CLANG.

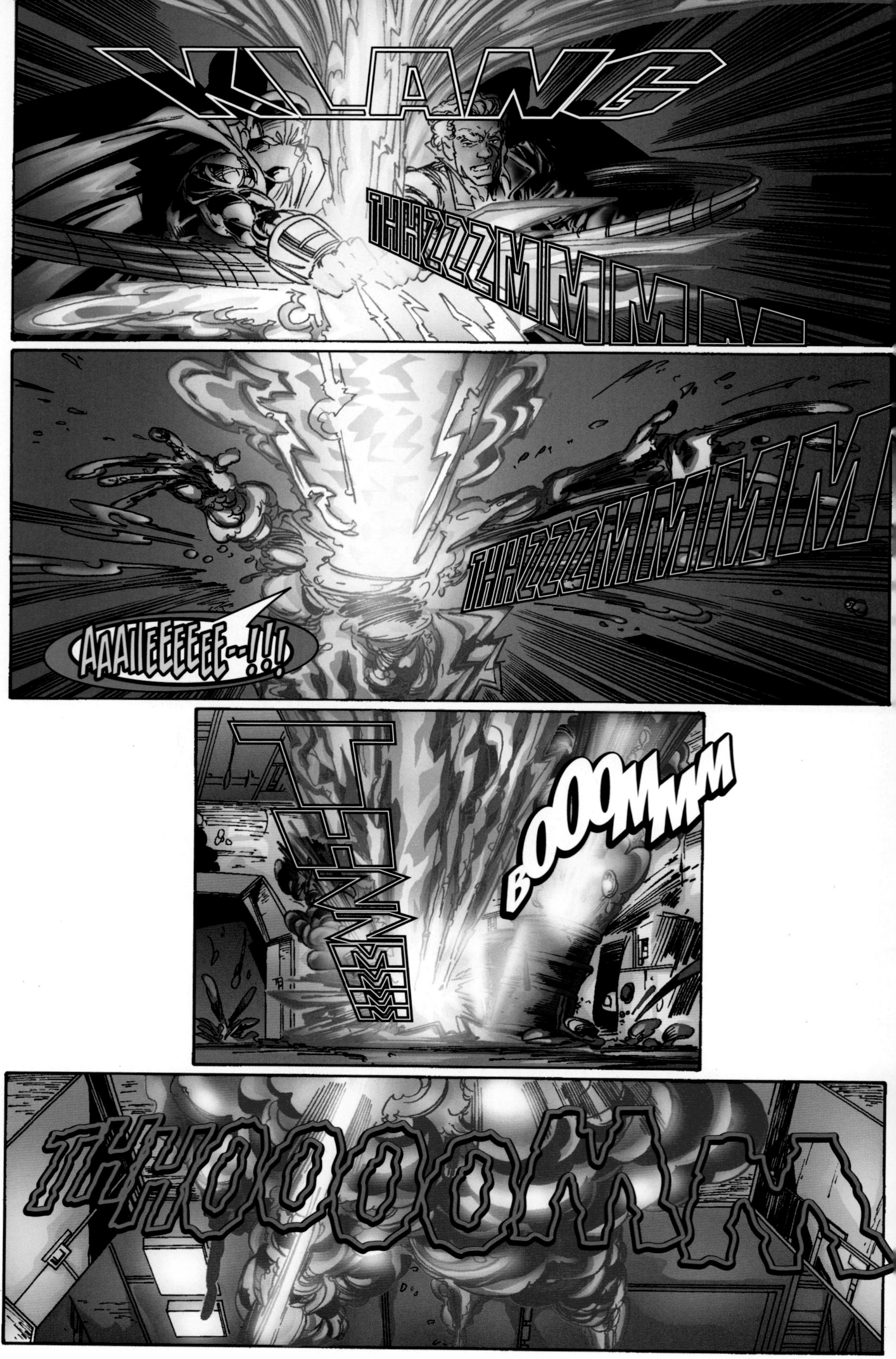
KLANG
THHZZZMMMM
THHZZZMMMMMM
AAAIEEEEEE--!!!
BOOOMMM
THOOOOM

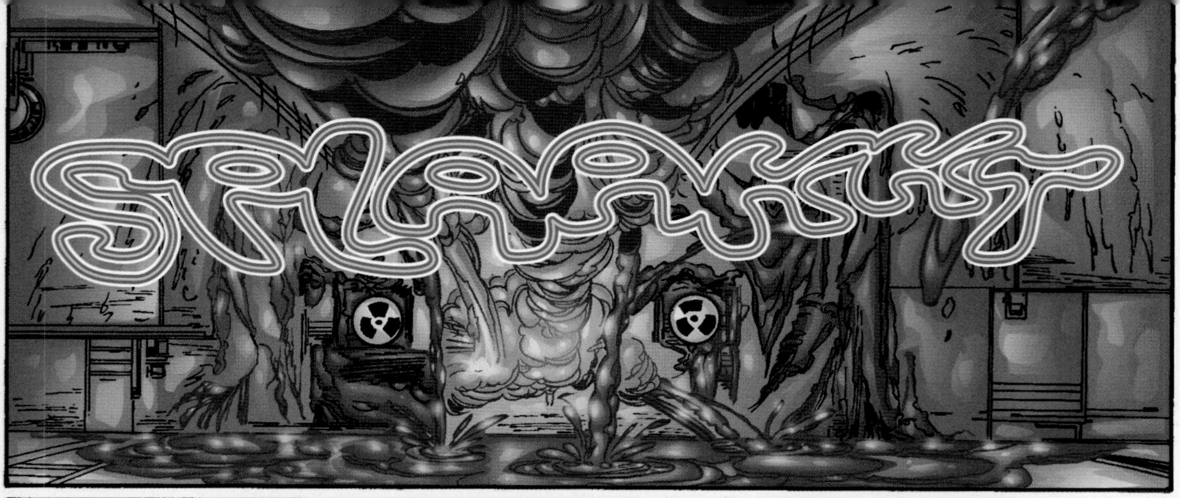

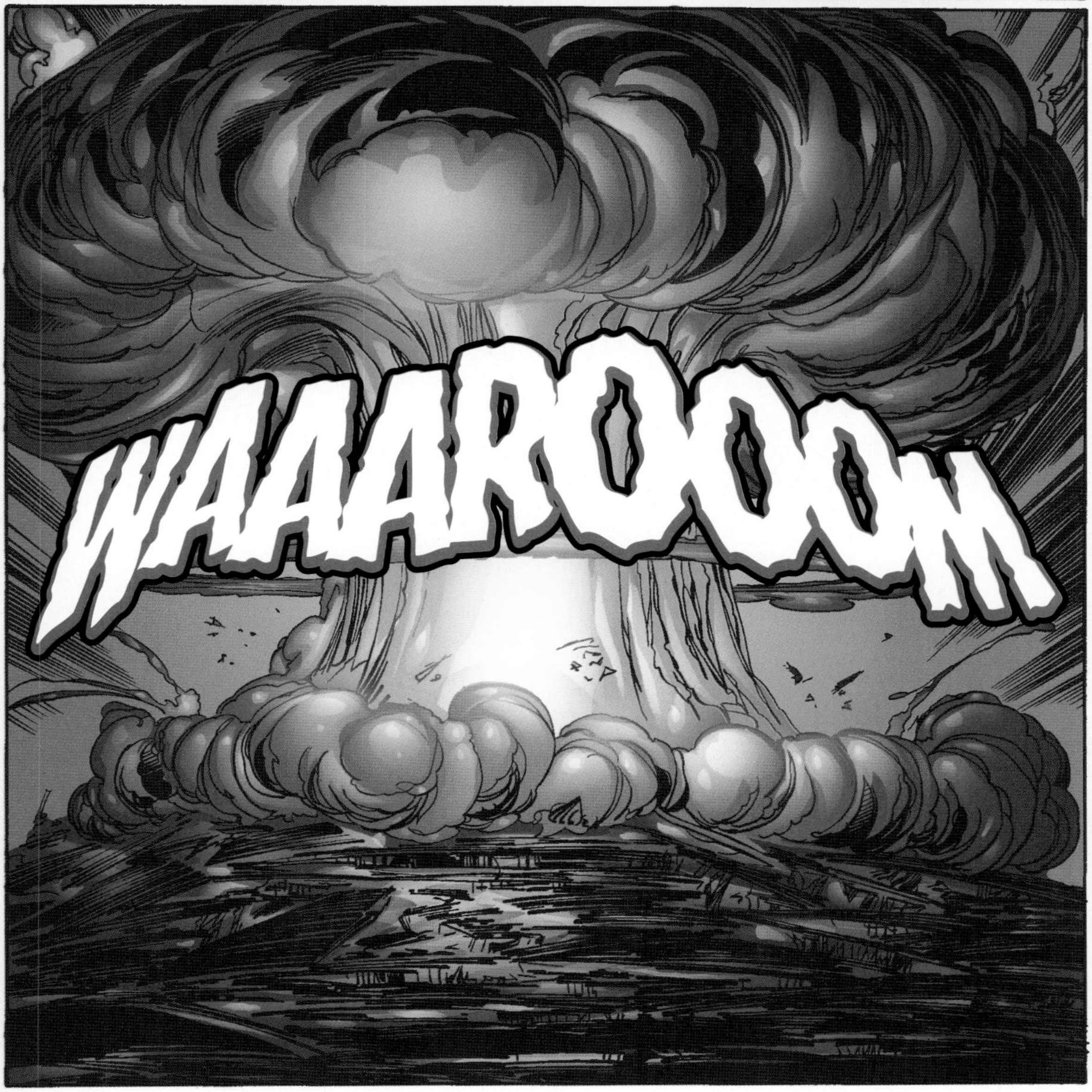
WAAAROOOM

Ducks: An Homage

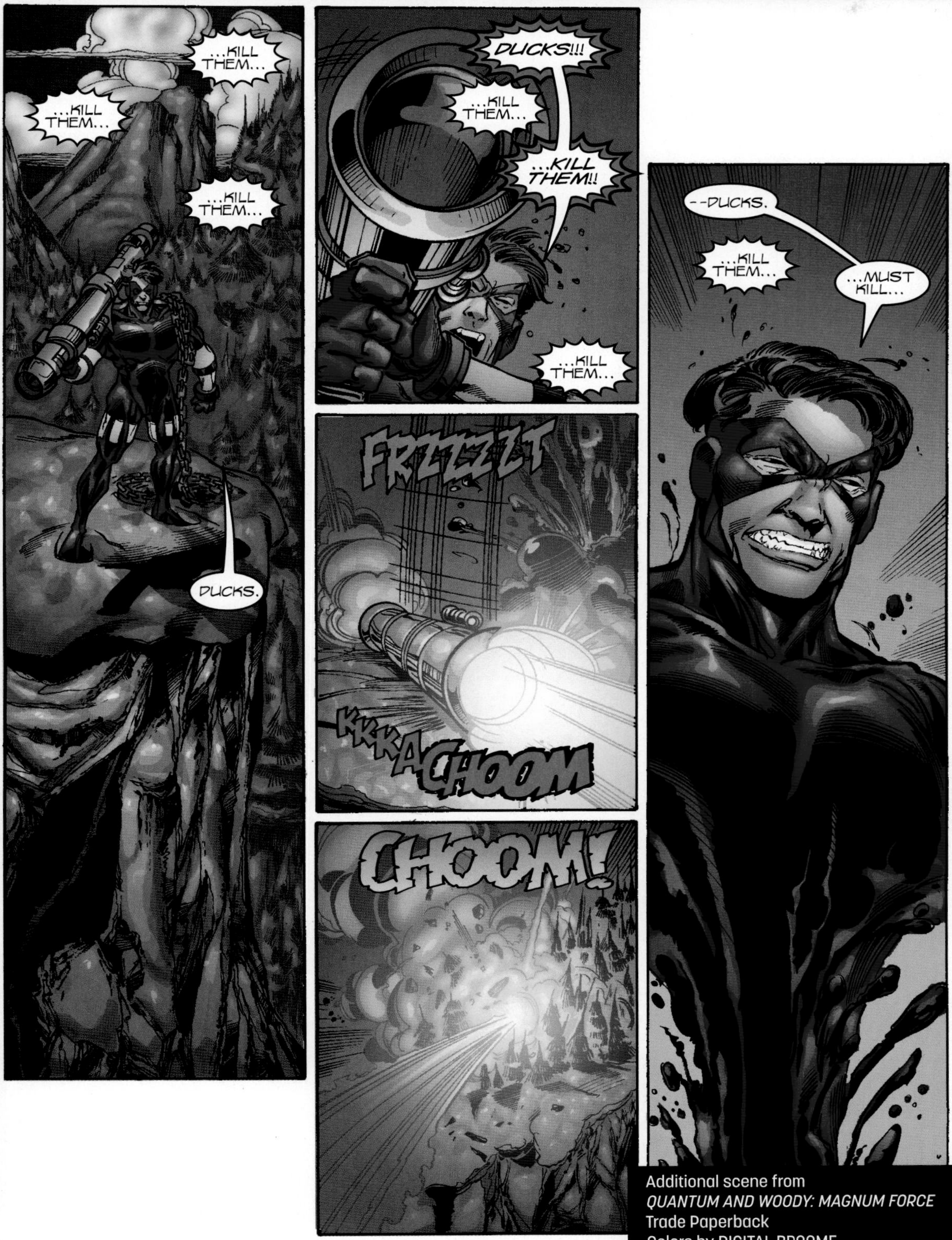
...KILL THEM...
...KILL THEM...
...KILL THEM...
DUCKS.
DUCKS!!!
...KILL THEM...
...KILL THEM!!
...KILL THEM...
FRZZZZT
KKKACHOOM
CHOOM!
--DUCKS.
...KILL THEM...
...MUST KILL...

Additional scene from
QUANTUM AND WOODY: MAGNUM FORCE
Trade Paperback
Colors by DIGITAL BROOME
Letters by DAVE SHARPE

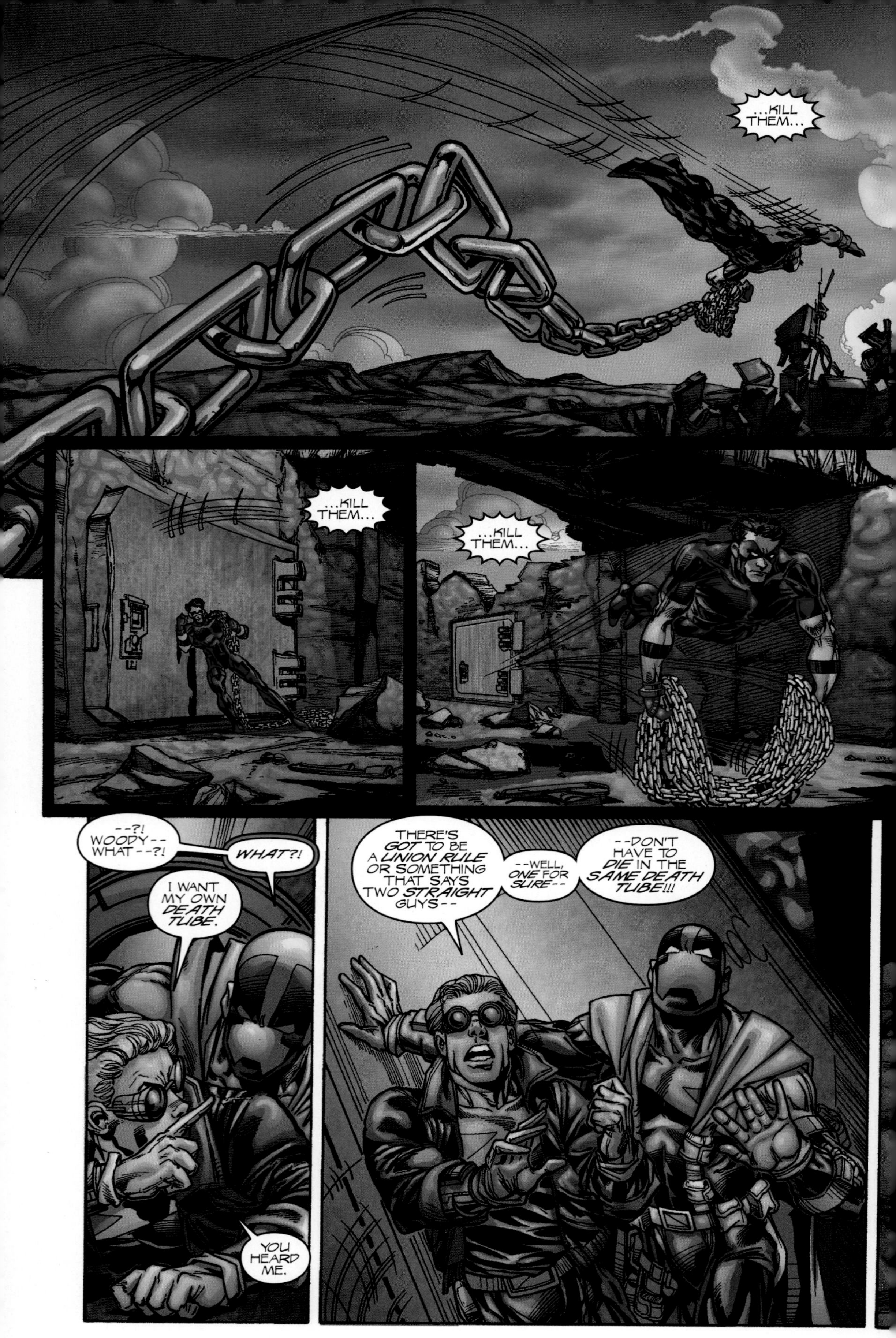
...KILL THEM...
...KILL THEM...
...KILL THEM...
--?! WOODY-- WHAT--?!
WHAT?!
I WANT MY OWN DEATH TUBE.
YOU HEARD ME.
THERE'S GOT TO BE A UNION RULE OR SOMETHING THAT SAYS TWO STRAIGHT GUYS--
--WELL, ONE FOR SURE--
--DON'T HAVE TO DIE IN THE SAME DEATH TUBE!!!

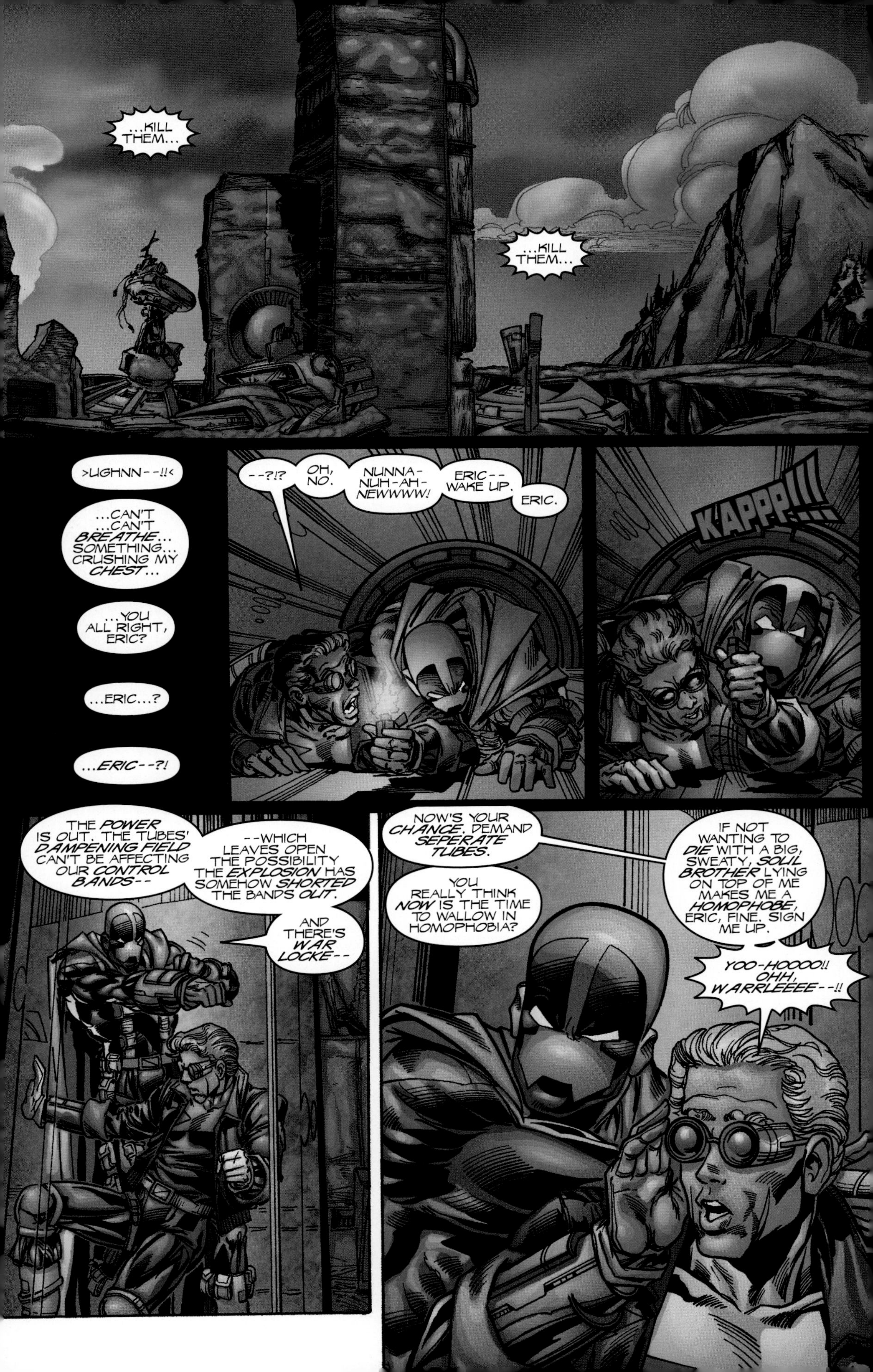

...KILL THEM...
...KILL THEM...
>UGHNN--!!<
...CAN'T ...CAN'T *BREATHE*... SOMETHING... CRUSHING MY *CHEST*...
...YOU ALL RIGHT, ERIC?
...ERIC...?
...*ERIC*--?!
--?!?
OH, NO.
NUNNA-NUH-AH-*NEWWWW!*
ERIC--WAKE UP.
ERIC.
KAPPP!!!!
THE *POWER* IS OUT. THE TUBES' *DAMPENING FIELD* CAN'T BE AFFECTING OUR *CONTROL BANDS*--
--WHICH LEAVES OPEN THE POSSIBILITY THE *EXPLOSION* HAS SOMEHOW *SHORTED* THE BANDS *OUT*.
AND THERE'S *WAR LOCKE*--
NOW'S YOUR *CHANCE*. DEMAND *SEPERATE TUBES*.
YOU REALLY THINK *NOW* IS THE TIME TO WALLOW IN HOMOPHOBIA?
IF NOT WANTING TO *DIE* WITH A BIG, SWEATY, *SOUL BROTHER* LYING ON TOP OF ME MAKES ME A *HOMOPHOBE*, ERIC, FINE. SIGN ME UP.
YOO-HOOOO!! OHH, WARRLEEEE--!!

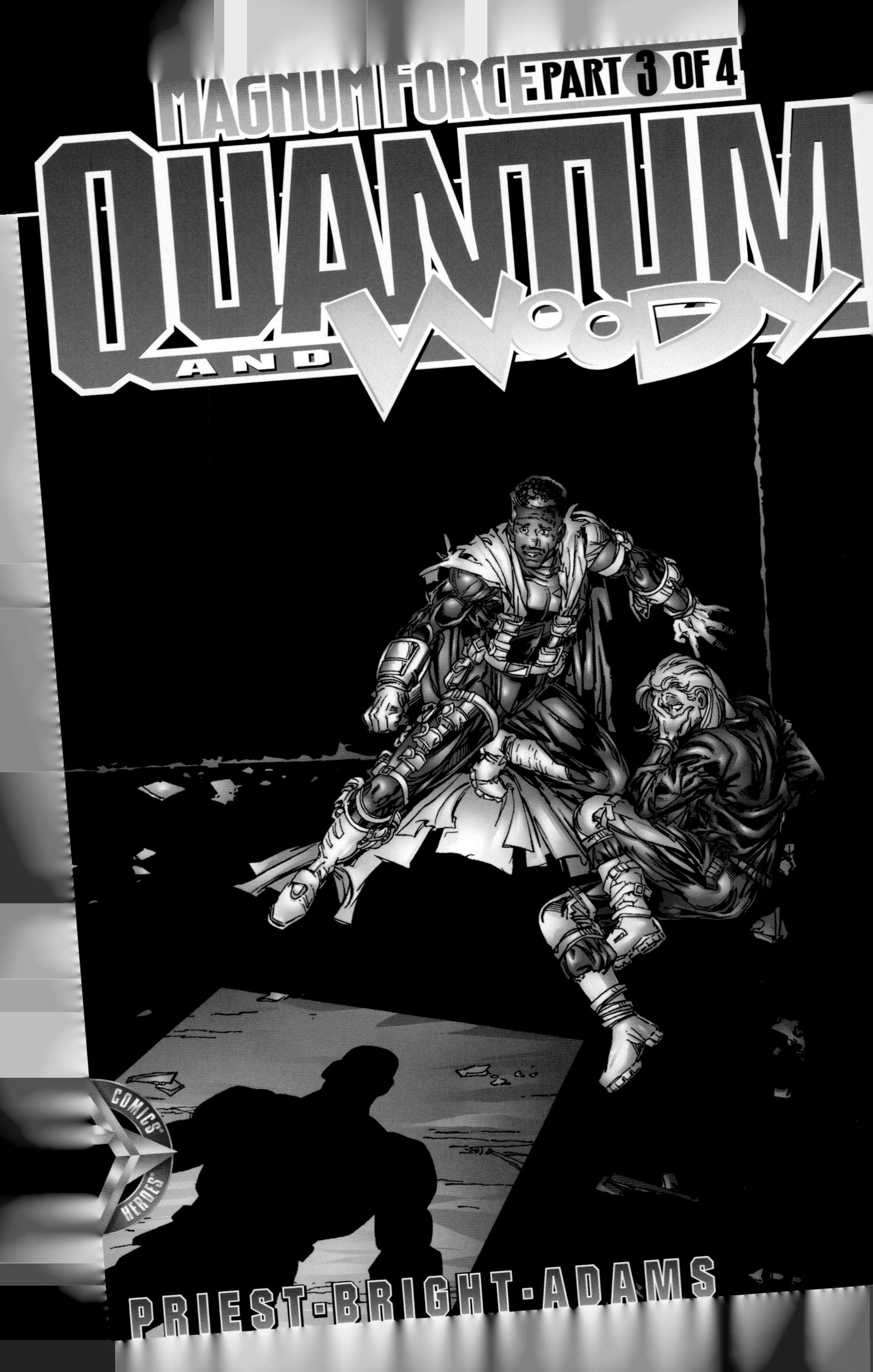
MAGNUM FORCE: PART 3 OF 4
QUANTUM AND WOODY
COMICS HEROES
PRIEST-BRIGHT-ADAMS

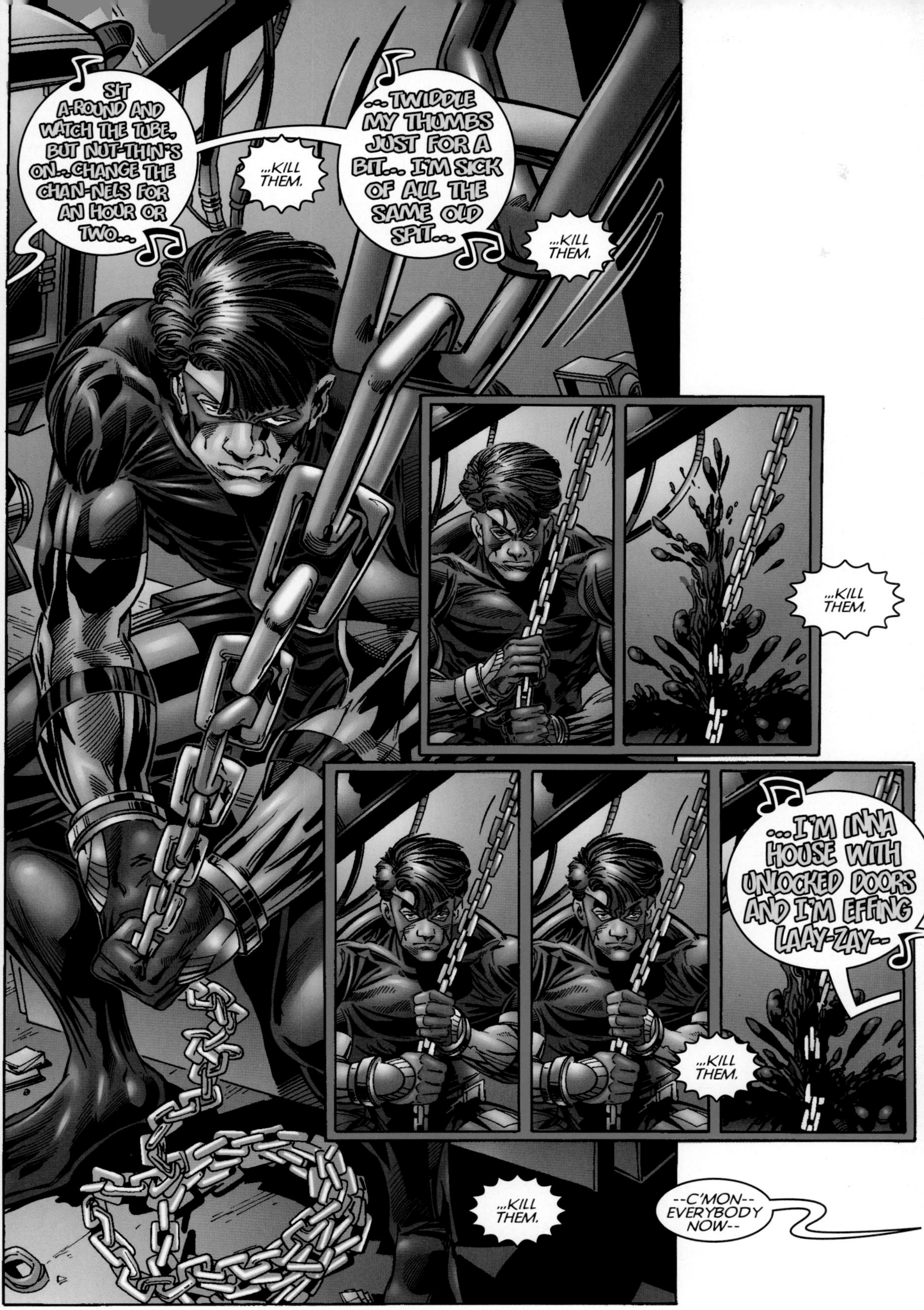
SIT A-ROUND AND WATCH THE TUBE, BUT NUT-THIN'S ON...CHANGE THE CHAN-NELS FOR AN HOUR OR TWO...
...KILL THEM.
...TWIDDLE MY THUMBS JUST FOR A BIT... I'M SICK OF ALL THE SAME OLD SPIT...
...KILL THEM.
...KILL THEM.
...I'M INNA HOUSE WITH UNLOCKED DOORS AND I'M EFFING LAAY-ZAY--
...KILL THEM.
...KILL THEM.
--C'MON-- EVERYBODY NOW--

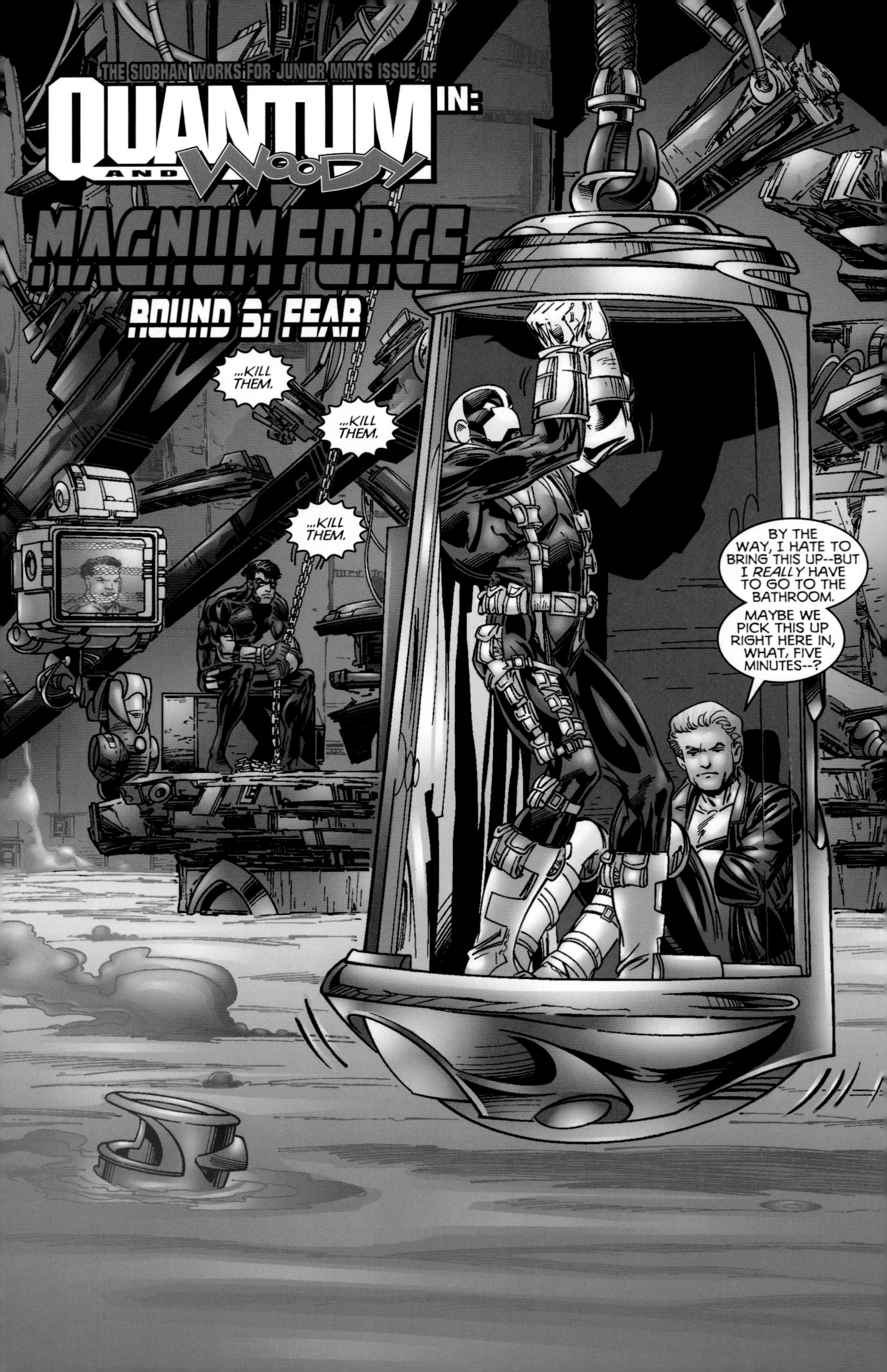
THE SIOBHAN WORKS FOR JUNIOR MINTS ISSUE OF
QUANTUM AND WOODY IN:
MAGNUM FORCE
ROUND 3: FEAR
...KILL THEM.
...KILL THEM.
...KILL THEM.
BY THE WAY, I HATE TO BRING THIS UP--BUT I REALLY HAVE TO GO TO THE BATHROOM.
MAYBE WE PICK THIS UP RIGHT HERE IN, WHAT, FIVE MINUTES--?

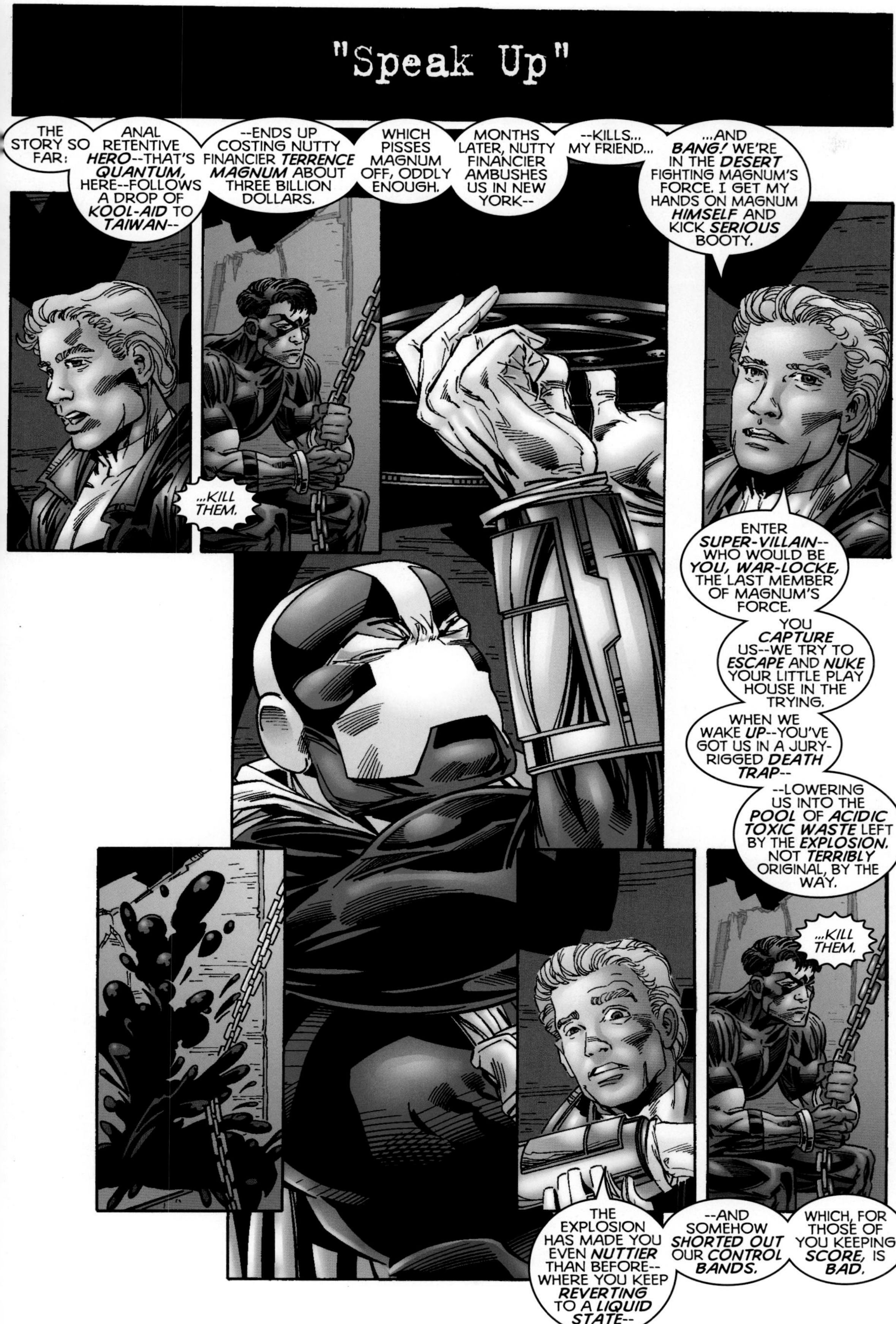
"Speak Up"
THE STORY SO FAR:
ANAL RETENTIVE HERO--THAT'S QUANTUM, HERE--FOLLOWS A DROP OF KOOL-AID TO TAIWAN--
--ENDS UP COSTING NUTTY FINANCIER TERRENCE MAGNUM ABOUT THREE BILLION DOLLARS.
WHICH PISSES MAGNUM OFF, ODDLY ENOUGH.
MONTHS LATER, NUTTY FINANCIER AMBUSHES US IN NEW YORK--
--KILLS... MY FRIEND...
...AND BANG! WE'RE IN THE DESERT FIGHTING MAGNUM'S FORCE. I GET MY HANDS ON MAGNUM HIMSELF AND KICK SERIOUS BOOTY.
...KILL THEM.
ENTER SUPER-VILLAIN--WHO WOULD BE YOU, WAR-LOCKE, THE LAST MEMBER OF MAGNUM'S FORCE.
YOU CAPTURE US--WE TRY TO ESCAPE AND NUKE YOUR LITTLE PLAY HOUSE IN THE TRYING.
WHEN WE WAKE UP--YOU'VE GOT US IN A JURY-RIGGED DEATH TRAP--
--LOWERING US INTO THE POOL OF ACIDIC TOXIC WASTE LEFT BY THE EXPLOSION. NOT TERRIBLY ORIGINAL, BY THE WAY.
...KILL THEM.
THE EXPLOSION HAS MADE YOU EVEN NUTTIER THAN BEFORE--WHERE YOU KEEP REVERTING TO A LIQUID STATE--
--AND SOMEHOW SHORTED OUT OUR CONTROL BANDS.
WHICH, FOR THOSE OF YOU KEEPING SCORE, IS BAD.

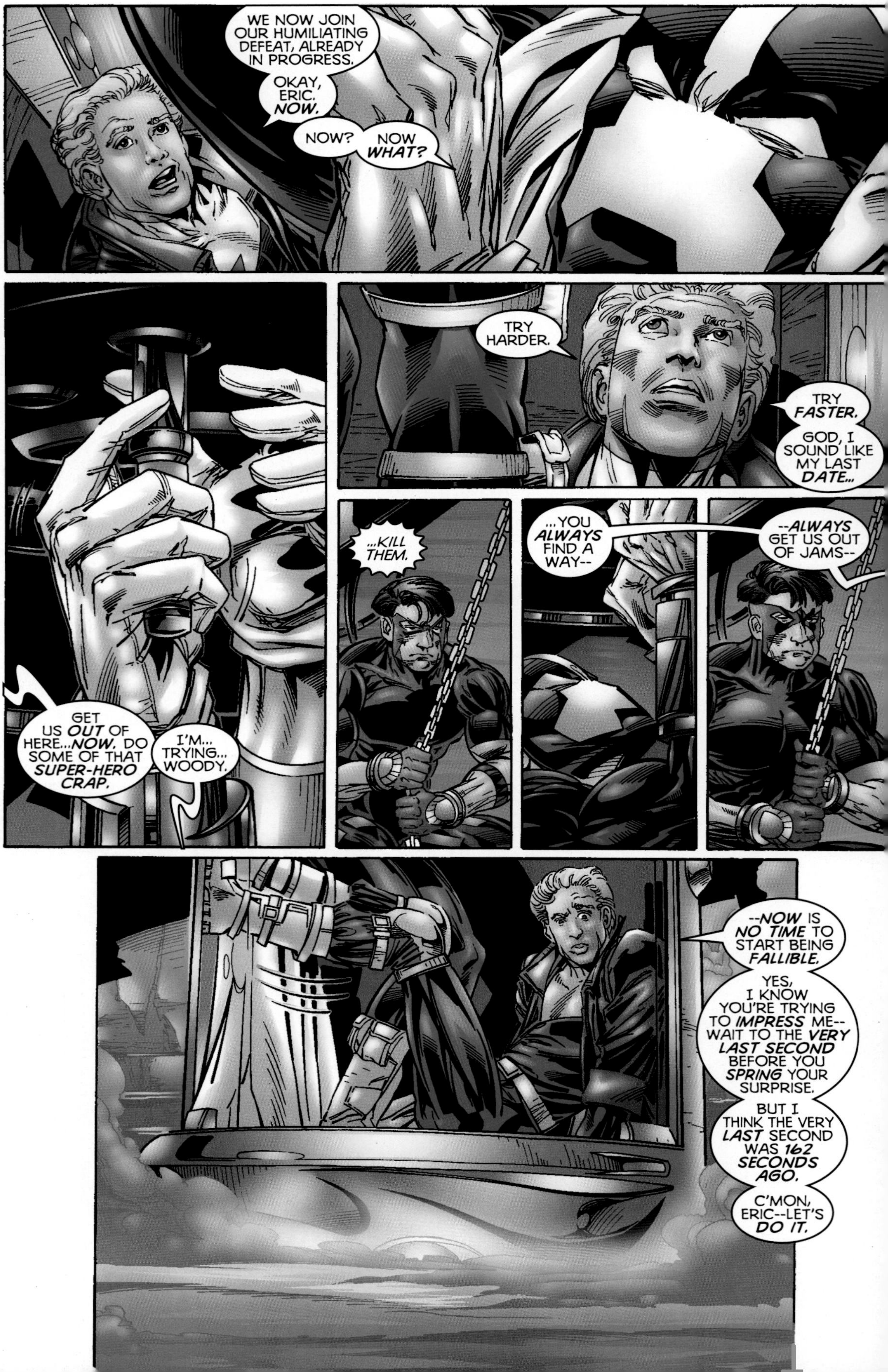
WE NOW JOIN OUR HUMILIATING DEFEAT, ALREADY IN PROGRESS.
OKAY, ERIC. NOW.
NOW?
NOW WHAT?
GET US OUT OF HERE...NOW. DO SOME OF THAT SUPER-HERO CRAP.
I'M... TRYING... WOODY.
TRY HARDER.
TRY FASTER.
GOD, I SOUND LIKE MY LAST DATE...
...KILL THEM.
...YOU ALWAYS FIND A WAY--
--ALWAYS GET US OUT OF JAMS--
--NOW IS NO TIME TO START BEING FALLIBLE.
YES, I KNOW YOU'RE TRYING TO IMPRESS ME-- WAIT TO THE VERY LAST SECOND BEFORE YOU SPRING YOUR SURPRISE.
BUT I THINK THE VERY LAST SECOND WAS 162 SECONDS AGO.
C'MON, ERIC--LET'S DO IT.

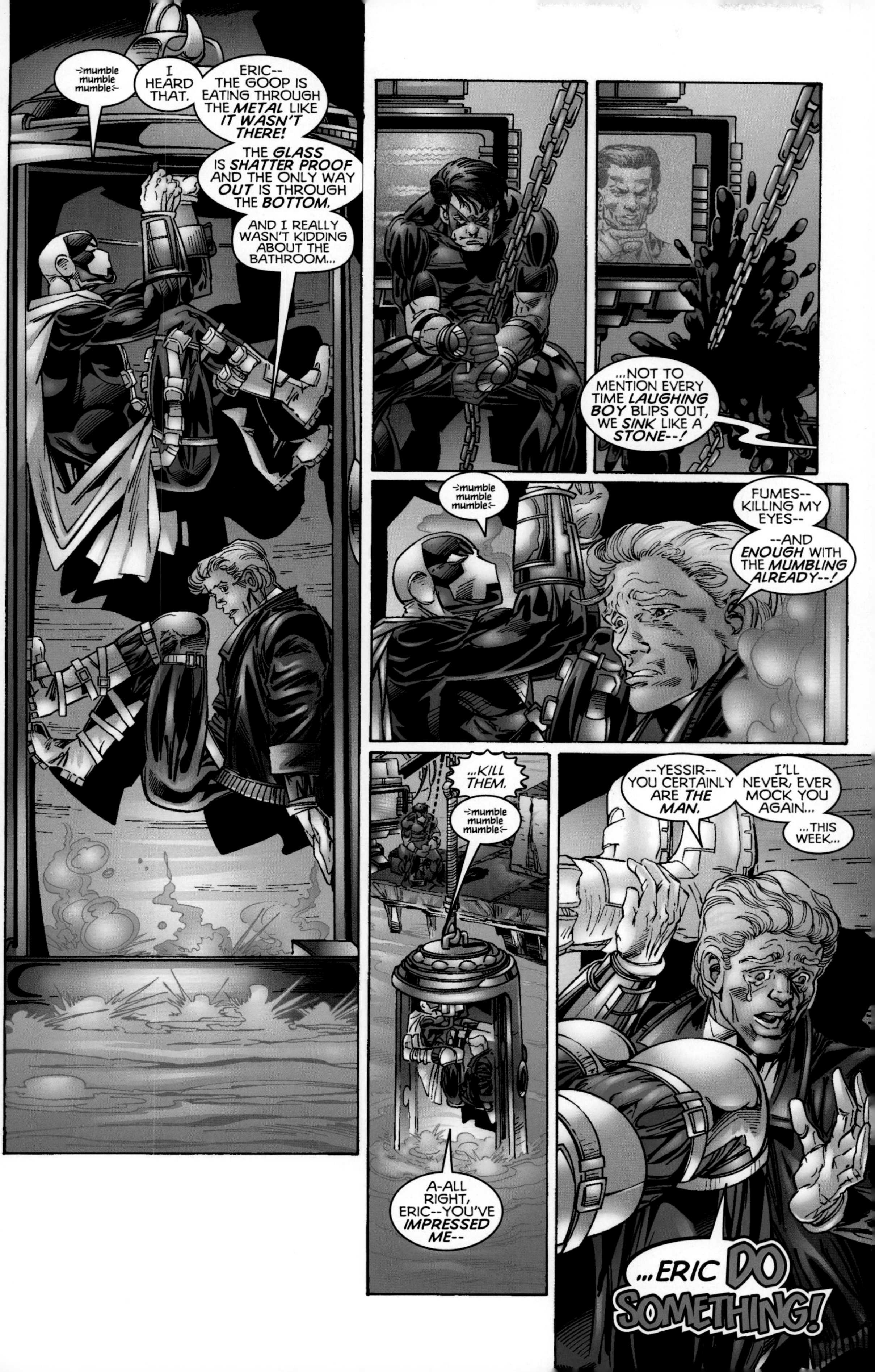

mumble mumble mumble
I HEARD THAT.
ERIC-- THE GOOP IS EATING THROUGH THE METAL LIKE IT WASN'T THERE!
THE GLASS IS SHATTER PROOF AND THE ONLY WAY OUT IS THROUGH THE BOTTOM.
AND I REALLY WASN'T KIDDING ABOUT THE BATHROOM...
...NOT TO MENTION EVERY TIME LAUGHING BOY BLIPS OUT, WE SINK LIKE A STONE--!
mumble mumble mumble
FUMES-- KILLING MY EYES--
--AND ENOUGH WITH THE MUMBLING ALREADY--!
...KILL THEM.
mumble mumble mumble
A-ALL RIGHT, ERIC--YOU'VE IMPRESSED ME--
--YESSIR-- YOU CERTAINLY ARE THE MAN.
I'LL NEVER, EVER MOCK YOU AGAIN...
...THIS WEEK...
...ERIC DO SOMETHING!

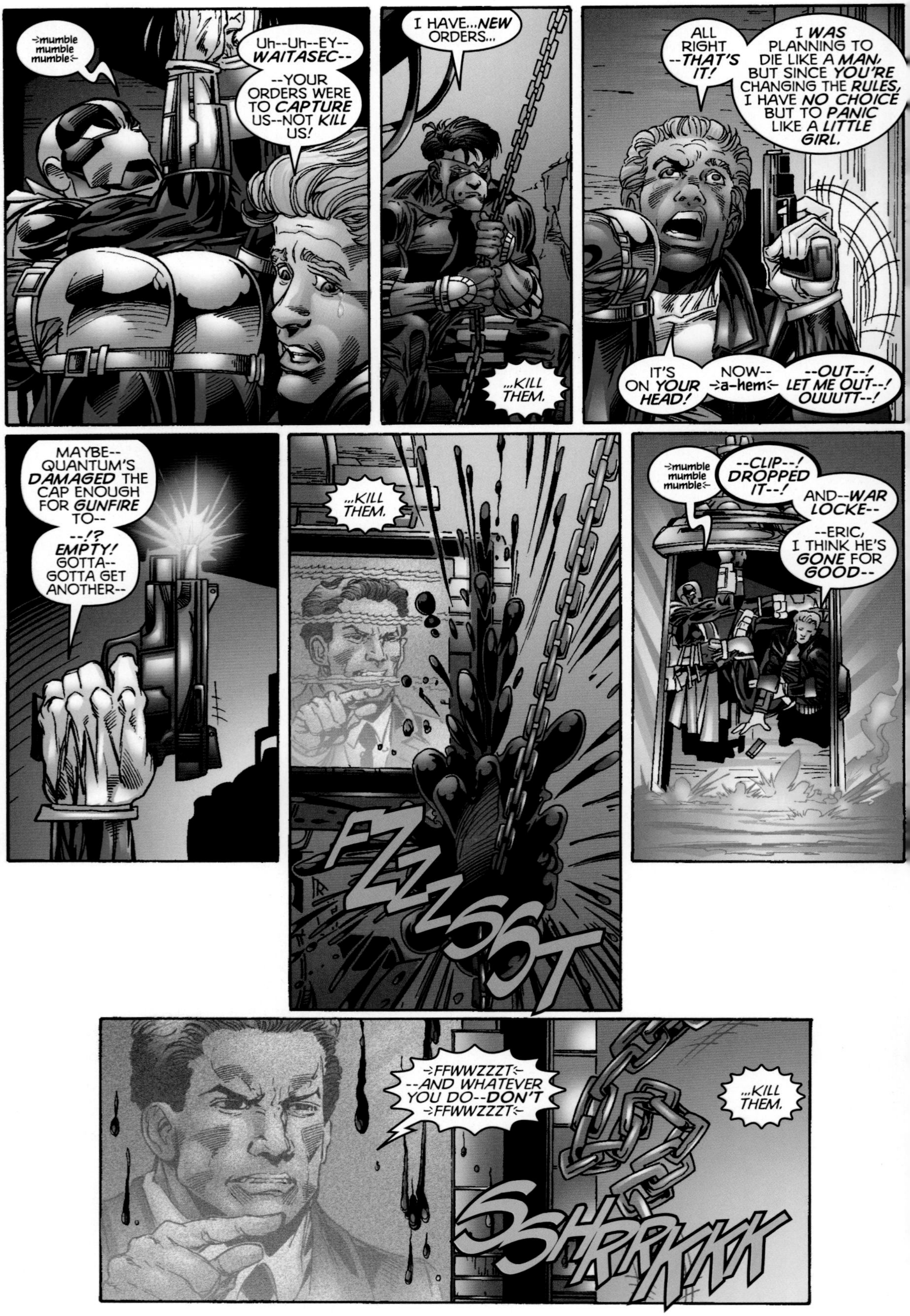

-mumble mumble mumble-
Uh--Uh--EY-- WAITASEC--
--YOUR ORDERS WERE TO CAPTURE US--NOT KILL US!
I HAVE...NEW ORDERS...
...KILL THEM.
ALL RIGHT --THAT'S IT!
I WAS PLANNING TO DIE LIKE A MAN, BUT SINCE YOU'RE CHANGING THE RULES, I HAVE NO CHOICE BUT TO PANIC LIKE A LITTLE GIRL.
IT'S ON YOUR HEAD!
NOW-- -a-hem-
--OUT--! LET ME OUT--! OUUUTT--!
MAYBE-- QUANTUM'S DAMAGED THE CAP ENOUGH FOR GUNFIRE TO--
--!? EMPTY! GOTTA-- GOTTA GET ANOTHER--
...KILL THEM.
FZZSST
-mumble mumble mumble-
--CLIP--! DROPPED IT--!
AND--WAR LOCKE--
--ERIC, I THINK HE'S GONE FOR GOOD--
-FFWWZZZT- --AND WHATEVER YOU DO--DON'T -FFWWZZZT-
...KILL THEM.
SSHRRKKK

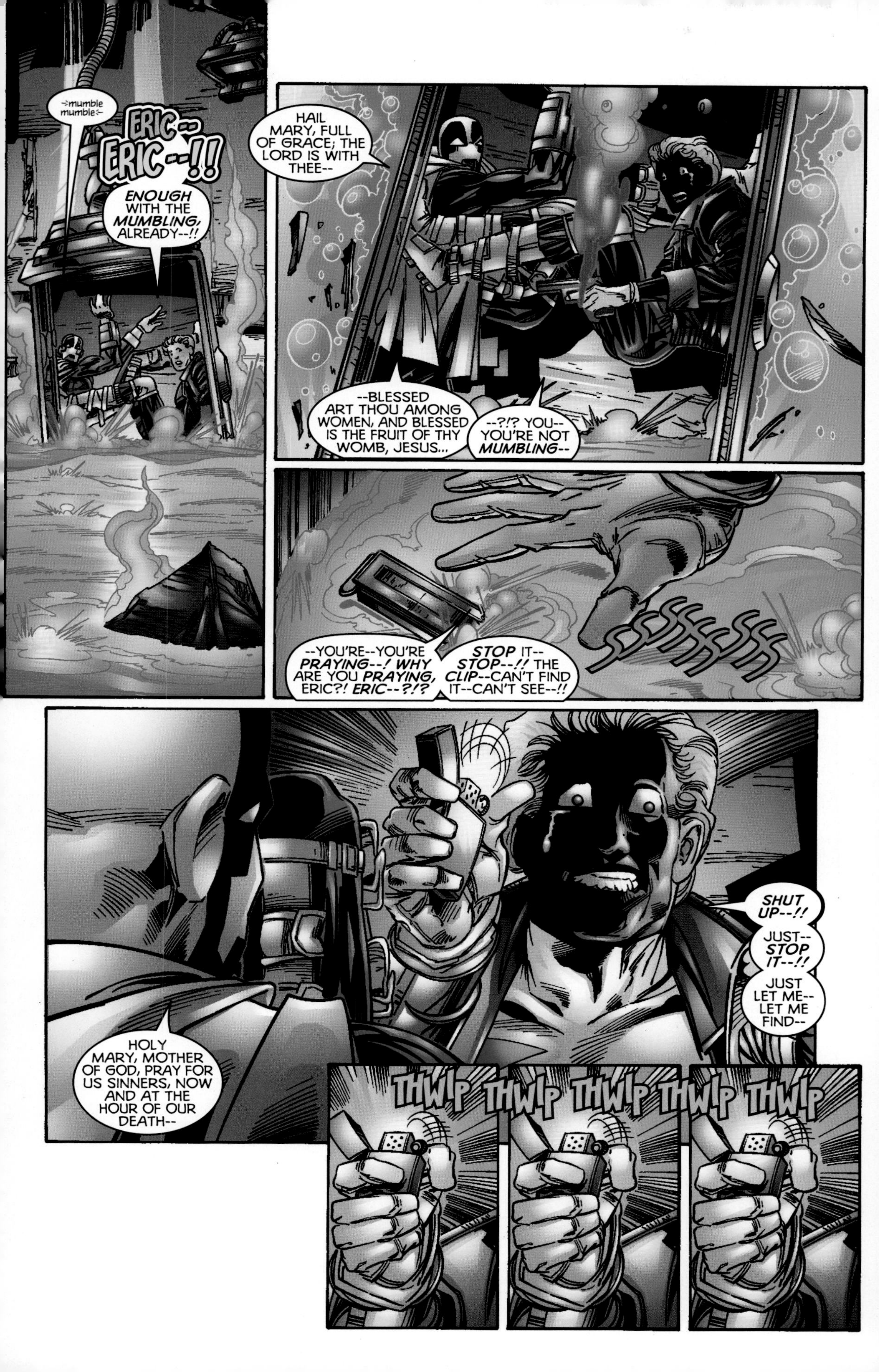

mumble mumble
ERIC--
ERIC--!!
ENOUGH WITH THE MUMBLING, ALREADY--!!
HAIL MARY, FULL OF GRACE; THE LORD IS WITH THEE--
--BLESSED ART THOU AMONG WOMEN, AND BLESSED IS THE FRUIT OF THY WOMB, JESUS...
--?!? YOU-- YOU'RE NOT MUMBLING--
--YOU'RE--YOU'RE PRAYING--! WHY ARE YOU PRAYING, ERIC?! ERIC--?!?
STOP IT-- STOP--!! THE CLIP--CAN'T FIND IT--CAN'T SEE--!!
SSSSSSSS
SHUT UP--!!
JUST-- STOP IT--!!
JUST LET ME-- LET ME FIND--
HOLY MARY, MOTHER OF GOD, PRAY FOR US SINNERS, NOW AND AT THE HOUR OF OUR DEATH--
THWIP THWIP THWIP THWIP THWIP

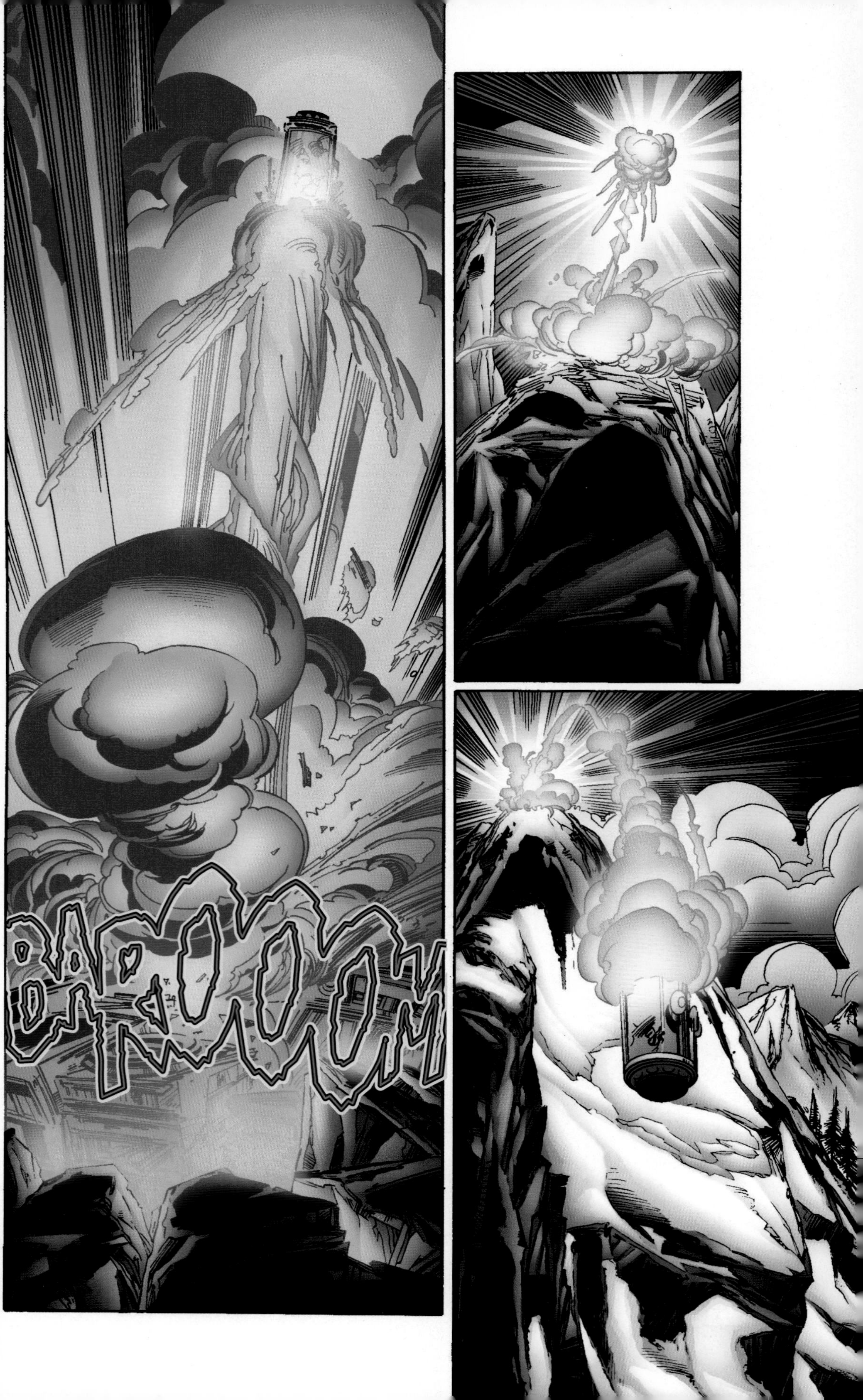
BRROOOOM

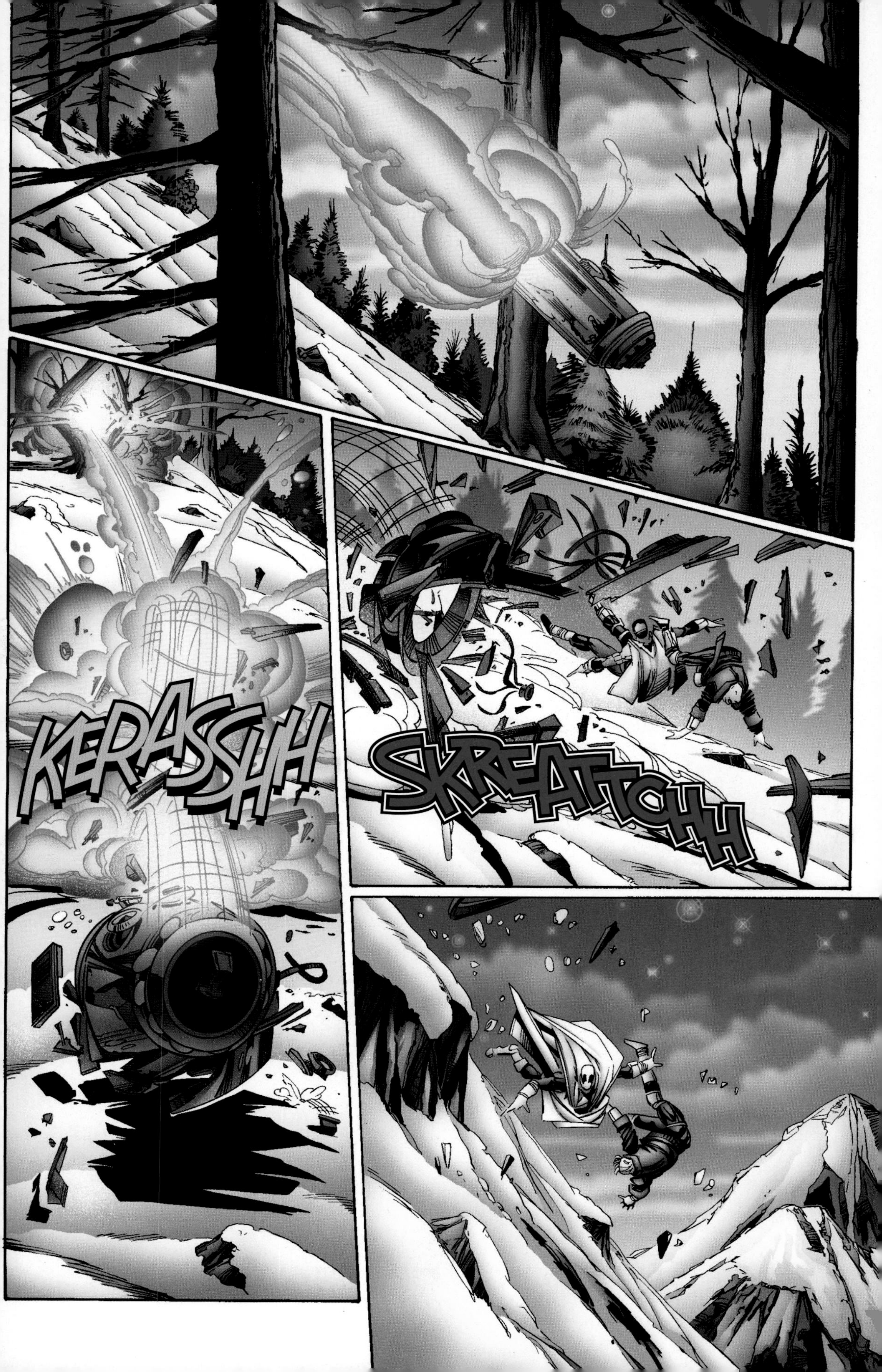
KERASSHH
SKREATTCHHH

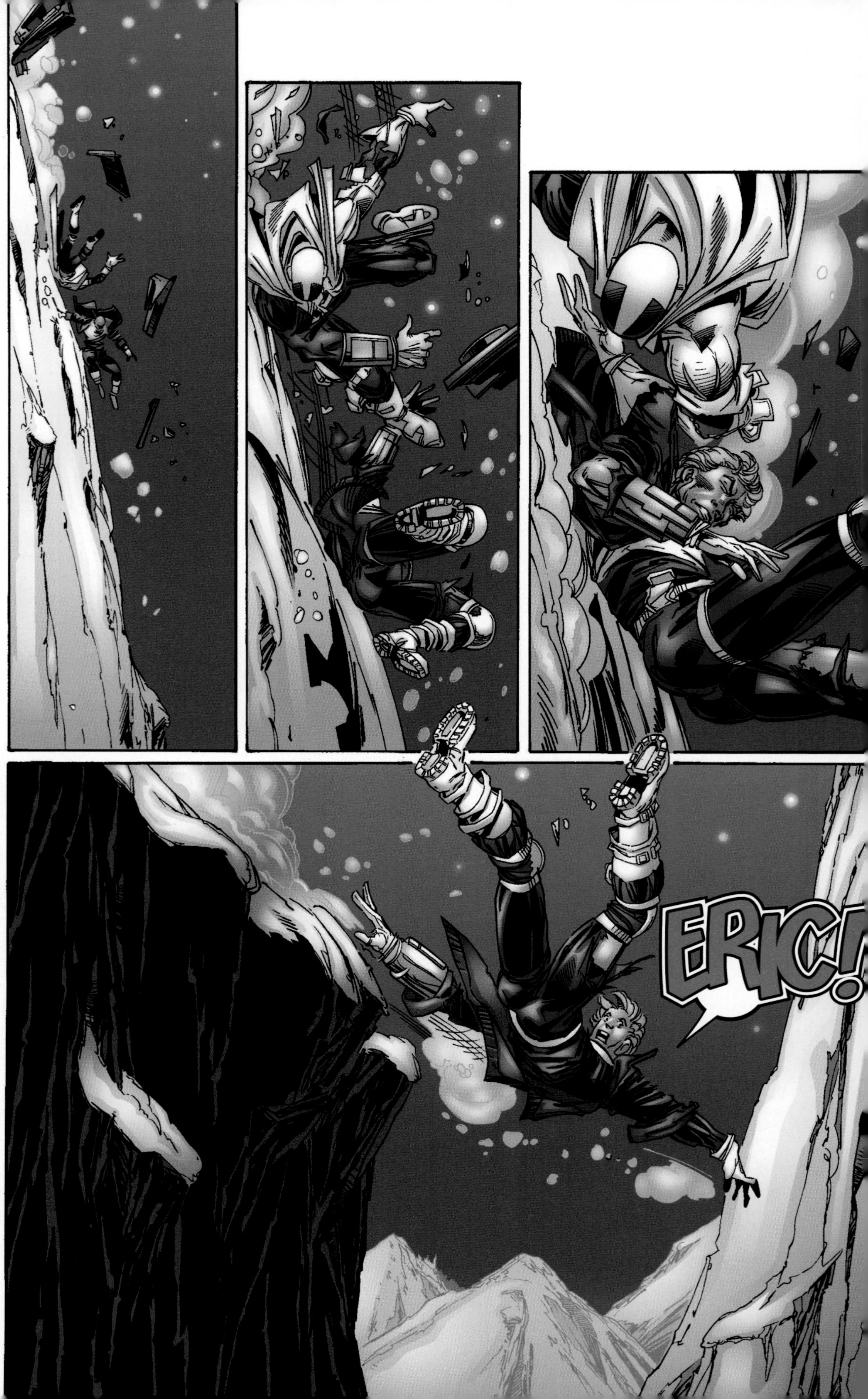
ERIC!

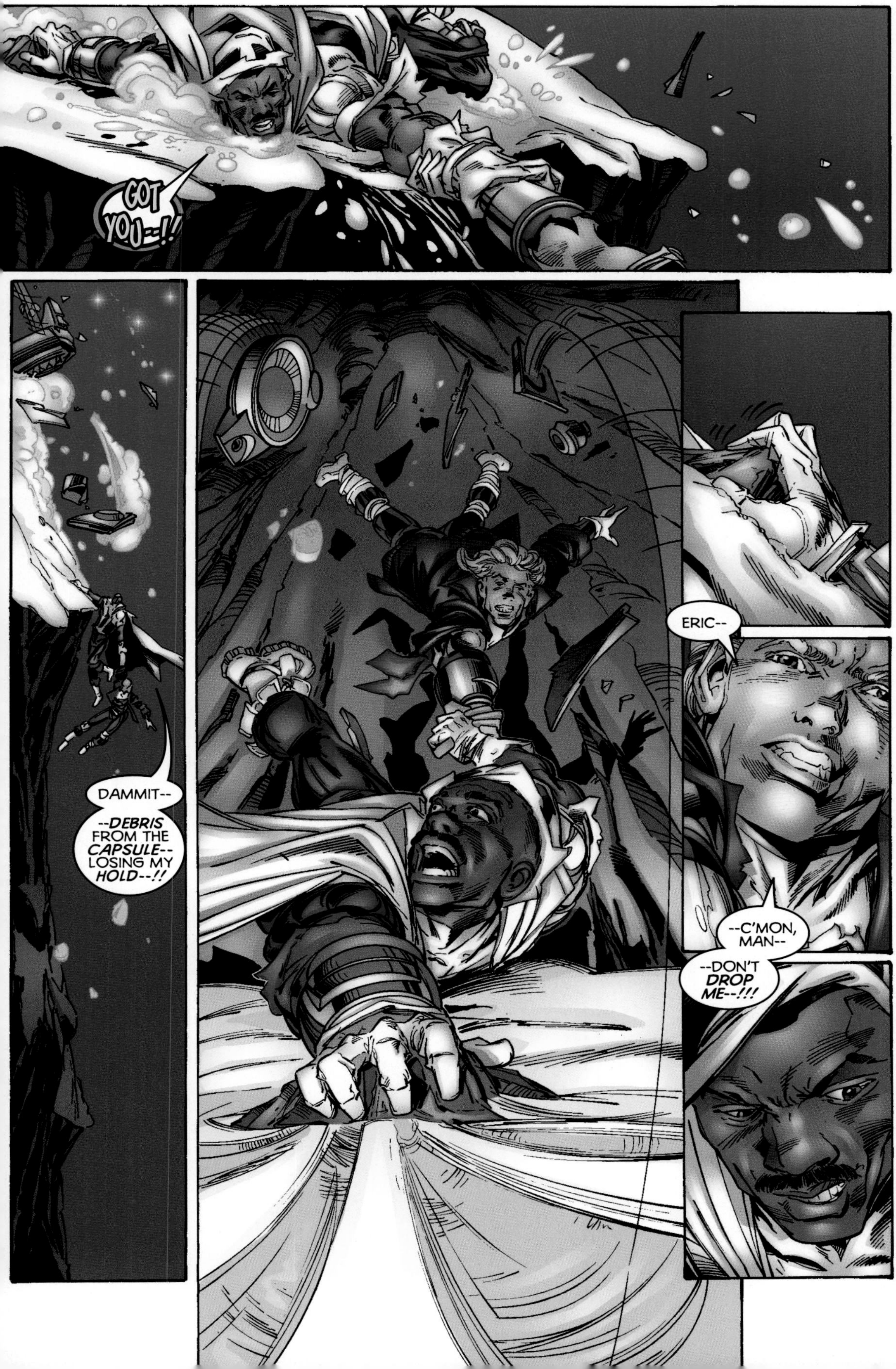
GOT YOU--!!
DAMMIT--
--DEBRIS FROM THE CAPSULE--
LOSING MY HOLD--!!
ERIC--
--C'MON, MAN--
--DON'T DROP ME--!!!

"Death and the Maidens"

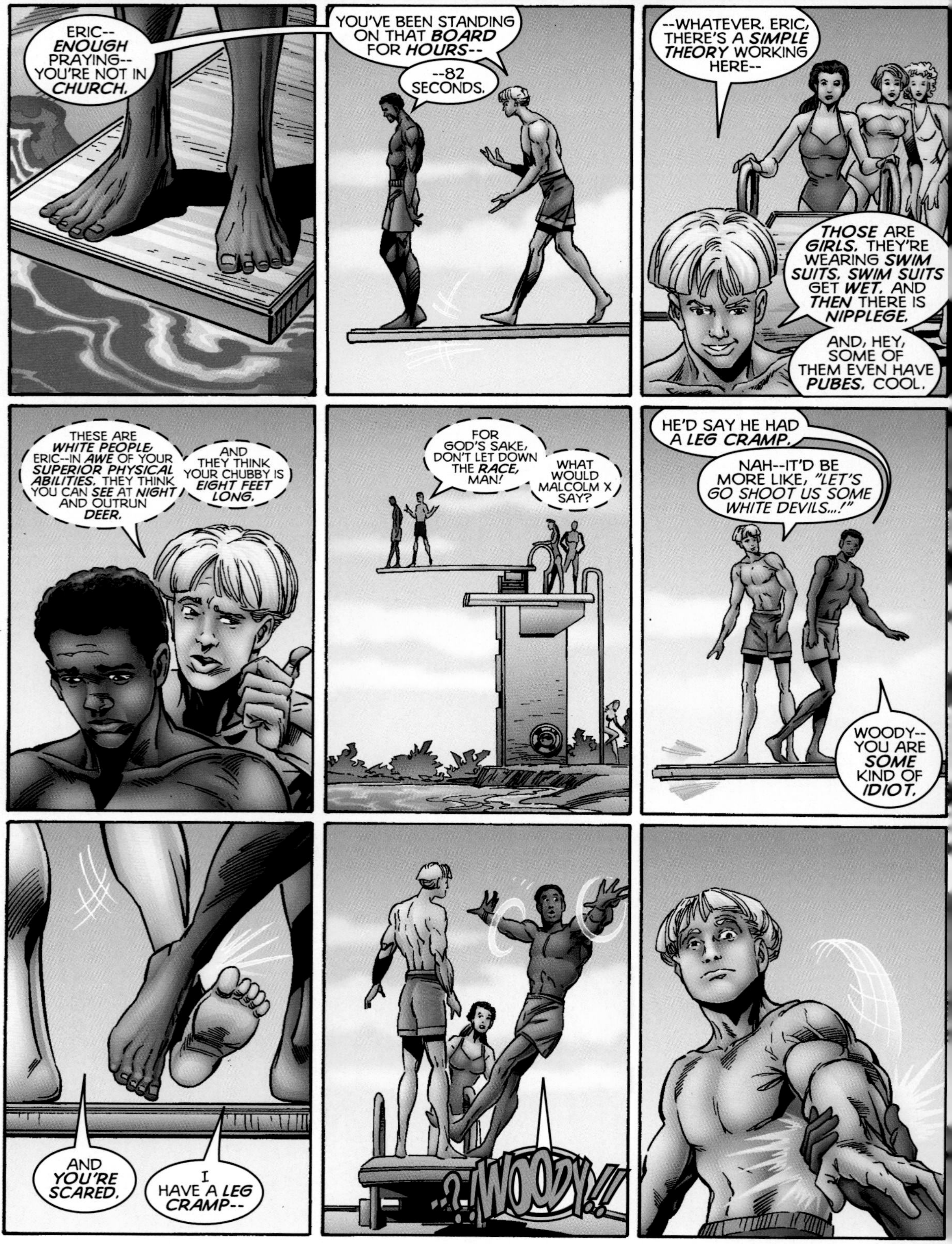
ERIC-- ENOUGH PRAYING-- YOU'RE NOT IN CHURCH.
YOU'VE BEEN STANDING ON THAT BOARD FOR HOURS--
--82 SECONDS.
--WHATEVER, ERIC, THERE'S A SIMPLE THEORY WORKING HERE--
THOSE ARE GIRLS, THEY'RE WEARING SWIM SUITS, SWIM SUITS GET WET, AND THEN THERE IS NIPPLEGE.
AND, HEY, SOME OF THEM EVEN HAVE PUBES, COOL.
THESE ARE WHITE PEOPLE, ERIC--IN AWE OF YOUR SUPERIOR PHYSICAL ABILITIES, THEY THINK YOU CAN SEE AT NIGHT AND OUTRUN DEER.
AND THEY THINK YOUR CHUBBY IS EIGHT FEET LONG.
FOR GOD'S SAKE, DON'T LET DOWN THE RACE, MAN!
WHAT WOULD MALCOLM X SAY?
HE'D SAY HE HAD A LEG CRAMP.
NAH--IT'D BE MORE LIKE, "LET'S GO SHOOT US SOME WHITE DEVILS...!"
WOODY-- YOU ARE SOME KIND OF IDIOT.
AND YOU'RE SCARED.
I HAVE A LEG CRAMP--
..?..!WOODY!!

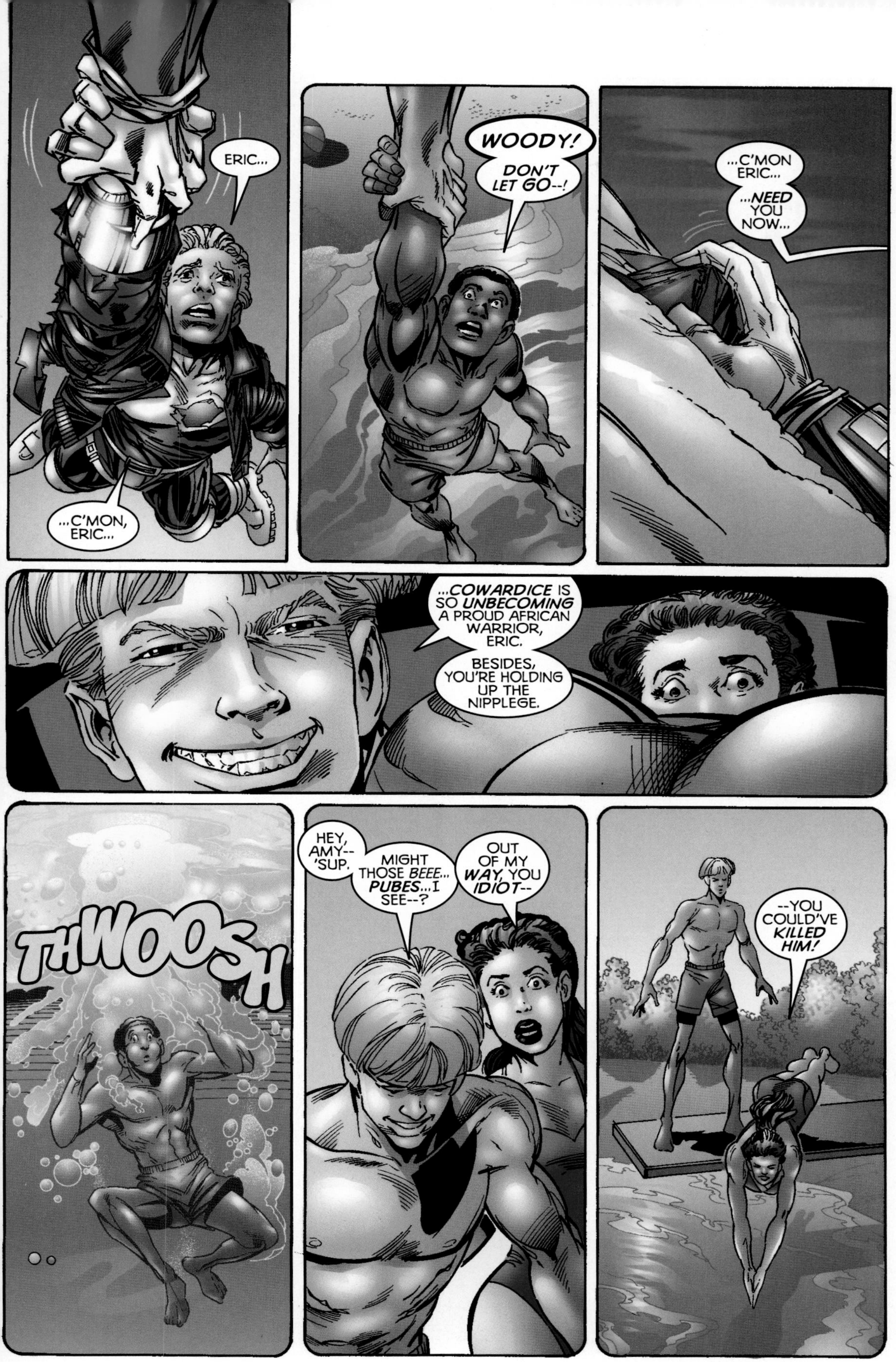
ERIC...
...C'MON, ERIC...
WOODY!
DON'T LET GO--!
...C'MON ERIC...
...NEED YOU NOW...
...COWARDICE IS SO UNBECOMING A PROUD AFRICAN WARRIOR, ERIC.
BESIDES, YOU'RE HOLDING UP THE NIPPLEGE.
THWOOSH
HEY, AMY-- 'SUP.
MIGHT THOSE BEEE... PUBES... I SEE--?
OUT OF MY WAY, YOU IDIOT--
--YOU COULD'VE KILLED HIM!

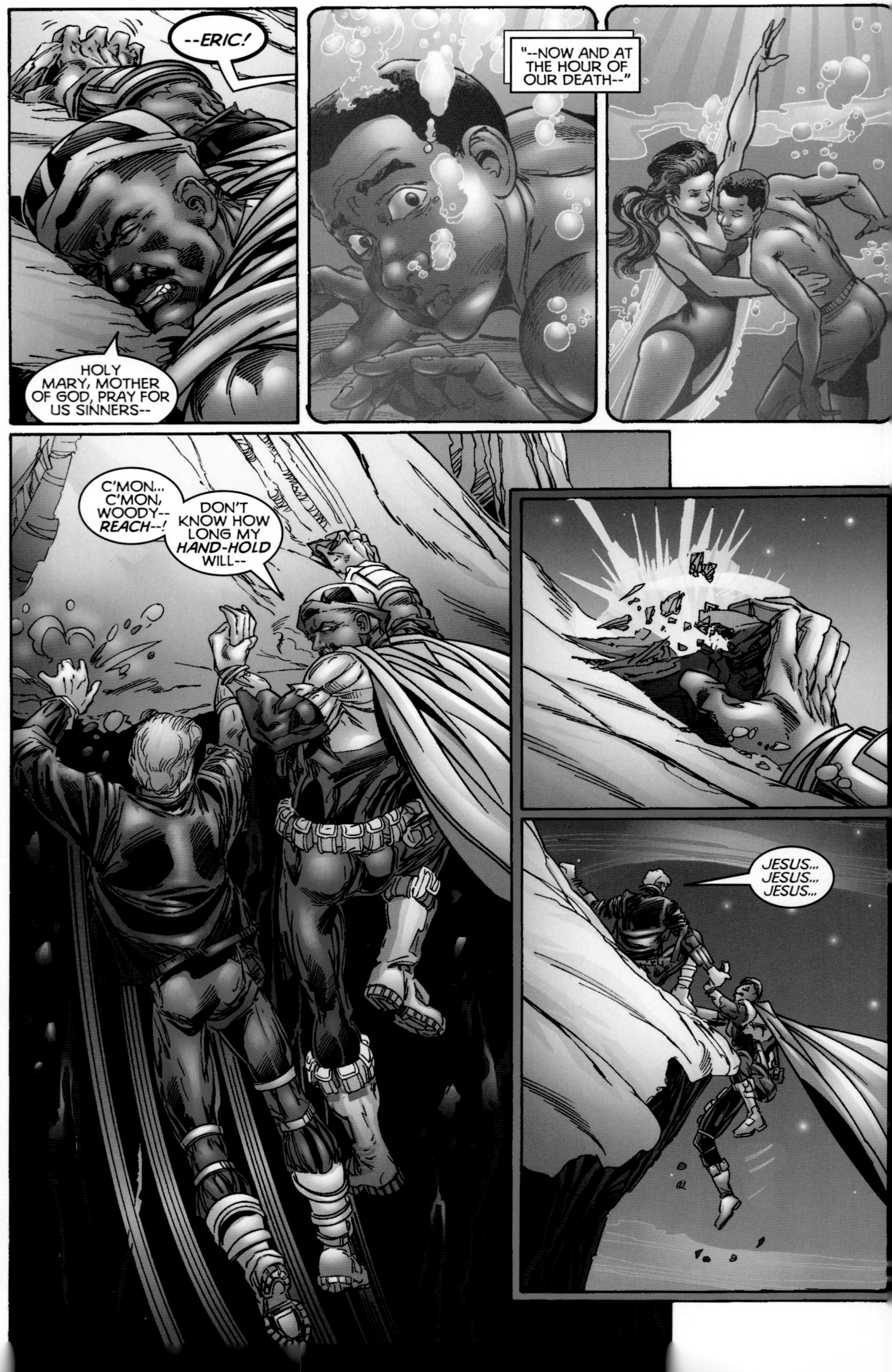
--ERIC!
HOLY MARY, MOTHER OF GOD, PRAY FOR US SINNERS--
"--NOW AND AT THE HOUR OF OUR DEATH--"
C'MON... C'MON, WOODY-- REACH--!
DON'T KNOW HOW LONG MY HAND-HOLD WILL--
JESUS... JESUS... JESUS...

"And Now The Bad News..."

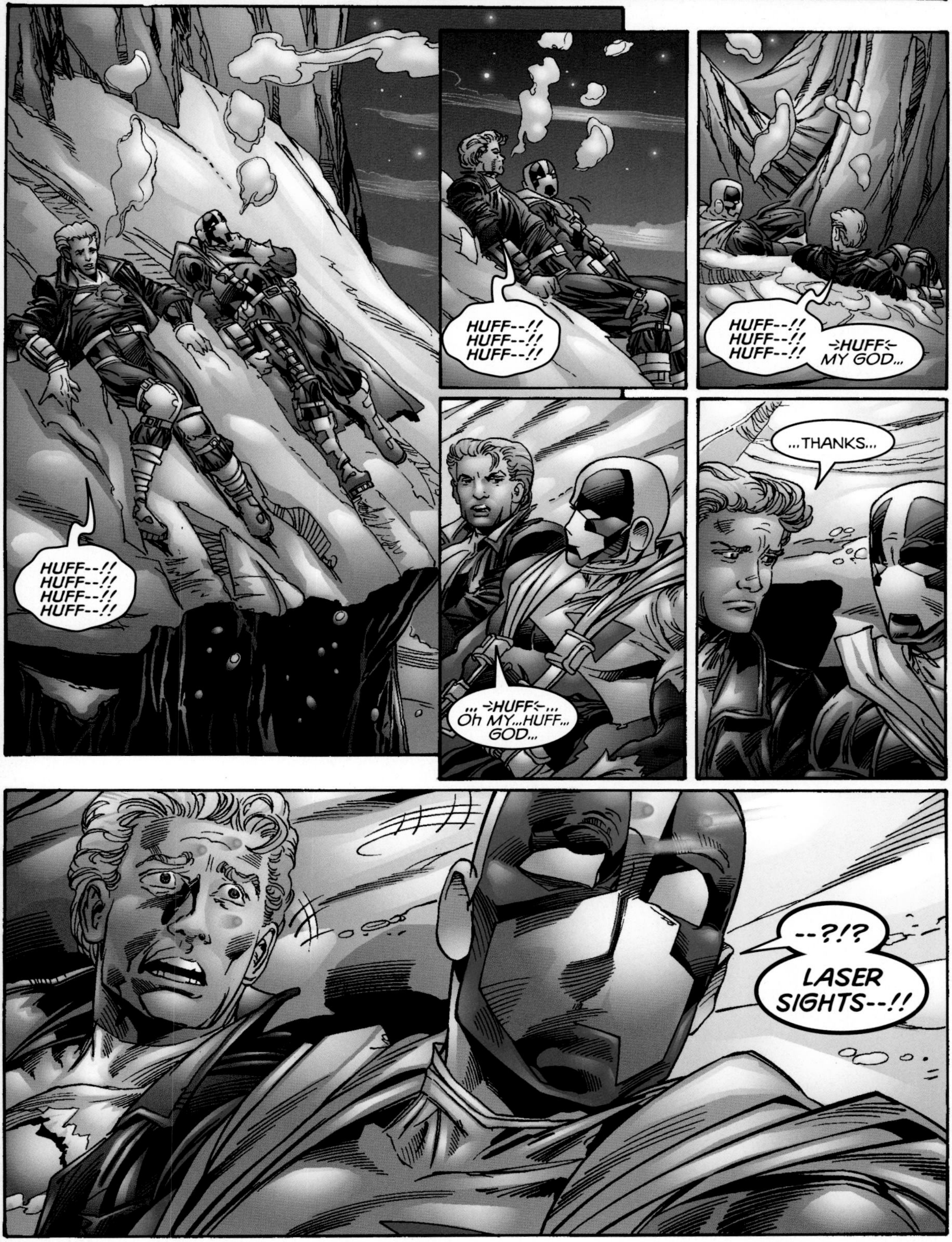
HUFF--!! HUFF--!! HUFF--!! HUFF--!!
HUFF--!! HUFF--!! HUFF--!!
HUFF--!! HUFF--!! HUFF--!!
HUFF MY GOD...
... HUFF... Oh MY... HUFF... GOD...
...THANKS...
--?!? LASER SIGHTS--!!

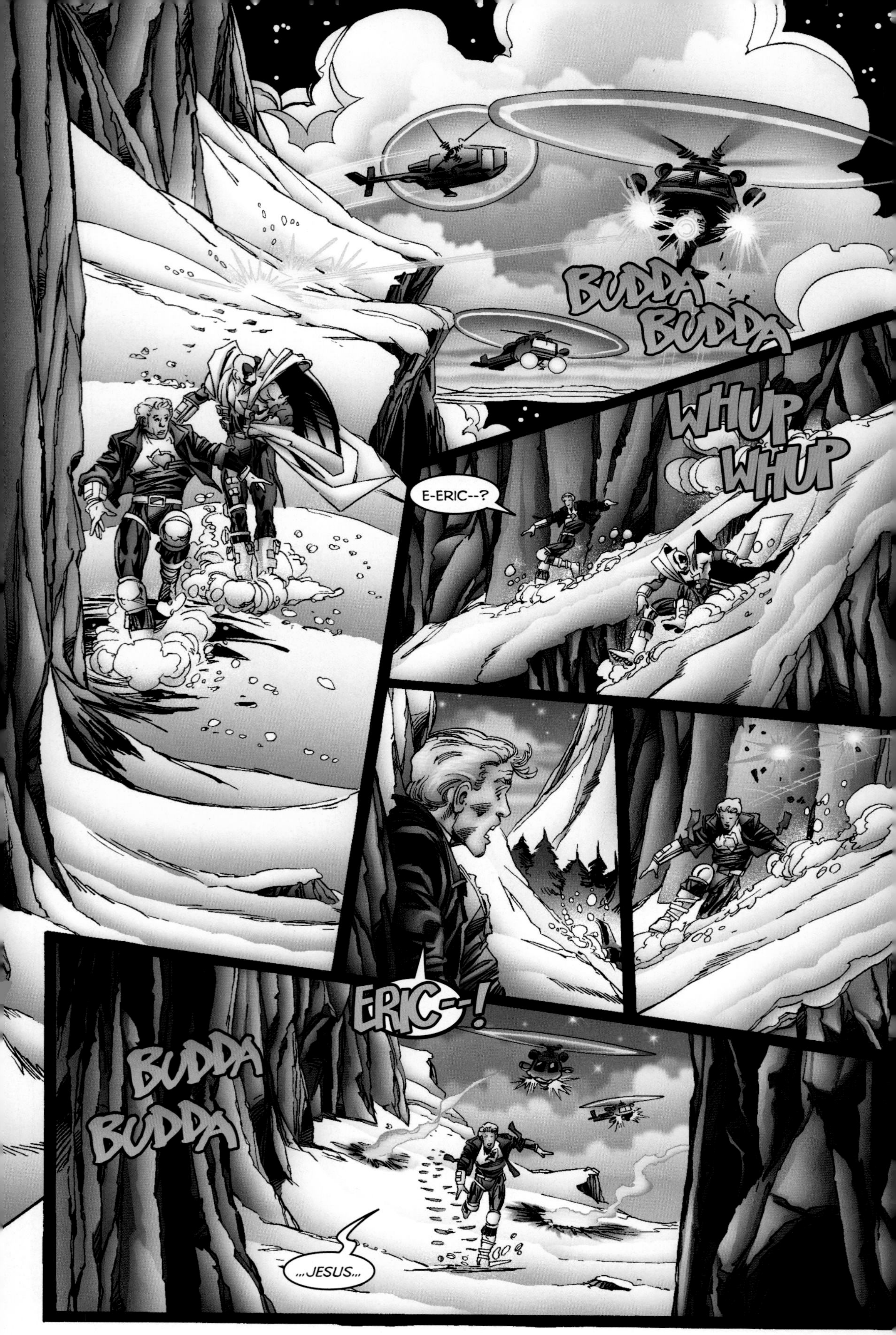
BUDDA BUDDA
WHUP WHUP
E-ERIC--?
ERIC--!
BUDDA BUDDA
...JESUS...

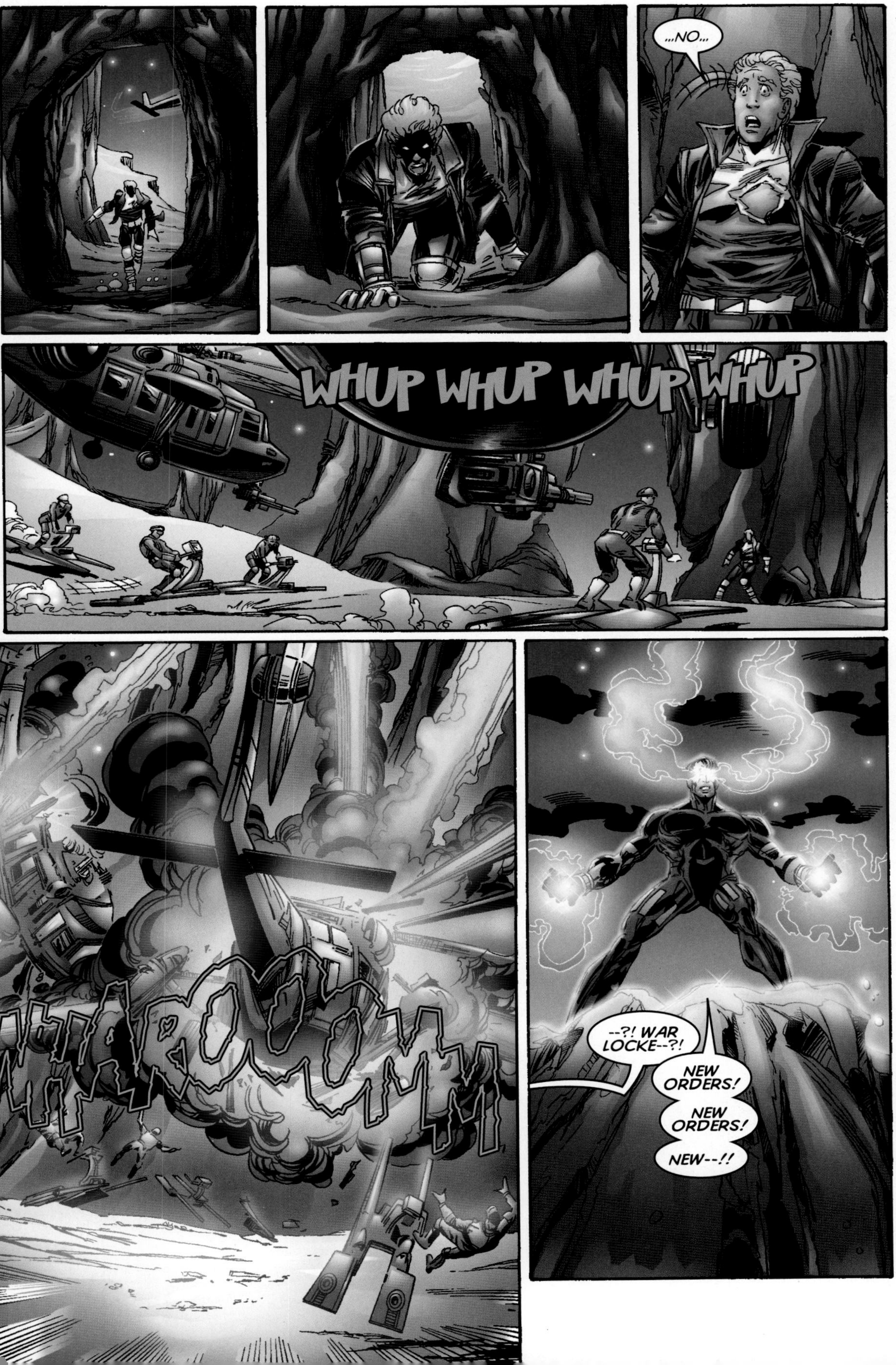
...NO...
WHUP WHUP WHUP WHUP
WHROOOOMM
--?! WAR LOCKE--?!
NEW ORDERS!
NEW ORDERS!
NEW--!!

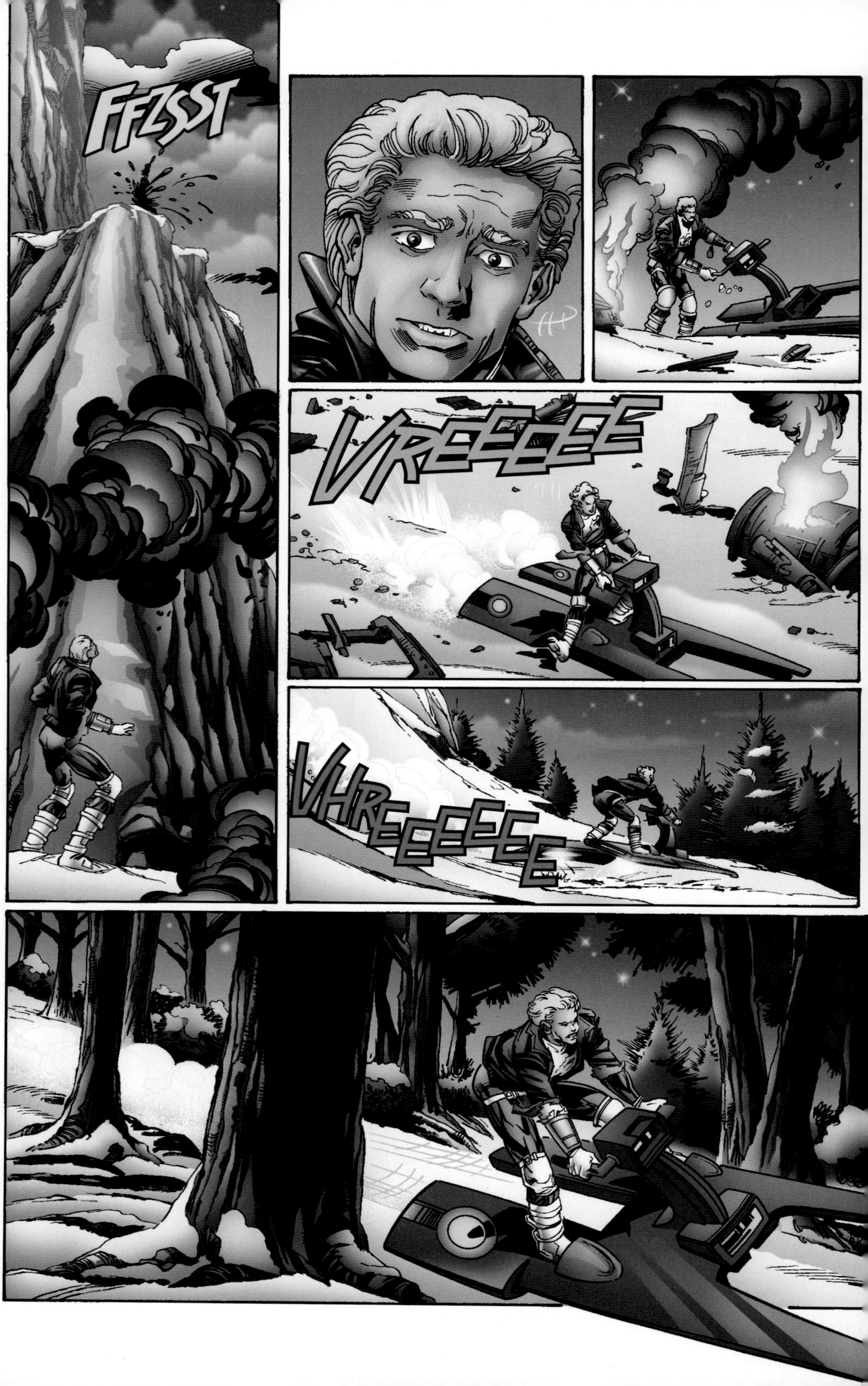
FFZSST
VREEEEEE
VHREEEEEEE

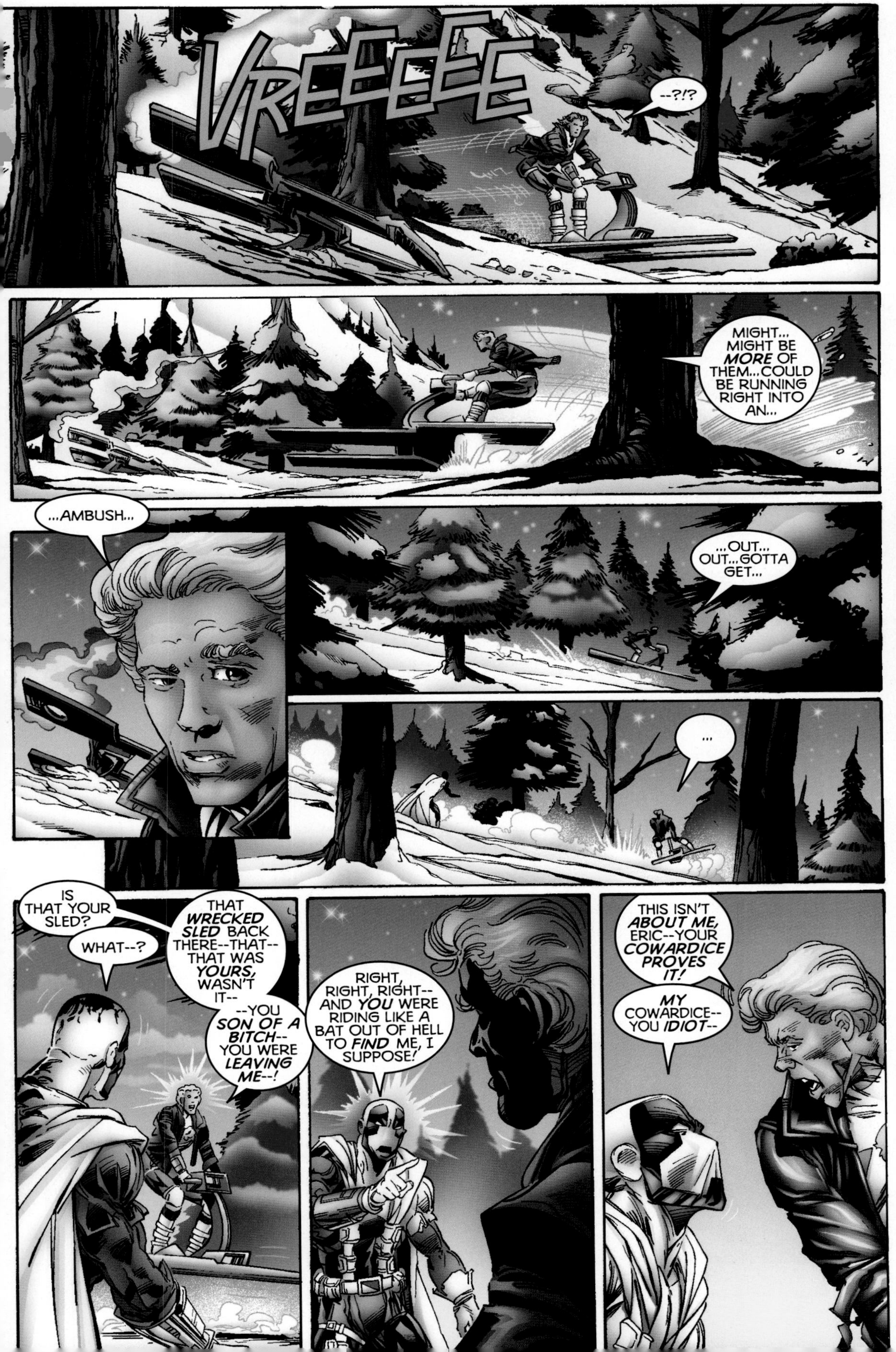
VREEEEEE
--?!?
MIGHT... MIGHT BE MORE OF THEM...COULD BE RUNNING RIGHT INTO AN...
...AMBUSH...
...OUT... OUT...GOTTA GET...
...
IS THAT YOUR SLED?
WHAT--?
THAT WRECKED SLED BACK THERE--THAT--THAT WAS YOURS, WASN'T IT--
--YOU SON OF A BITCH--YOU WERE LEAVING ME--!
RIGHT, RIGHT, RIGHT--AND YOU WERE RIDING LIKE A BAT OUT OF HELL TO FIND ME, I SUPPOSE!
THIS ISN'T ABOUT ME, ERIC--YOUR COWARDICE PROVES IT!
MY COWARDICE--YOU IDIOT--

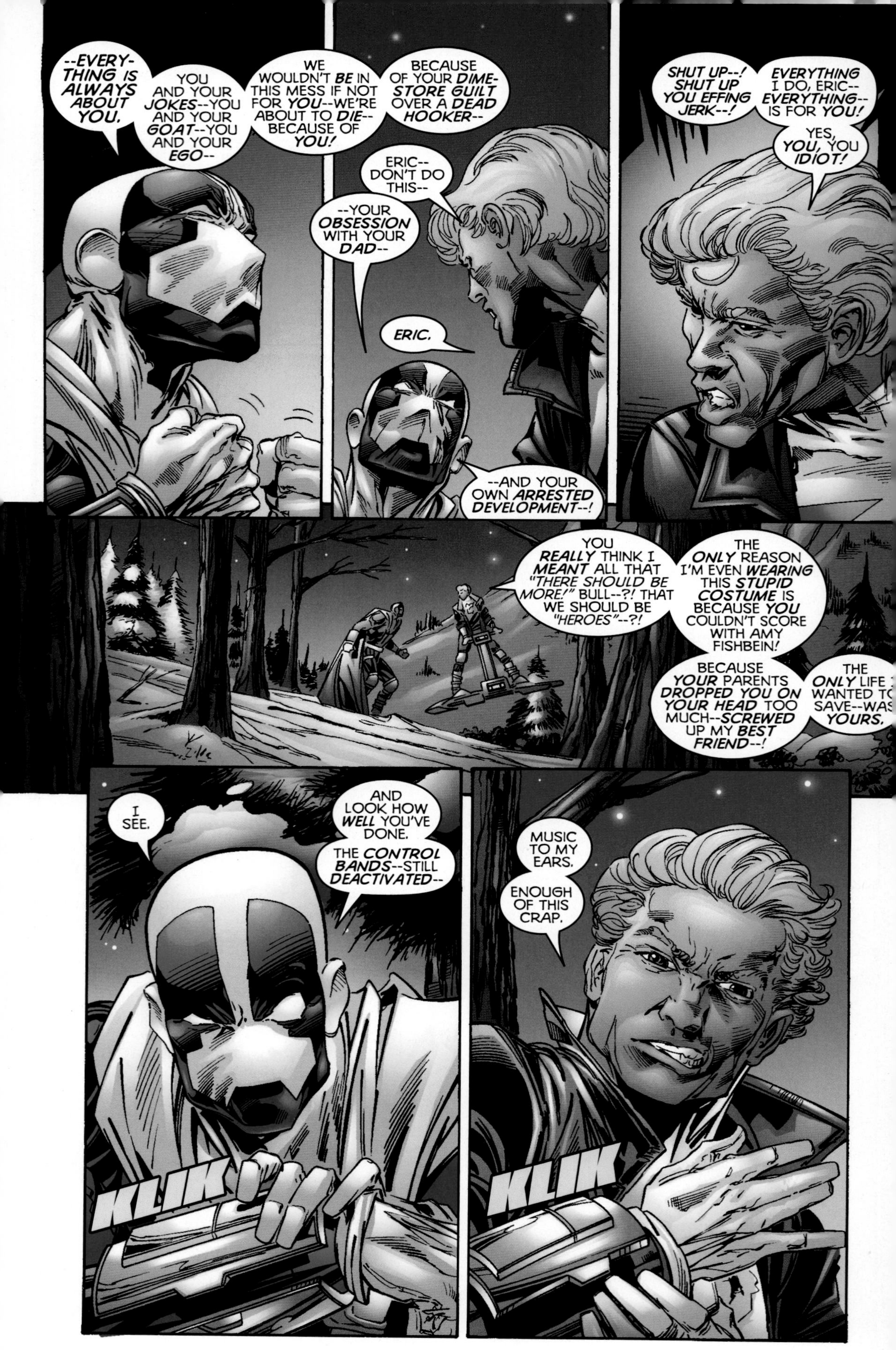
--EVERYTHING IS ALWAYS ABOUT YOU.
YOU AND YOUR JOKES--YOU AND YOUR GOAT--YOU AND YOUR EGO--
WE WOULDN'T BE IN THIS MESS IF NOT FOR YOU--WE'RE ABOUT TO DIE--BECAUSE OF YOU!
BECAUSE OF YOUR DIME-STORE GUILT OVER A DEAD HOOKER--
ERIC--DON'T DO THIS--
--YOUR OBSESSION WITH YOUR DAD--
ERIC.
--AND YOUR OWN ARRESTED DEVELOPMENT--!
SHUT UP--! SHUT UP YOU EFFING JERK--!
EVERYTHING I DO, ERIC--EVERYTHING--IS FOR YOU!
YES, YOU, YOU IDIOT!
YOU REALLY THINK I MEANT ALL THAT "THERE SHOULD BE MORE!" BULL--?! THAT WE SHOULD BE "HEROES"--?!
THE ONLY REASON I'M EVEN WEARING THIS STUPID COSTUME IS BECAUSE YOU COULDN'T SCORE WITH AMY FISHBEIN!
BECAUSE YOUR PARENTS DROPPED YOU ON YOUR HEAD TOO MUCH--SCREWED UP MY BEST FRIEND--!
THE ONLY LIFE I WANTED TO SAVE--WAS YOURS.
I SEE.
AND LOOK HOW WELL YOU'VE DONE.
THE CONTROL BANDS--STILL DEACTIVATED--
KLIK
MUSIC TO MY EARS.
ENOUGH OF THIS CRAP.
KLIK

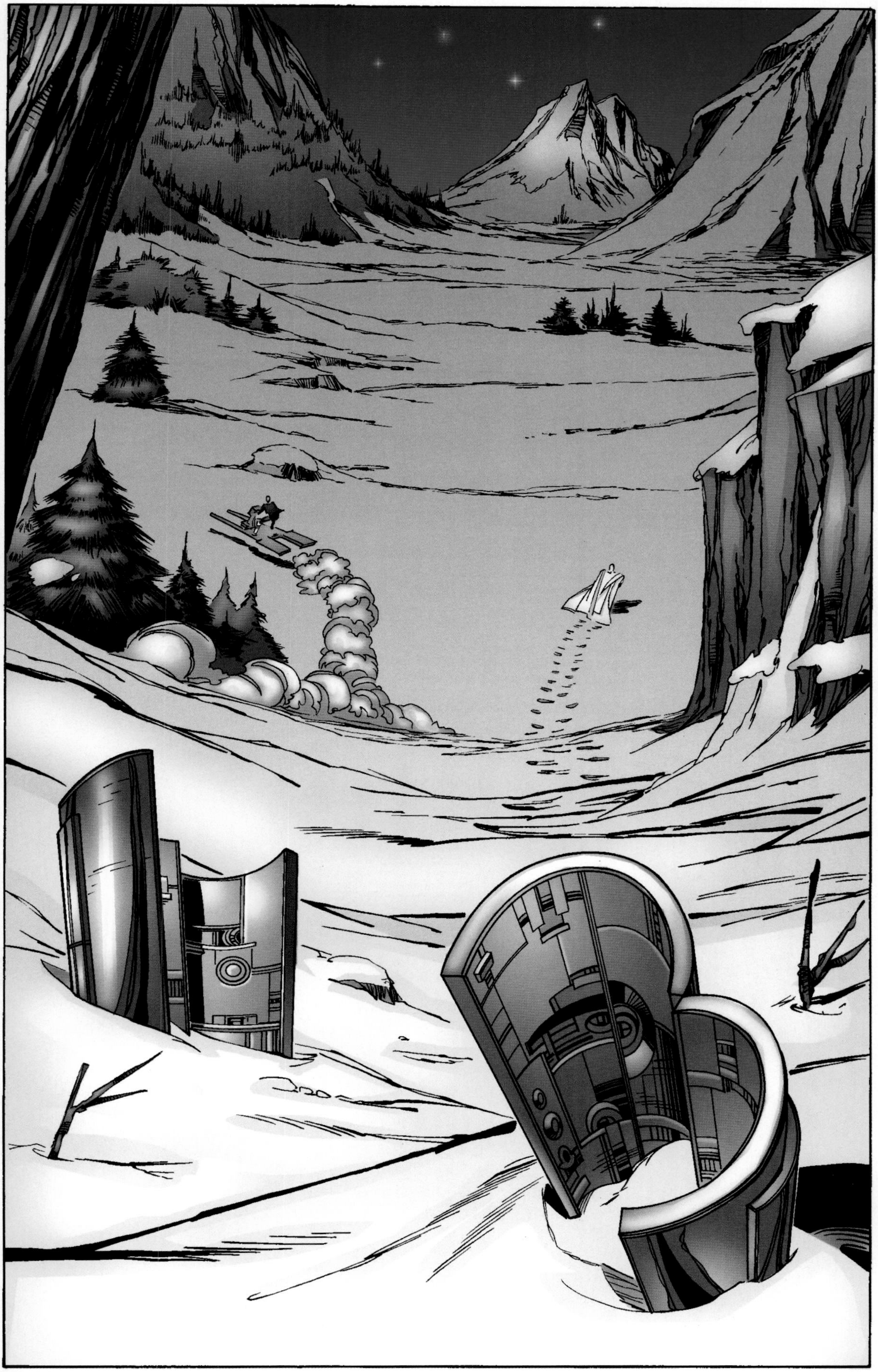

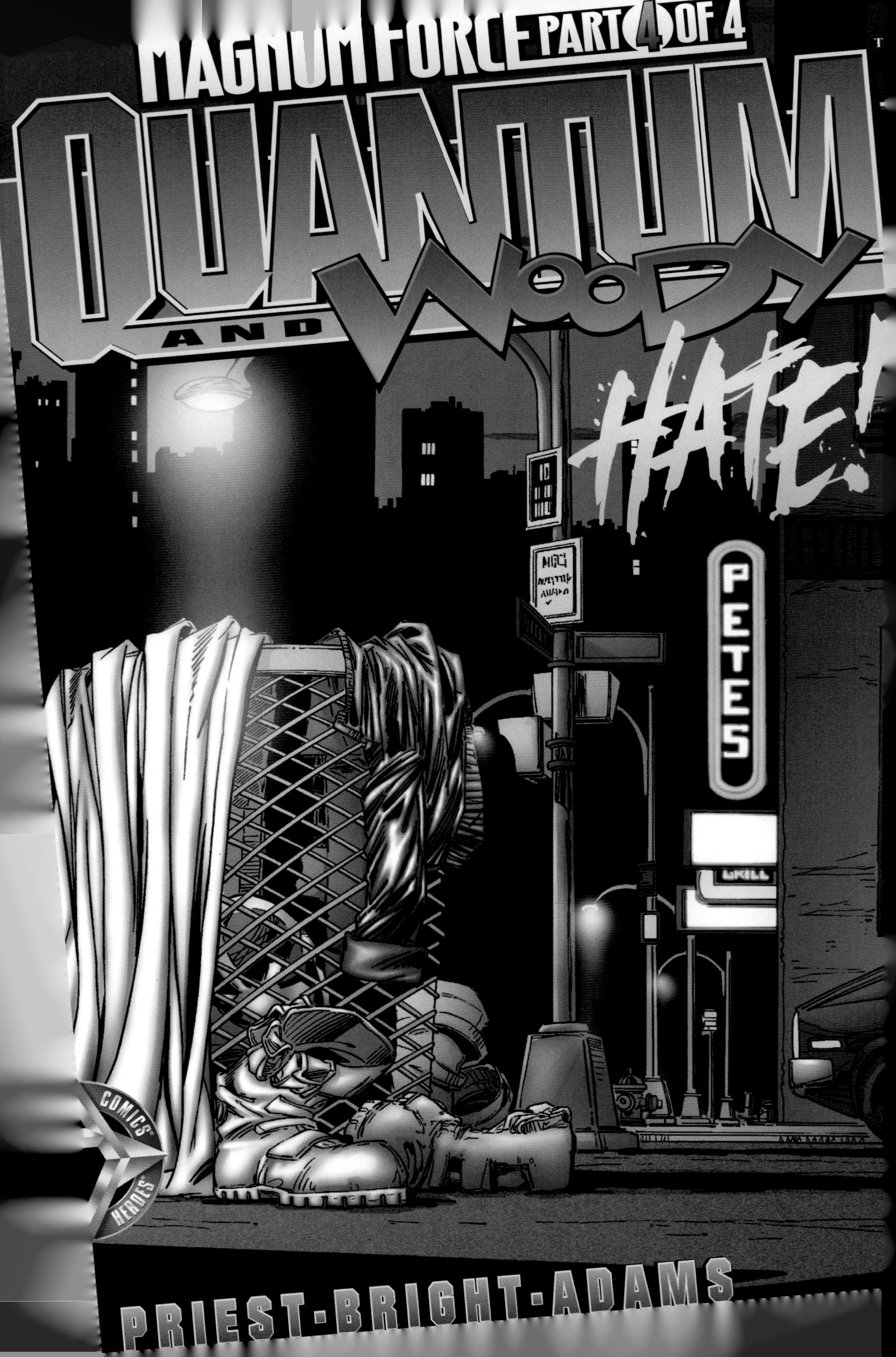
MAGNUM FORCE PART 4 OF 4
QUANTUM AND WOODY
HATE!
PETES
GRILL
PRIEST-BRIGHT-ADAMS

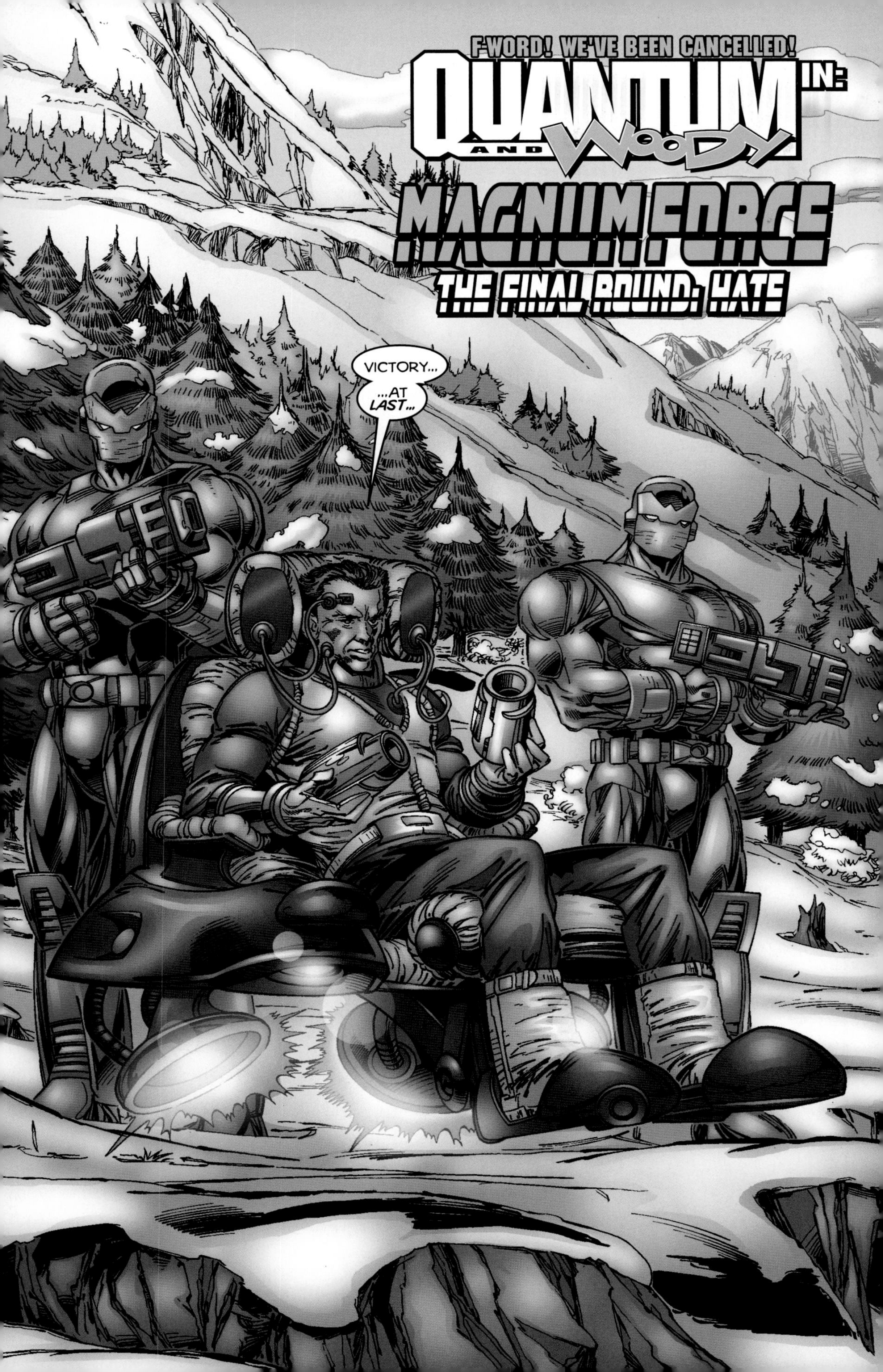
F-WORD! WE'VE BEEN CANCELLED!
QUANTUM AND WOODY IN:
MAGNUM FORCE
THE FINAL ROUND: HATE
VICTORY...
...AT LAST...

"Victory"

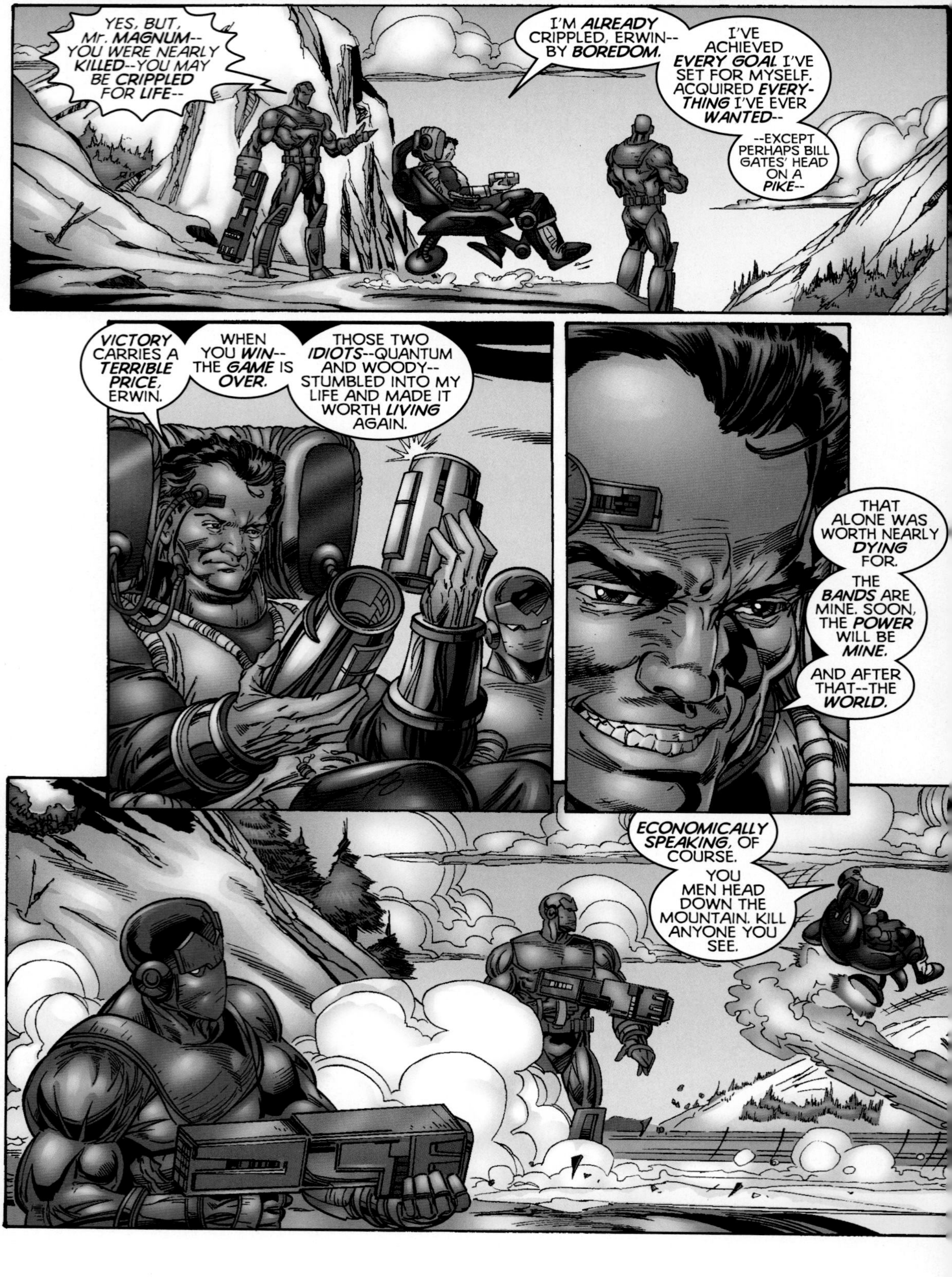
YES, BUT, Mr. MAGNUM--YOU WERE NEARLY KILLED--YOU MAY BE CRIPPLED FOR LIFE--
I'M ALREADY CRIPPLED, ERWIN--BY BOREDOM.
I'VE ACHIEVED EVERY GOAL I'VE SET FOR MYSELF. ACQUIRED EVERY-THING I'VE EVER WANTED--
--EXCEPT PERHAPS BILL GATES' HEAD ON A PIKE--
VICTORY CARRIES A TERRIBLE PRICE, ERWIN.
WHEN YOU WIN--THE GAME IS OVER.
THOSE TWO IDIOTS--QUANTUM AND WOODY--STUMBLED INTO MY LIFE AND MADE IT WORTH LIVING AGAIN.
THAT ALONE WAS WORTH NEARLY DYING FOR.
THE BANDS ARE MINE. SOON, THE POWER WILL BE MINE.
AND AFTER THAT--THE WORLD.
ECONOMICALLY SPEAKING, OF COURSE.
YOU MEN HEAD DOWN THE MOUNTAIN. KILL ANYONE YOU SEE.

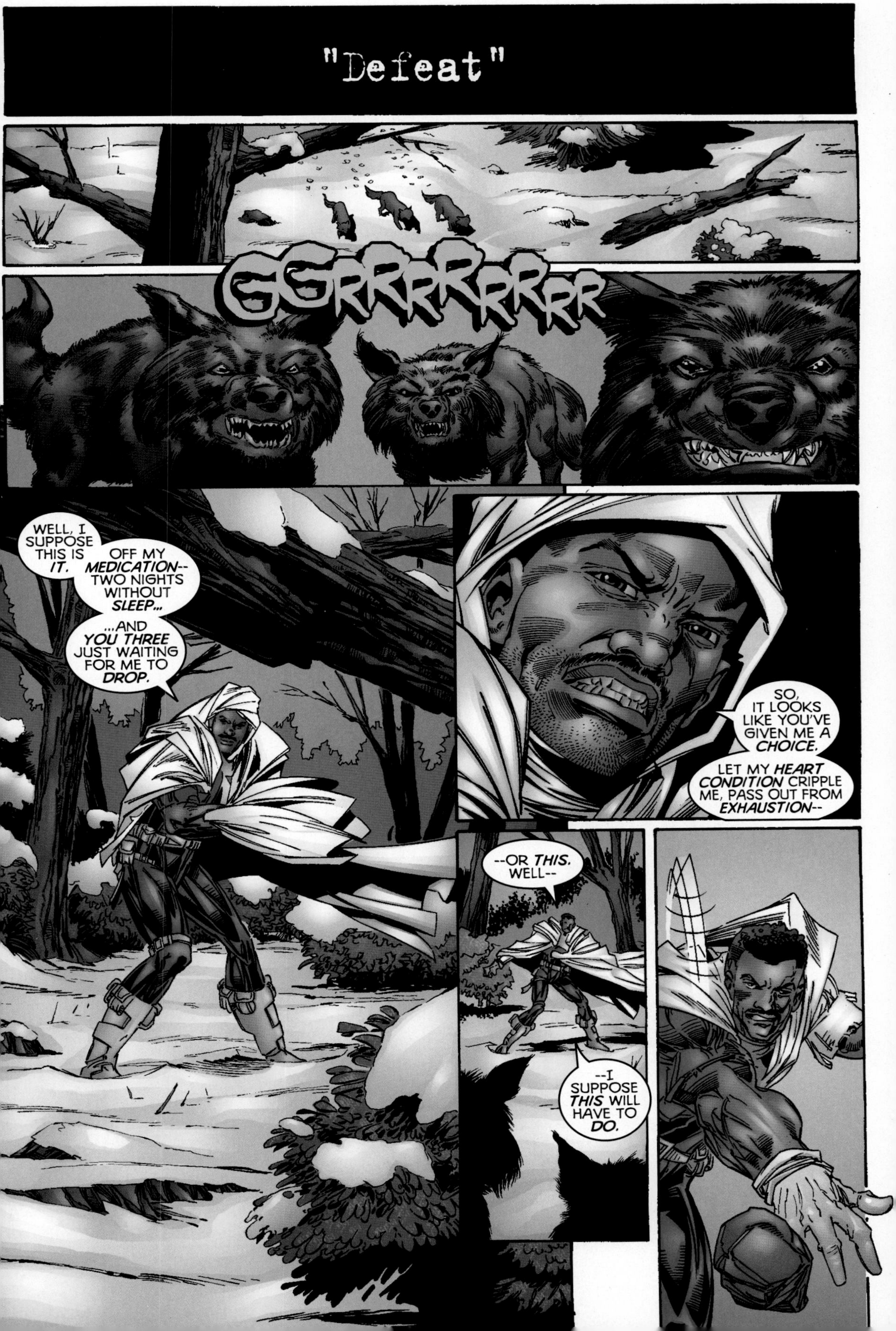
"Defeat"
GSRRRRRRRR
WELL, I SUPPOSE THIS IS IT.
OFF MY MEDICATION--TWO NIGHTS WITHOUT SLEEP...
...AND YOU THREE JUST WAITING FOR ME TO DROP.
SO, IT LOOKS LIKE YOU'VE GIVEN ME A CHOICE.
LET MY HEART CONDITION CRIPPLE ME, PASS OUT FROM EXHAUSTION--
--OR THIS. WELL--
--I SUPPOSE THIS WILL HAVE TO DO.

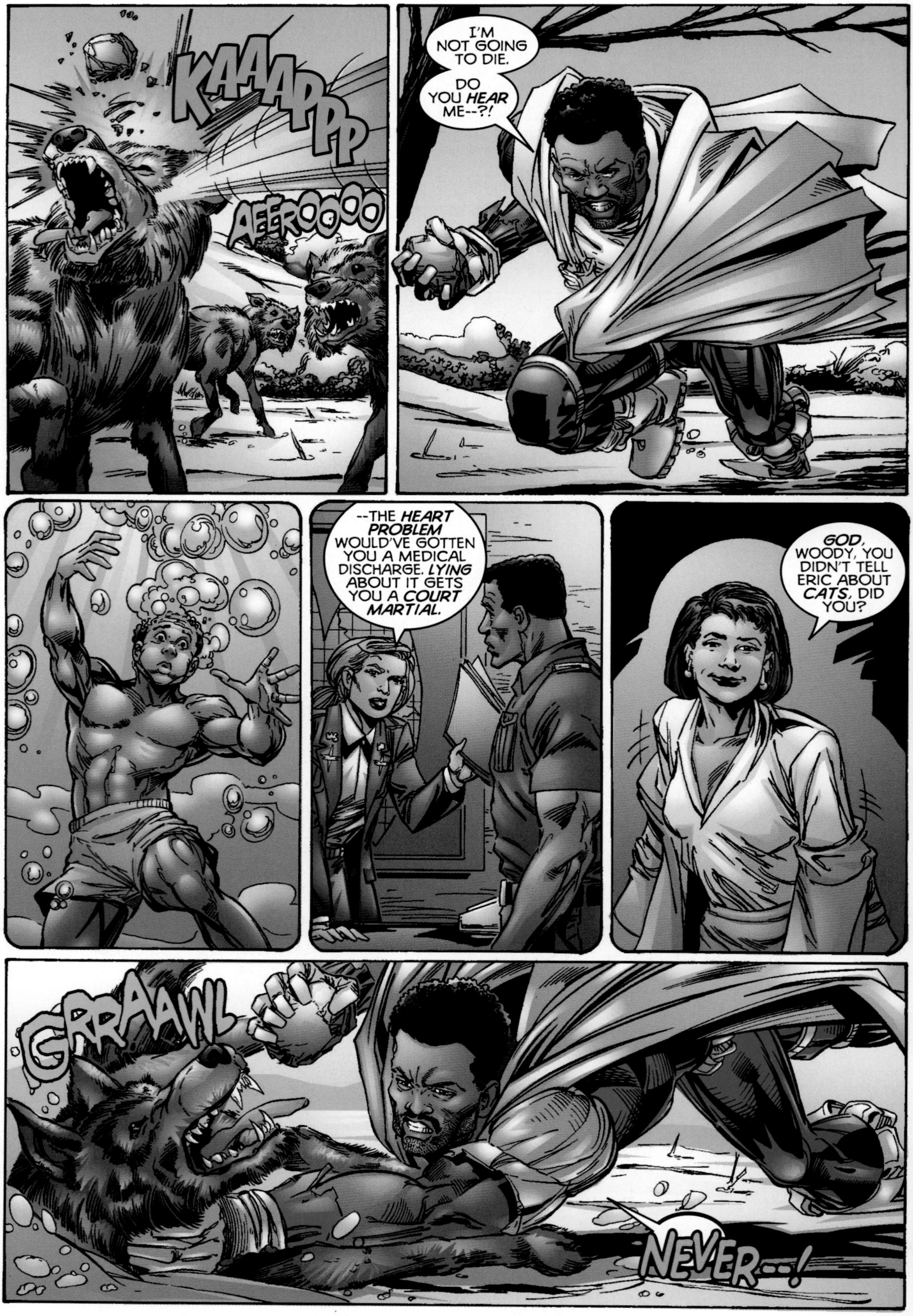
KAAAAPPPP
AEEROOOO
I'M NOT GOING TO DIE.
DO YOU HEAR ME--?!
--THE HEART PROBLEM WOULD'VE GOTTEN YOU A MEDICAL DISCHARGE. LYING ABOUT IT GETS YOU A COURT MARTIAL.
GOD, WOODY, YOU DIDN'T TELL ERIC ABOUT CATS, DID YOU?
GRRAAWL
NEVER--!

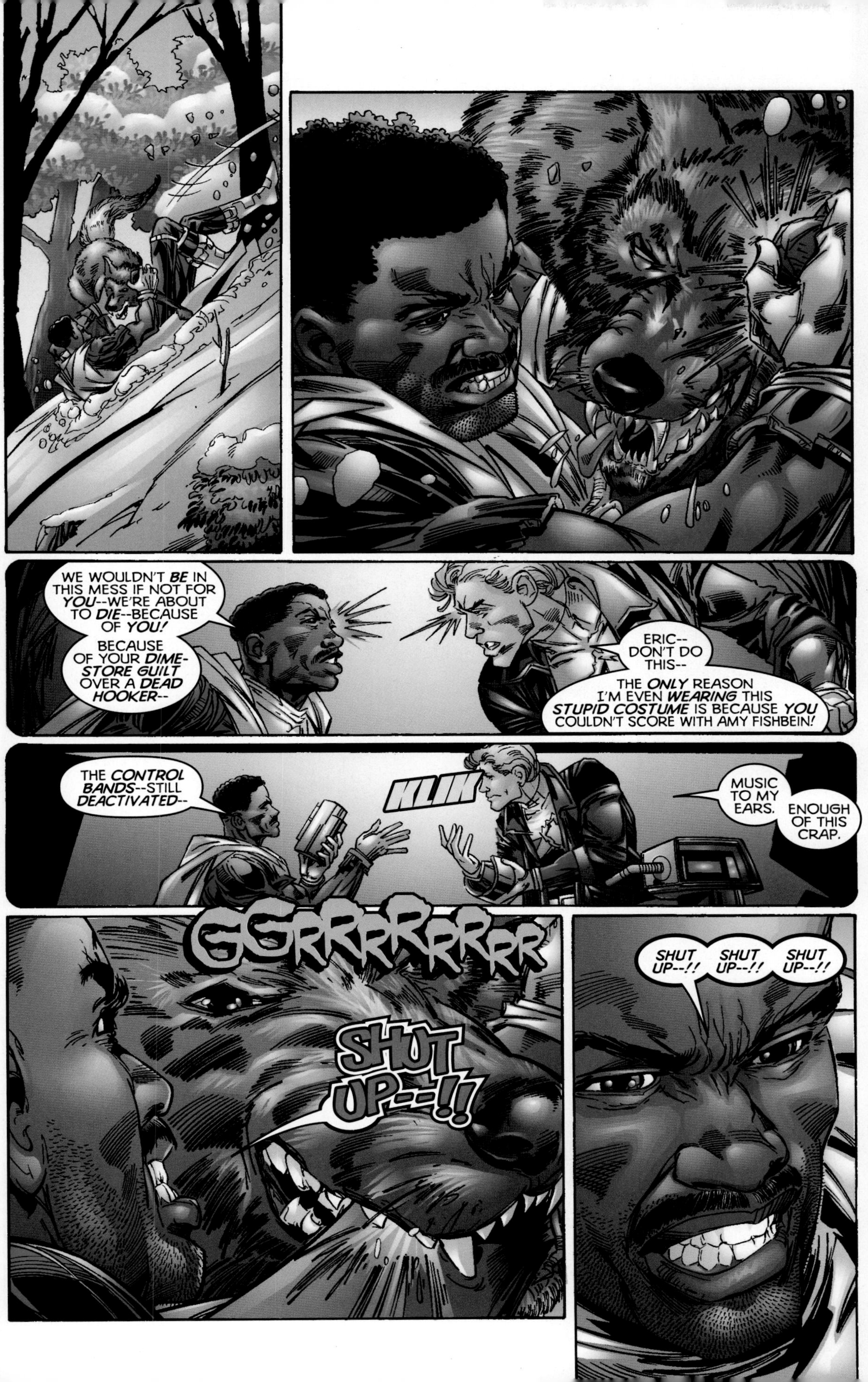
WE WOULDN'T BE IN THIS MESS IF NOT FOR YOU--WE'RE ABOUT TO DIE--BECAUSE OF YOU!
BECAUSE OF YOUR DIME-STORE GUILT OVER A DEAD HOOKER--
ERIC-- DON'T DO THIS--
THE ONLY REASON I'M EVEN WEARING THIS STUPID COSTUME IS BECAUSE YOU COULDN'T SCORE WITH AMY FISHBEIN!
THE CONTROL BANDS--STILL DEACTIVATED--
KLIK
MUSIC TO MY EARS.
ENOUGH OF THIS CRAP.
GGRRRRRRRRR
SHUT UP--!!
SHUT UP--!!
SHUT UP--!!
SHUT UP--!!

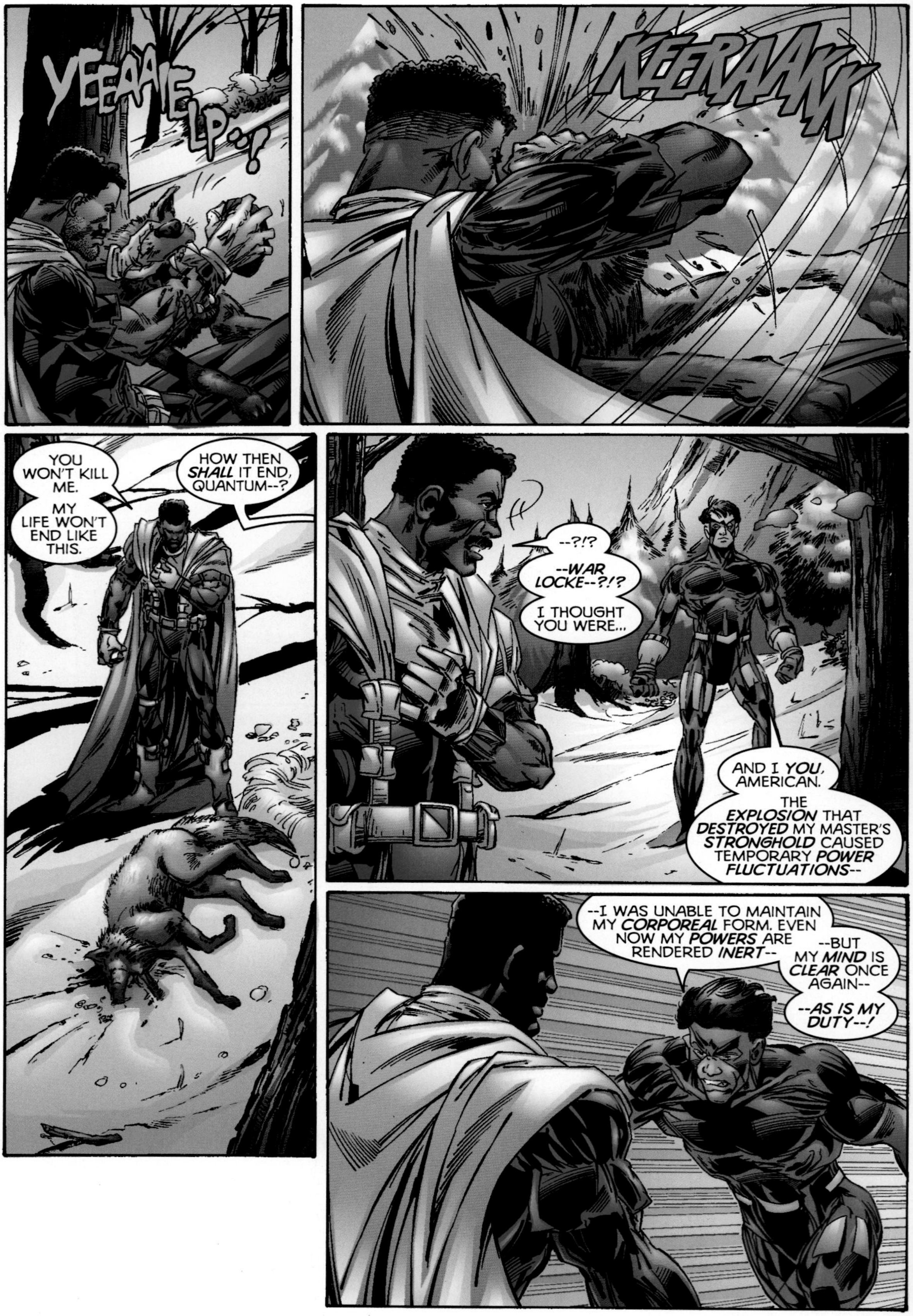
YEEAAIE
ELP--!
KEERAAKK
YOU WON'T KILL ME.
MY LIFE WON'T END LIKE THIS.
HOW THEN SHALL IT END, QUANTUM--?
--?!?
--WAR LOCKE--?!?
I THOUGHT YOU WERE...
AND I YOU, AMERICAN.
THE EXPLOSION THAT DESTROYED MY MASTER'S STRONGHOLD CAUSED TEMPORARY POWER FLUCTUATIONS--
--I WAS UNABLE TO MAINTAIN MY CORPOREAL FORM. EVEN NOW MY POWERS ARE RENDERED INERT--
--BUT MY MIND IS CLEAR ONCE AGAIN--
--AS IS MY DUTY--!

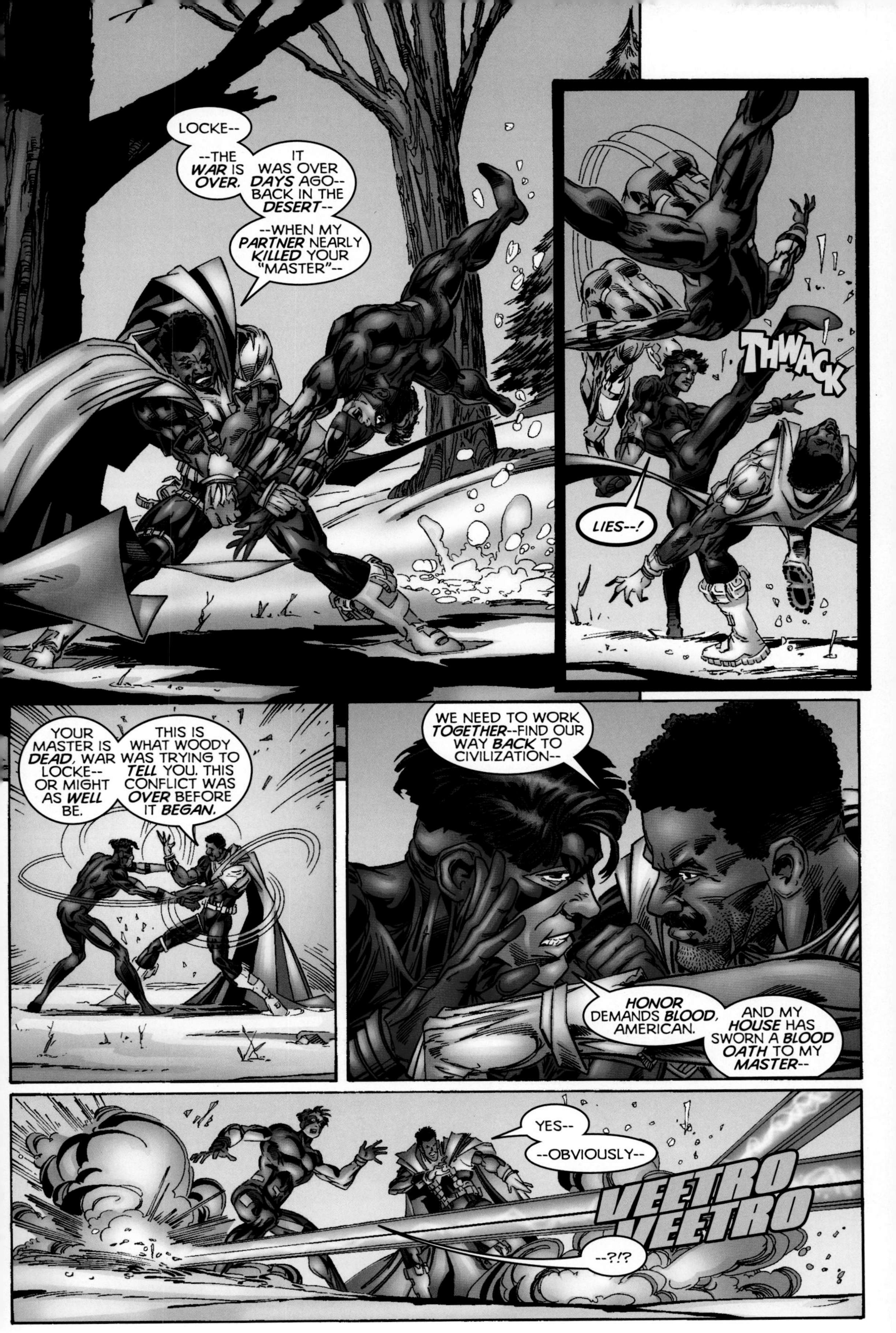
LOCKE--
--THE WAR IS OVER.
IT WAS OVER DAYS AGO-- BACK IN THE DESERT--
--WHEN MY PARTNER NEARLY KILLED YOUR "MASTER"--
THWACK
LIES--!
YOUR MASTER IS DEAD, WAR LOCKE-- OR MIGHT AS WELL BE.
THIS IS WHAT WOODY WAS TRYING TO TELL YOU. THIS CONFLICT WAS OVER BEFORE IT BEGAN.
WE NEED TO WORK TOGETHER--FIND OUR WAY BACK TO CIVILIZATION--
HONOR DEMANDS BLOOD, AMERICAN.
AND MY HOUSE HAS SWORN A BLOOD OATH TO MY MASTER--
YES--
--OBVIOUSLY--
VEETRO VEETRO
--?!?

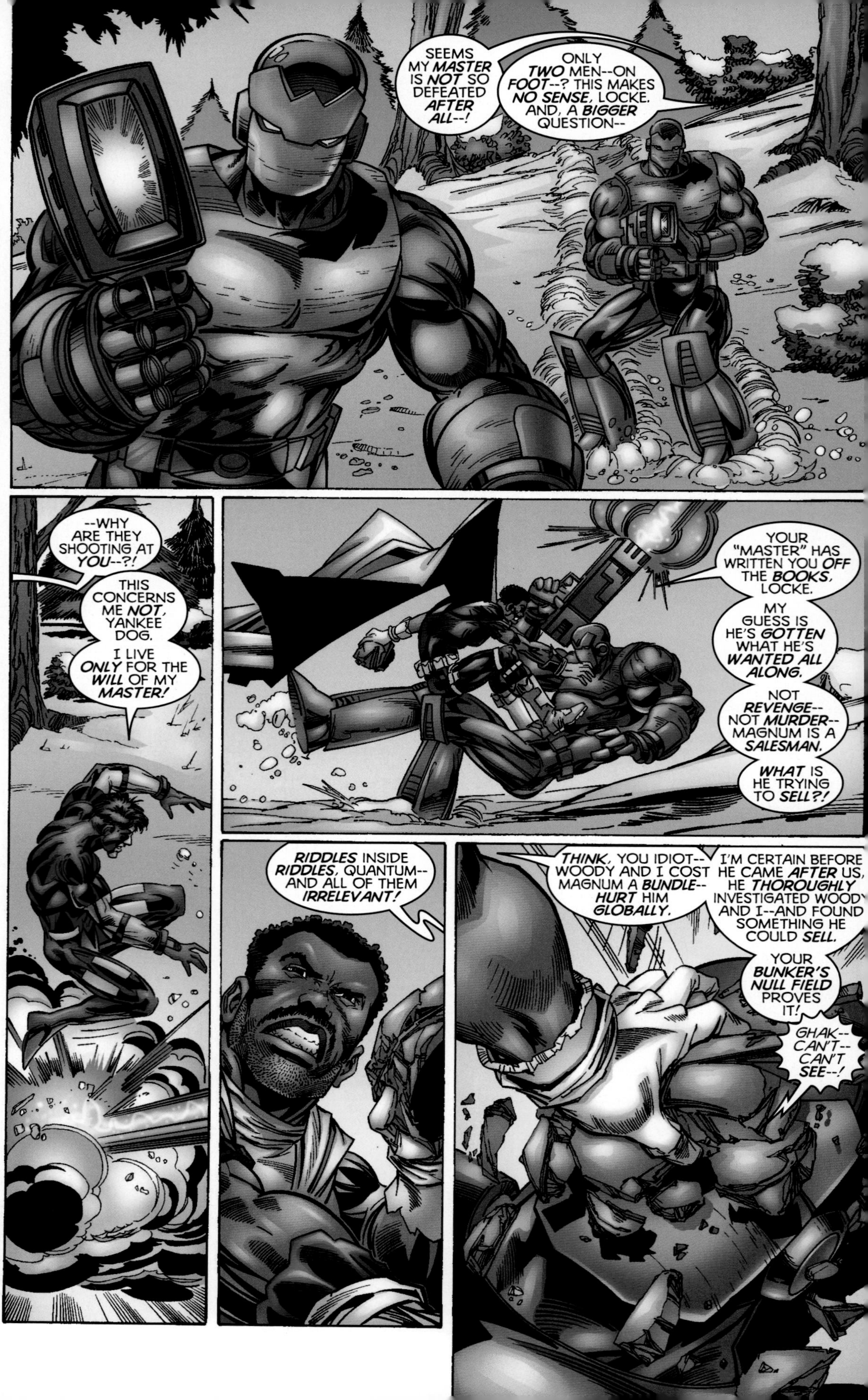
SEEMS MY MASTER IS NOT SO DEFEATED AFTER ALL--!
ONLY TWO MEN--ON FOOT--? THIS MAKES NO SENSE, LOCKE. AND, A BIGGER QUESTION--
--WHY ARE THEY SHOOTING AT YOU--?!
THIS CONCERNS ME NOT, YANKEE DOG.
I LIVE ONLY FOR THE WILL OF MY MASTER!
YOUR "MASTER" HAS WRITTEN YOU OFF THE BOOKS, LOCKE.
MY GUESS IS HE'S GOTTEN WHAT HE'S WANTED ALL ALONG.
NOT REVENGE-- NOT MURDER-- MAGNUM IS A SALESMAN.
WHAT IS HE TRYING TO SELL?!
RIDDLES INSIDE RIDDLES, QUANTUM-- AND ALL OF THEM IRRELEVANT!
THINK, YOU IDIOT-- WOODY AND I COST MAGNUM A BUNDLE-- HURT HIM GLOBALLY.
I'M CERTAIN BEFORE HE CAME AFTER US, HE THOROUGHLY INVESTIGATED WOODY AND I--AND FOUND SOMETHING HE COULD SELL.
YOUR BUNKER'S NULL FIELD PROVES IT!
GHAK-- CAN'T-- CAN'T SEE--!

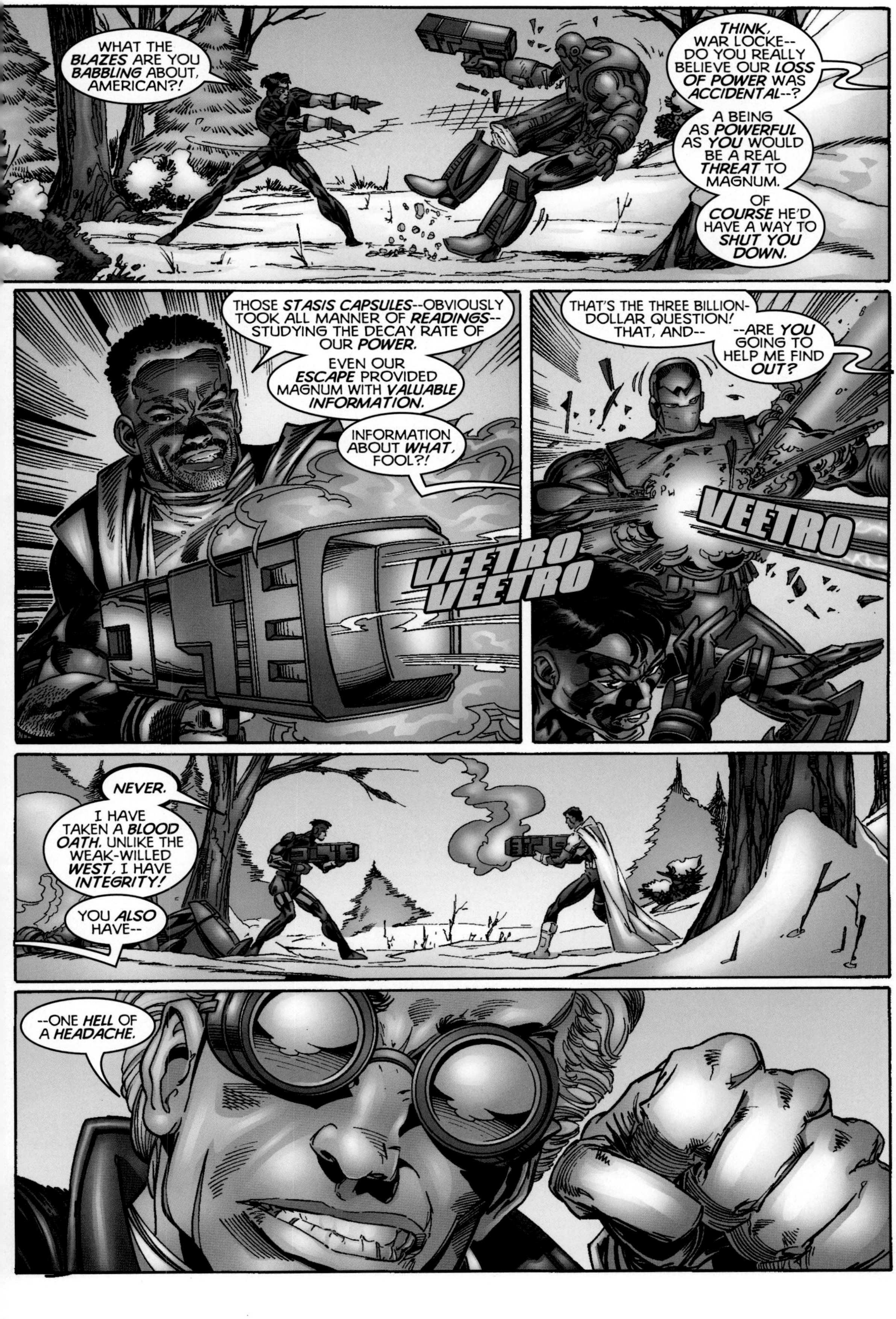
WHAT THE BLAZES ARE YOU BABBLING ABOUT, AMERICAN?!
THINK, WAR LOCKE-- DO YOU REALLY BELIEVE OUR LOSS OF POWER WAS ACCIDENTAL--?
A BEING AS POWERFUL AS YOU WOULD BE A REAL THREAT TO MAGNUM.
OF COURSE HE'D HAVE A WAY TO SHUT YOU DOWN.
THOSE STASIS CAPSULES--OBVIOUSLY TOOK ALL MANNER OF READINGS-- STUDYING THE DECAY RATE OF OUR POWER.
EVEN OUR ESCAPE PROVIDED MAGNUM WITH VALUABLE INFORMATION.
INFORMATION ABOUT WHAT, FOOL?!
VEETRO
VEETRO
THAT'S THE THREE BILLION-DOLLAR QUESTION! THAT, AND--
--ARE YOU GOING TO HELP ME FIND OUT?
VEETRO
NEVER.
I HAVE TAKEN A BLOOD OATH, UNLIKE THE WEAK-WILLED WEST, I HAVE INTEGRITY!
YOU ALSO HAVE--
--ONE HELL OF A HEADACHE.

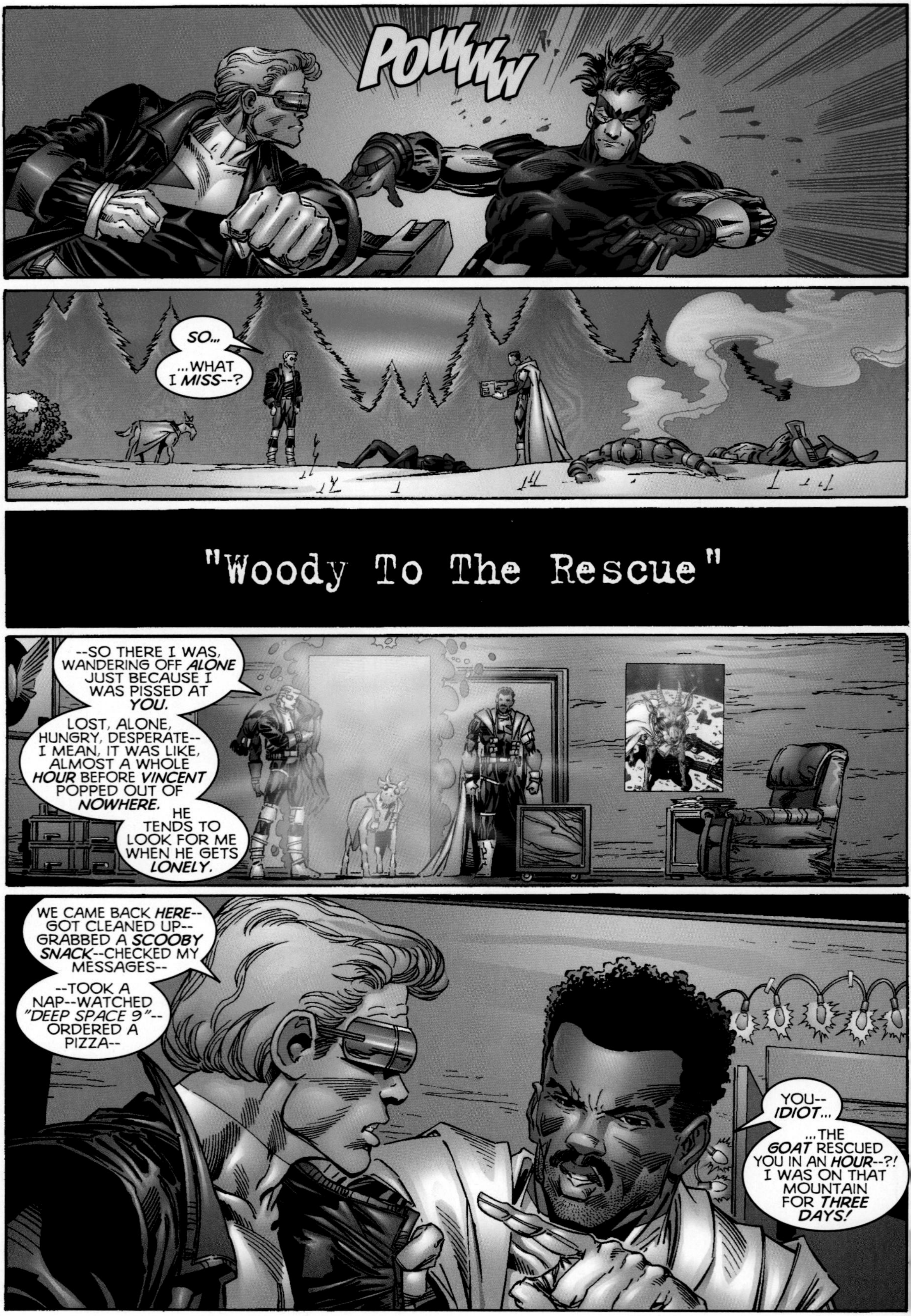
POWWW
SO...
...WHAT I MISS--?
"Woody To The Rescue"
--SO THERE I WAS, WANDERING OFF ALONE JUST BECAUSE I WAS PISSED AT YOU.
LOST, ALONE, HUNGRY, DESPERATE-- I MEAN, IT WAS LIKE, ALMOST A WHOLE HOUR BEFORE VINCENT POPPED OUT OF NOWHERE.
HE TENDS TO LOOK FOR ME WHEN HE GETS LONELY.
WE CAME BACK HERE-- GOT CLEANED UP-- GRABBED A SCOOBY SNACK--CHECKED MY MESSAGES--
--TOOK A NAP--WATCHED "DEEP SPACE 9"-- ORDERED A PIZZA--
YOU-- IDIOT...
...THE GOAT RESCUED YOU IN AN HOUR--?! I WAS ON THAT MOUNTAIN FOR THREE DAYS!

YOU PUT *YOURSELF* ON THAT MOUNTAIN, ERIC, WHEN YOU *DESERTED* ME.

UNLESS YOU *FORGOT*, WE'RE *NOT PARTNERS* ANYMORE.

BUT, FOR YOUR INFORMATION, I *TRIED* TO FIND YOU. GOATS DON'T EXACTLY *JUMP* WHEN YOU *ORDER* THEM TO.

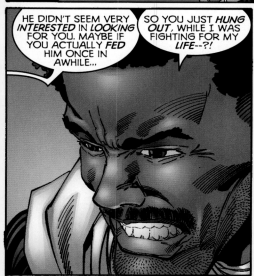

HE DIDN'T SEEM VERY *INTERESTED* IN *LOOKING* FOR YOU. MAYBE IF YOU ACTUALLY *FED* HIM ONCE IN AWHILE...

SO YOU JUST *HUNG OUT*, WHILE I WAS FIGHTING FOR MY *LIFE*--?!

YUP. WATCHED MTV, PLAYED *"FORSAKEN"*-- WATCHED THE WOODY- MOBILE--

--CALLED UP A *FEW* CHICKS.

HEY-- ERIC. GREAT *LEGS.*

HOLLY-- AND *AGENT SHERIDAN*--

TEMPEST, ERIC. I THINK WE'RE *THERE* NOW.

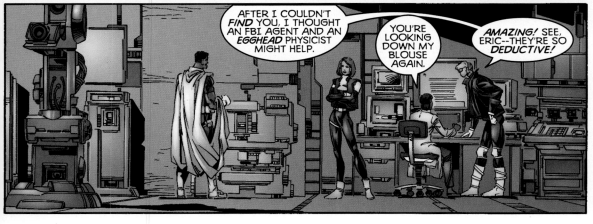

AFTER I COULDN'T *FIND* YOU, I THOUGHT AN FBI AGENT AND AN *EGGHEAD* PHYSICIST MIGHT HELP.

YOU'RE LOOKING DOWN MY BLOUSE AGAIN.

AMAZING! SEE, ERIC--THEY'RE SO *DEDUCTIVE!*

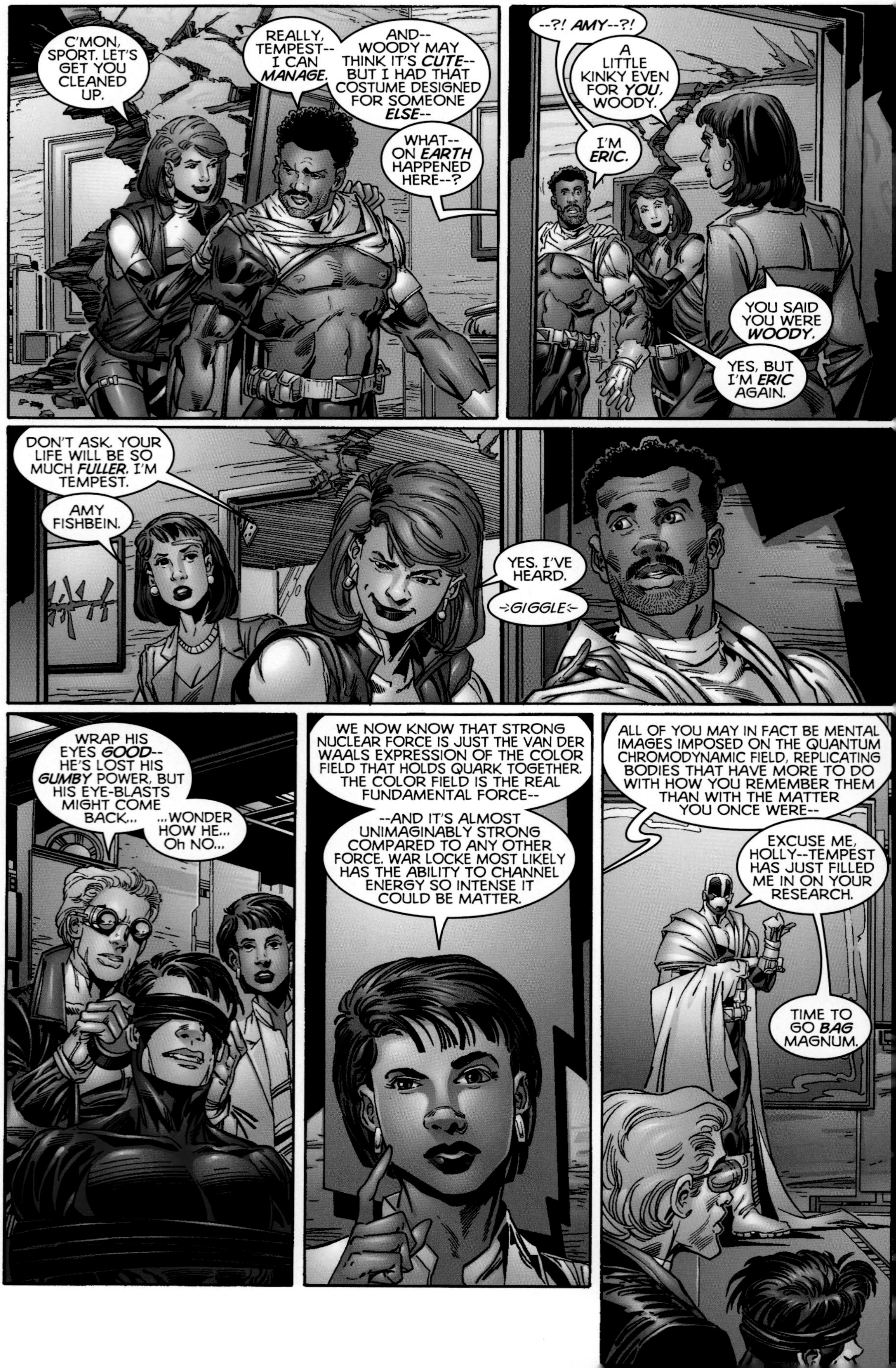
C'MON, SPORT. LET'S GET YOU CLEANED UP.
REALLY, TEMPEST-- I CAN MANAGE.
AND-- WOODY MAY THINK IT'S CUTE-- BUT I HAD THAT COSTUME DESIGNED FOR SOMEONE ELSE--
WHAT-- ON EARTH HAPPENED HERE--?
--?! AMY--?!
A LITTLE KINKY EVEN FOR YOU, WOODY.
I'M ERIC.
YOU SAID YOU WERE WOODY.
YES, BUT I'M ERIC AGAIN.
DON'T ASK. YOUR LIFE WILL BE SO MUCH FULLER. I'M TEMPEST.
AMY FISHBEIN.
YES. I'VE HEARD.
GIGGLE
WRAP HIS EYES GOOD-- HE'S LOST HIS GUMBY POWER, BUT HIS EYE-BLASTS MIGHT COME BACK...
...WONDER HOW HE... Oh NO...
WE NOW KNOW THAT STRONG NUCLEAR FORCE IS JUST THE VAN DER WAALS EXPRESSION OF THE COLOR FIELD THAT HOLDS QUARK TOGETHER. THE COLOR FIELD IS THE REAL FUNDAMENTAL FORCE--
--AND IT'S ALMOST UNIMAGINABLY STRONG COMPARED TO ANY OTHER FORCE. WAR LOCKE MOST LIKELY HAS THE ABILITY TO CHANNEL ENERGY SO INTENSE IT COULD BE MATTER.
ALL OF YOU MAY IN FACT BE MENTAL IMAGES IMPOSED ON THE QUANTUM CHROMODYNAMIC FIELD, REPLICATING BODIES THAT HAVE MORE TO DO WITH HOW YOU REMEMBER THEM THAN WITH THE MATTER YOU ONCE WERE--
EXCUSE ME, HOLLY--TEMPEST HAS JUST FILLED ME IN ON YOUR RESEARCH.
TIME TO GO BAG MAGNUM.

"Death Of A Salesman"

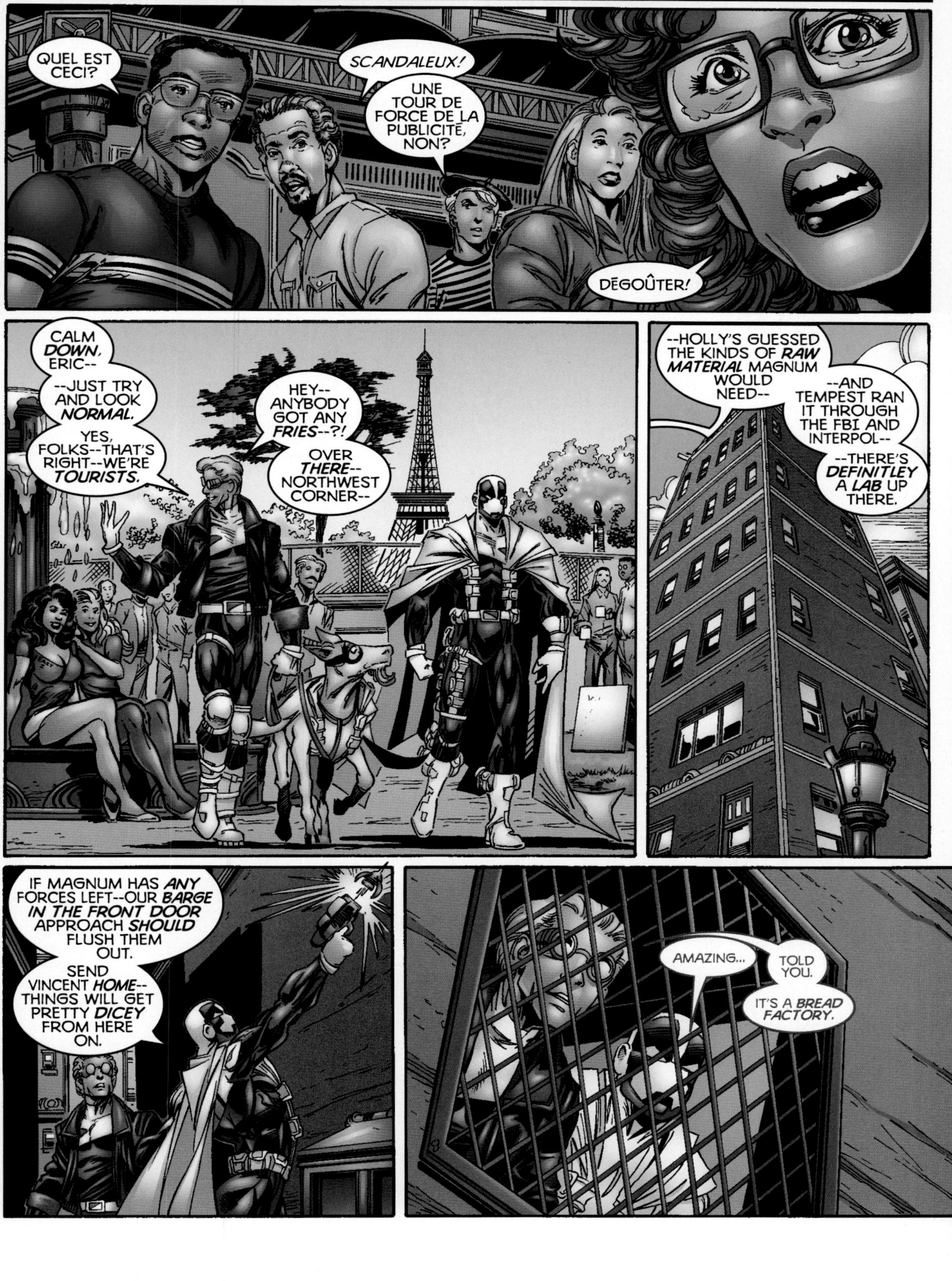
QUEL EST CECI?
SCANDALEUX!
UNE TOUR DE FORCE DE LA PUBLICITÉ, NON?
DĒGOÛTER!
CALM DOWN, ERIC--
--JUST TRY AND LOOK NORMAL.
YES, FOLKS--THAT'S RIGHT--WE'RE TOURISTS.
HEY--ANYBODY GOT ANY FRIES--?!
OVER THERE--NORTHWEST CORNER--
--HOLLY'S GUESSED THE KINDS OF RAW MATERIAL MAGNUM WOULD NEED--
--AND TEMPEST RAN IT THROUGH THE FBI AND INTERPOL--
--THERE'S DEFINITLEY A LAB UP THERE.
IF MAGNUM HAS ANY FORCES LEFT--OUR BARGE IN THE FRONT DOOR APPROACH SHOULD FLUSH THEM OUT.
SEND VINCENT HOME--THINGS WILL GET PRETTY DICEY FROM HERE ON.
AMAZING...
TOLD YOU.
IT'S A BREAD FACTORY.

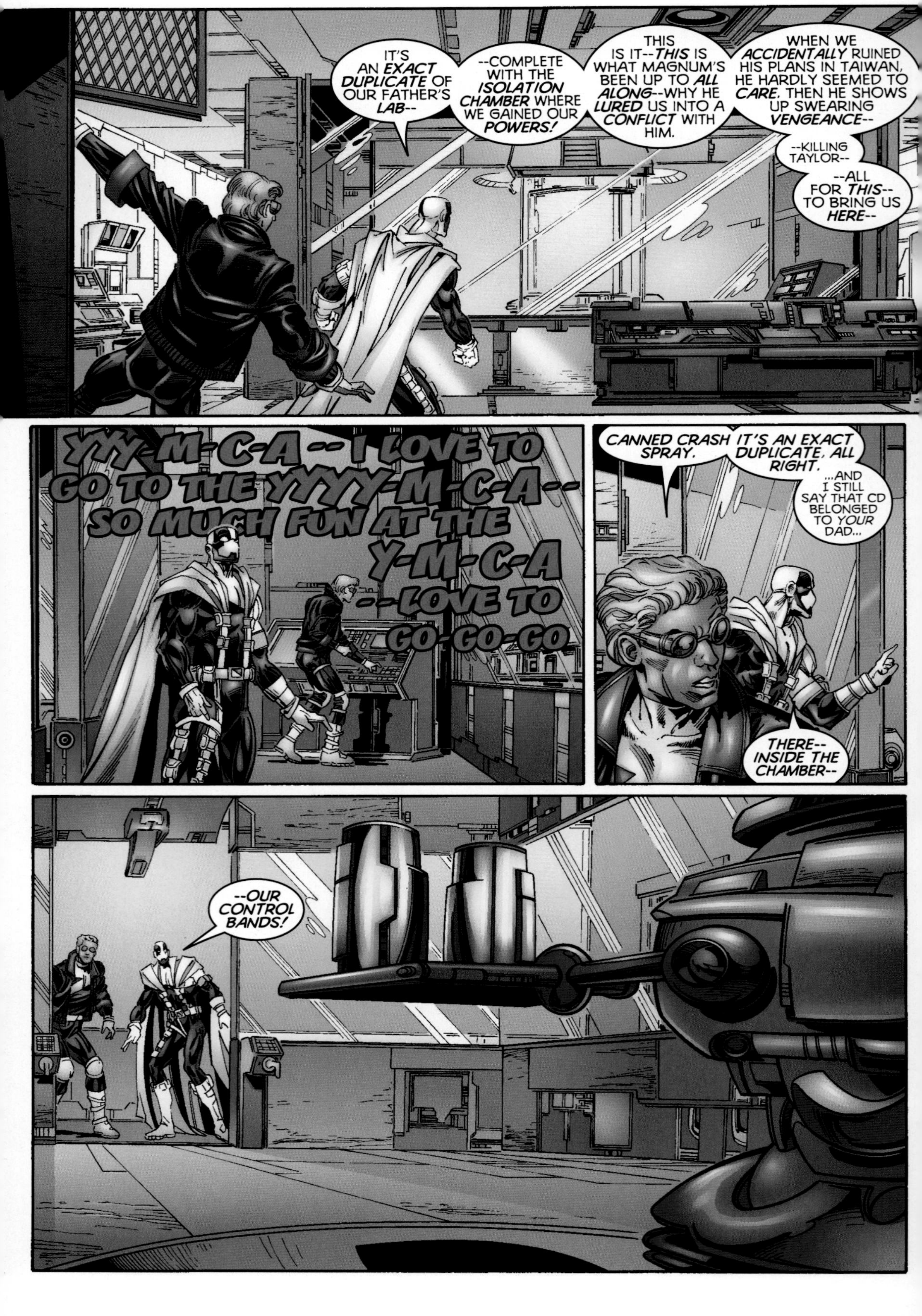
IT'S AN EXACT DUPLICATE OF OUR FATHER'S LAB--
--COMPLETE WITH THE ISOLATION CHAMBER WHERE WE GAINED OUR POWERS!
THIS IS IT--THIS IS WHAT MAGNUM'S BEEN UP TO ALL ALONG--WHY HE LURED US INTO A CONFLICT WITH HIM.
WHEN WE ACCIDENTALLY RUINED HIS PLANS IN TAIWAN, HE HARDLY SEEMED TO CARE. THEN HE SHOWS UP SWEARING VENGEANCE--
--KILLING TAYLOR--
--ALL FOR THIS-- TO BRING US HERE--
YYY-M-C-A -- I LOVE TO GO TO THE YYYY-M-C-A-- SO MUCH FUN AT THE Y-M-C-A --LOVE TO GO-GO-GO
CANNED CRASH SPRAY.
IT'S AN EXACT DUPLICATE, ALL RIGHT.
...AND I STILL SAY THAT CD BELONGED TO YOUR DAD...
THERE-- INSIDE THE CHAMBER--
--OUR CONTROL BANDS!

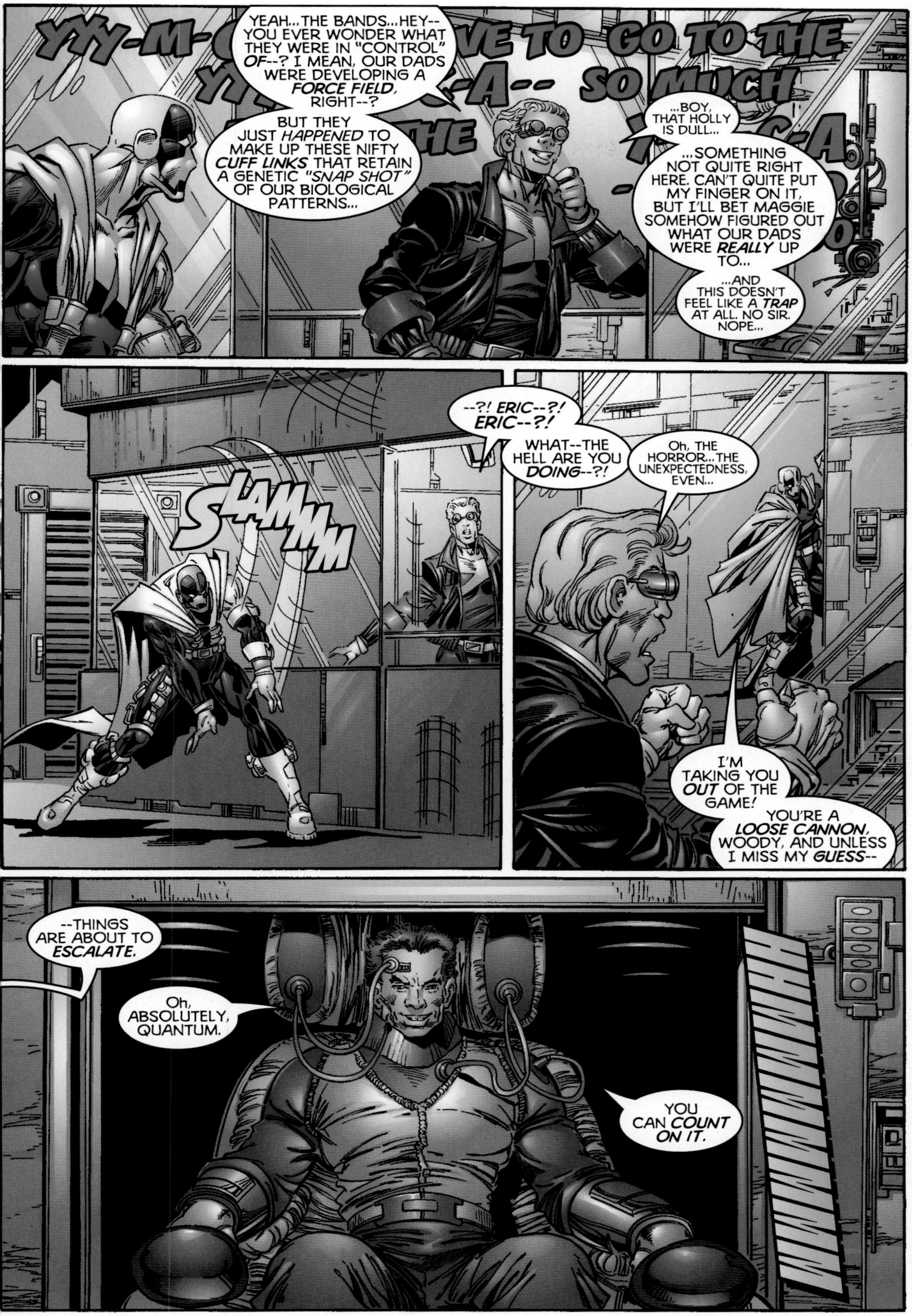
YEAH... THE BANDS... HEY-- YOU EVER WONDER WHAT THEY WERE IN "CONTROL" OF--? I MEAN, OUR DADS WERE DEVELOPING A *FORCE FIELD*, RIGHT--?
BUT THEY JUST *HAPPENED* TO MAKE UP THESE NIFTY *CUFF LINKS* THAT RETAIN A GENETIC *"SNAP SHOT"* OF OUR BIOLOGICAL PATTERNS...
...BOY, THAT HOLLY IS DULL...
...SOMETHING NOT QUITE RIGHT HERE. CAN'T QUITE PUT MY FINGER ON IT, BUT I'LL BET MAGGIE SOMEHOW FIGURED OUT WHAT OUR DADS WERE *REALLY* UP TO...
...AND THIS DOESN'T FEEL LIKE A *TRAP* AT ALL. NO SIR. NOPE...
SLAMMMM
--?! *ERIC--?! ERIC--?!*
WHAT--THE HELL ARE YOU *DOING*--?!
Oh, THE HORROR... THE UNEXPECTEDNESS, EVEN...
I'M TAKING YOU *OUT* OF THE GAME!
YOU'RE A *LOOSE CANNON*, WOODY, AND UNLESS I MISS MY *GUESS*--
--THINGS ARE ABOUT TO *ESCALATE*.
Oh, ABSOLUTELY, QUANTUM.
YOU CAN *COUNT ON IT*.

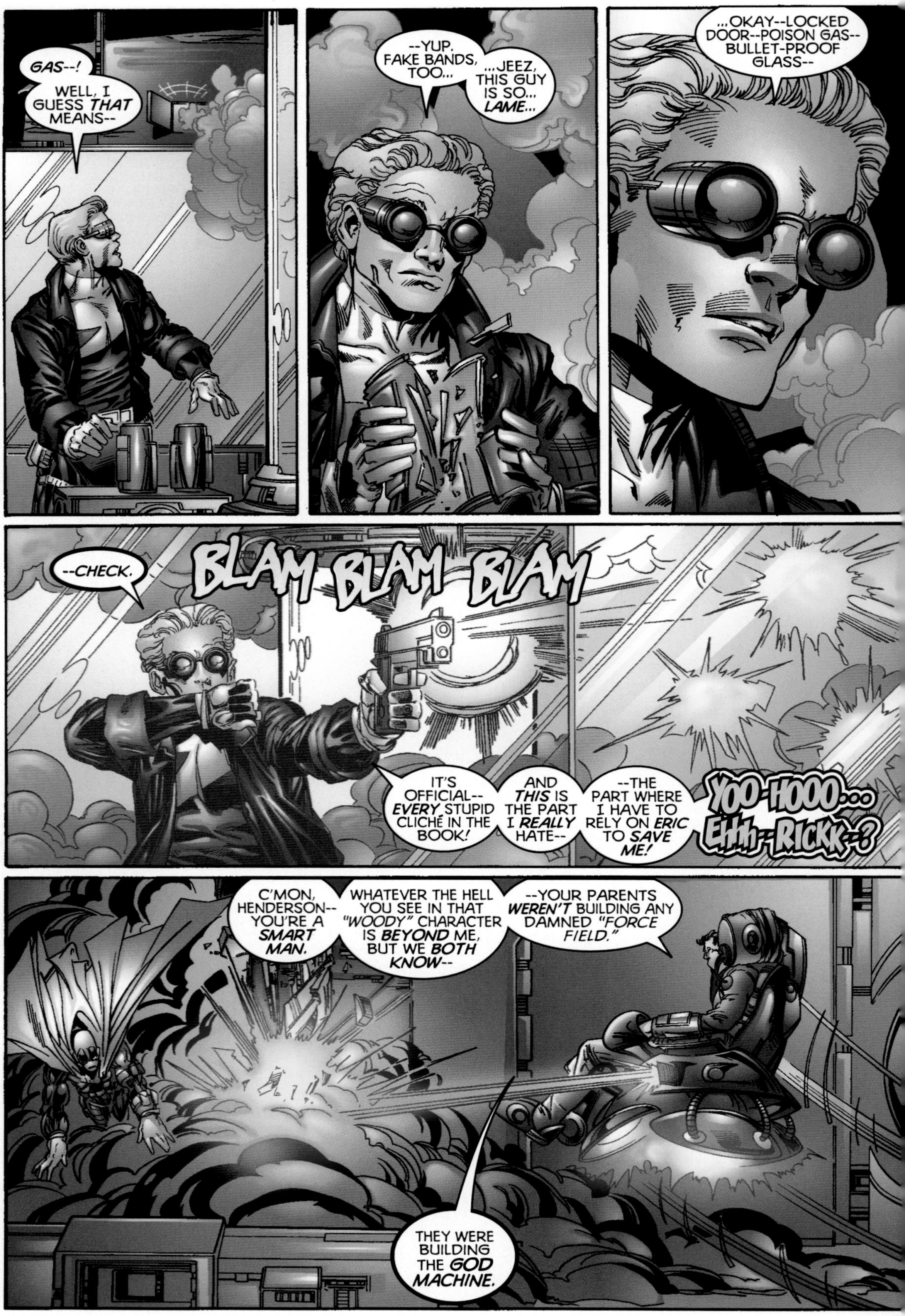
GAS--!
WELL, I GUESS THAT MEANS--
--YUP. FAKE BANDS, TOO...
...JEEZ, THIS GUY IS SO... LAME...
...OKAY--LOCKED DOOR--POISON GAS--BULLET-PROOF GLASS--
--CHECK.
BLAM BLAM BLAM
IT'S OFFICIAL--EVERY STUPID CLICHÉ IN THE BOOK!
AND THIS IS THE PART I REALLY HATE--
--THE PART WHERE I HAVE TO RELY ON ERIC TO SAVE ME!
YOO-HOOO... Ehhh-RICKK--?
C'MON, HENDERSON--YOU'RE A SMART MAN.
WHATEVER THE HELL YOU SEE IN THAT "WOODY" CHARACTER IS BEYOND ME, BUT WE BOTH KNOW--
--YOUR PARENTS WEREN'T BUILDING ANY DAMNED "FORCE FIELD."
THEY WERE BUILDING THE GOD MACHINE.

"IT'LL BE A TRAAAP. HERE, TAKE THIS PLASTEEEK."

MY *GOD*, I HATE IT WHEN ERIC'S *RIGHT*.

THIS GLASS CAN HANDLE BULLETS--

THE *GOD MACHINE*, QUANTUM--

--THE NEXT *EVOLUTION* OF *MANKIND*. THAT'S WHAT THE *CONTROL BANDS* WERE FOR!

THEY WERE *NEVER INTENDED* FOR *INDIVIDUAL* USE-- BUT, USED *TOGETHER*--

--LET'S SEE HOW YA DO WITH SOMETHING A LOT *UGLIER*.

BLAM

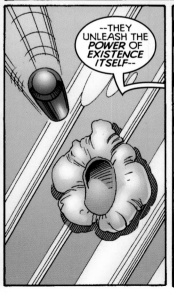

--THEY UNLEASH THE *POWER* OF *EXISTENCE* ITSELF--

GOWAAAMMM

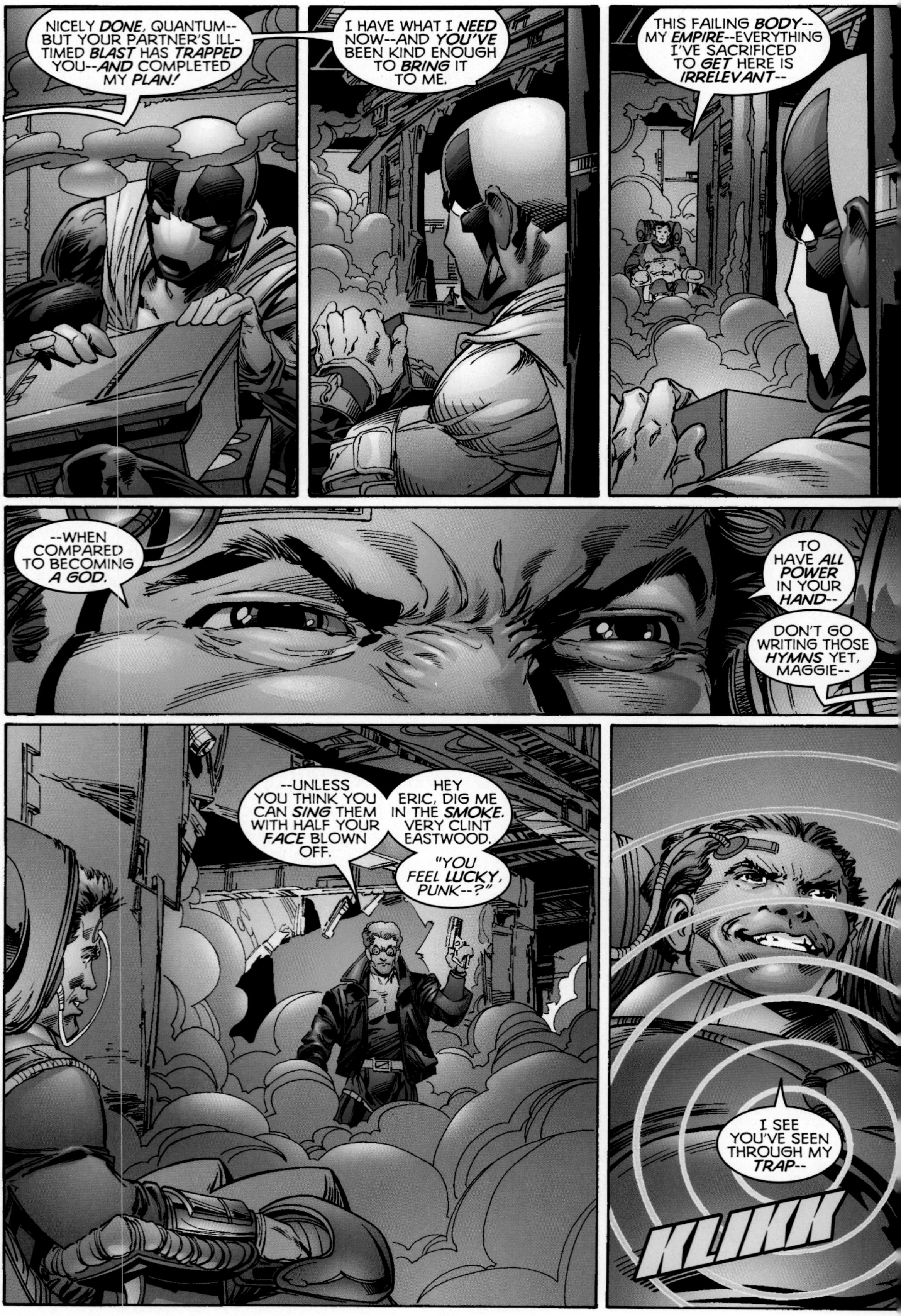
NICELY DONE, QUANTUM--BUT YOUR PARTNER'S ILL-TIMED BLAST HAS TRAPPED YOU--AND COMPLETED MY PLAN!
I HAVE WHAT I NEED NOW--AND YOU'VE BEEN KIND ENOUGH TO BRING IT TO ME.
THIS FAILING BODY--MY EMPIRE--EVERYTHING I'VE SACRIFICED TO GET HERE IS IRRELEVANT--
--WHEN COMPARED TO BECOMING A GOD.
TO HAVE ALL POWER IN YOUR HAND--
DON'T GO WRITING THOSE HYMNS YET, MAGGIE--
--UNLESS YOU THINK YOU CAN SING THEM WITH HALF YOUR FACE BLOWN OFF.
HEY ERIC, DIG ME IN THE SMOKE. VERY CLINT EASTWOOD.
"YOU FEEL LUCKY, PUNK--?"
I SEE YOU'VE SEEN THROUGH MY TRAP--
KLIKK

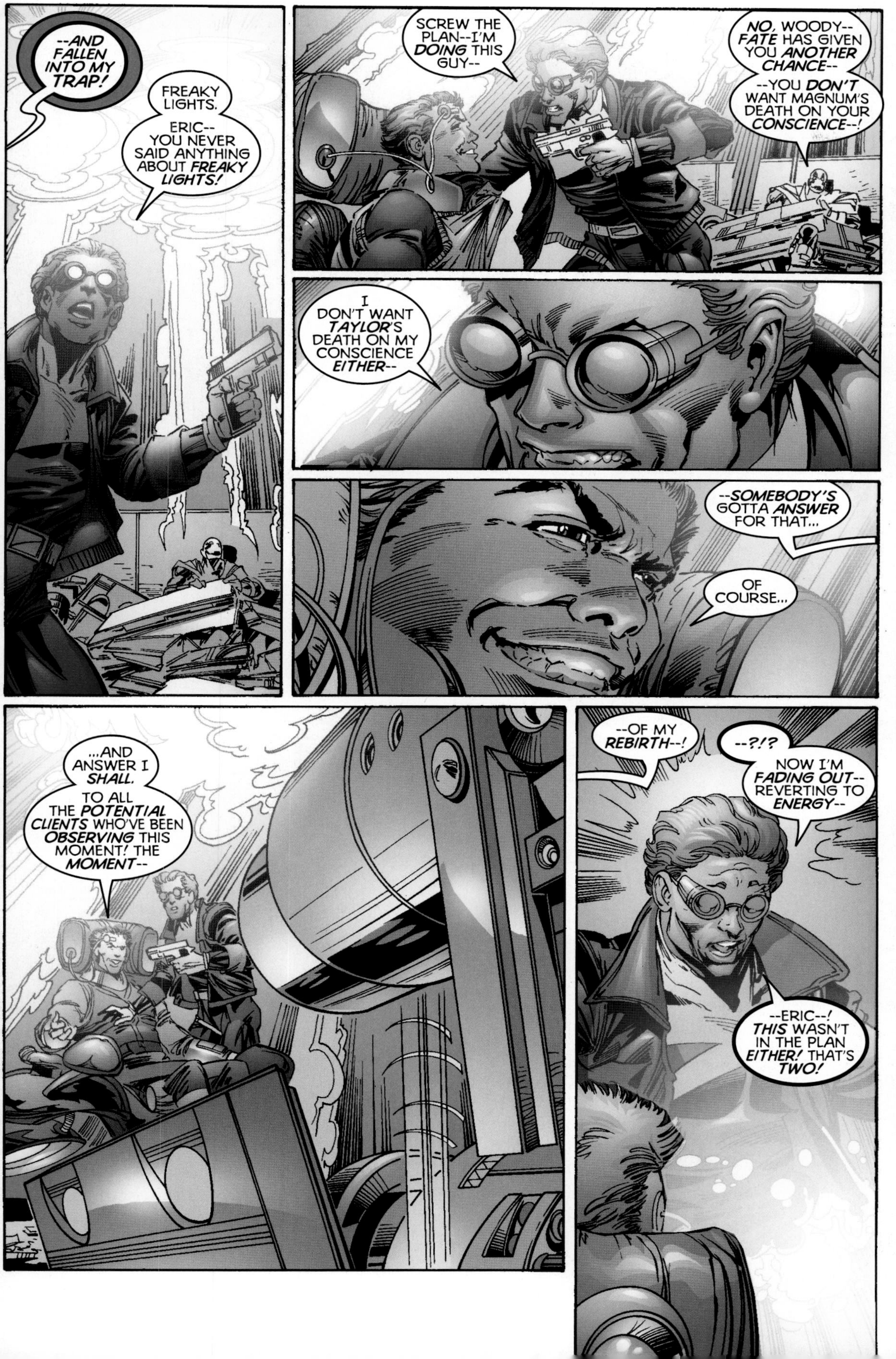
--AND FALLEN INTO MY TRAP!
FREAKY LIGHTS.
ERIC-- YOU NEVER SAID ANYTHING ABOUT FREAKY LIGHTS!
SCREW THE PLAN--I'M DOING THIS GUY--
NO, WOODY-- FATE HAS GIVEN YOU ANOTHER CHANCE--
--YOU DON'T WANT MAGNUM'S DEATH ON YOUR CONSCIENCE--!
I DON'T WANT TAYLOR'S DEATH ON MY CONSCIENCE EITHER--
--SOMEBODY'S GOTTA ANSWER FOR THAT...
OF COURSE...
...AND ANSWER I SHALL.
TO ALL THE POTENTIAL CLIENTS WHO'VE BEEN OBSERVING THIS MOMENT! THE MOMENT--
--OF MY REBIRTH--!
--?!?
NOW I'M FADING OUT-- REVERTING TO ENERGY--
--ERIC--! THIS WASN'T IN THE PLAN EITHER! THAT'S TWO!

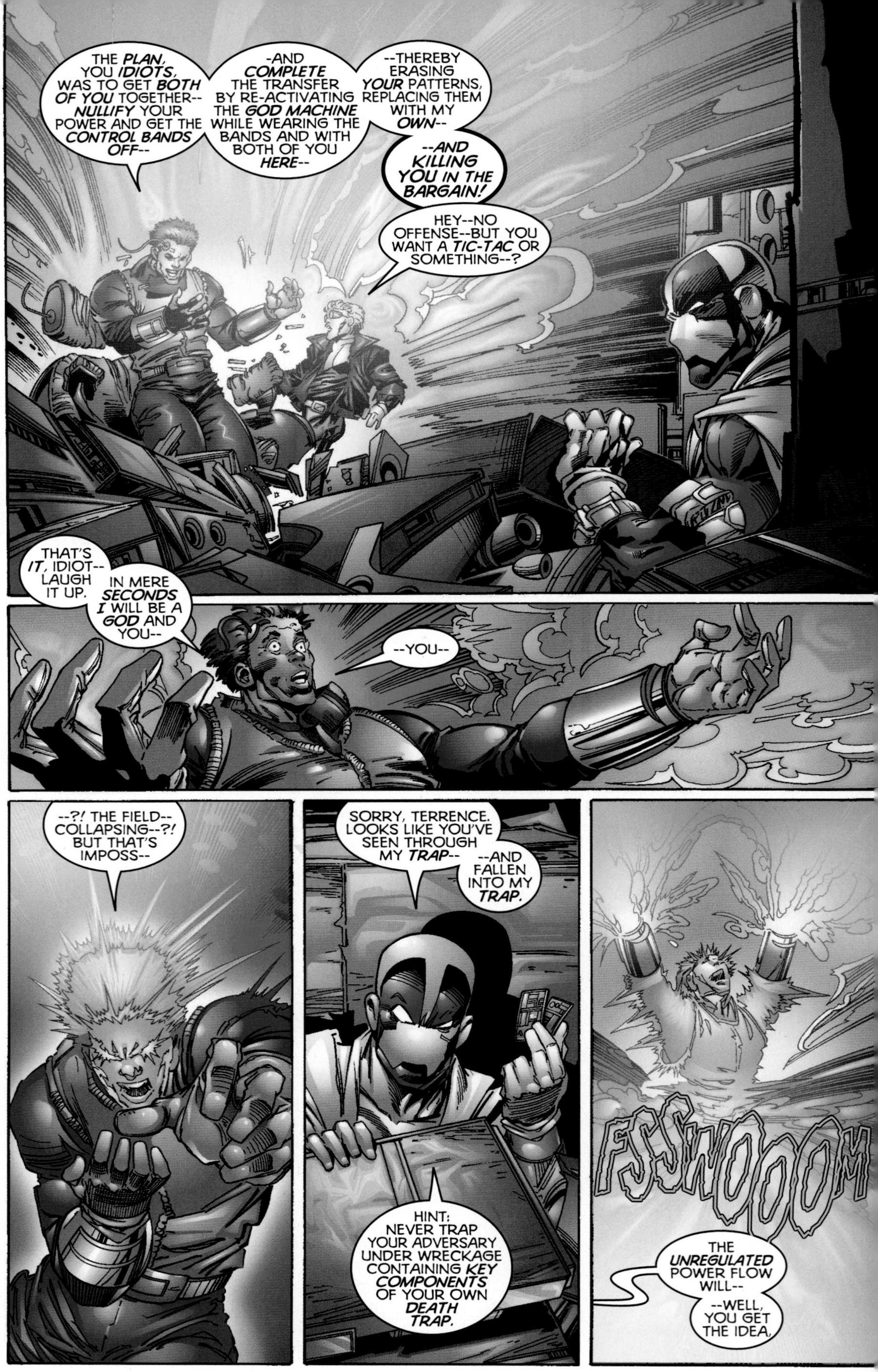
THE PLAN, YOU IDIOTS, WAS TO GET BOTH OF YOU TOGETHER-- NULLIFY YOUR POWER AND GET THE CONTROL BANDS OFF--
-AND COMPLETE THE TRANSFER BY RE-ACTIVATING THE GOD MACHINE WHILE WEARING THE BANDS AND WITH BOTH OF YOU HERE--
--THEREBY ERASING YOUR PATTERNS, REPLACING THEM WITH MY OWN--
--AND KILLING YOU IN THE BARGAIN!
HEY--NO OFFENSE--BUT YOU WANT A TIC-TAC OR SOMETHING--?
THAT'S IT, IDIOT-- LAUGH IT UP.
IN MERE SECONDS I WILL BE A GOD AND YOU--
--YOU--
--?! THE FIELD-- COLLAPSING--?! BUT THAT'S IMPOSS--
SORRY, TERRENCE. LOOKS LIKE YOU'VE SEEN THROUGH MY TRAP--
--AND FALLEN INTO MY TRAP.
HINT: NEVER TRAP YOUR ADVERSARY UNDER WRECKAGE CONTAINING KEY COMPONENTS OF YOUR OWN DEATH TRAP.
FSSWOOOOM
THE UNREGULATED POWER FLOW WILL--
--WELL, YOU GET THE IDEA.

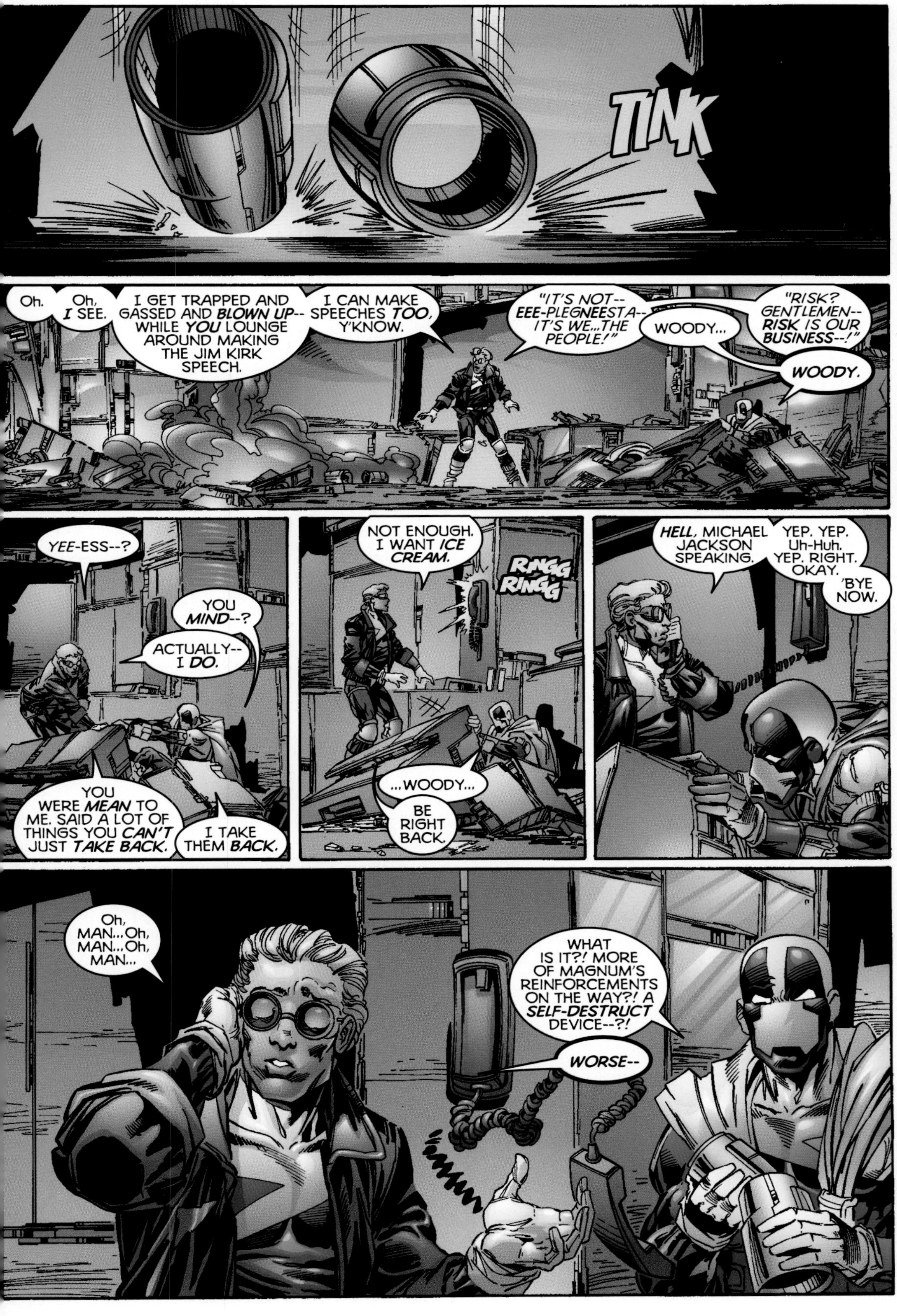
TINK
Oh.
Oh, I SEE.
I GET TRAPPED AND GASSED AND BLOWN UP-- WHILE YOU LOUNGE AROUND MAKING THE JIM KIRK SPEECH.
I CAN MAKE SPEECHES TOO, Y'KNOW.
"IT'S NOT-- EEE-PLEGNEESTA-- IT'S WE...THE PEOPLE!"
WOODY...
"RISK? GENTLEMEN-- RISK IS OUR BUSINESS--!"
WOODY.
YEE-ESS--?
YOU MIND--?
ACTUALLY-- I DO.
YOU WERE MEAN TO ME. SAID A LOT OF THINGS YOU CAN'T JUST TAKE BACK.
I TAKE THEM BACK.
NOT ENOUGH. I WANT ICE CREAM.
RINGG RINGG
...WOODY...
BE RIGHT BACK.
HELL, MICHAEL JACKSON SPEAKING.
YEP. YEP. Uh-Huh. YEP. RIGHT. OKAY. 'BYE NOW.
Oh, MAN...Oh, MAN...Oh, MAN...
WHAT IS IT?! MORE OF MAGNUM'S REINFORCEMENTS ON THE WAY?! A SELF-DESTRUCT DEVICE--?!
WORSE--

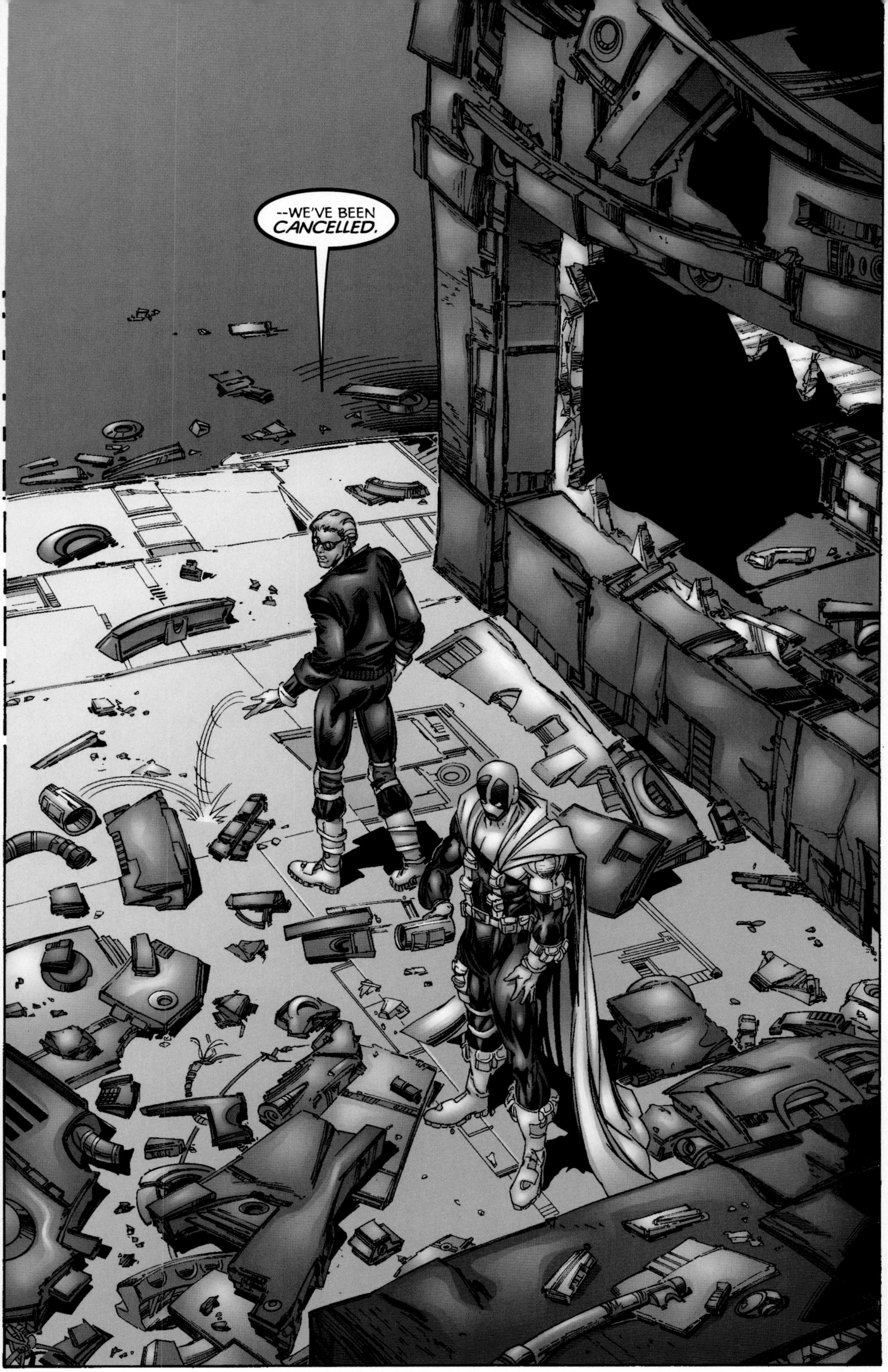
--WE'VE BEEN *CANCELLED.*

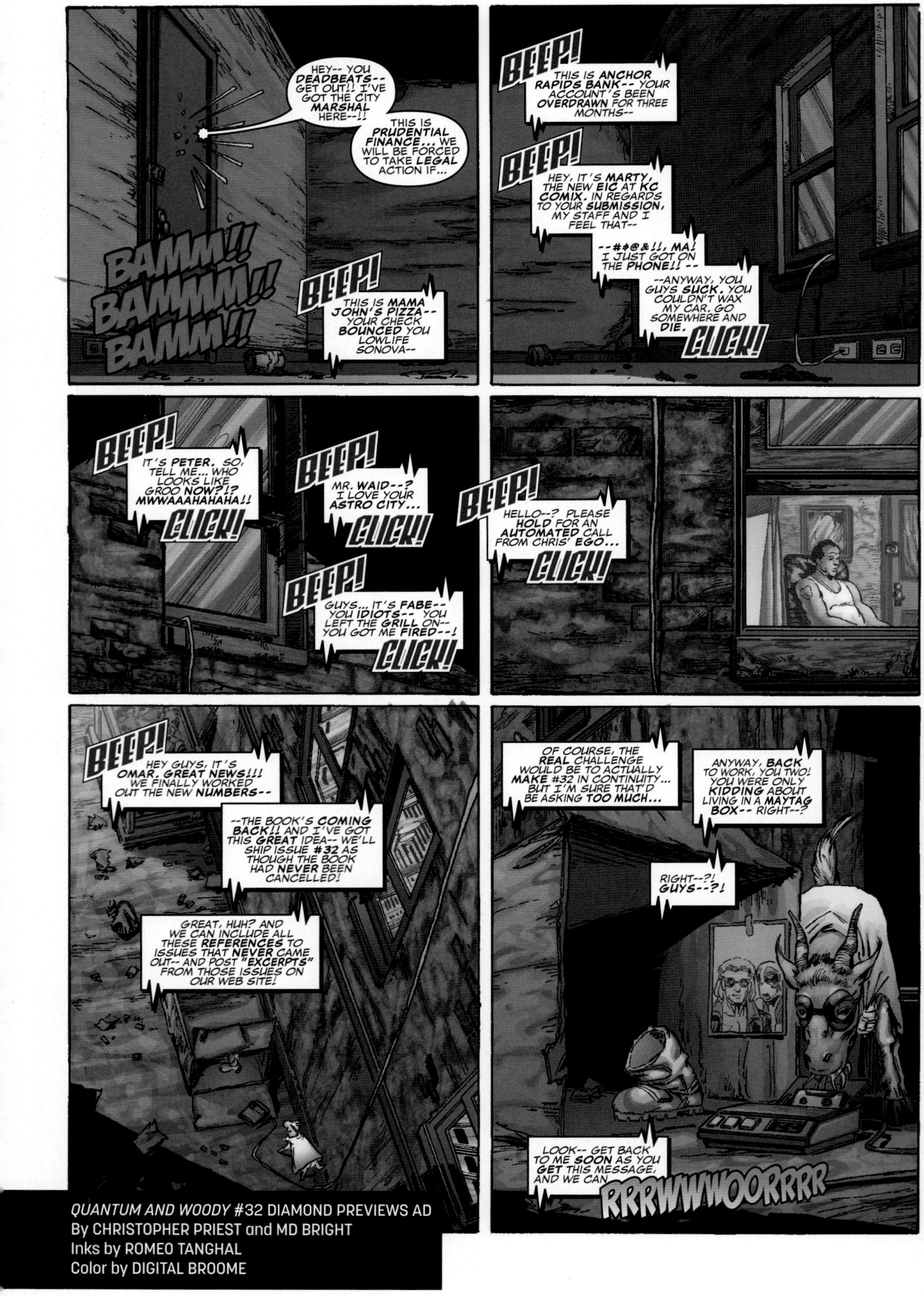
HEY-- YOU DEADBEATS-- GET OUT!! I'VE GOT THE CITY MARSHAL HERE--!!
THIS IS PRUDENTIAL FINANCE... WE WILL BE FORCED TO TAKE LEGAL ACTION IF...
BAMM!! BAMMM!! BAMM!!
BEEP!
THIS IS MAMA JOHN'S PIZZA-- YOUR CHECK BOUNCED YOU LOWLIFE SONOVA--
BEEP!
THIS IS ANCHOR RAPIDS BANK-- YOUR ACCOUNT'S BEEN OVERDRAWN FOR THREE MONTHS--
BEEP!
HEY, IT'S MARTY, THE NEW EIC AT KC COMIX. IN REGARDS TO YOUR SUBMISSION, MY STAFF AND I FEEL THAT--
--#$@&!!, MA! I JUST GOT ON THE PHONE!! --
--ANYWAY, YOU GUYS SUCK. YOU COULDN'T WAX MY CAR. GO SOMEWHERE AND DIE.
CLICK!
BEEP!
IT'S PETER. SO, TELL ME... WHO LOOKS LIKE GROO NOW?!? MWWAAAHAHAHA!!
CLICK!
BEEP!
MR. WAID--? I LOVE YOUR ASTRO CITY...
CLICK!
BEEP!
GUYS... IT'S FABE-- YOU IDIOTS-- YOU LEFT THE GRILL ON-- YOU GOT ME FIRED--!
CLICK!
BEEP!
HELLO--? PLEASE HOLD FOR AN AUTOMATED CALL FROM CHRIS' EGO...
CLICK!
BEEP!
HEY GUYS, IT'S OMAR. GREAT NEWS!!! WE FINALLY WORKED OUT THE NEW NUMBERS--
--THE BOOK'S COMING BACK!! AND I'VE GOT THIS GREAT IDEA-- WE'LL SHIP ISSUE #32 AS THOUGH THE BOOK HAD NEVER BEEN CANCELLED!
GREAT, HUH? AND WE CAN INCLUDE ALL THESE REFERENCES TO ISSUES THAT NEVER CAME OUT-- AND POST "EXCERPTS" FROM THOSE ISSUES ON OUR WEB SITE!
OF COURSE, THE REAL CHALLENGE WOULD BE TO ACTUALLY MAKE #32 IN CONTINUITY... BUT I'M SURE THAT'D BE ASKING TOO MUCH...
ANYWAY, BACK TO WORK, YOU TWO! YOU WERE ONLY KIDDING ABOUT LIVING IN A MAYTAG BOX-- RIGHT--?
RIGHT--?! GUYS--?!
LOOK-- GET BACK TO ME SOON AS YOU GET THIS MESSAGE, AND WE CAN
RRRWWWOORRRR

QUANTUM AND WOODY #32 DIAMOND PREVIEWS AD
By CHRISTOPHER PRIEST and MD BRIGHT
Inks by ROMEO TANGHAL
Color by DIGITAL BROOME

QUANTUM AND WOODY

#32
Sept.

ECLIPSE PART

PRIEST•BRIGHT

QUANTUM AND WOODY™
ECLIPSE™ PART THREE OF FOUR

PREVIOUSLY:

Returning from the moon, Quantum and Woody narrowly survived Dr. Eclipse's onslaught that left them pinned under the wreckage of their space shuttle. Using their combined Quantum energy (and with a little timely chewing from their intrepid mascot), the heroes escaped to pursue Master Darque's evil minion through the labyrinthine bowels of New York City in a risky attempt to wear Dr. Eclipse down by forcing him to drain his power to below-nominal levels.

The desperate battle has exacted a price on both the heroes and their arch enemy, whom they have finally cornered in a Chelsea alleyway...

special thanks to:

GREG MORROW, PhD

ELMO
PSEUDOSCIENCE

"Tomorrow"

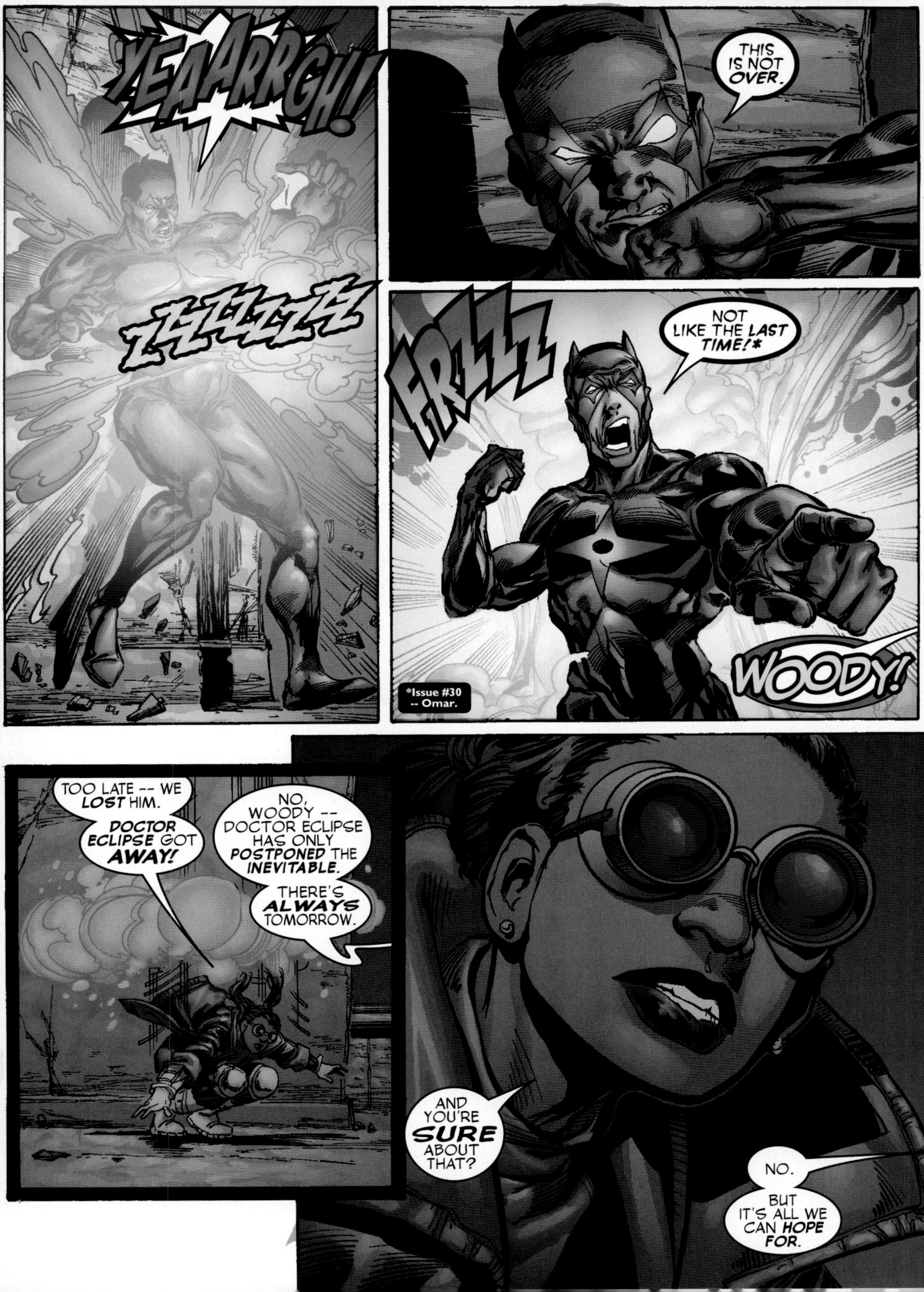
YEAARRGH!
ZZZZZZZZ
THIS IS NOT OVER.
FRZZZ
NOT LIKE THE LAST TIME!*
WOODY!
*Issue #30 -- Omar.
TOO LATE -- WE LOST HIM. DOCTOR ECLIPSE GOT AWAY!
NO, WOODY -- DOCTOR ECLIPSE HAS ONLY POSTPONED THE INEVITABLE.
THERE'S ALWAYS TOMORROW.
AND YOU'RE SURE ABOUT THAT?
NO.
BUT IT'S ALL WE CAN HOPE FOR.

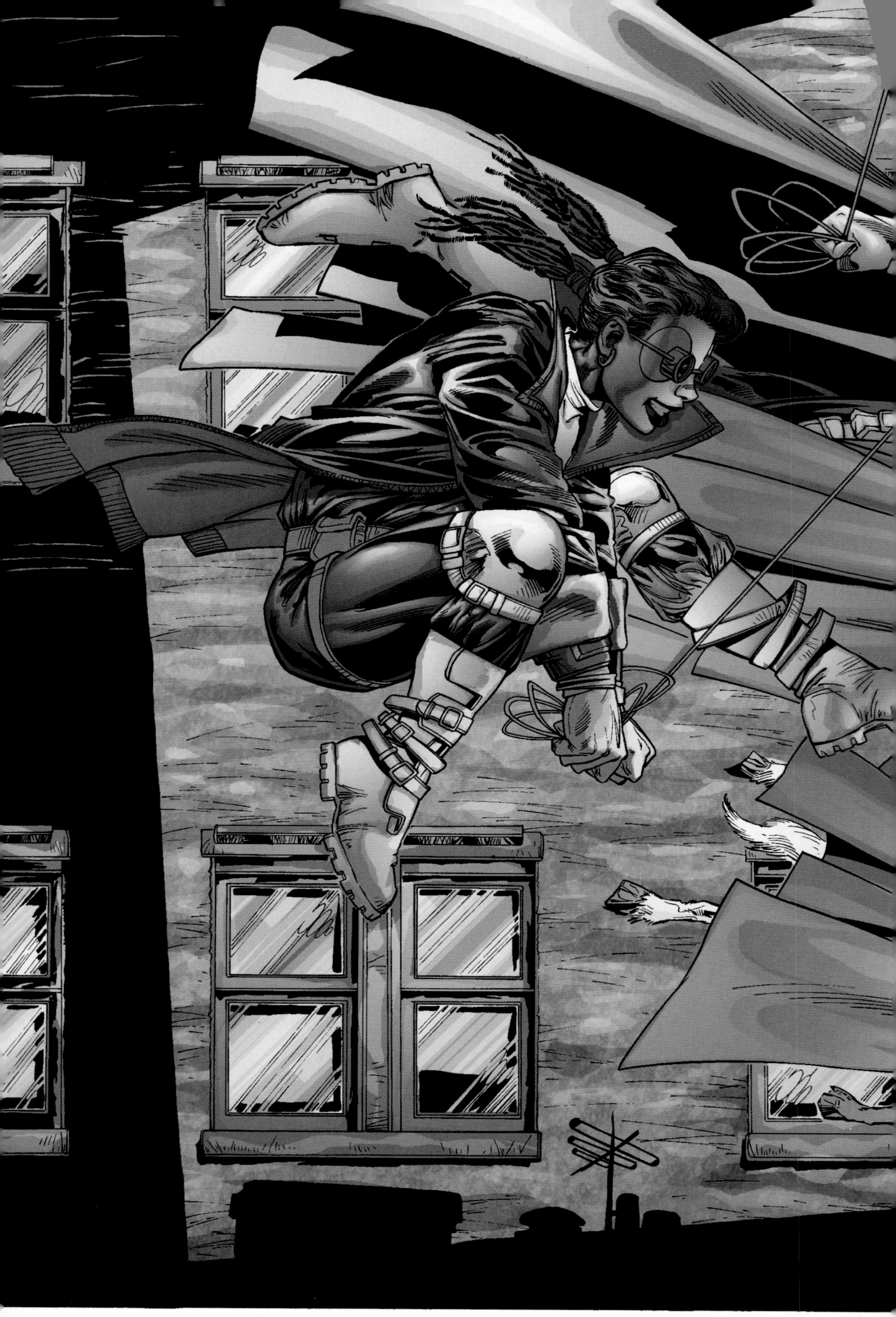

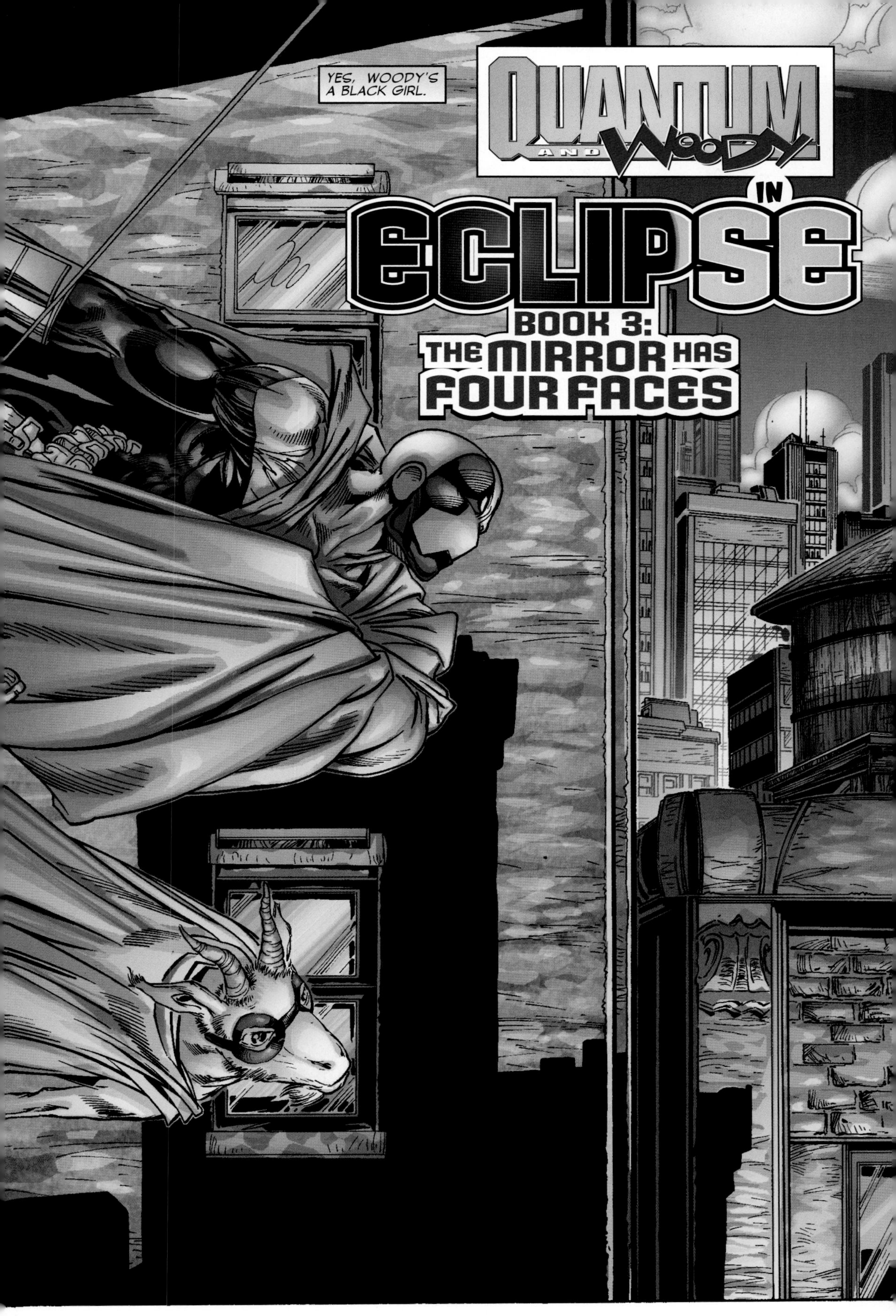
YES, WOODY'S A BLACK GIRL.
QUANTUM AND WOODY
IN
ECLIPSE
BOOK 3: THE MIRROR HAS FOUR FACES

"Tamara"

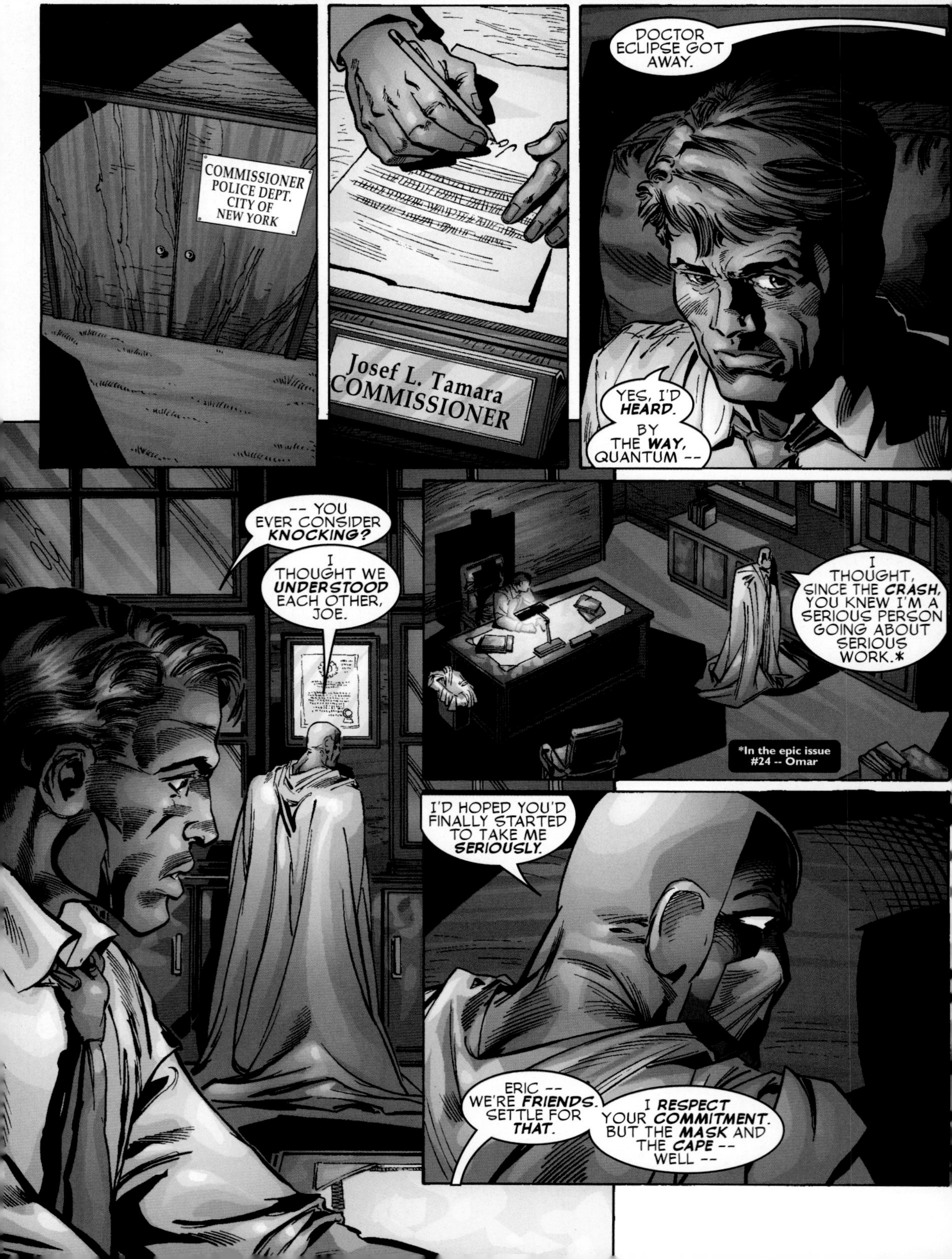
COMMISSIONER
POLICE DEPT.
CITY OF
NEW YORK
Josef L. Tamara
COMMISSIONER
DOCTOR ECLIPSE GOT AWAY.
YES, I'D HEARD.
BY THE WAY, QUANTUM --
-- YOU EVER CONSIDER KNOCKING?
I THOUGHT WE UNDERSTOOD EACH OTHER, JOE.
I THOUGHT, SINCE THE CRASH, YOU KNEW I'M A SERIOUS PERSON GOING ABOUT SERIOUS WORK.*
*In the epic issue #24 -- Omar
I'D HOPED YOU'D FINALLY STARTED TO TAKE ME SERIOUSLY.
ERIC -- WE'RE FRIENDS. SETTLE FOR THAT.
I RESPECT YOUR COMMITMENT. BUT THE MASK AND THE CAPE -- WELL --

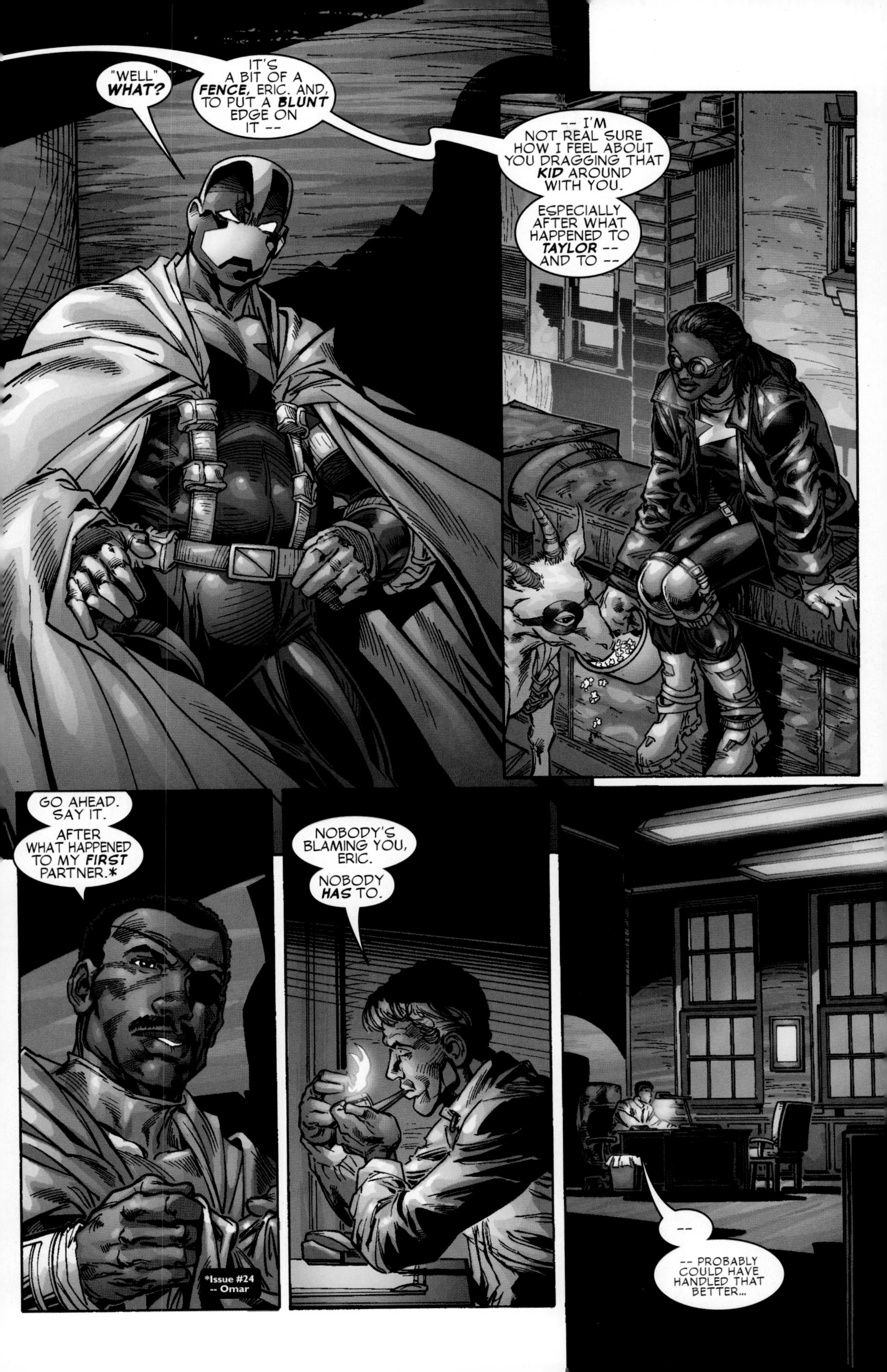

"WELL" WHAT?
IT'S A BIT OF A FENCE, ERIC. AND, TO PUT A BLUNT EDGE ON IT --
-- I'M NOT REAL SURE HOW I FEEL ABOUT YOU DRAGGING THAT KID AROUND WITH YOU.
ESPECIALLY AFTER WHAT HAPPENED TO TAYLOR -- AND TO --
GO AHEAD. SAY IT.
AFTER WHAT HAPPENED TO MY FIRST PARTNER.*
*Issue #24 -- Omar
NOBODY'S BLAMING YOU, ERIC.
NOBODY HAS TO.
--
-- PROBABLY COULD HAVE HANDLED THAT BETTER...

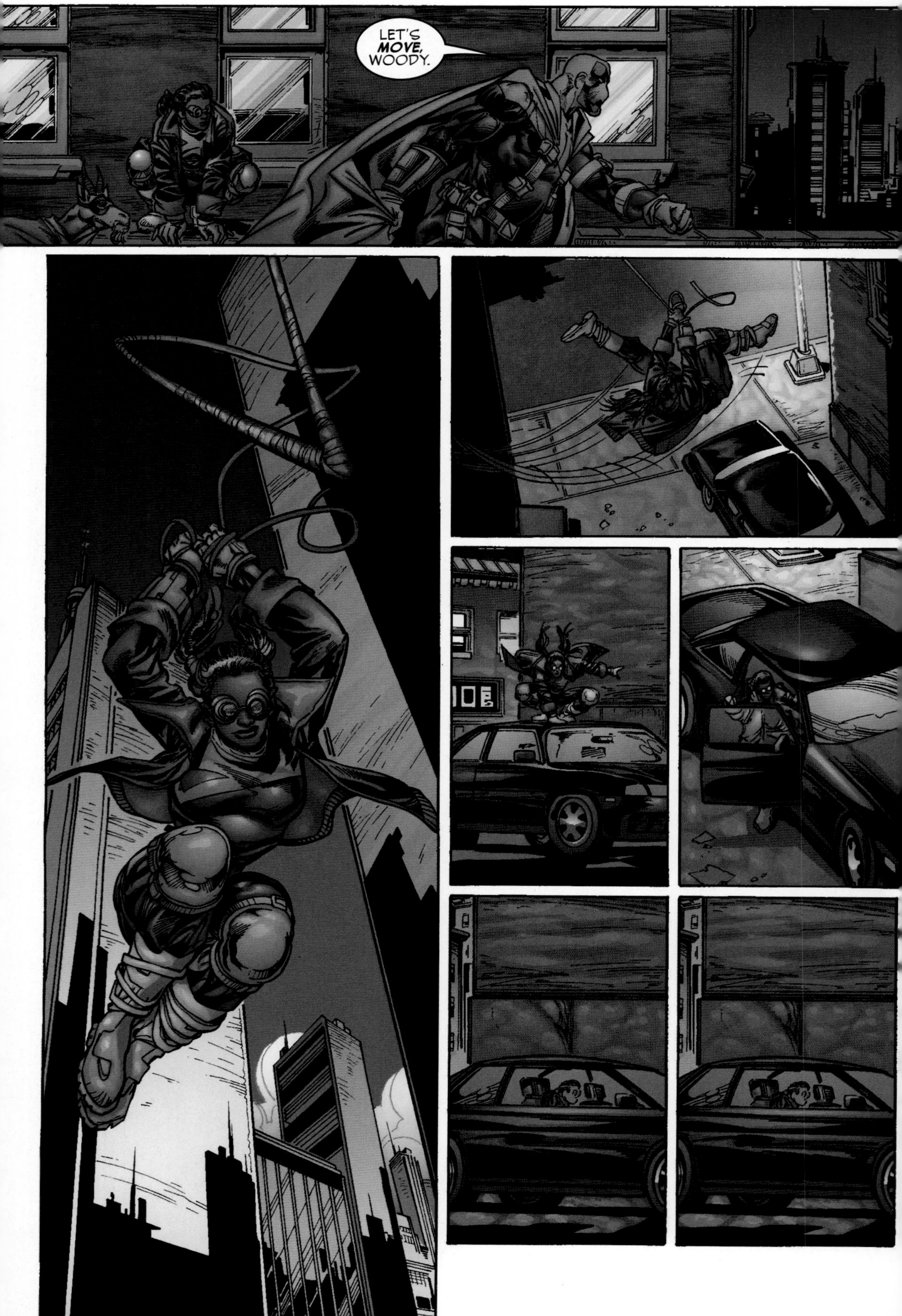
LET'S MOVE, WOODY.

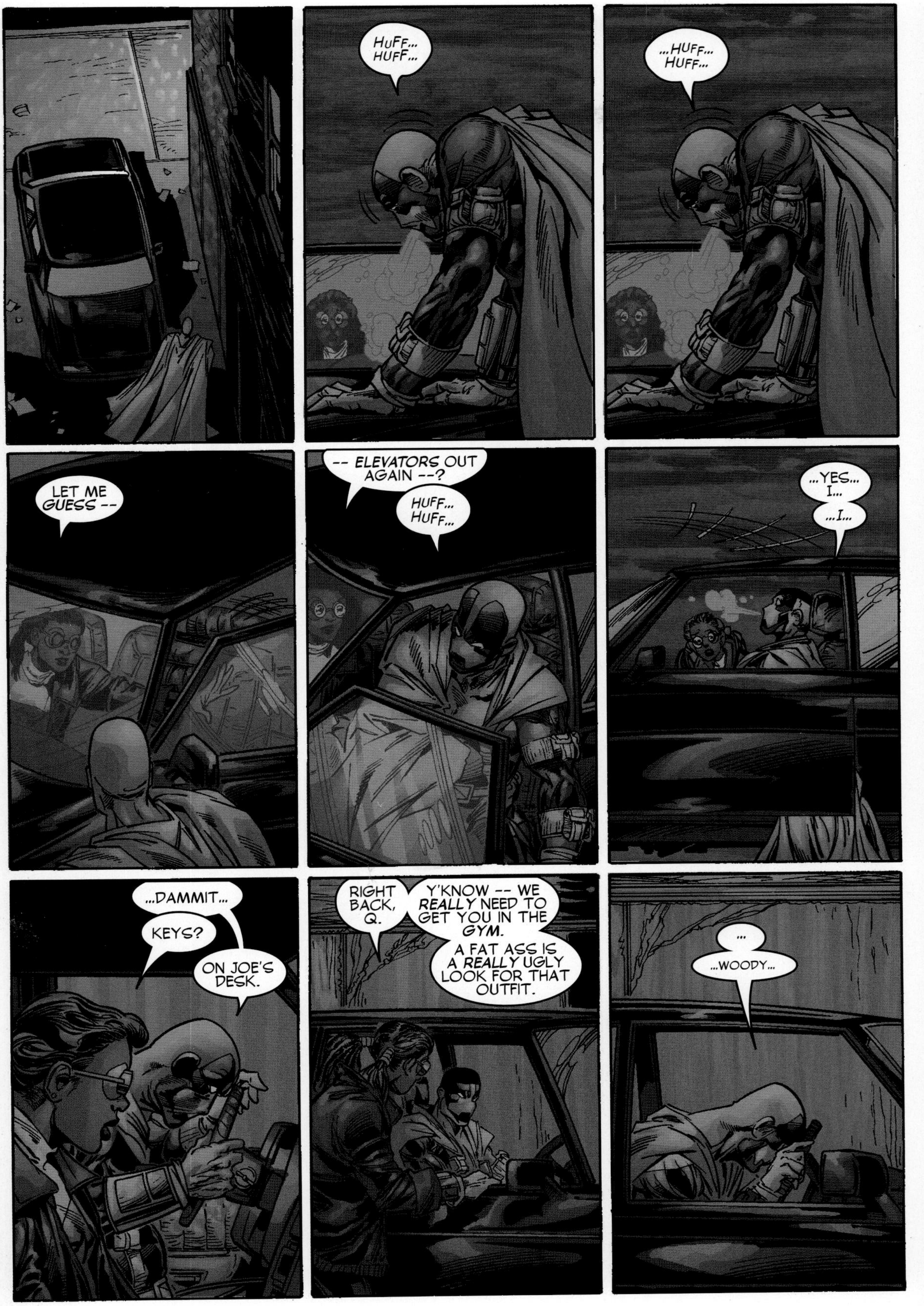
HUFF... HUFF...
...HUFF... HUFF...
LET ME GUESS --
-- ELEVATORS OUT AGAIN --?
HUFF... HUFF...
...YES... I...
...I...
...DAMMIT...
KEYS?
ON JOE'S DESK.
RIGHT BACK, Q.
Y'KNOW -- WE REALLY NEED TO GET YOU IN THE GYM.
A FAT ASS IS A REALLY UGLY LOOK FOR THAT OUTFIT.
...
...WOODY...

"Him"

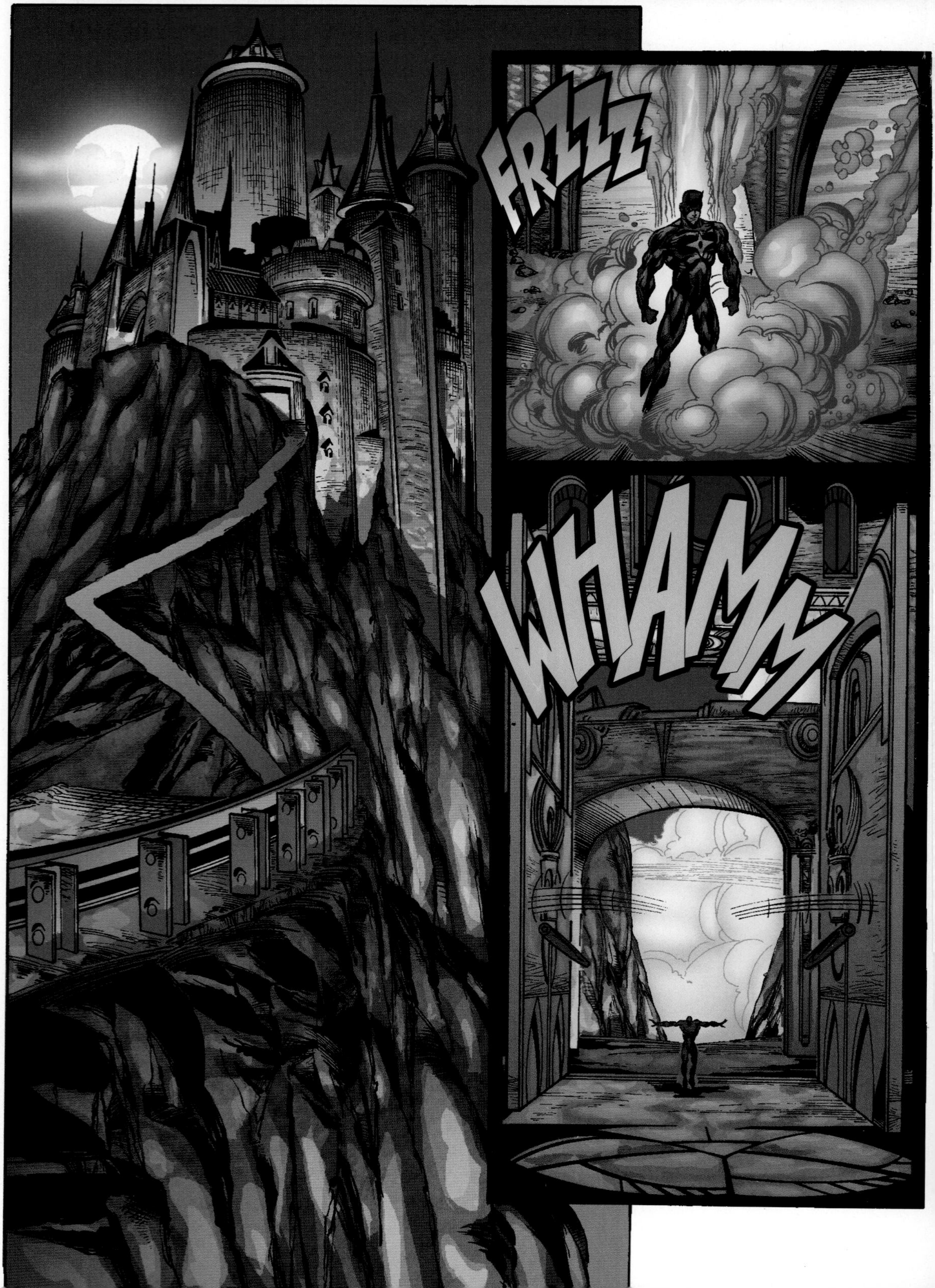
FRZZZ
WHAMM

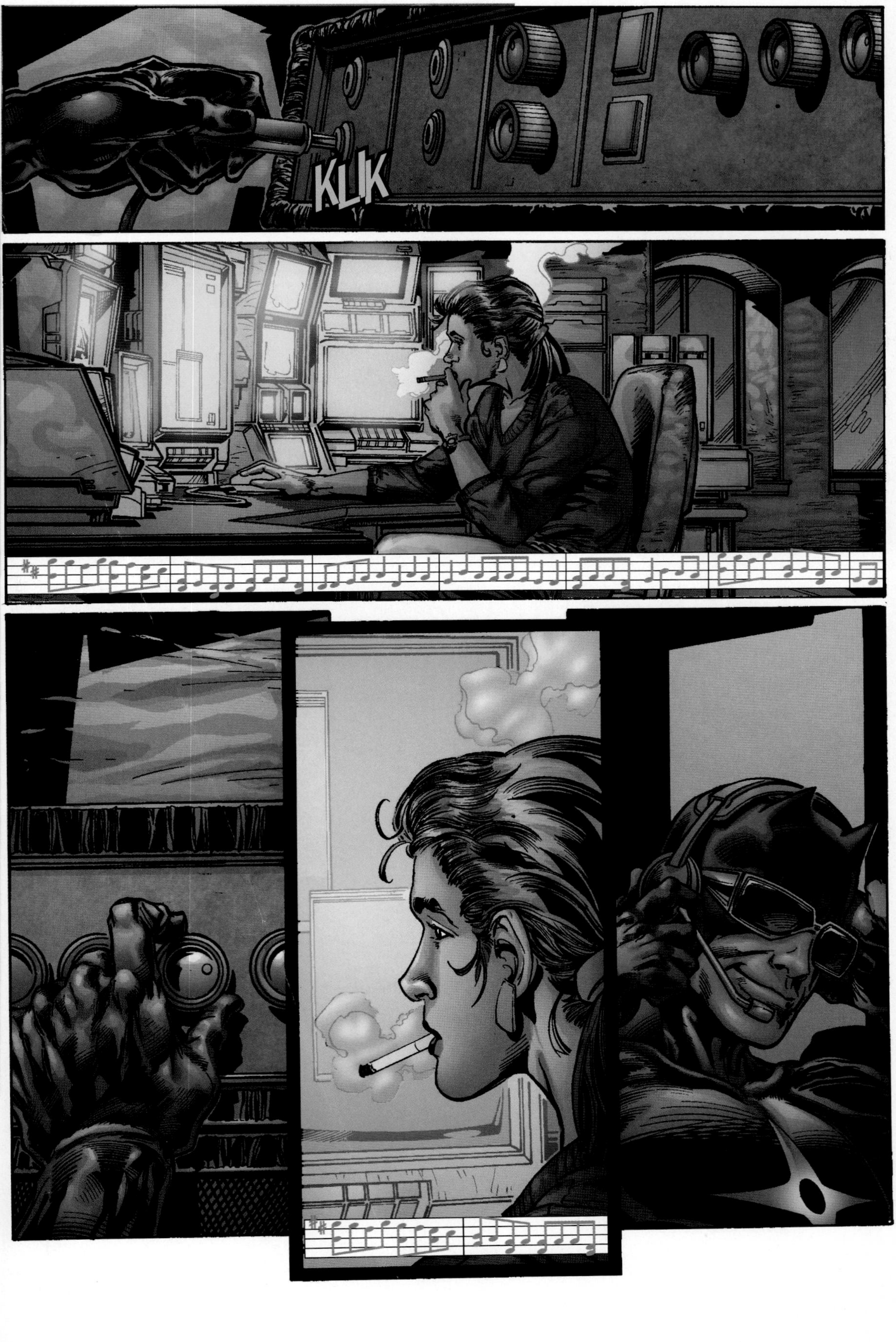
KLIK

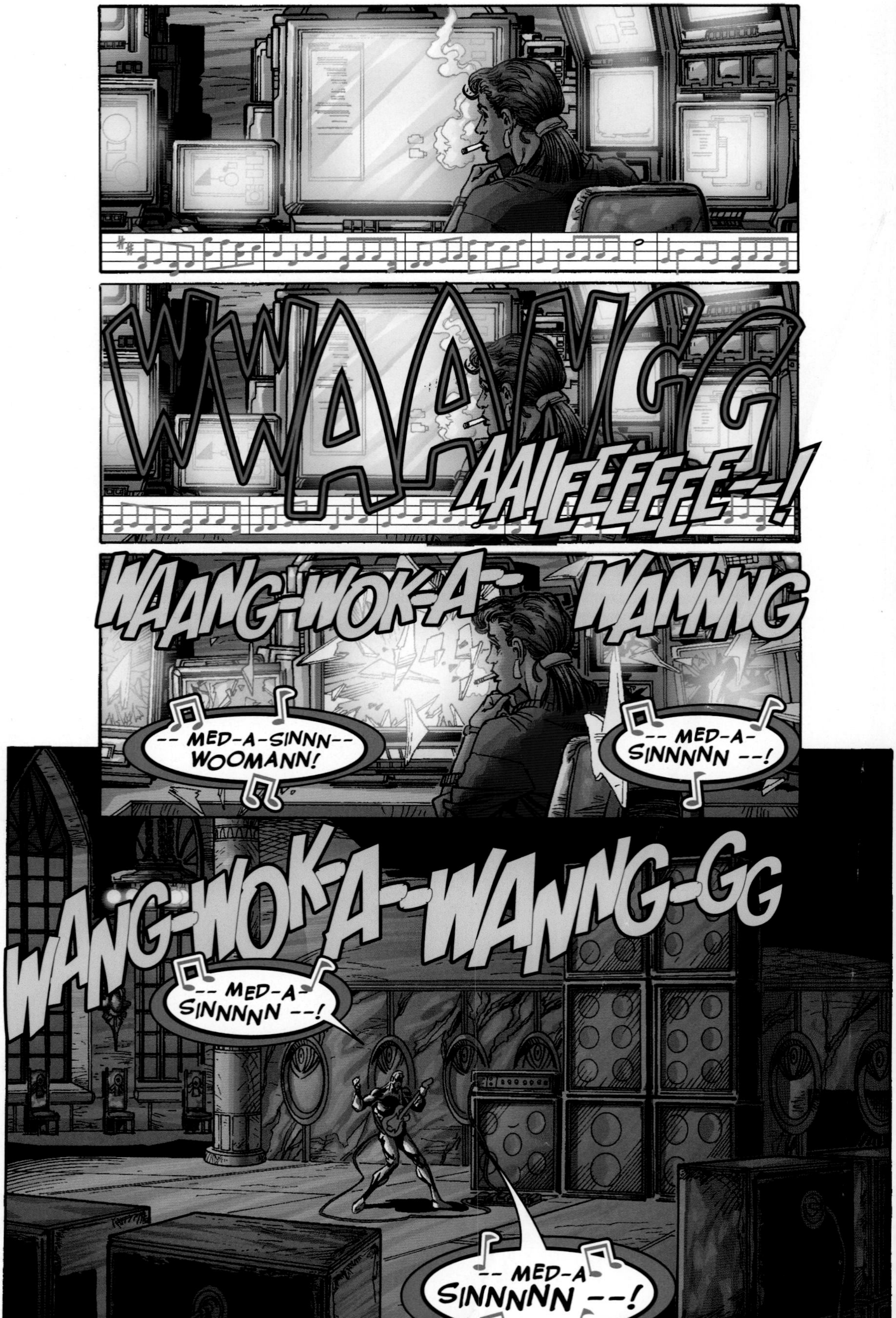

WWAAANGG
AAIIEEEEEE--!
WAANG-WOK-A- WANNNG
-- MED-A-SINNN-- WOOMANN!
-- MED-A- SINNNNN --!
WANG-WOK-A--WANNG-GG
-- MED-A- SINNNNN --!
-- MED-A SINNNNN --!

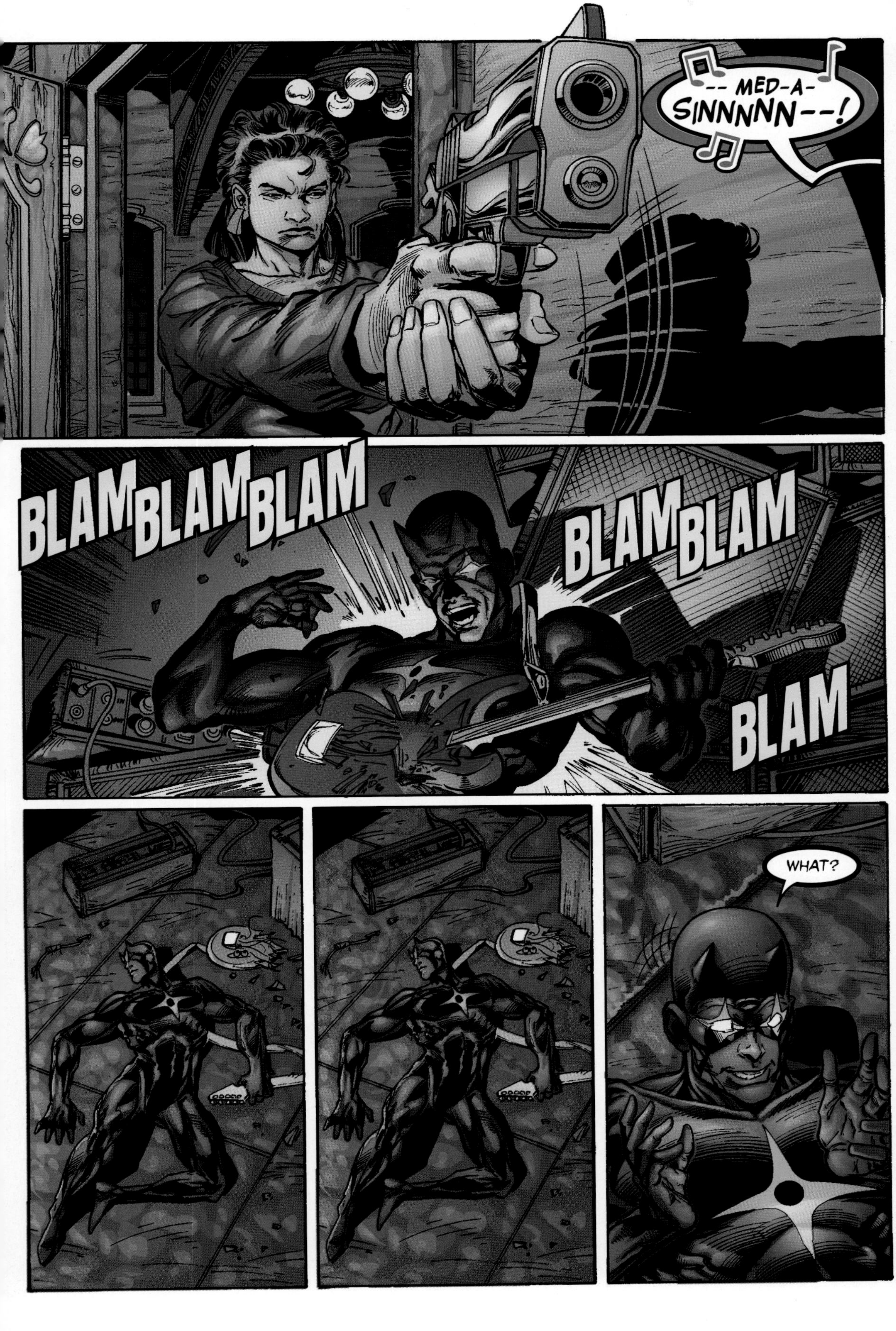
-- MED-A-
SINNNNN--!
BLAM BLAM BLAM
BLAM BLAM
BLAM
WHAT?

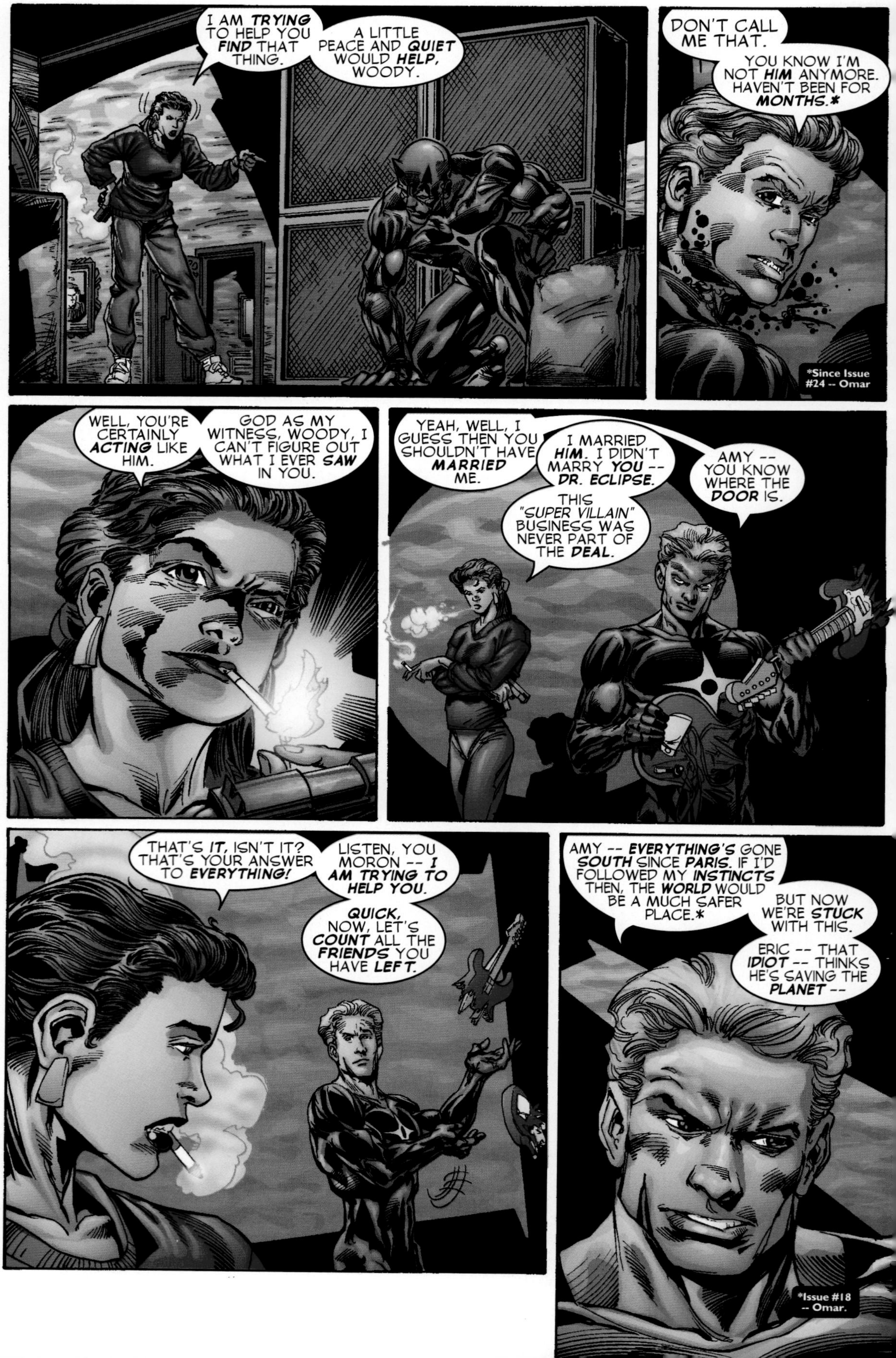
I AM TRYING TO HELP YOU FIND THAT THING.
A LITTLE PEACE AND QUIET WOULD HELP, WOODY.
DON'T CALL ME THAT.
YOU KNOW I'M NOT HIM ANYMORE. HAVEN'T BEEN FOR MONTHS.*
*Since Issue #24 -- Omar
WELL, YOU'RE CERTAINLY ACTING LIKE HIM.
GOD AS MY WITNESS, WOODY, I CAN'T FIGURE OUT WHAT I EVER SAW IN YOU.
YEAH, WELL, I GUESS THEN YOU SHOULDN'T HAVE MARRIED ME.
I MARRIED HIM. I DIDN'T MARRY YOU -- DR. ECLIPSE.
THIS "SUPER VILLAIN" BUSINESS WAS NEVER PART OF THE DEAL.
AMY -- YOU KNOW WHERE THE DOOR IS.
THAT'S IT, ISN'T IT? THAT'S YOUR ANSWER TO EVERYTHING!
LISTEN, YOU MORON -- I AM TRYING TO HELP YOU.
QUICK, NOW, LET'S COUNT ALL THE FRIENDS YOU HAVE LEFT.
AMY -- EVERYTHING'S GONE SOUTH SINCE PARIS. IF I'D FOLLOWED MY INSTINCTS THEN, THE WORLD WOULD BE A MUCH SAFER PLACE.*
BUT NOW WE'RE STUCK WITH THIS.
ERIC -- THAT IDIOT -- THINKS HE'S SAVING THE PLANET --
*Issue #18 -- Omar.

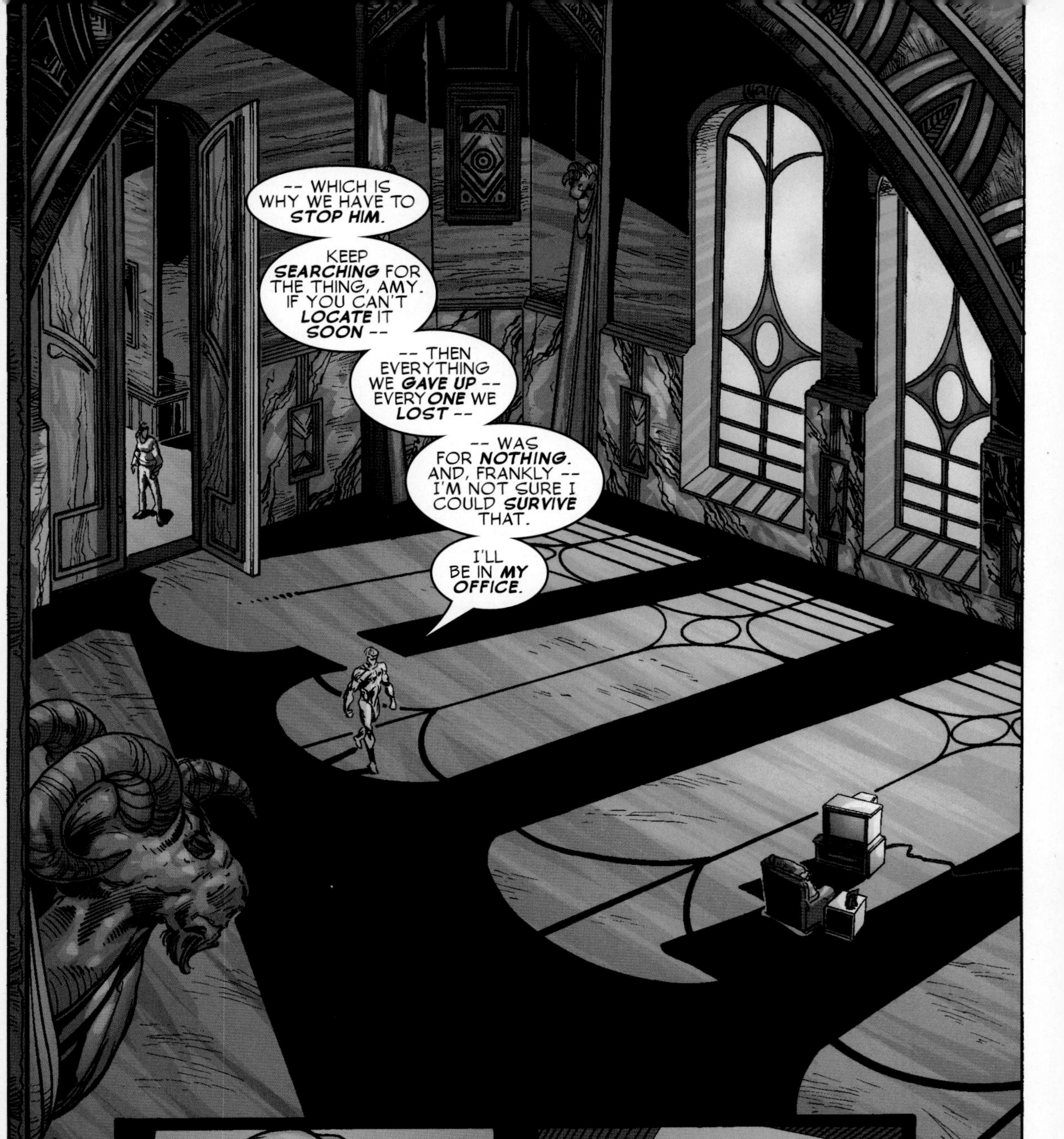
-- WHICH IS WHY WE HAVE TO STOP HIM.
KEEP SEARCHING FOR THE THING, AMY. IF YOU CAN'T LOCATE IT SOON --
-- THEN EVERYTHING WE GAVE UP -- EVERYONE WE LOST --
-- WAS FOR NOTHING. AND, FRANKLY -- I'M NOT SURE I COULD SURVIVE THAT.
I'LL BE IN MY OFFICE.

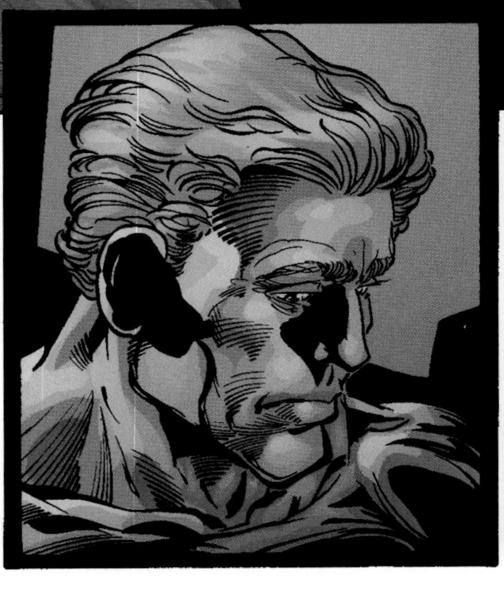

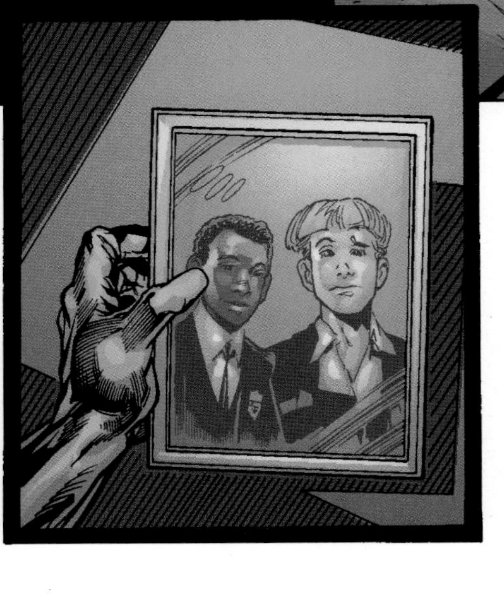

"The Child"

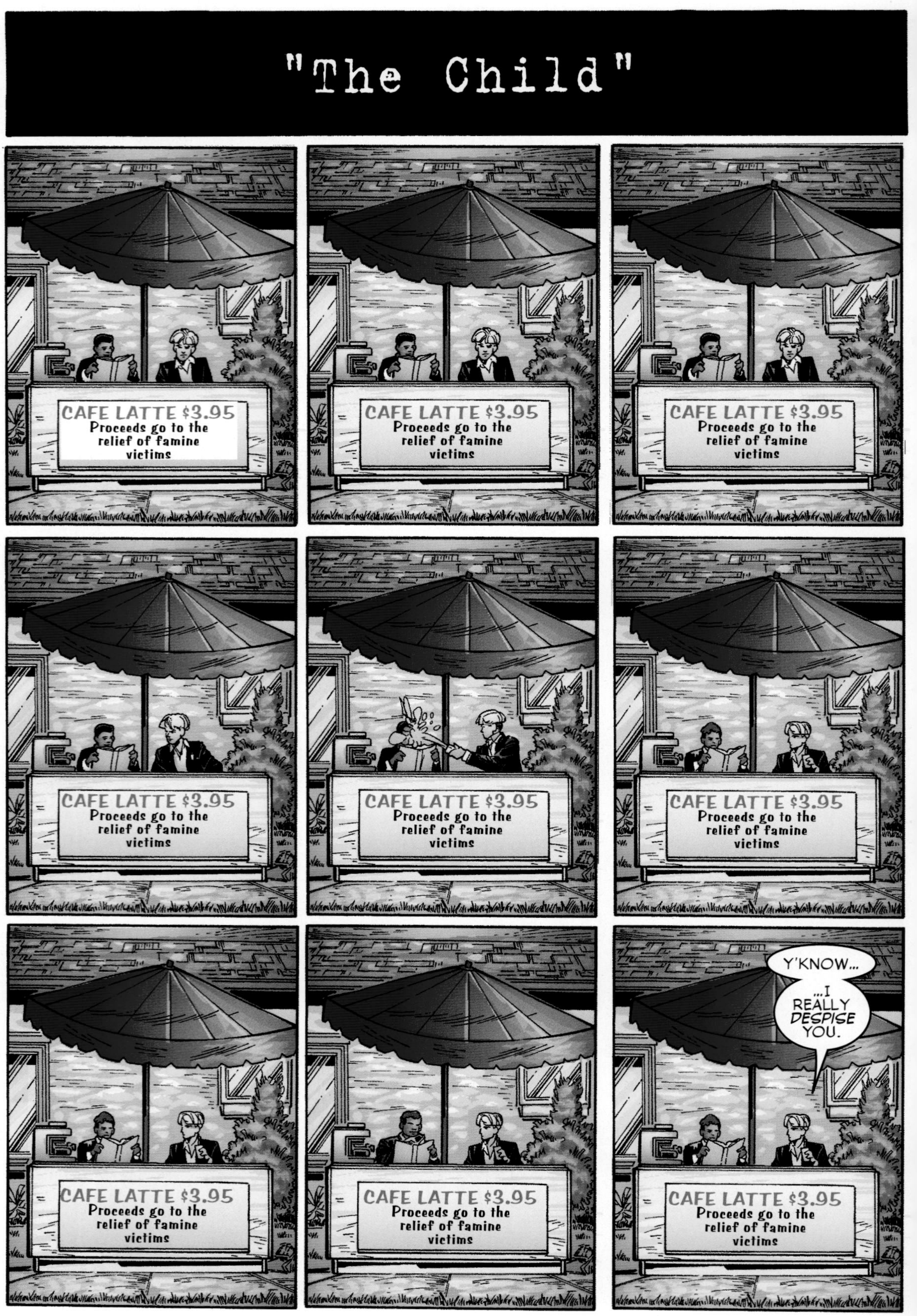
CAFE LATTE $3.95
Proceeds go to the relief of famine victims
CAFE LATTE $3.95
Proceeds go to the relief of famine victims
CAFE LATTE $3.95
Proceeds go to the relief of famine victims
CAFE LATTE $3.95
Proceeds go to the relief of famine victims
CAFE LATTE $3.95
Proceeds go to the relief of famine victims
CAFE LATTE $3.95
Proceeds go to the relief of famine victims
CAFE LATTE $3.95
Proceeds go to the relief of famine victims
CAFE LATTE $3.95
Proceeds go to the relief of famine victims
Y'KNOW...
...I REALLY DESPISE YOU.
CAFE LATTE $3.95
Proceeds go to the relief of famine victims

ERIC -- WE'VE BEEN SITTING OUT HERE FOR *HOURS.*

NOBODY -- AND I MEAN *NOBODY* -- IS GONNA BUY COFFEE FROM A *NEGRO* IN *GREENWICH,* CONNECTICUT.

IT'S JUST *NOT DONE.*

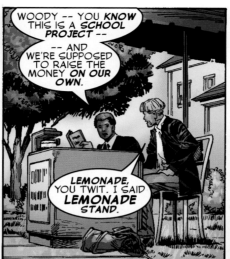

WOODY -- YOU *KNOW* THIS IS A *SCHOOL PROJECT* --

-- AND WE'RE SUPPOSED TO RAISE THE MONEY *ON OUR OWN.*

LEMONADE, YOU TWIT. I SAID *LEMONADE STAND.*

A COUPLE OF OLD *CRATES* AND SOME *PAINT.*

WOODY -- THERE'S NOTHING WRONG WITH GOING A COUPLE YARDS *FARTHER.*

ERIC --

-- THIS THING COST *SEVEN THOUSAND DOLLARS.*

WHAT'S YOUR POINT --?

HEY, FELLAS.

CAFE LATTE $3.95
Proceeds go to the
relief of famine
victims

HI, AMY.

HEY, FISHFACE.

MISSED YOU AT THE LIBRARY YESTERDAY.

MATH CLUB.

SO -- I'LL SEE YOU *LATER,* RIGHT --?

COUNT ON IT.

ERIC -- SHE'S A *JEWISH WHITE GIRL.*

YOU'LL BURST INTO FLAMES.

Y'KNOW -- YOU ARE *SUCH* A CHILD.

MAYBE, BUT I'M A CHILD WITH A *POLAROID* OF YOUR WOMAN'S *DRAWERS.*

WOODY -- *NO ONE* IS GOING TO PAY --

SEE FISHBEIN'S PANTIES $75
AFTER ALL the
ERIC: NEVER... WILL
victims

YOU TAKE *VISA* --?

SEE THAT *LOOK* ON YOUR FACE?

IT'S WHAT I *LIVE* FOR.

"Friends"

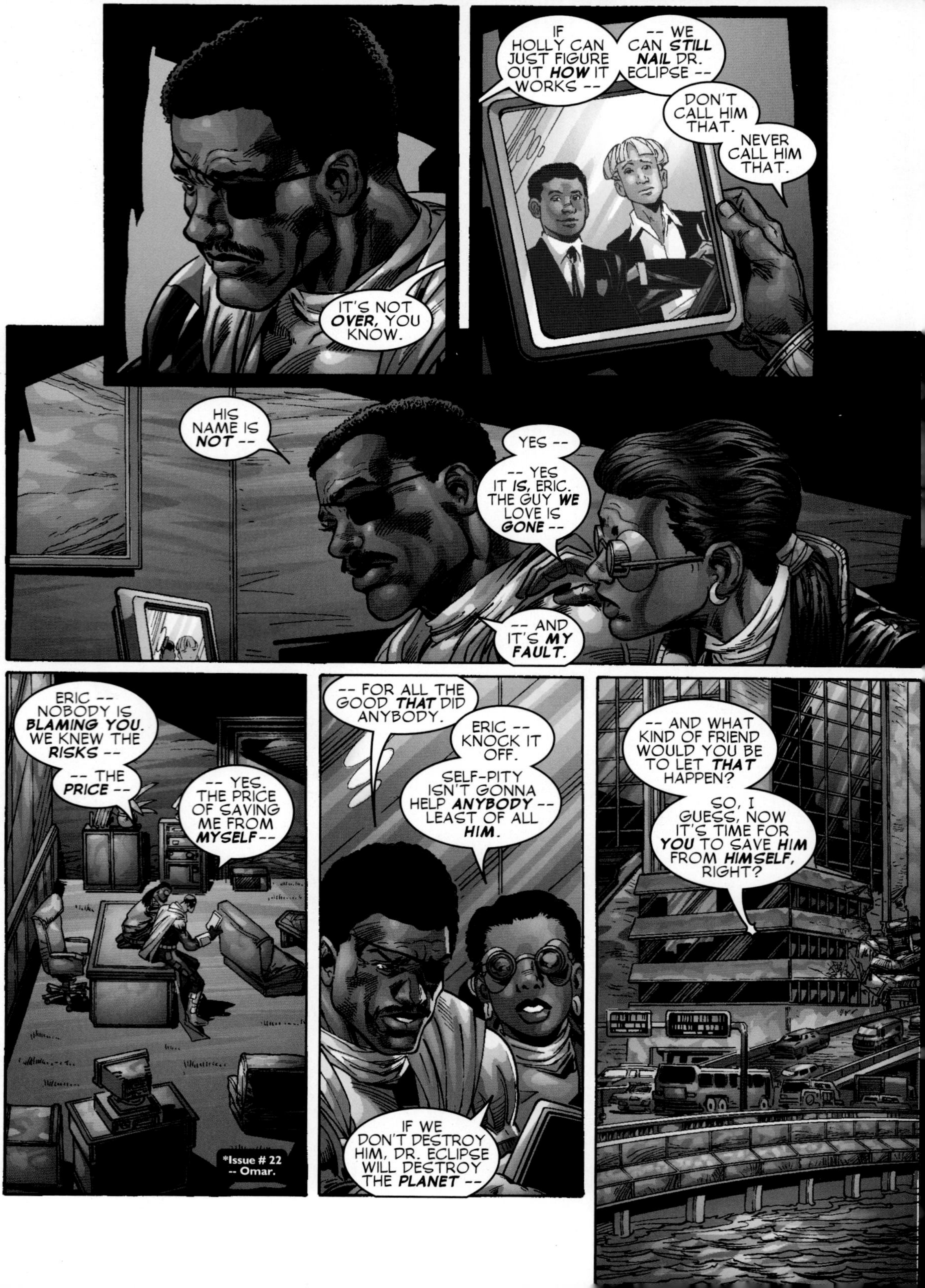
IT'S NOT OVER, YOU KNOW.
IF HOLLY CAN JUST FIGURE OUT HOW IT WORKS --
-- WE CAN STILL NAIL DR. ECLIPSE --
DON'T CALL HIM THAT.
NEVER CALL HIM THAT.
HIS NAME IS NOT --
YES --
-- YES IT IS, ERIC. THE GUY WE LOVE IS GONE --
-- AND IT'S MY FAULT.
ERIC -- NOBODY IS BLAMING YOU. WE KNEW THE RISKS --
-- THE PRICE --
-- YES. THE PRICE OF SAVING ME FROM MYSELF --
*Issue # 22 -- Omar.
-- FOR ALL THE GOOD THAT DID ANYBODY.
ERIC -- KNOCK IT OFF.
SELF-PITY ISN'T GONNA HELP ANYBODY -- LEAST OF ALL HIM.
IF WE DON'T DESTROY HIM, DR. ECLIPSE WILL DESTROY THE PLANET --
-- AND WHAT KIND OF FRIEND WOULD YOU BE TO LET THAT HAPPEN?
SO, I GUESS, NOW IT'S TIME FOR YOU TO SAVE HIM FROM HIMSELF, RIGHT?

"We're Not Sure, But This Might Be A Lesbo-Type Deal"

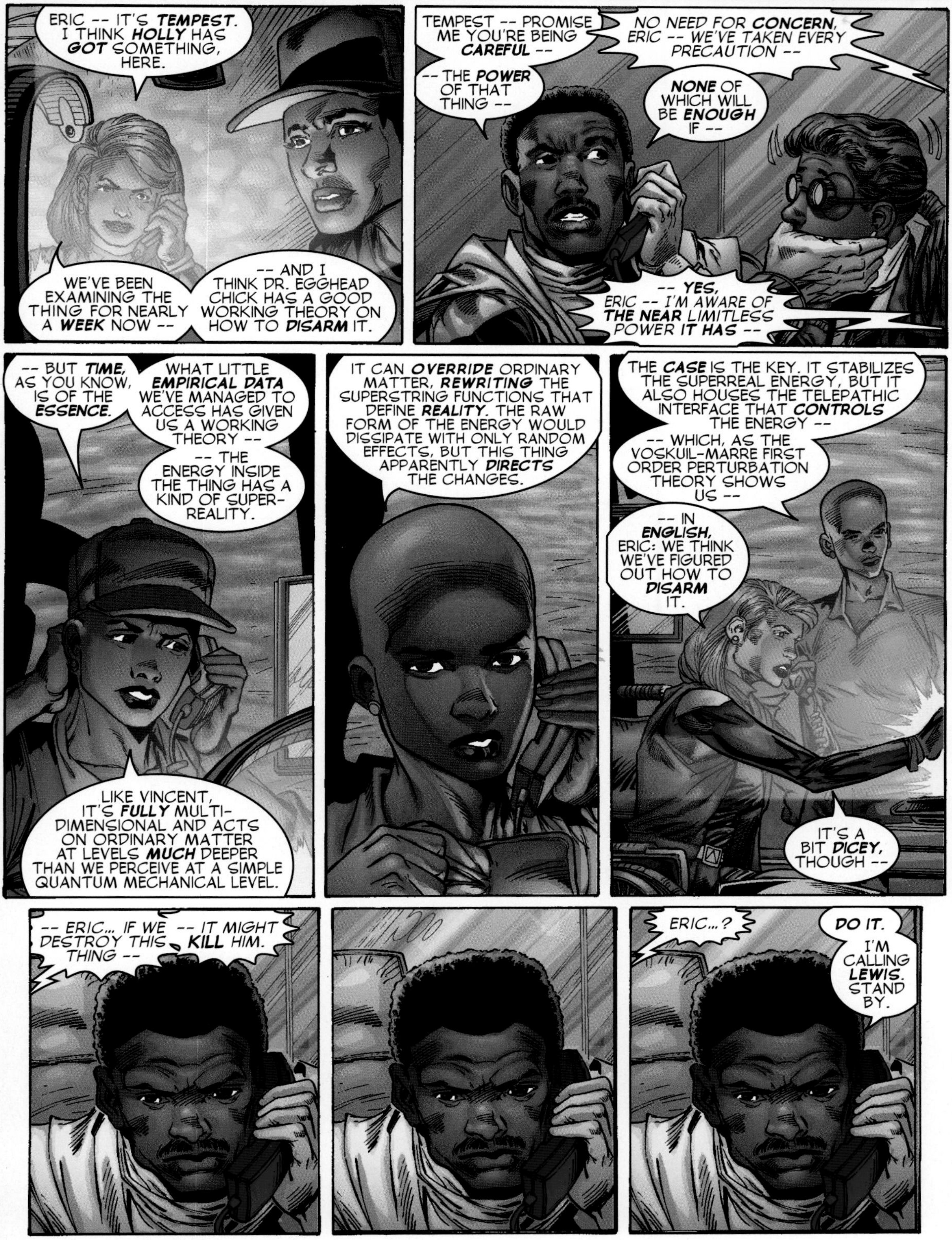
ERIC -- IT'S TEMPEST. I THINK HOLLY HAS GOT SOMETHING, HERE.
WE'VE BEEN EXAMINING THE THING FOR NEARLY A WEEK NOW --
-- AND I THINK DR. EGGHEAD CHICK HAS A GOOD WORKING THEORY ON HOW TO DISARM IT.
TEMPEST -- PROMISE ME YOU'RE BEING CAREFUL --
-- THE POWER OF THAT THING --
NO NEED FOR CONCERN, ERIC -- WE'VE TAKEN EVERY PRECAUTION --
NONE OF WHICH WILL BE ENOUGH IF --
-- YES, ERIC -- I'M AWARE OF THE NEAR LIMITLESS POWER IT HAS --
-- BUT TIME, AS YOU KNOW, IS OF THE ESSENCE.
WHAT LITTLE EMPIRICAL DATA WE'VE MANAGED TO ACCESS HAS GIVEN US A WORKING THEORY --
-- THE ENERGY INSIDE THE THING HAS A KIND OF SUPER-REALITY.
LIKE VINCENT, IT'S FULLY MULTI-DIMENSIONAL AND ACTS ON ORDINARY MATTER AT LEVELS MUCH DEEPER THAN WE PERCEIVE AT A SIMPLE QUANTUM MECHANICAL LEVEL.
IT CAN OVERRIDE ORDINARY MATTER, REWRITING THE SUPERSTRING FUNCTIONS THAT DEFINE REALITY. THE RAW FORM OF THE ENERGY WOULD DISSIPATE WITH ONLY RANDOM EFFECTS, BUT THIS THING APPARENTLY DIRECTS THE CHANGES.
THE CASE IS THE KEY. IT STABILIZES THE SUPERREAL ENERGY, BUT IT ALSO HOUSES THE TELEPATHIC INTERFACE THAT CONTROLS THE ENERGY --
-- WHICH, AS THE VOSKUIL-MARRE FIRST ORDER PERTURBATION THEORY SHOWS US --
-- IN ENGLISH, ERIC: WE THINK WE'VE FIGURED OUT HOW TO DISARM IT.
IT'S A BIT DICEY, THOUGH --
-- ERIC... IF WE DESTROY THIS THING --
-- IT MIGHT KILL HIM.
ERIC...?
DO IT.
I'M CALLING LEWIS. STAND BY.

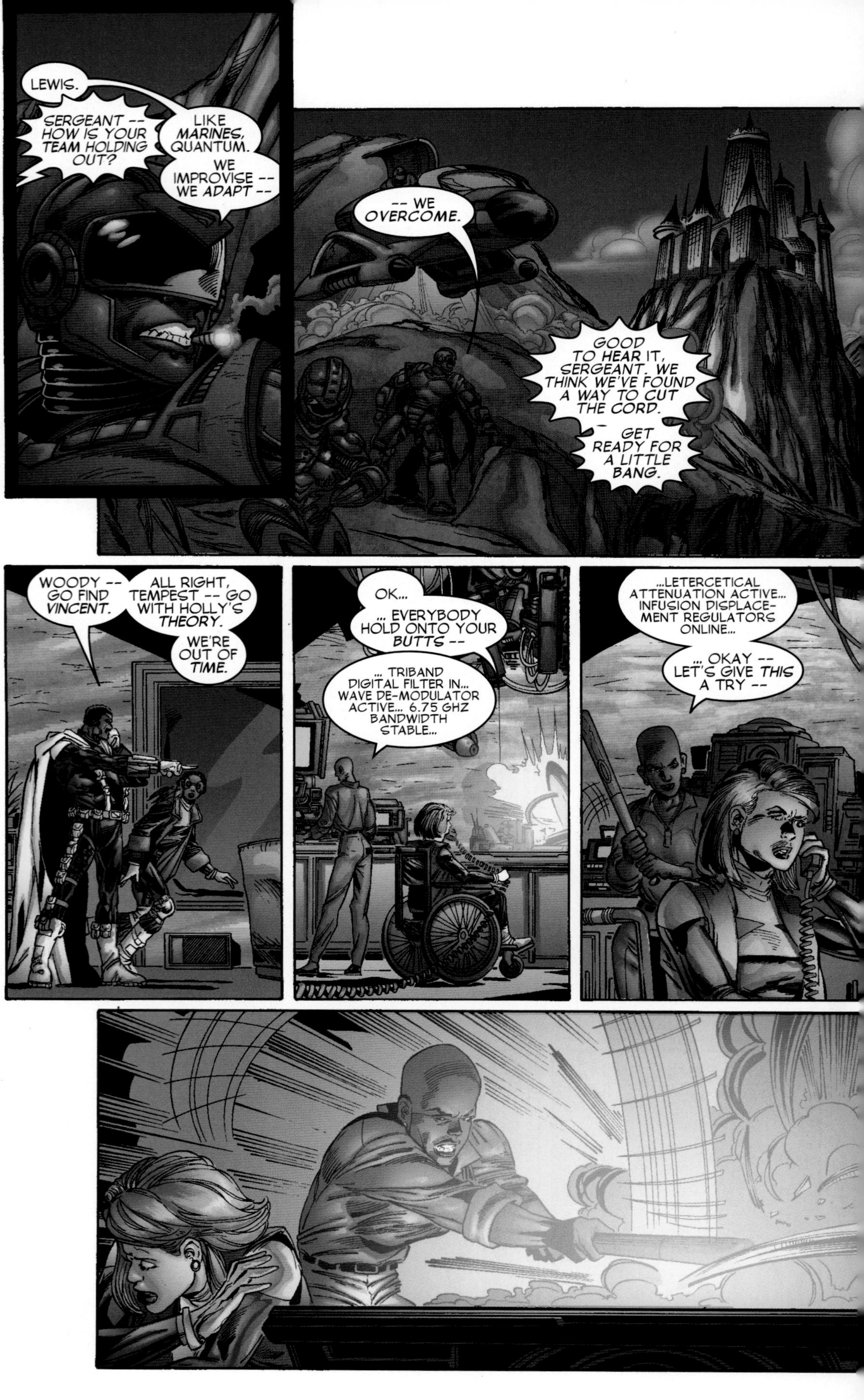
LEWIS.
SERGEANT -- HOW IS YOUR TEAM HOLDING OUT?
LIKE MARINES, QUANTUM.
WE IMPROVISE -- WE ADAPT --
-- WE OVERCOME.
GOOD TO HEAR IT, SERGEANT. WE THINK WE'VE FOUND A WAY TO CUT THE CORD.
GET READY FOR A LITTLE BANG.
WOODY -- GO FIND VINCENT.
ALL RIGHT, TEMPEST -- GO WITH HOLLY'S THEORY.
WE'RE OUT OF TIME.
OK...
... EVERYBODY HOLD ONTO YOUR BUTTS --
... TRIBAND DIGITAL FILTER IN... WAVE DE-MODULATOR ACTIVE... 6.75 GHZ BANDWIDTH STABLE...
...LETERCETICAL ATTENUATION ACTIVE... INFUSION DISPLACEMENT REGULATORS ONLINE...
... OKAY -- LET'S GIVE THIS A TRY --

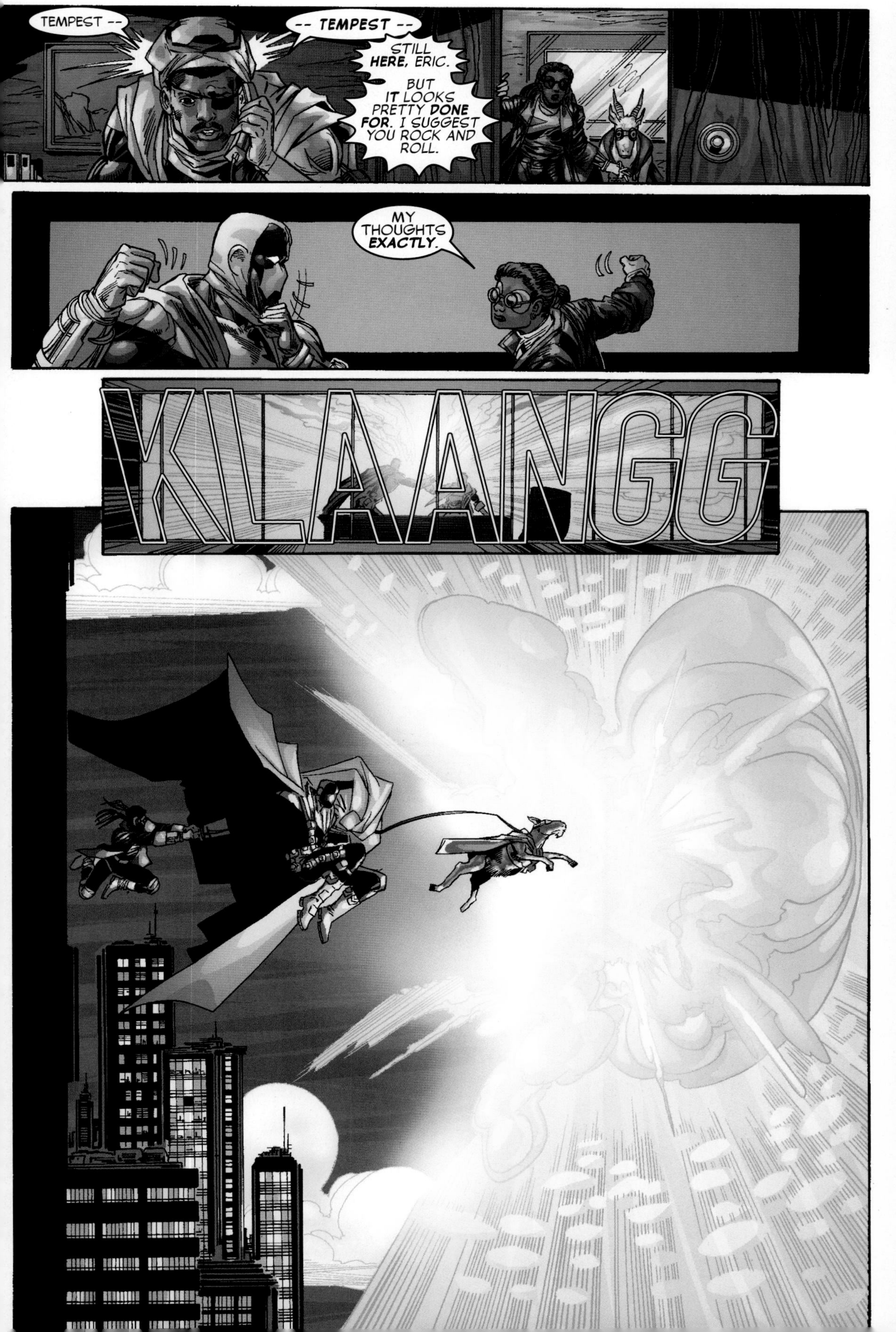
TEMPEST --
-- TEMPEST --
STILL HERE, ERIC.
BUT IT LOOKS PRETTY DONE FOR. I SUGGEST YOU ROCK AND ROLL.
MY THOUGHTS EXACTLY.
KILAANGG

"'G' is for 'Ghaahh!!'"

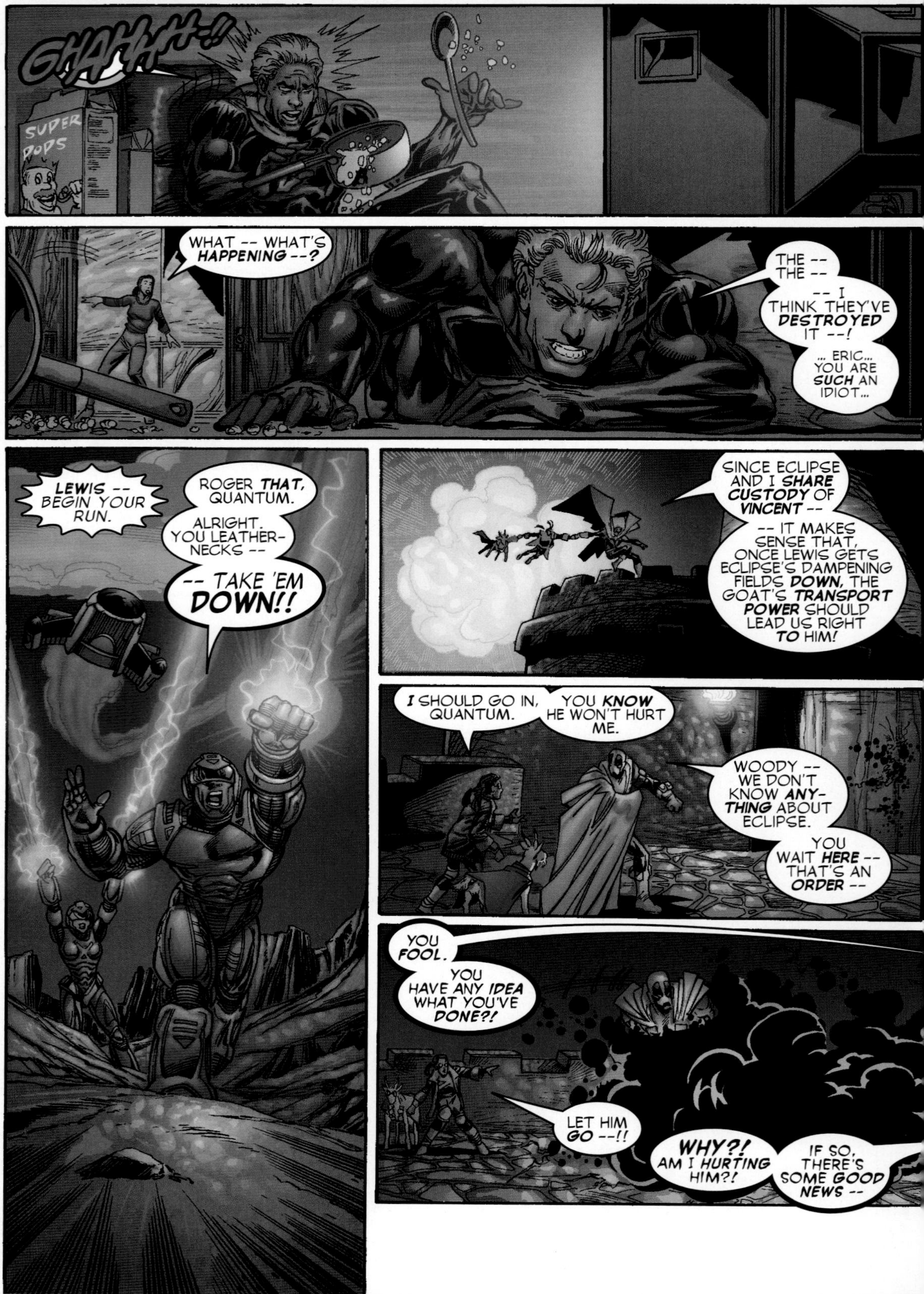
GHAHHH-!!
SUPER POPS
WHAT -- WHAT'S HAPPENING --?
THE -- THE -- -- I THINK THEY'VE DESTROYED IT --!
... ERIC... YOU ARE SUCH AN IDIOT...
LEWIS -- BEGIN YOUR RUN.
ROGER THAT, QUANTUM.
ALRIGHT. YOU LEATHER-NECKS --
-- TAKE 'EM DOWN!!
SINCE ECLIPSE AND I SHARE CUSTODY OF VINCENT --
-- IT MAKES SENSE THAT, ONCE LEWIS GETS ECLIPSE'S DAMPENING FIELDS DOWN, THE GOAT'S TRANSPORT POWER SHOULD LEAD US RIGHT TO HIM!
I SHOULD GO IN, QUANTUM.
YOU KNOW HE WON'T HURT ME.
WOODY -- WE DON'T KNOW ANY-THING ABOUT ECLIPSE.
YOU WAIT HERE -- THAT'S AN ORDER --
YOU FOOL.
YOU HAVE ANY IDEA WHAT YOU'VE DONE?!
LET HIM GO --!!
WHY?! AM I HURTING HIM?!
IF SO, THERE'S SOME GOOD NEWS --

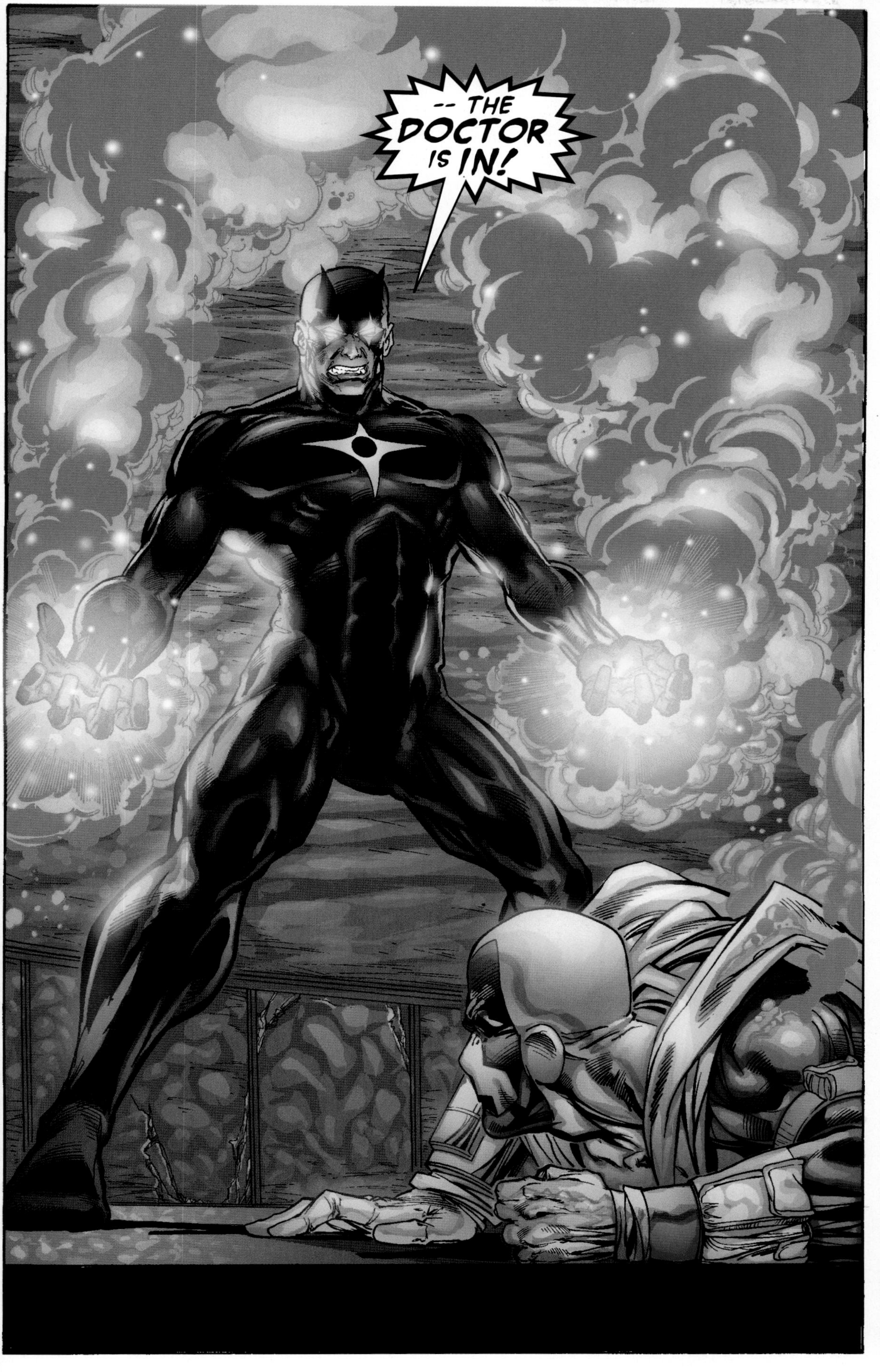
-- THE DOCTOR IS IN!

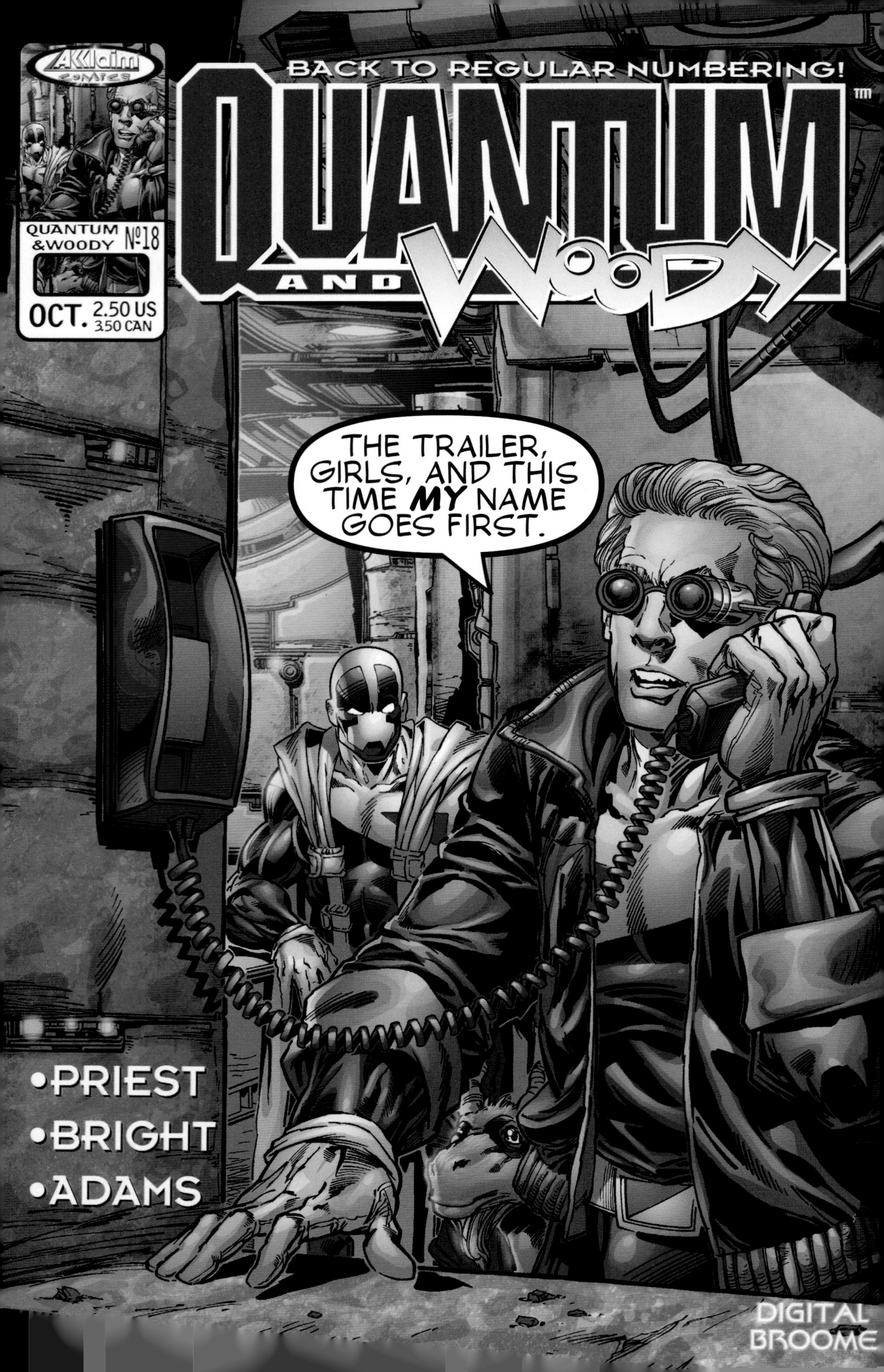

ACCLAIM COMICS
QUANTUM &WOODY №18
OCT. 2.50 US 3.50 CAN
BACK TO REGULAR NUMBERING!
QUANTUM AND WOODY™
THE TRAILER, GIRLS, AND THIS TIME MY NAME GOES FIRST.
•PRIEST
•BRIGHT
•ADAMS
DIGITAL BROOME

"This Just In"

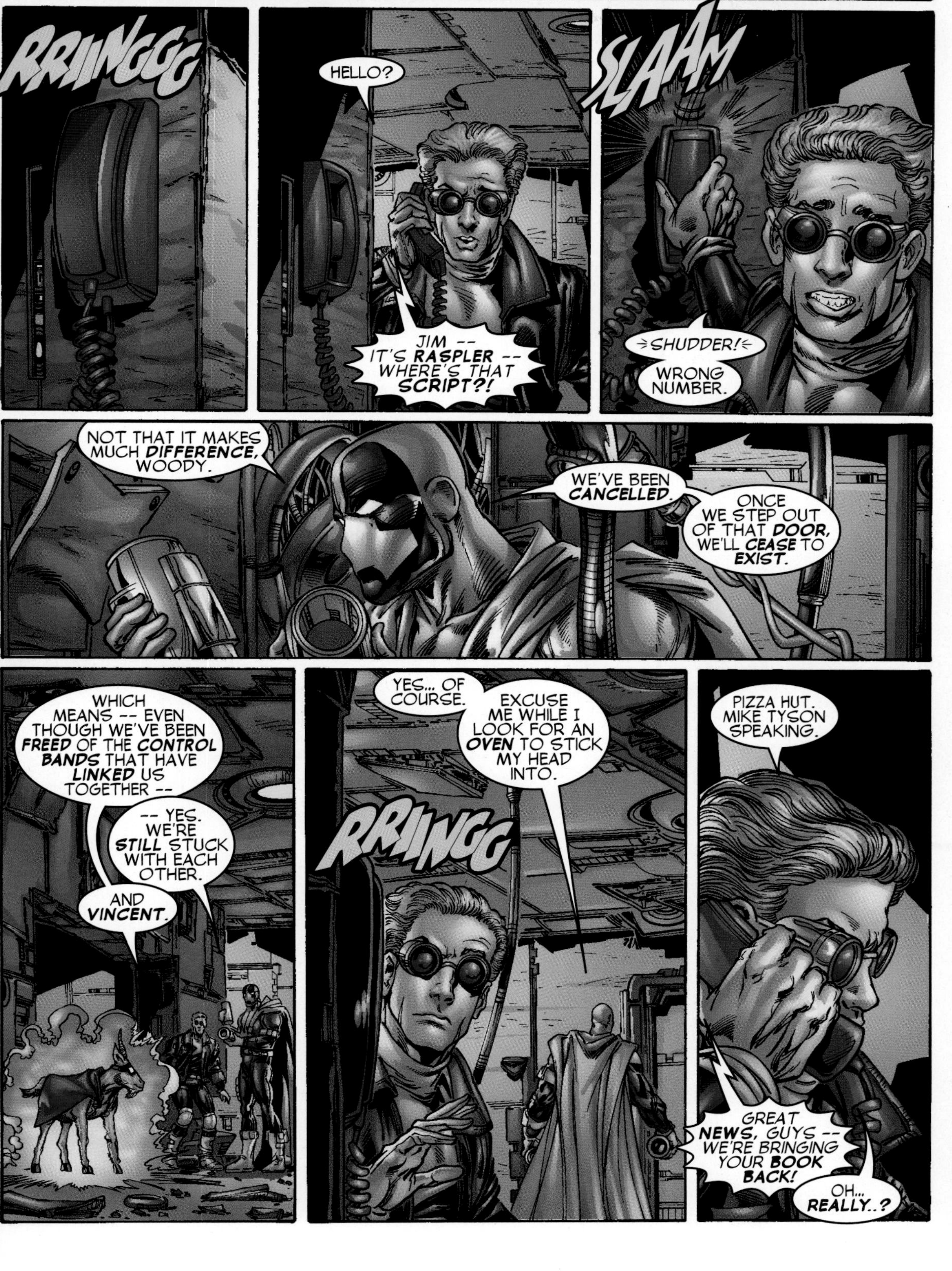
RRIINGGG
HELLO?
JIM -- IT'S RASPLER -- WHERE'S THAT SCRIPT?!
SLAAM
SHUDDER!
WRONG NUMBER.
NOT THAT IT MAKES MUCH DIFFERENCE, WOODY.
WE'VE BEEN CANCELLED.
ONCE WE STEP OUT OF THAT DOOR, WE'LL CEASE TO EXIST.
WHICH MEANS -- EVEN THOUGH WE'VE BEEN FREED OF THE CONTROL BANDS THAT HAVE LINKED US TOGETHER --
-- YES. WE'RE STILL STUCK WITH EACH OTHER.
AND VINCENT.
YES... OF COURSE.
EXCUSE ME WHILE I LOOK FOR AN OVEN TO STICK MY HEAD INTO.
RRIINGG
PIZZA HUT. MIKE TYSON SPEAKING.
GREAT NEWS, GUYS -- WE'RE BRINGING YOUR BOOK BACK!
OH... REALLY..?

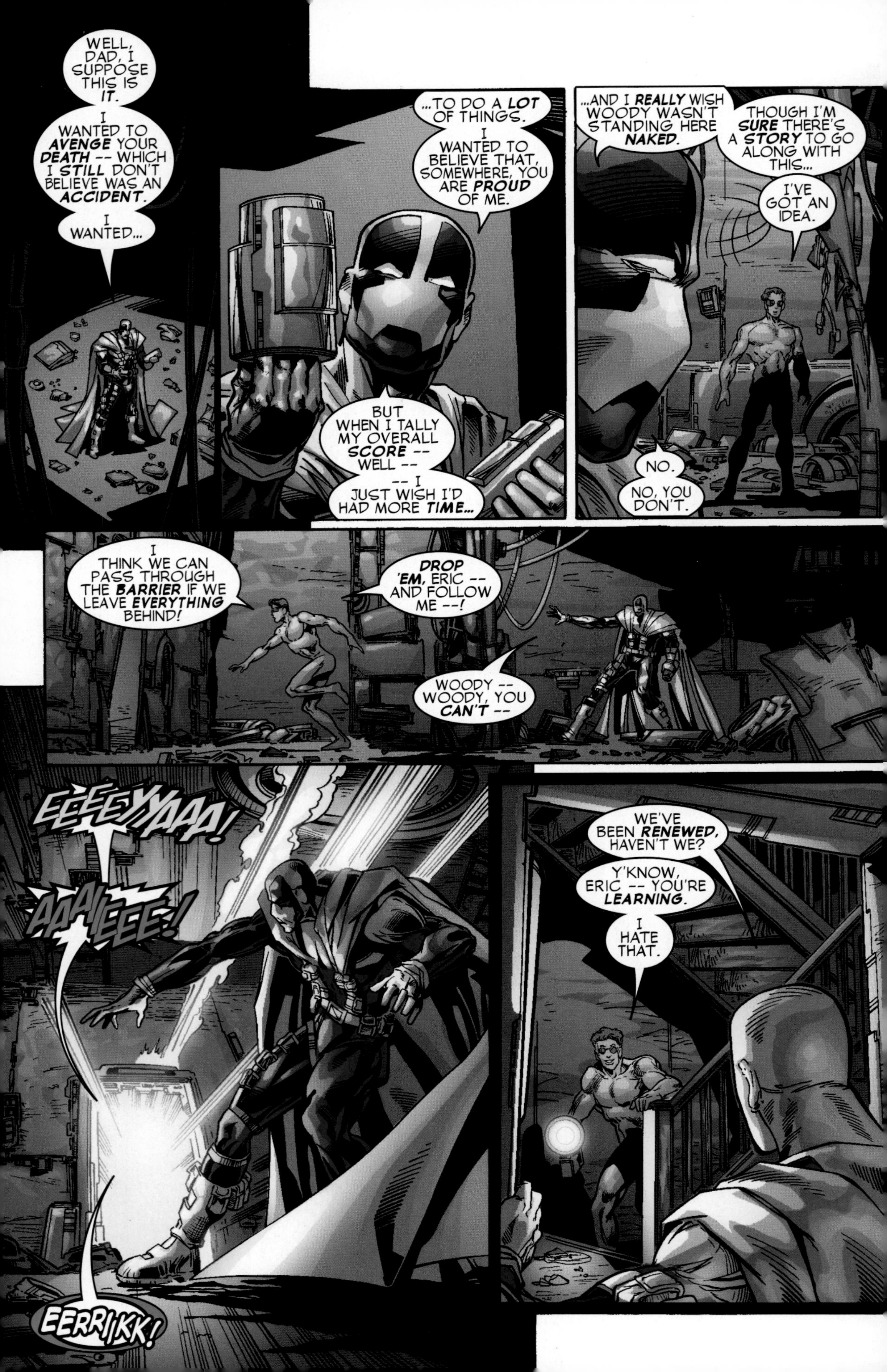
WELL, DAD, I SUPPOSE THIS IS IT.
I WANTED TO AVENGE YOUR DEATH -- WHICH I STILL DON'T BELIEVE WAS AN ACCIDENT.
I WANTED...
...TO DO A LOT OF THINGS.
I WANTED TO BELIEVE THAT, SOMEWHERE, YOU ARE PROUD OF ME.
BUT WHEN I TALLY MY OVERALL SCORE -- WELL --
-- I JUST WISH I'D HAD MORE TIME...
...AND I REALLY WISH WOODY WASN'T STANDING HERE NAKED.
THOUGH I'M SURE THERE'S A STORY TO GO ALONG WITH THIS...
I'VE GOT AN IDEA.
NO.
NO, YOU DON'T.
I THINK WE CAN PASS THROUGH THE BARRIER IF WE LEAVE EVERYTHING BEHIND!
DROP 'EM, ERIC -- AND FOLLOW ME --!
WOODY -- WOODY, YOU CAN'T --
EEEEYYAAA!
AAAIEEEE!
EERRIIKK!
WE'VE BEEN RENEWED, HAVEN'T WE?
Y'KNOW, ERIC -- YOU'RE LEARNING.
I HATE THAT.

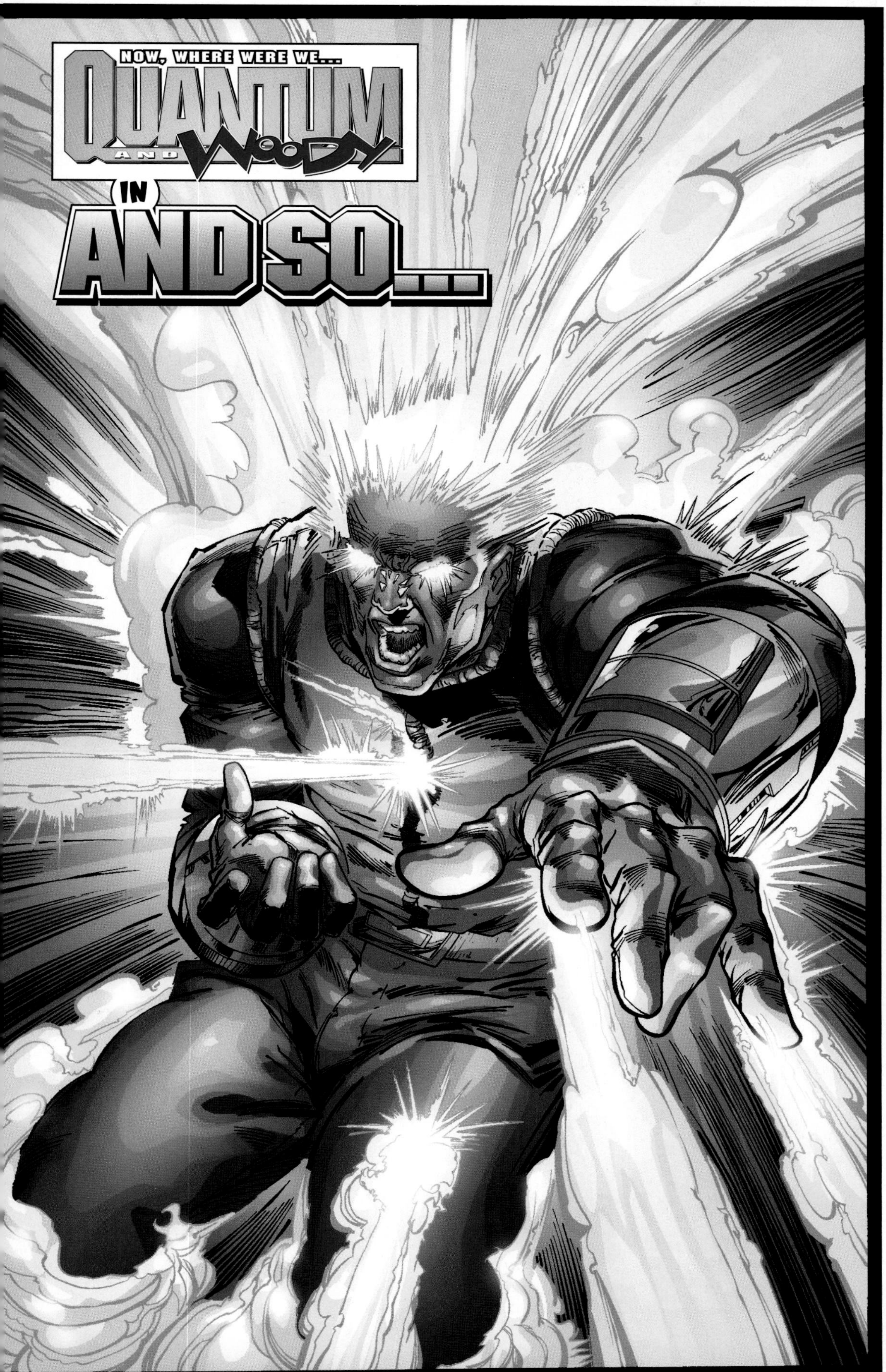

NOW, WHERE WERE WE...
QUANTUM AND WOODY
IN
AND SO...

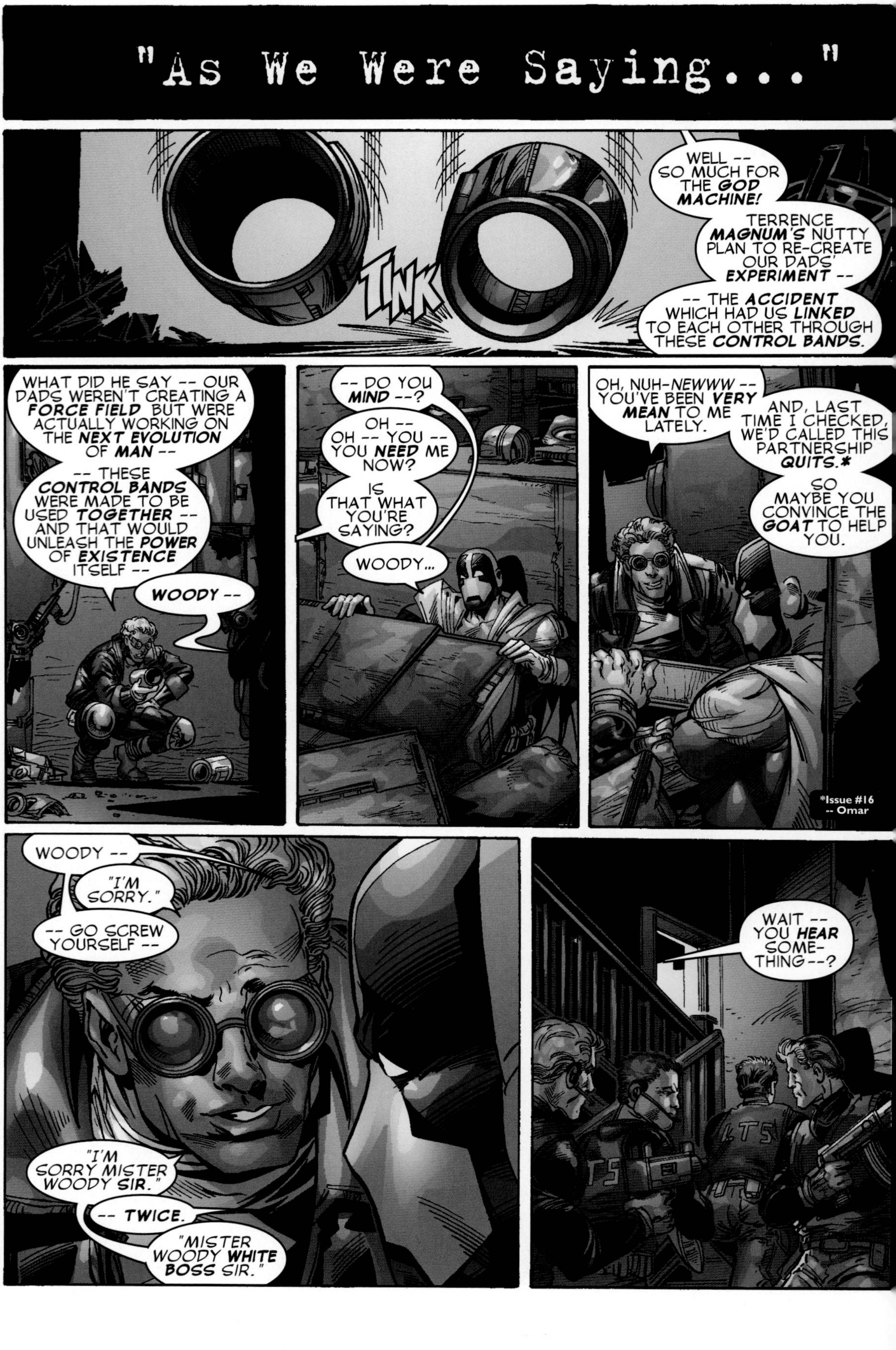
"As We Were Saying..."
WELL -- SO MUCH FOR THE GOD MACHINE!
TERRENCE MAGNUM'S NUTTY PLAN TO RE-CREATE OUR DADS' EXPERIMENT --
-- THE ACCIDENT WHICH HAD US LINKED TO EACH OTHER THROUGH THESE CONTROL BANDS.
TINK
WHAT DID HE SAY -- OUR DADS WEREN'T CREATING A FORCE FIELD BUT WERE ACTUALLY WORKING ON THE NEXT EVOLUTION OF MAN --
-- THESE CONTROL BANDS WERE MADE TO BE USED TOGETHER -- AND THAT WOULD UNLEASH THE POWER OF EXISTENCE ITSELF --
WOODY --
-- DO YOU MIND --?
OH -- OH -- YOU -- YOU NEED ME NOW?
IS THAT WHAT YOU'RE SAYING?
WOODY...
OH, NUH-NEWWW -- YOU'VE BEEN VERY MEAN TO ME LATELY.
AND, LAST TIME I CHECKED, WE'D CALLED THIS PARTNERSHIP QUITS.*
SO MAYBE YOU CONVINCE THE GOAT TO HELP YOU.
*Issue #16 -- Omar
WOODY --
"I'M SORRY."
-- GO SCREW YOURSELF --
"I'M SORRY MISTER WOODY SIR."
-- TWICE.
"MISTER WOODY WHITE BOSS SIR."
WAIT -- YOU HEAR SOME-THING--?

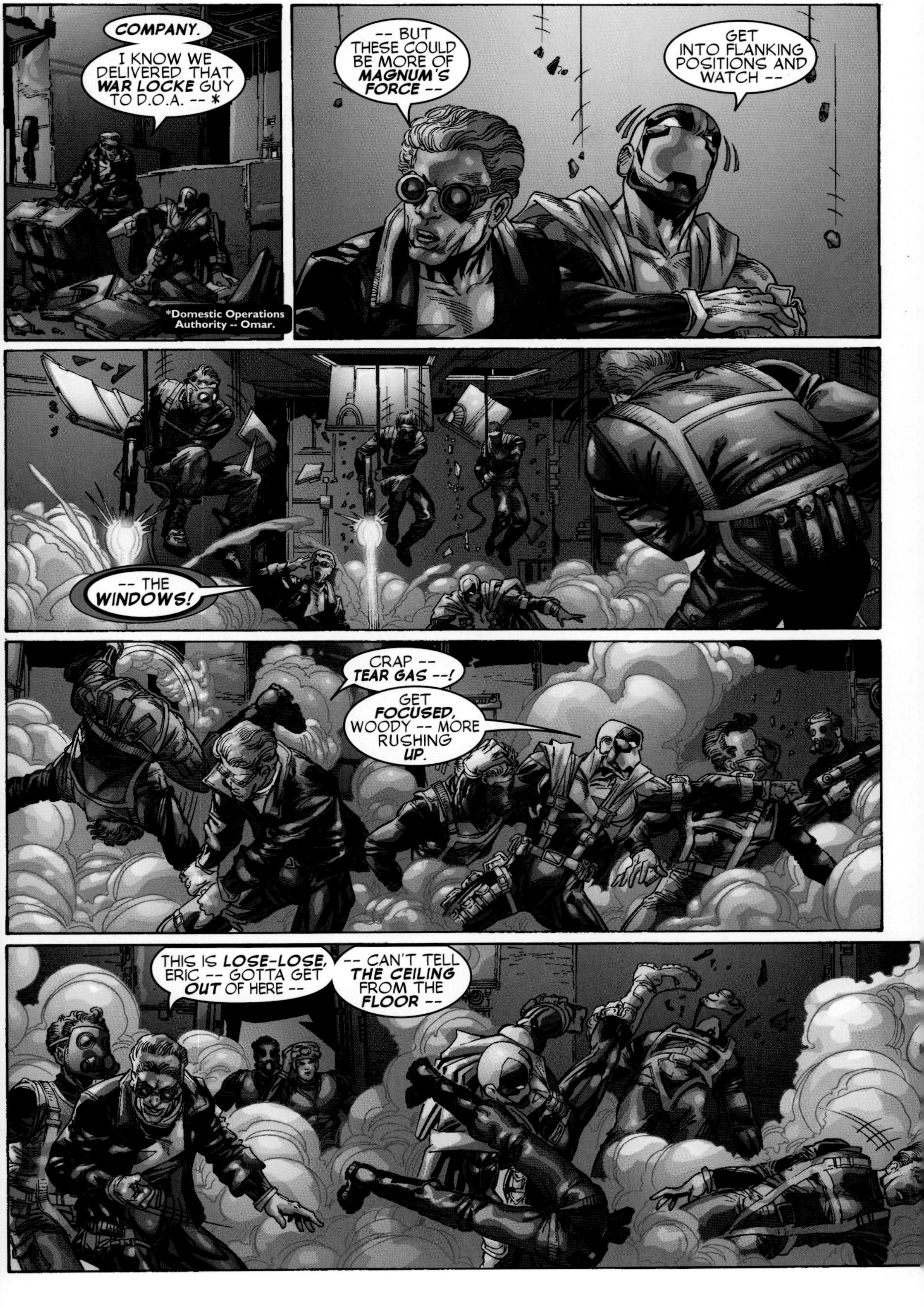
COMPANY.
I KNOW WE DELIVERED THAT WAR LOCKE GUY TO D.O.A. -- *
*Domestic Operations Authority -- Omar.
-- BUT THESE COULD BE MORE OF MAGNUM'S FORCE --
GET INTO FLANKING POSITIONS AND WATCH --
-- THE WINDOWS!
CRAP -- TEAR GAS --!
GET FOCUSED, WOODY -- MORE RUSHING UP.
THIS IS LOSE-LOSE, ERIC -- GOTTA GET OUT OF HERE --
-- CAN'T TELL THE CEILING FROM THE FLOOR --

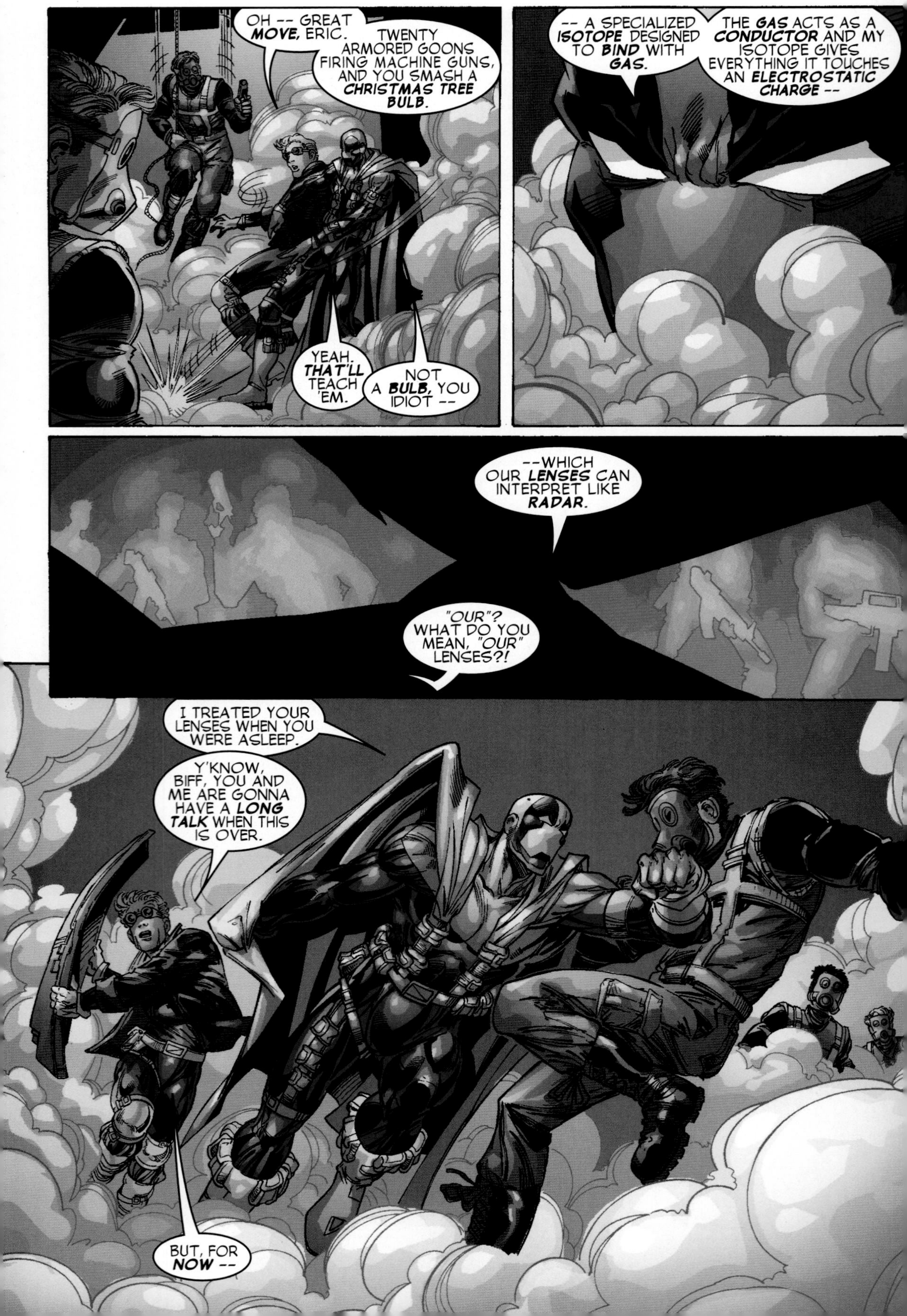
OH -- GREAT MOVE, ERIC.
TWENTY ARMORED GOONS FIRING MACHINE GUNS, AND YOU SMASH A CHRISTMAS TREE BULB.
YEAH. THAT'LL TEACH 'EM.
NOT A BULB, YOU IDIOT --
-- A SPECIALIZED ISOTOPE DESIGNED TO BIND WITH GAS.
THE GAS ACTS AS A CONDUCTOR AND MY ISOTOPE GIVES EVERYTHING IT TOUCHES AN ELECTROSTATIC CHARGE --
--WHICH OUR LENSES CAN INTERPRET LIKE RADAR.
"OUR"? WHAT DO YOU MEAN, "OUR" LENSES?!
I TREATED YOUR LENSES WHEN YOU WERE ASLEEP.
Y'KNOW, BIFF, YOU AND ME ARE GONNA HAVE A LONG TALK WHEN THIS IS OVER.
BUT, FOR NOW --

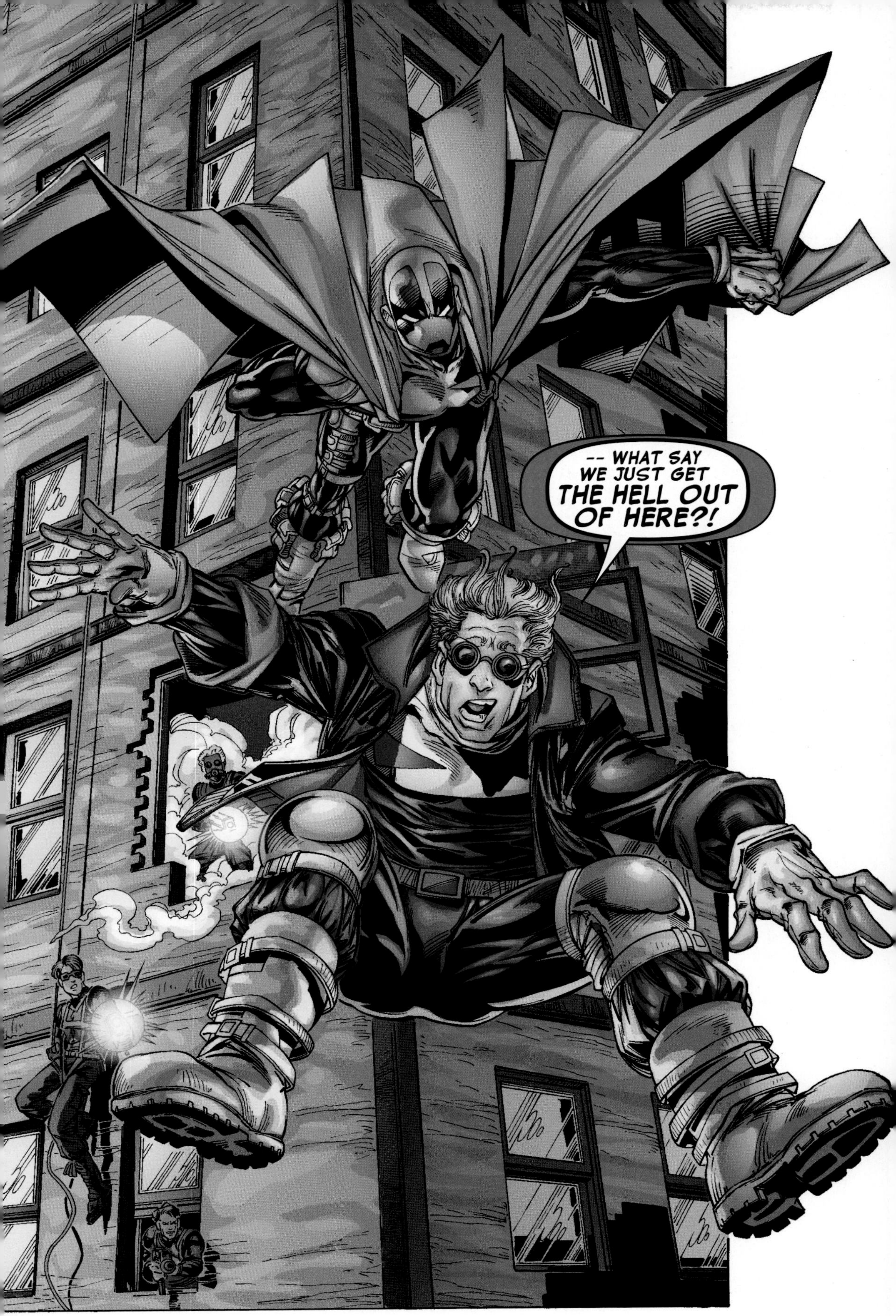
-- WHAT SAY WE JUST GET THE HELL OUT OF HERE?!

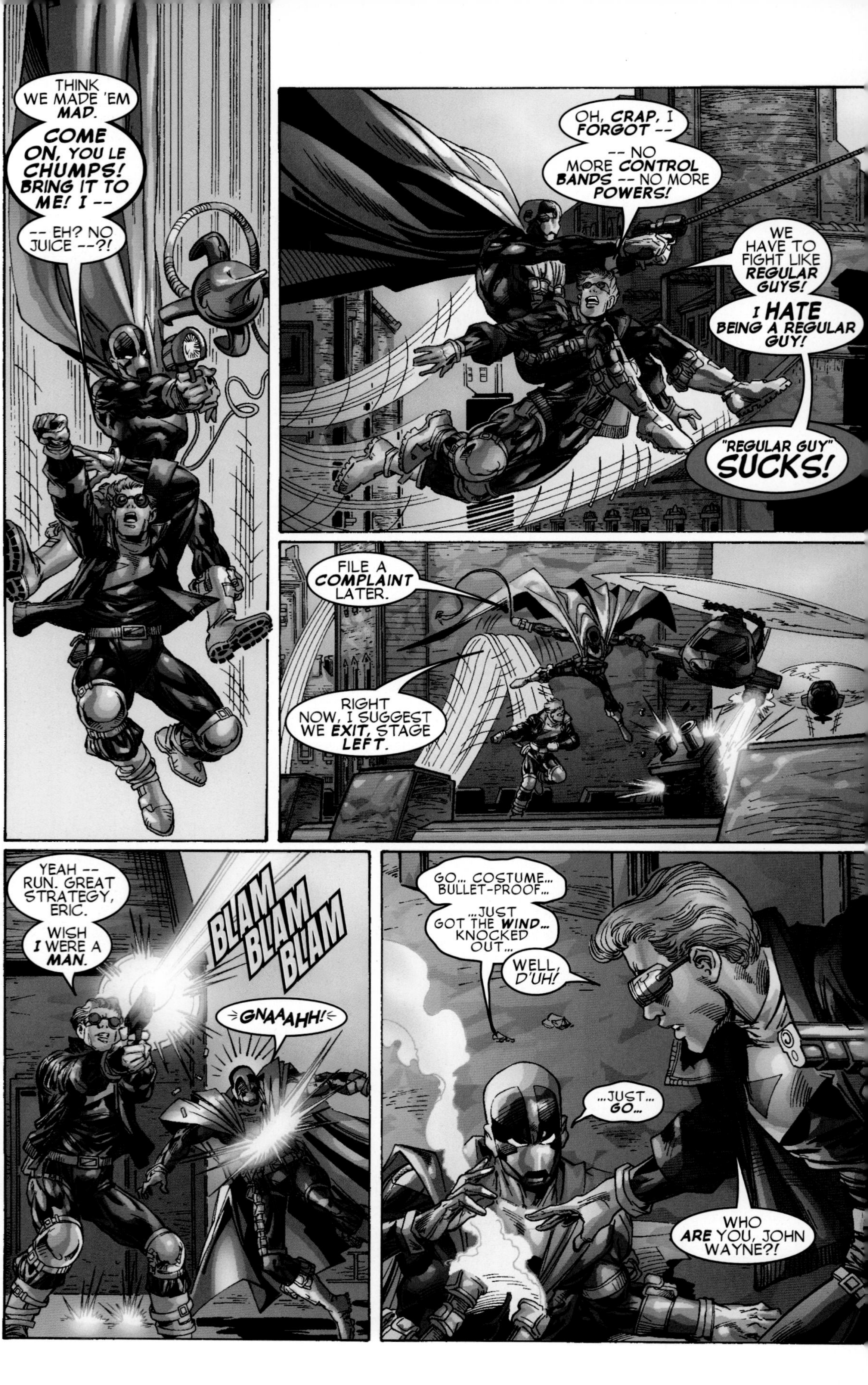
THINK WE MADE 'EM MAD.
COME ON, YOU LE CHUMPS! BRING IT TO ME! I --
-- EH? NO JUICE --?!
OH, CRAP, I FORGOT --
-- NO MORE CONTROL BANDS -- NO MORE POWERS!
WE HAVE TO FIGHT LIKE REGULAR GUYS!
I HATE BEING A REGULAR GUY!
"REGULAR GUY" SUCKS!
FILE A COMPLAINT LATER.
RIGHT NOW, I SUGGEST WE EXIT, STAGE LEFT.
YEAH -- RUN. GREAT STRATEGY, ERIC.
WISH I WERE A MAN.
BLAM BLAM BLAM
GNAAAHH!
GO... COSTUME... BULLET-PROOF...
...JUST GOT THE WIND... KNOCKED OUT...
WELL, D'UH!
...JUST... GO...
WHO ARE YOU, JOHN WAYNE?!

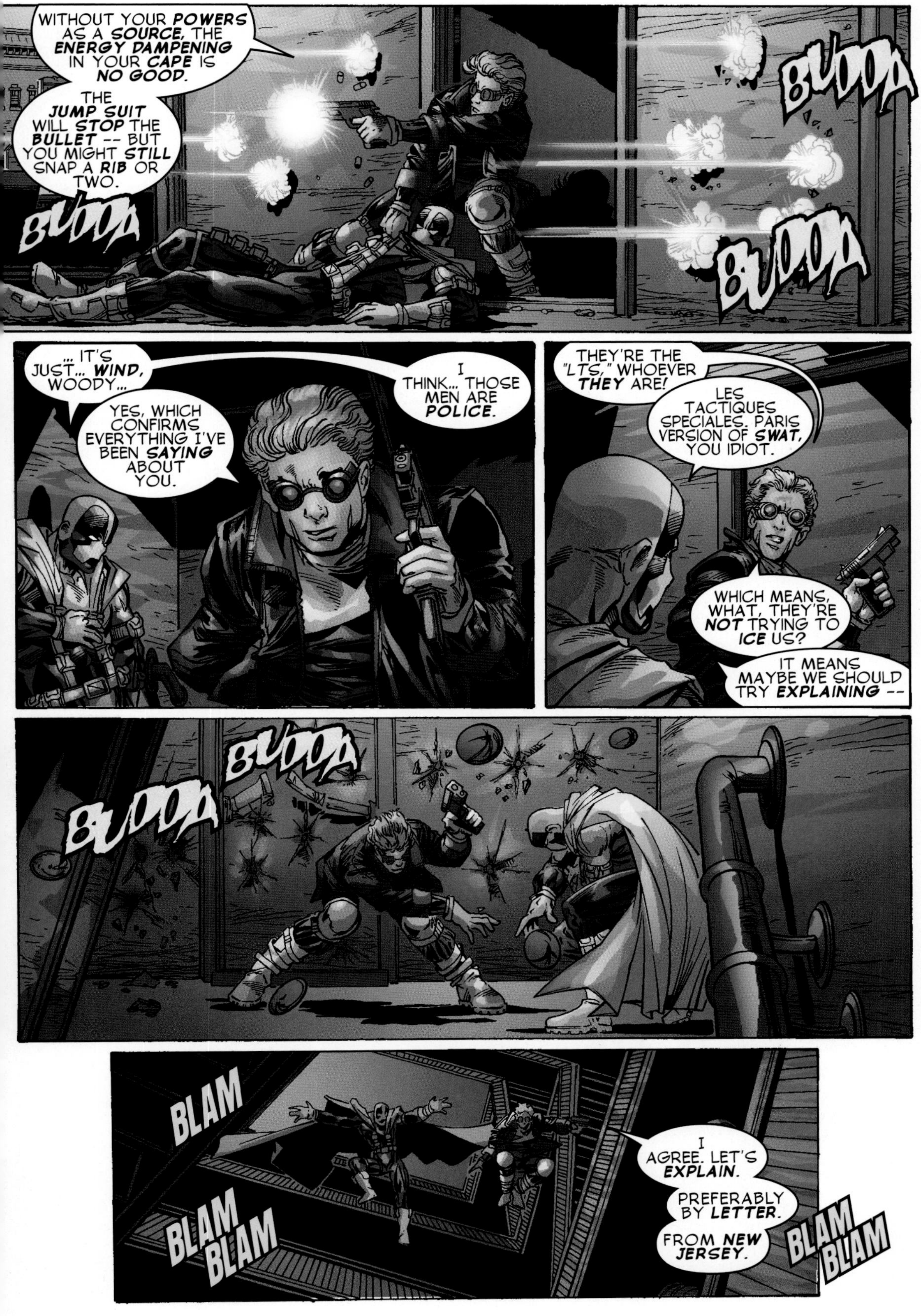
WITHOUT YOUR POWERS AS A SOURCE, THE ENERGY DAMPENING IN YOUR CAPE IS NO GOOD.
THE JUMP SUIT WILL STOP THE BULLET -- BUT YOU MIGHT STILL SNAP A RIB OR TWO.
BUDDA
BUDDA
BUDDA
... IT'S JUST... WIND, WOODY...
YES, WHICH CONFIRMS EVERYTHING I'VE BEEN SAYING ABOUT YOU.
I THINK... THOSE MEN ARE POLICE.
THEY'RE THE "LTS," WHOEVER THEY ARE!
LES TACTIQUES SPECIALES. PARIS VERSION OF SWAT, YOU IDIOT.
WHICH MEANS, WHAT, THEY'RE NOT TRYING TO ICE US?
IT MEANS MAYBE WE SHOULD TRY EXPLAINING --
BUDDA
BUDDA
BLAM
BLAM BLAM
I AGREE. LET'S EXPLAIN.
PREFERABLY BY LETTER.
FROM NEW JERSEY.
BLAM BLAM

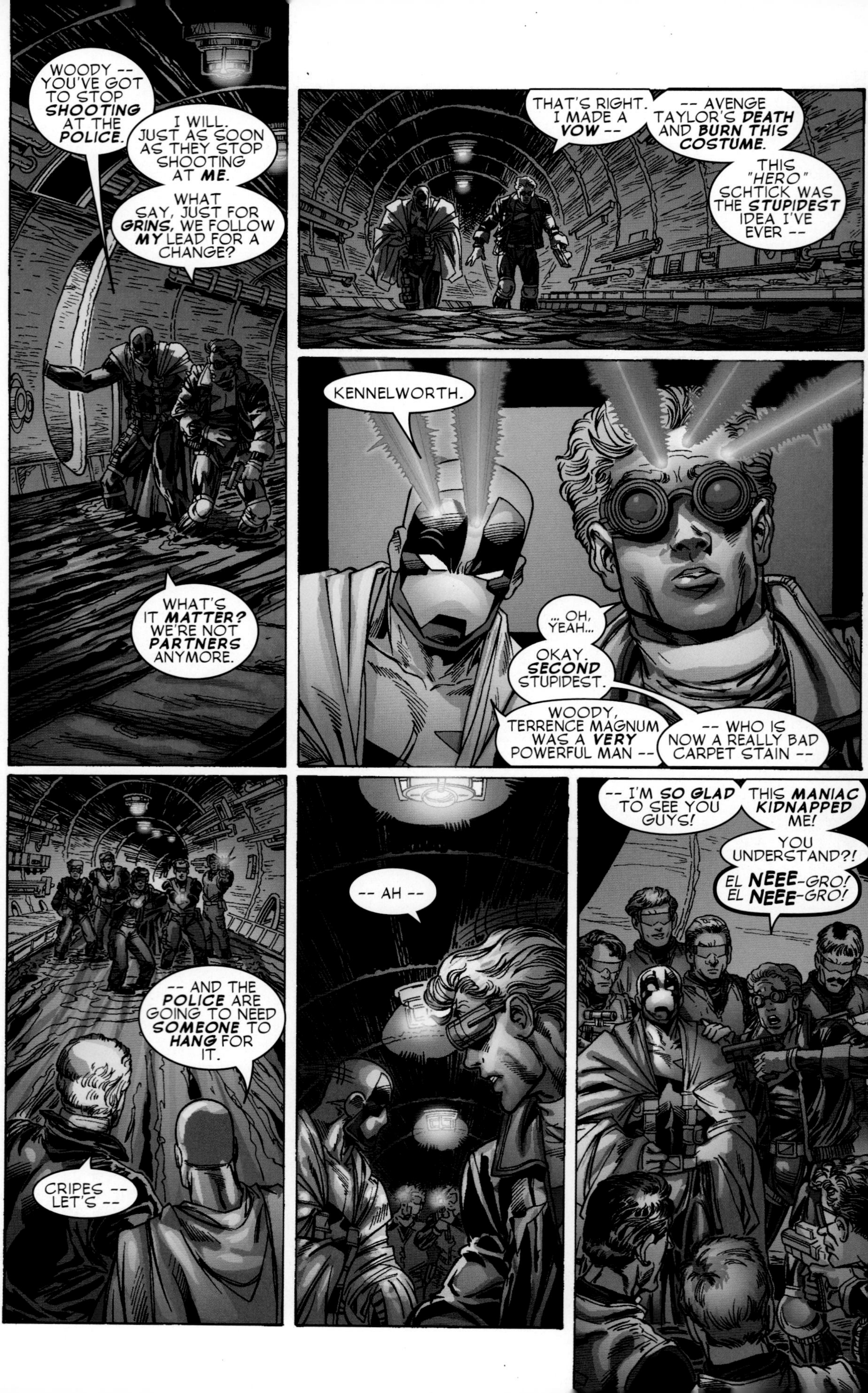
WOODY -- YOU'VE GOT TO STOP SHOOTING AT THE POLICE.
I WILL. JUST AS SOON AS THEY STOP SHOOTING AT ME.
WHAT SAY, JUST FOR GRINS, WE FOLLOW MY LEAD FOR A CHANGE?
WHAT'S IT MATTER? WE'RE NOT PARTNERS ANYMORE.
THAT'S RIGHT. I MADE A VOW --
-- AVENGE TAYLOR'S DEATH AND BURN THIS COSTUME.
THIS "HERO" SCHTICK WAS THE STUPIDEST IDEA I'VE EVER --
KENNELWORTH.
...OH, YEAH...
OKAY. SECOND STUPIDEST.
WOODY, TERRENCE MAGNUM WAS A VERY POWERFUL MAN --
-- WHO IS NOW A REALLY BAD CARPET STAIN --
-- AND THE POLICE ARE GOING TO NEED SOMEONE TO HANG FOR IT.
CRIPES -- LET'S --
-- AH --
-- I'M SO GLAD TO SEE YOU GUYS!
THIS MANIAC KIDNAPPED ME!
YOU UNDERSTAND?!
EL NEEE-GRO! EL NEEE-GRO!

"Mooned"

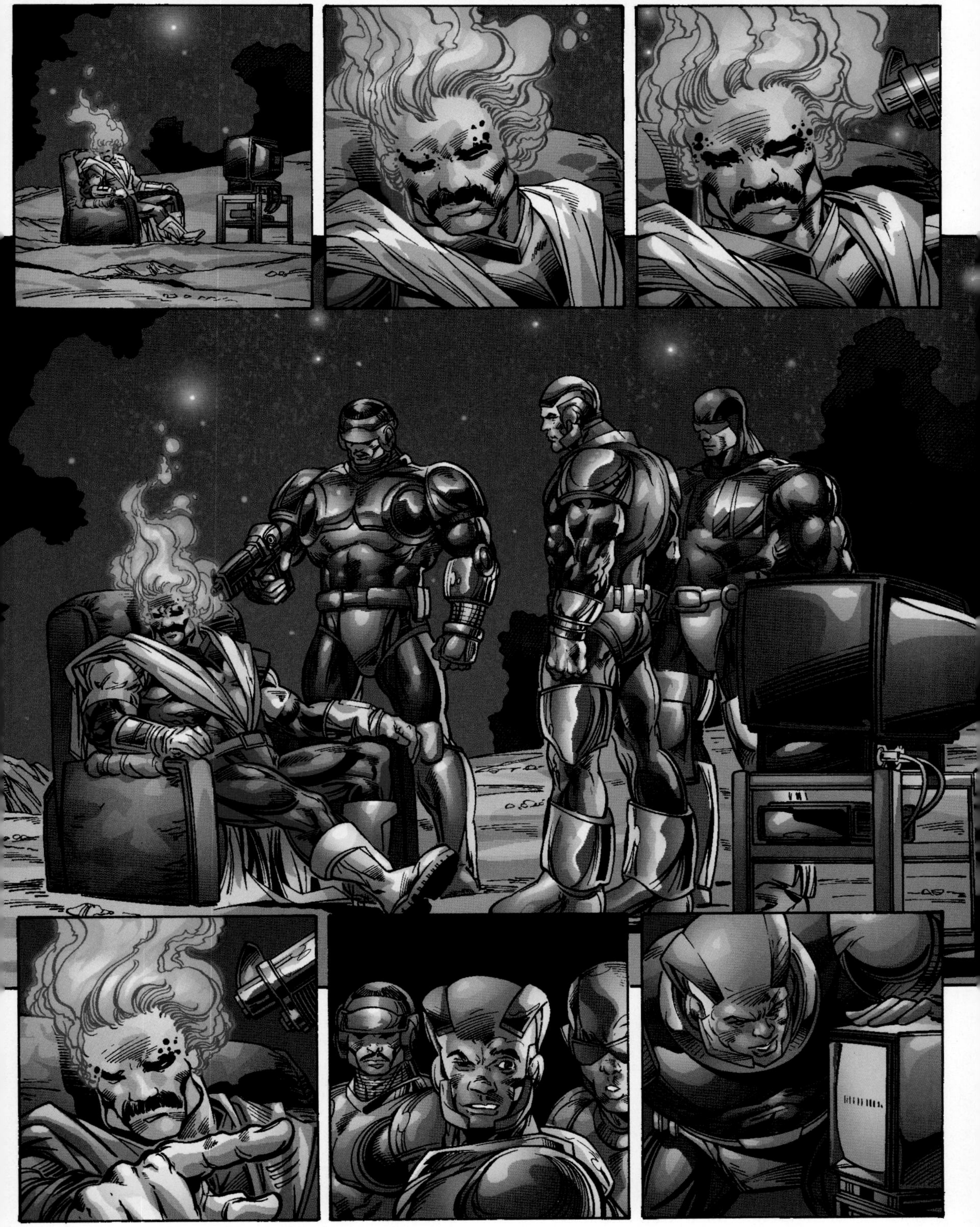

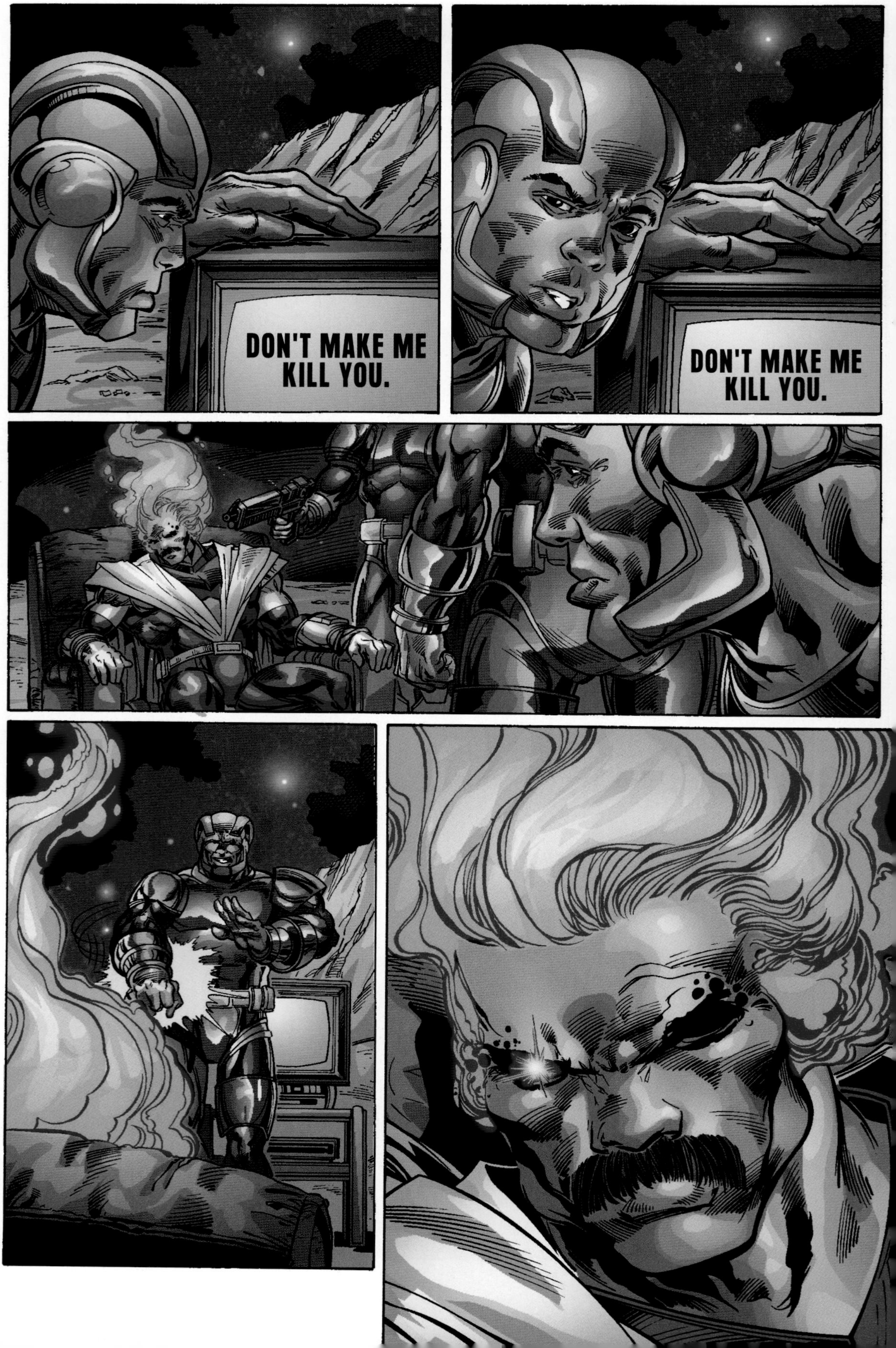
DON'T MAKE ME KILL YOU.
DON'T MAKE ME KILL YOU.

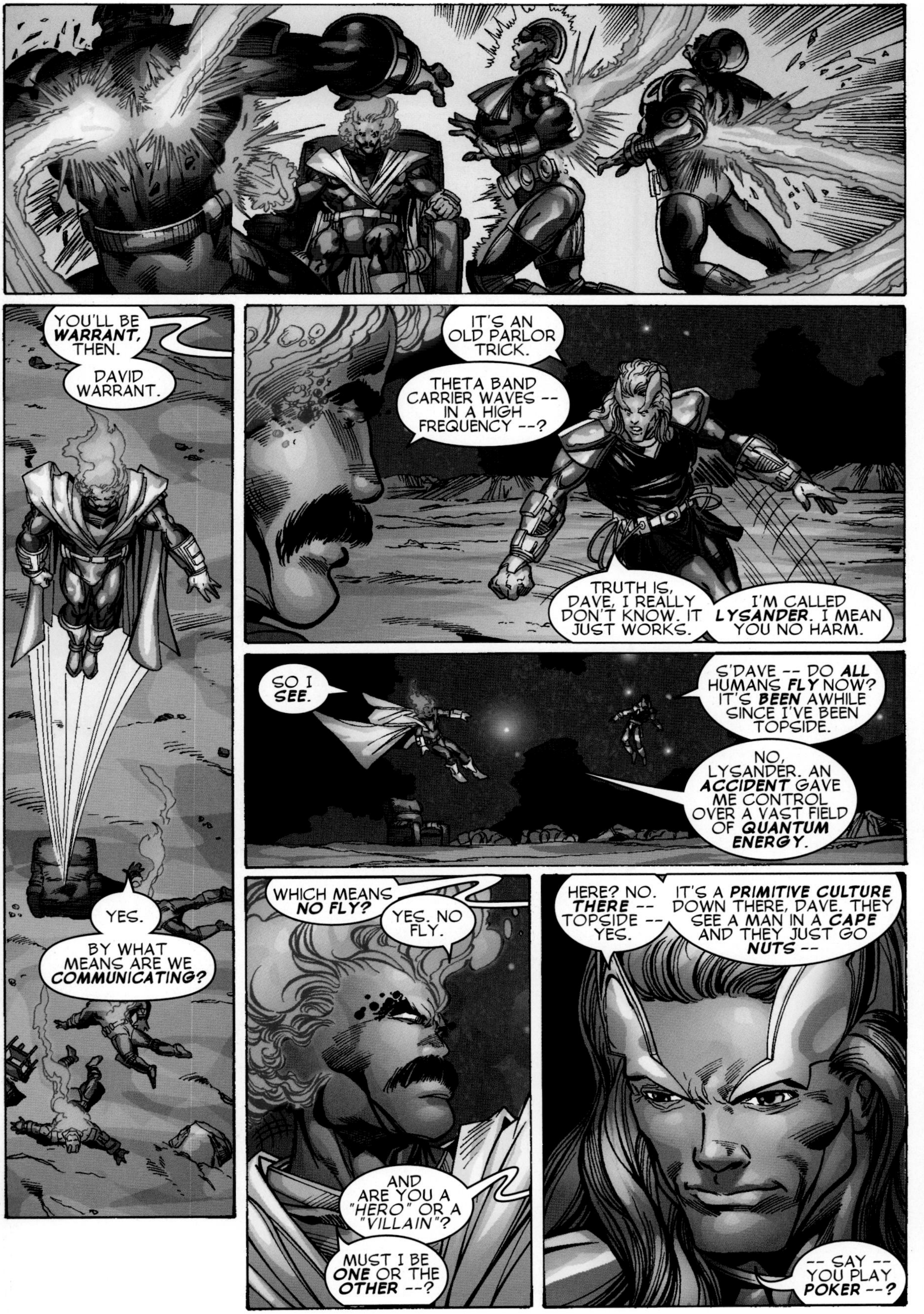
YOU'LL BE **WARRANT,** THEN.
DAVID WARRANT.
YES.
BY WHAT MEANS ARE WE **COMMUNICATING?**
IT'S AN OLD PARLOR TRICK.
THETA BAND CARRIER WAVES -- IN A HIGH FREQUENCY --?
TRUTH IS, DAVE, I REALLY DON'T KNOW. IT JUST WORKS.
I'M CALLED **LYSANDER.** I MEAN YOU NO HARM.
SO I **SEE.**
S'DAVE -- DO **ALL** HUMANS **FLY** NOW? IT'S **BEEN** AWHILE SINCE I'VE BEEN TOPSIDE.
NO, LYSANDER. AN **ACCIDENT** GAVE ME CONTROL OVER A VAST FIELD OF **QUANTUM ENERGY.**
WHICH MEANS **NO FLY?**
YES. NO FLY.
AND ARE YOU A "HERO" OR A "VILLAIN"?
MUST I BE **ONE** OR THE **OTHER** --?
HERE? NO. **THERE** -- TOPSIDE -- YES.
IT'S A **PRIMITIVE CULTURE** DOWN THERE, DAVE. THEY SEE A MAN IN A **CAPE** AND THEY JUST GO **NUTS** --
-- SAY -- YOU PLAY **POKER** --?

"Waiting For Vincent"

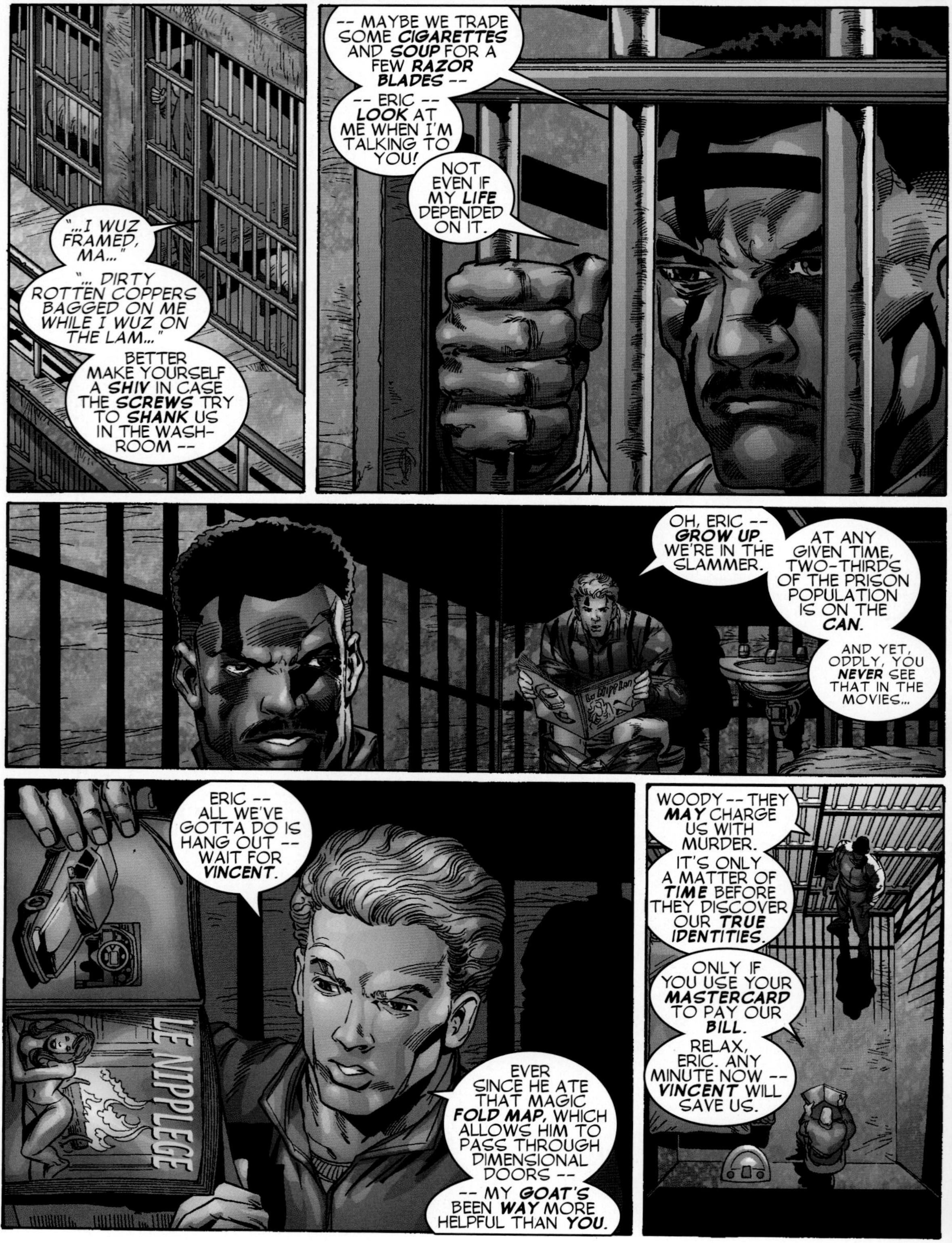
"...I WUZ FRAMED, MA..."
"... DIRTY ROTTEN COPPERS BAGGED ON ME WHILE I WUZ ON THE LAM..."
BETTER MAKE YOURSELF A SHIV IN CASE THE SCREWS TRY TO SHANK US IN THE WASH-ROOM --
-- MAYBE WE TRADE SOME CIGARETTES AND SOUP FOR A FEW RAZOR BLADES --
-- ERIC -- LOOK AT ME WHEN I'M TALKING TO YOU!
NOT EVEN IF MY LIFE DEPENDED ON IT.
OH, ERIC -- GROW UP. WE'RE IN THE SLAMMER.
AT ANY GIVEN TIME, TWO-THIRDS OF THE PRISON POPULATION IS ON THE CAN.
AND YET, ODDLY, YOU NEVER SEE THAT IN THE MOVIES...
ERIC -- ALL WE'VE GOTTA DO IS HANG OUT -- WAIT FOR VINCENT.
LE NIPPLEGE
EVER SINCE HE ATE THAT MAGIC FOLD MAP, WHICH ALLOWS HIM TO PASS THROUGH DIMENSIONAL DOORS --
-- MY GOAT'S BEEN WAY MORE HELPFUL THAN YOU.
WOODY -- THEY MAY CHARGE US WITH MURDER.
IT'S ONLY A MATTER OF TIME BEFORE THEY DISCOVER OUR TRUE IDENTITIES.
ONLY IF YOU USE YOUR MASTERCARD TO PAY OUR BILL.
RELAX, ERIC. ANY MINUTE NOW -- VINCENT WILL SAVE US.

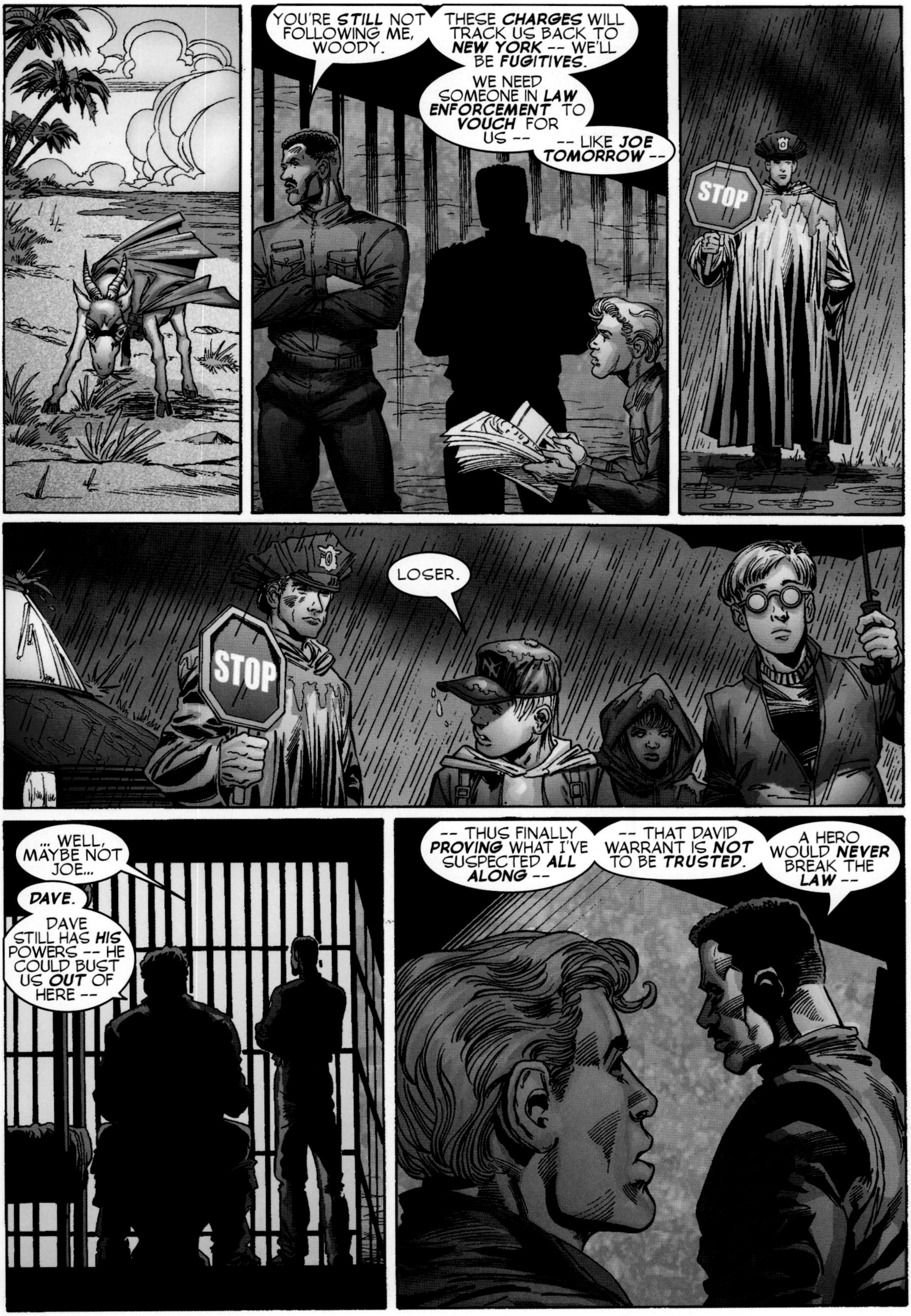

YOU'RE STILL NOT FOLLOWING ME, WOODY.
THESE CHARGES WILL TRACK US BACK TO NEW YORK -- WE'LL BE FUGITIVES.
WE NEED SOMEONE IN LAW ENFORCEMENT TO VOUCH FOR US --
-- LIKE JOE TOMORROW --
STOP
STOP
LOSER.
... WELL, MAYBE NOT JOE...
DAVE.
DAVE STILL HAS HIS POWERS -- HE COULD BUST US OUT OF HERE --
-- THUS FINALLY PROVING WHAT I'VE SUSPECTED ALL ALONG --
-- THAT DAVID WARRANT IS NOT TO BE TRUSTED.
A HERO WOULD NEVER BREAK THE LAW --

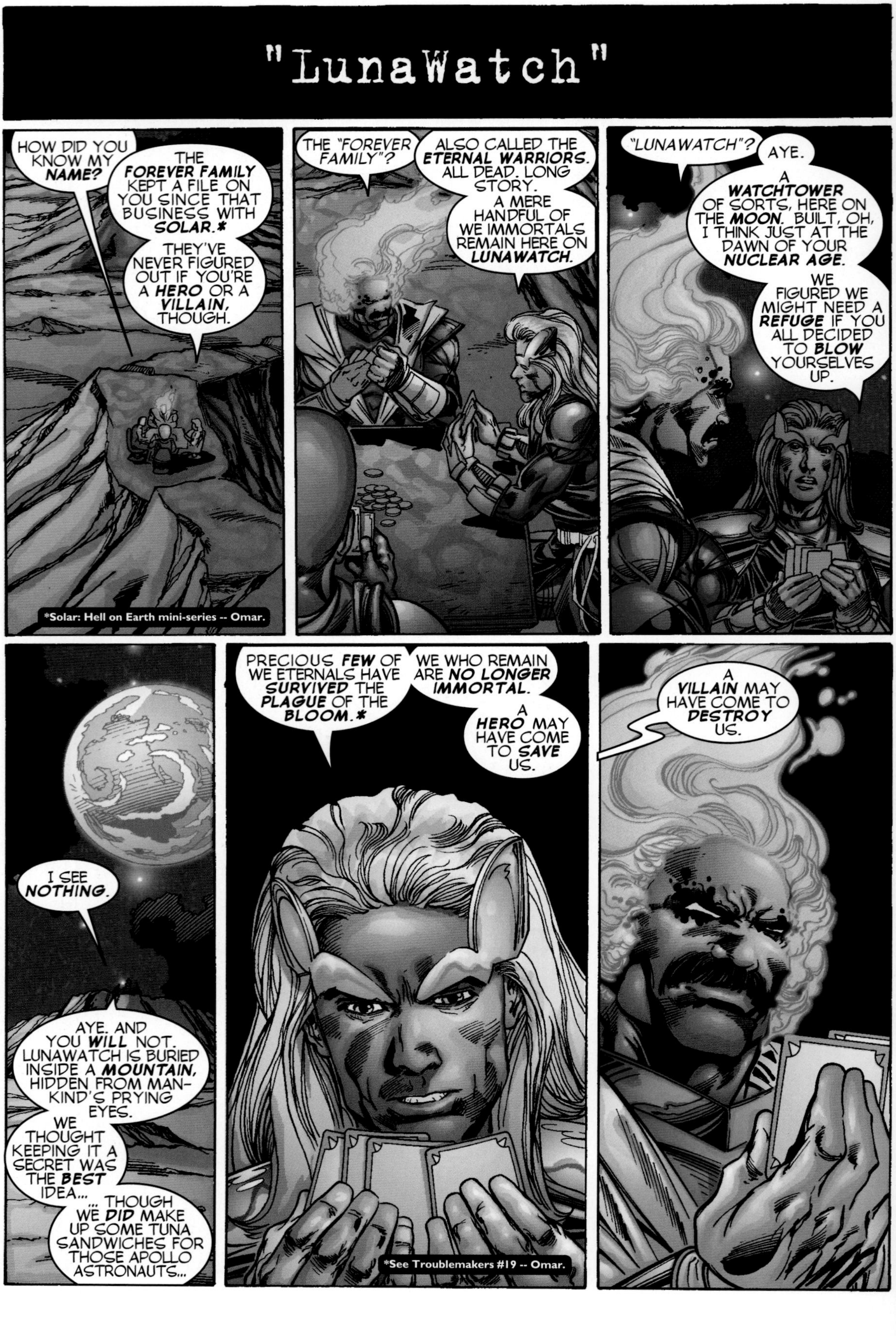
"LunaWatch"
HOW DID YOU KNOW MY NAME?
THE FOREVER FAMILY KEPT A FILE ON YOU SINCE THAT BUSINESS WITH SOLAR.*
THEY'VE NEVER FIGURED OUT IF YOU'RE A HERO OR A VILLAIN, THOUGH.
*Solar: Hell on Earth mini-series -- Omar.
THE "FOREVER FAMILY"?
ALSO CALLED THE ETERNAL WARRIORS. ALL DEAD. LONG STORY.
A MERE HANDFUL OF WE IMMORTALS REMAIN HERE ON LUNAWATCH.
"LUNAWATCH"?
AYE.
A WATCHTOWER OF SORTS, HERE ON THE MOON. BUILT, OH, I THINK JUST AT THE DAWN OF YOUR NUCLEAR AGE.
WE FIGURED WE MIGHT NEED A REFUGE IF YOU ALL DECIDED TO BLOW YOURSELVES UP.
I SEE NOTHING.
AYE. AND YOU WILL NOT. LUNAWATCH IS BURIED INSIDE A MOUNTAIN, HIDDEN FROM MAN-KIND'S PRYING EYES.
WE THOUGHT KEEPING IT A SECRET WAS THE BEST IDEA...
... THOUGH WE DID MAKE UP SOME TUNA SANDWICHES FOR THOSE APOLLO ASTRONAUTS...
PRECIOUS FEW OF WE ETERNALS HAVE SURVIVED THE PLAGUE OF THE BLOOM.*
WE WHO REMAIN ARE NO LONGER IMMORTAL.
A HERO MAY HAVE COME TO SAVE US.
*See Troublemakers #19 -- Omar.
A VILLAIN MAY HAVE COME TO DESTROY US.

"Shadows"

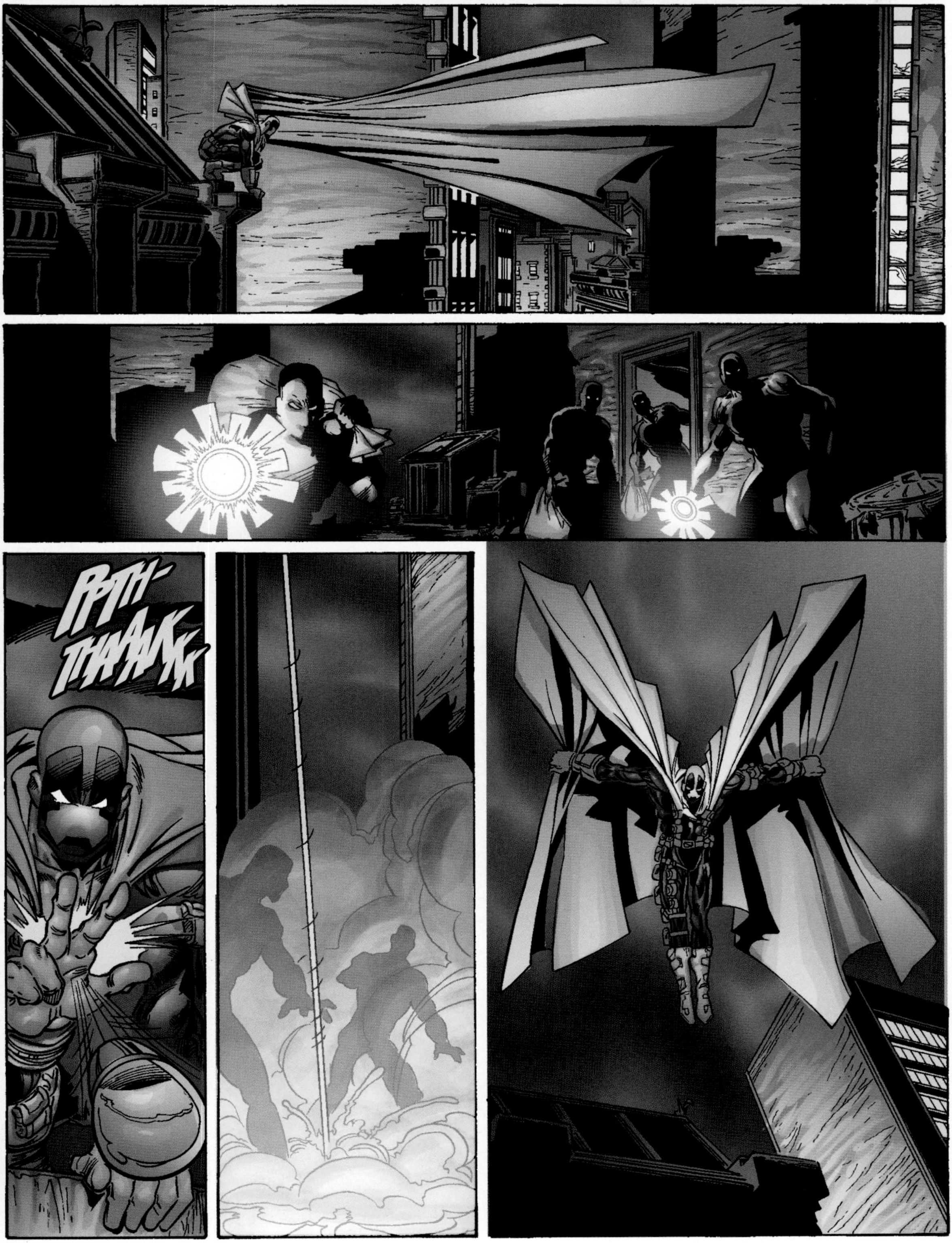
PPTH-
THAAAKK

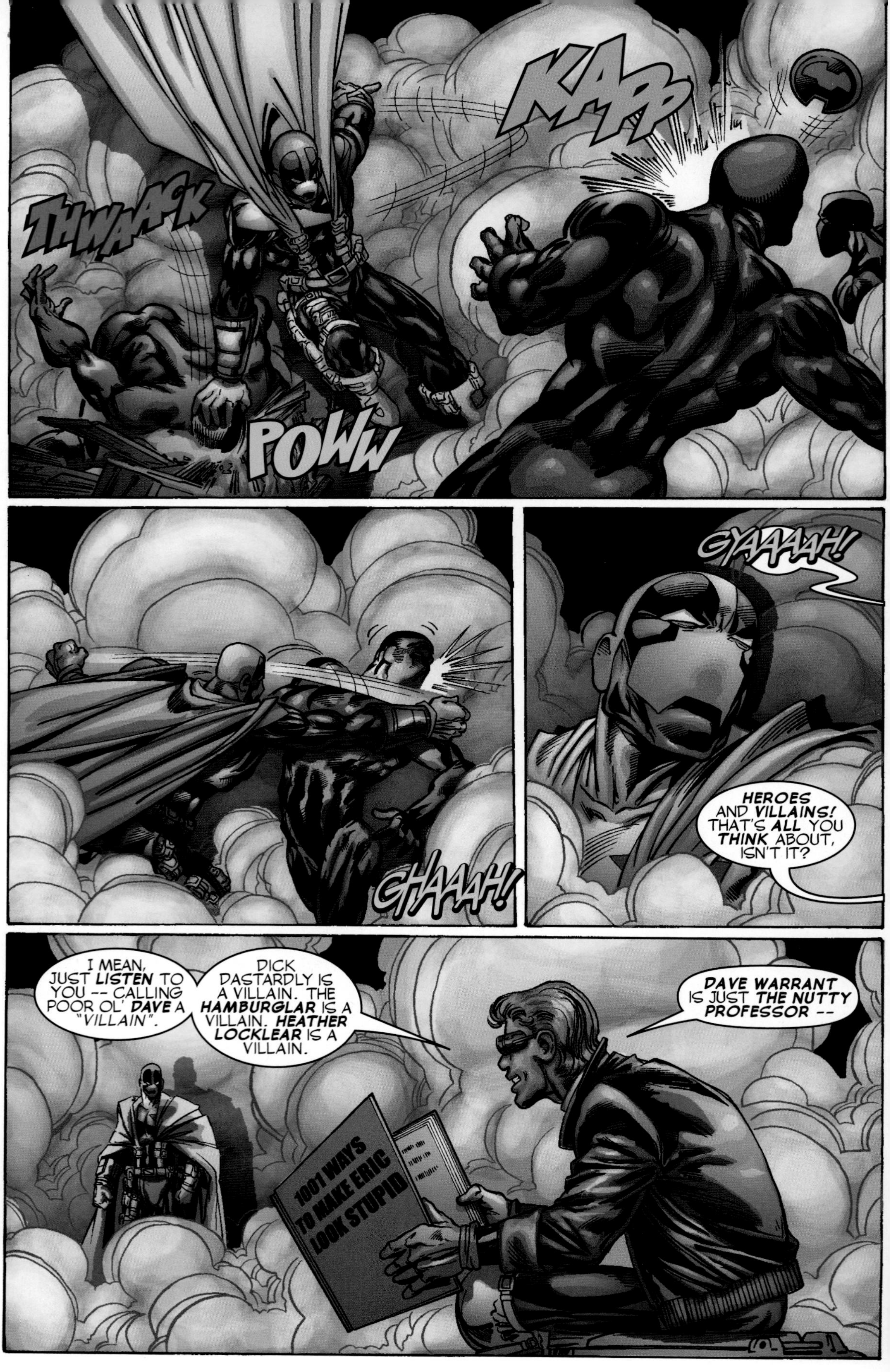
KAPP
THWAACK
POWW
CHAAAH!
GYAAAAH!
HEROES AND VILLAINS! THAT'S ALL YOU THINK ABOUT, ISN'T IT?
I MEAN, JUST LISTEN TO YOU -- CALLING POOR OL' DAVE A "VILLAIN".
DICK DASTARDLY IS A VILLAIN. THE HAMBURGLAR IS A VILLAIN. HEATHER LOCKLEAR IS A VILLAIN.
DAVE WARRANT IS JUST THE NUTTY PROFESSOR --
1001 WAYS TO MAKE ERIC LOOK STUPID

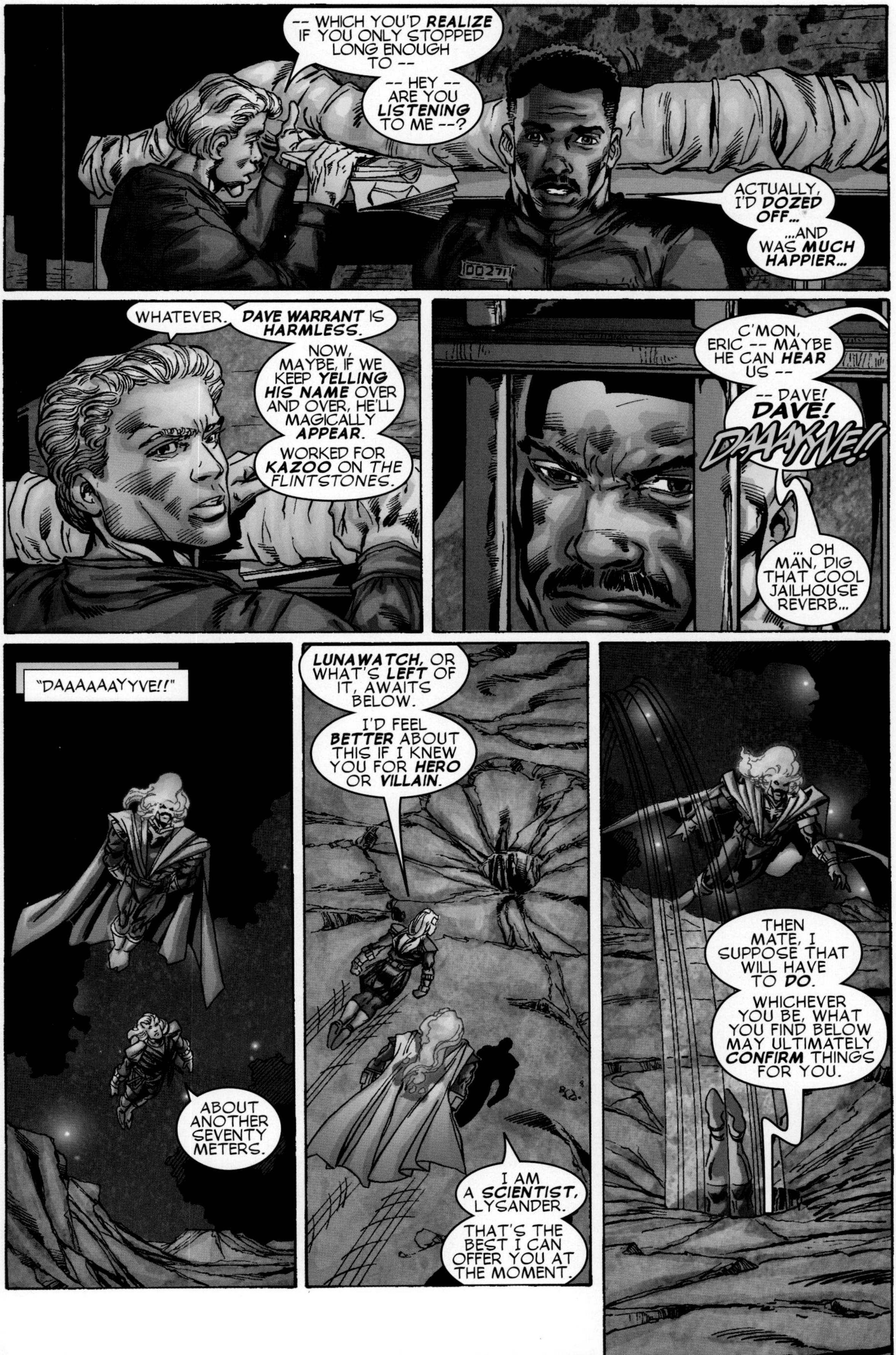
-- WHICH YOU'D REALIZE IF YOU ONLY STOPPED LONG ENOUGH TO --
-- HEY -- ARE YOU LISTENING TO ME --?
ACTUALLY, I'D DOZED OFF...
...AND WAS MUCH HAPPIER...
00271
WHATEVER. DAVE WARRANT IS HARMLESS.
NOW, MAYBE, IF WE KEEP YELLING HIS NAME OVER AND OVER, HE'LL MAGICALLY APPEAR.
WORKED FOR KAZOO ON THE FLINTSTONES.
C'MON, ERIC -- MAYBE HE CAN HEAR US --
-- DAVE! DAVE! DAAAYYVE!!
... OH MAN, DIG THAT COOL JAILHOUSE REVERB...
"DAAAAAAYYVE!!"
ABOUT ANOTHER SEVENTY METERS.
LUNAWATCH, OR WHAT'S LEFT OF IT, AWAITS BELOW.
I'D FEEL BETTER ABOUT THIS IF I KNEW YOU FOR HERO OR VILLAIN.
I AM A SCIENTIST, LYSANDER.
THAT'S THE BEST I CAN OFFER YOU AT THE MOMENT.
THEN MATE, I SUPPOSE THAT WILL HAVE TO DO.
WHICHEVER YOU BE, WHAT YOU FIND BELOW MAY ULTIMATELY CONFIRM THINGS FOR YOU.

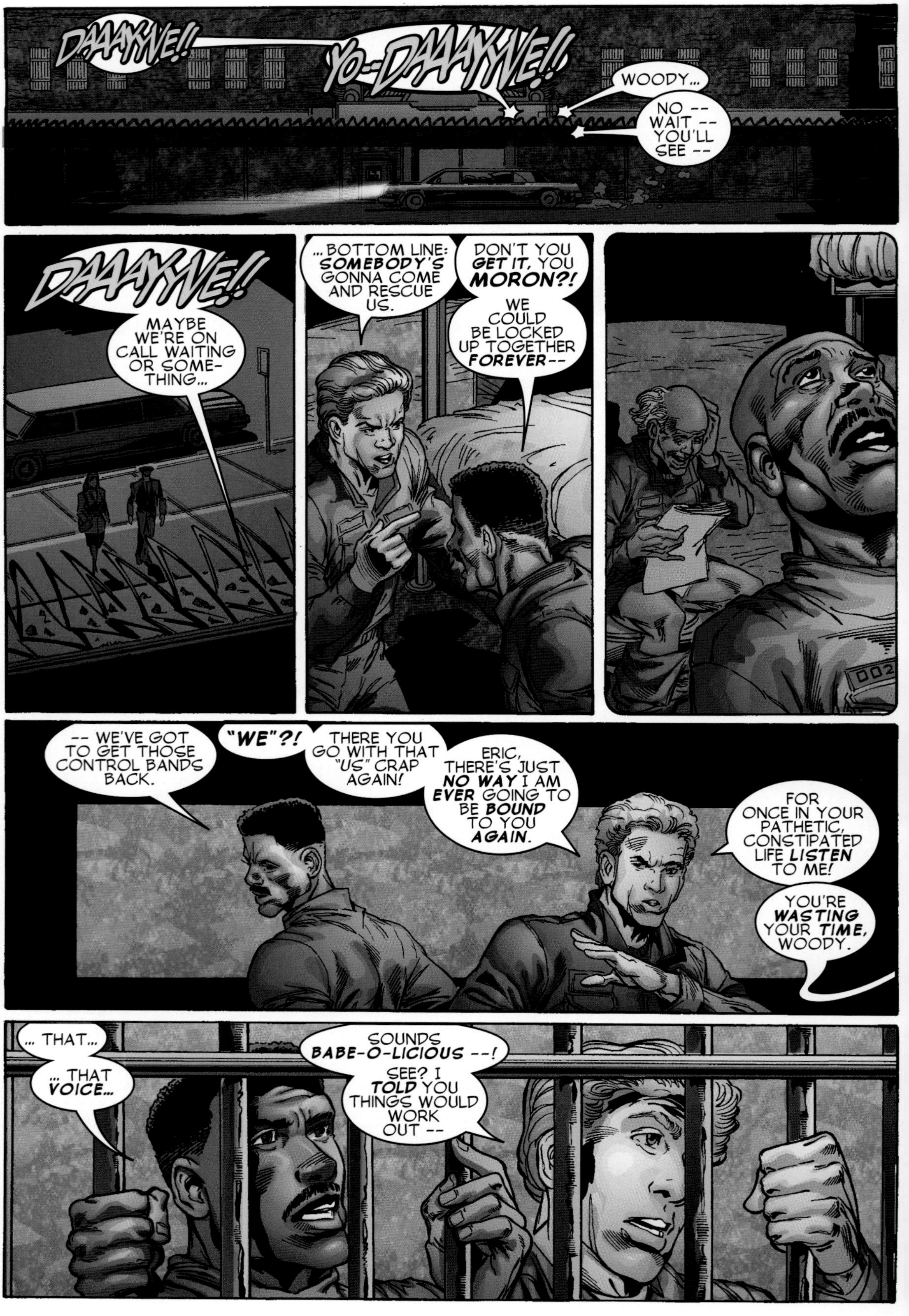
DAAAYYNE!!
YO-DAAAYYNE!!
WOODY...
NO -- WAIT -- YOU'LL SEE --
DAAAYYNE!!
MAYBE WE'RE ON CALL WAITING OR SOME-THING...
...BOTTOM LINE: SOMEBODY'S GONNA COME AND RESCUE US.
DON'T YOU GET IT, YOU MORON?!
WE COULD BE LOCKED UP TOGETHER FOREVER--
-- WE'VE GOT TO GET THOSE CONTROL BANDS BACK.
"WE"?!
THERE YOU GO WITH THAT "US" CRAP AGAIN!
ERIC, THERE'S JUST NO WAY I AM EVER GOING TO BE BOUND TO YOU AGAIN.
FOR ONCE IN YOUR PATHETIC, CONSTIPATED LIFE LISTEN TO ME!
YOU'RE WASTING YOUR TIME, WOODY.
... THAT...
... THAT VOICE...
SOUNDS BABE-O-LICIOUS --!
SEE? I TOLD YOU THINGS WOULD WORK OUT --

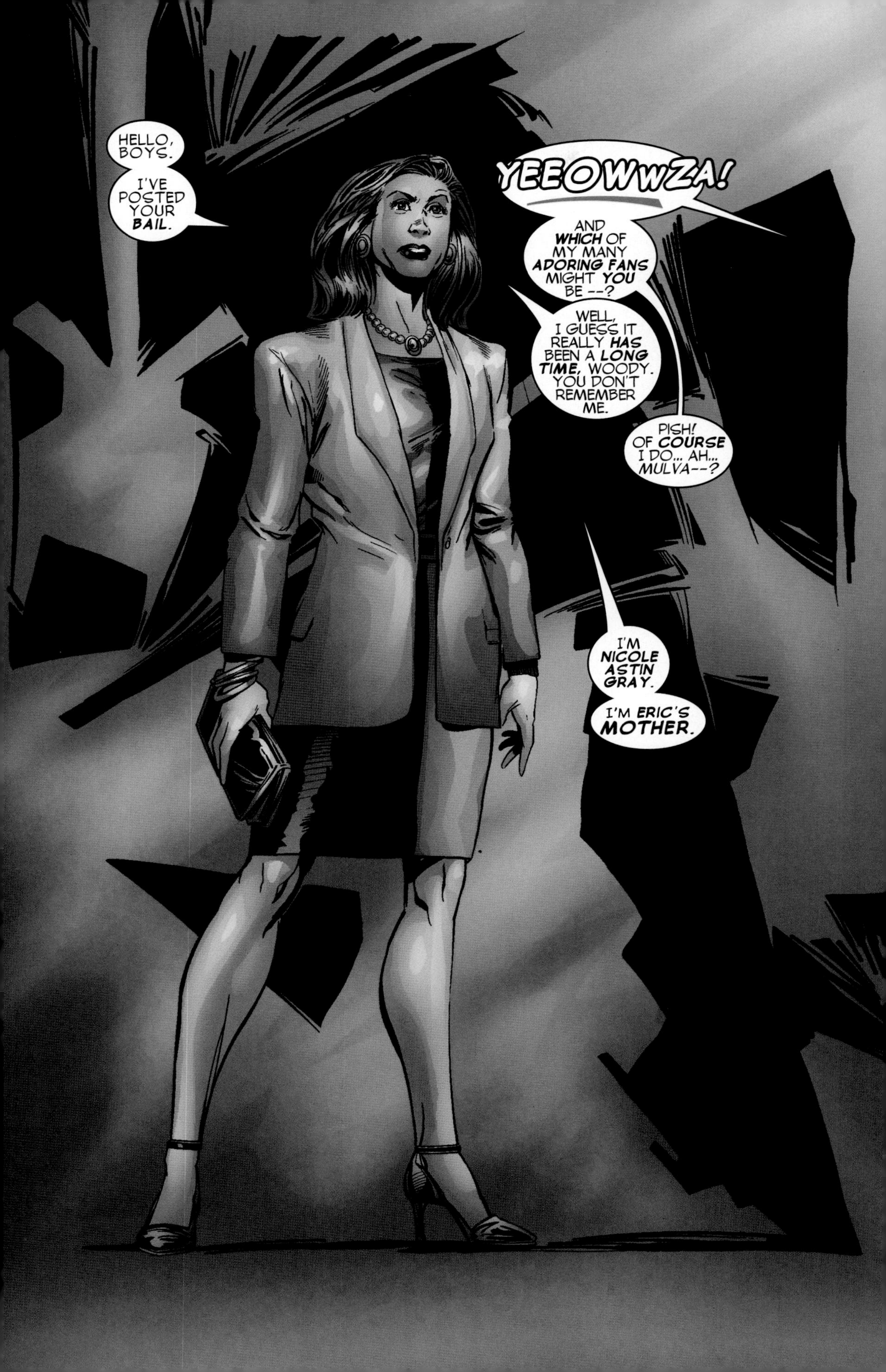
HELLO, BOYS.
I'VE POSTED YOUR BAIL.
YEEOWWWZA!
AND WHICH OF MY MANY ADORING FANS MIGHT YOU BE --?
WELL, I GUESS IT REALLY HAS BEEN A LONG TIME, WOODY. YOU DON'T REMEMBER ME.
PISH! OF COURSE I DO... AH... MULVA--?
I'M NICOLE ASTIN GRAY.
I'M ERIC'S MOTHER.

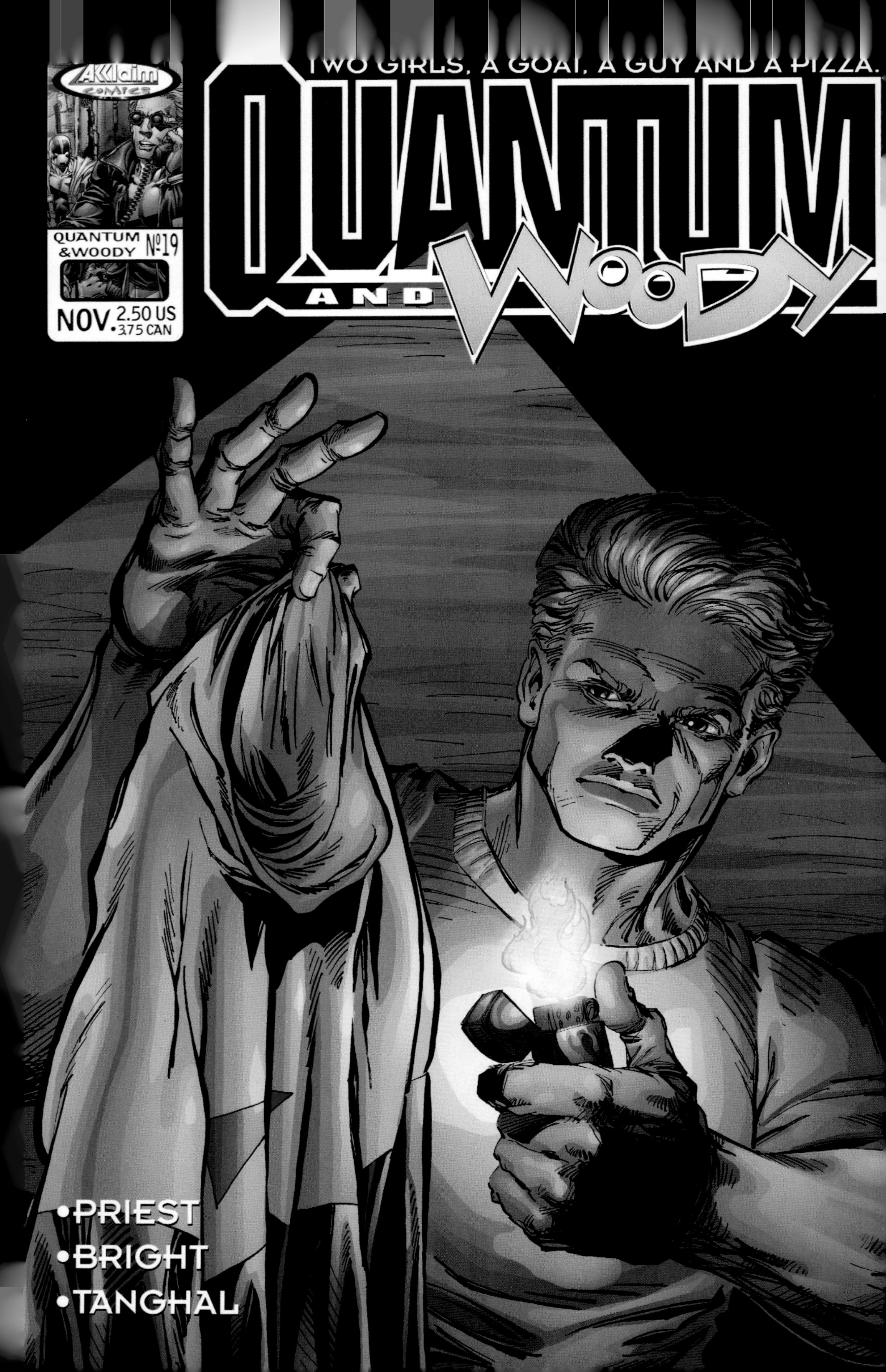

TWO GIRLS, A GOAT, A GUY AND A PIZZA.
QUANTUM AND WOODY
ACCLAIM COMICS
QUANTUM &WOODY №19
NOV. 2.50 US •3.75 CAN
•PRIEST
•BRIGHT
•TANGHAL

"The Devil and Miss Lucy"

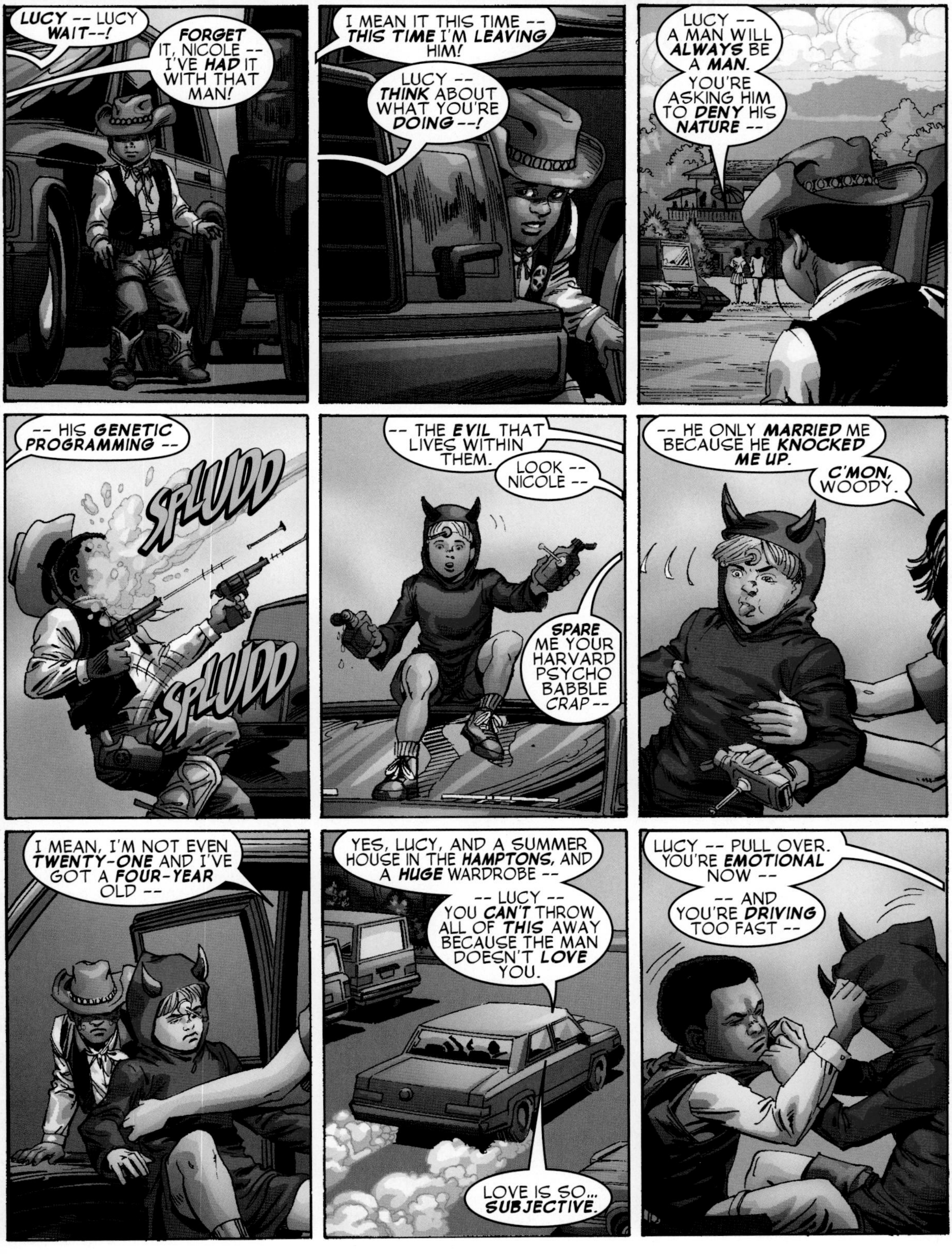
LUCY -- LUCY WAIT--!
FORGET IT, NICOLE -- I'VE HAD IT WITH THAT MAN!
I MEAN IT THIS TIME -- THIS TIME I'M LEAVING HIM!
LUCY -- THINK ABOUT WHAT YOU'RE DOING --!
LUCY -- A MAN WILL ALWAYS BE A MAN.
YOU'RE ASKING HIM TO DENY HIS NATURE --
-- HIS GENETIC PROGRAMMING --
SPLUDD
SPLUDD
-- THE EVIL THAT LIVES WITHIN THEM.
LOOK -- NICOLE --
SPARE ME YOUR HARVARD PSYCHO BABBLE CRAP --
-- HE ONLY MARRIED ME BECAUSE HE KNOCKED ME UP.
C'MON, WOODY.
I MEAN, I'M NOT EVEN TWENTY-ONE AND I'VE GOT A FOUR-YEAR OLD --
YES, LUCY, AND A SUMMER HOUSE IN THE HAMPTONS, AND A HUGE WARDROBE --
-- LUCY -- YOU CAN'T THROW ALL OF THIS AWAY BECAUSE THE MAN DOESN'T LOVE YOU.
LOVE IS SO... SUBJECTIVE.
LUCY -- PULL OVER. YOU'RE EMOTIONAL NOW --
-- AND YOU'RE DRIVING TOO FAST --

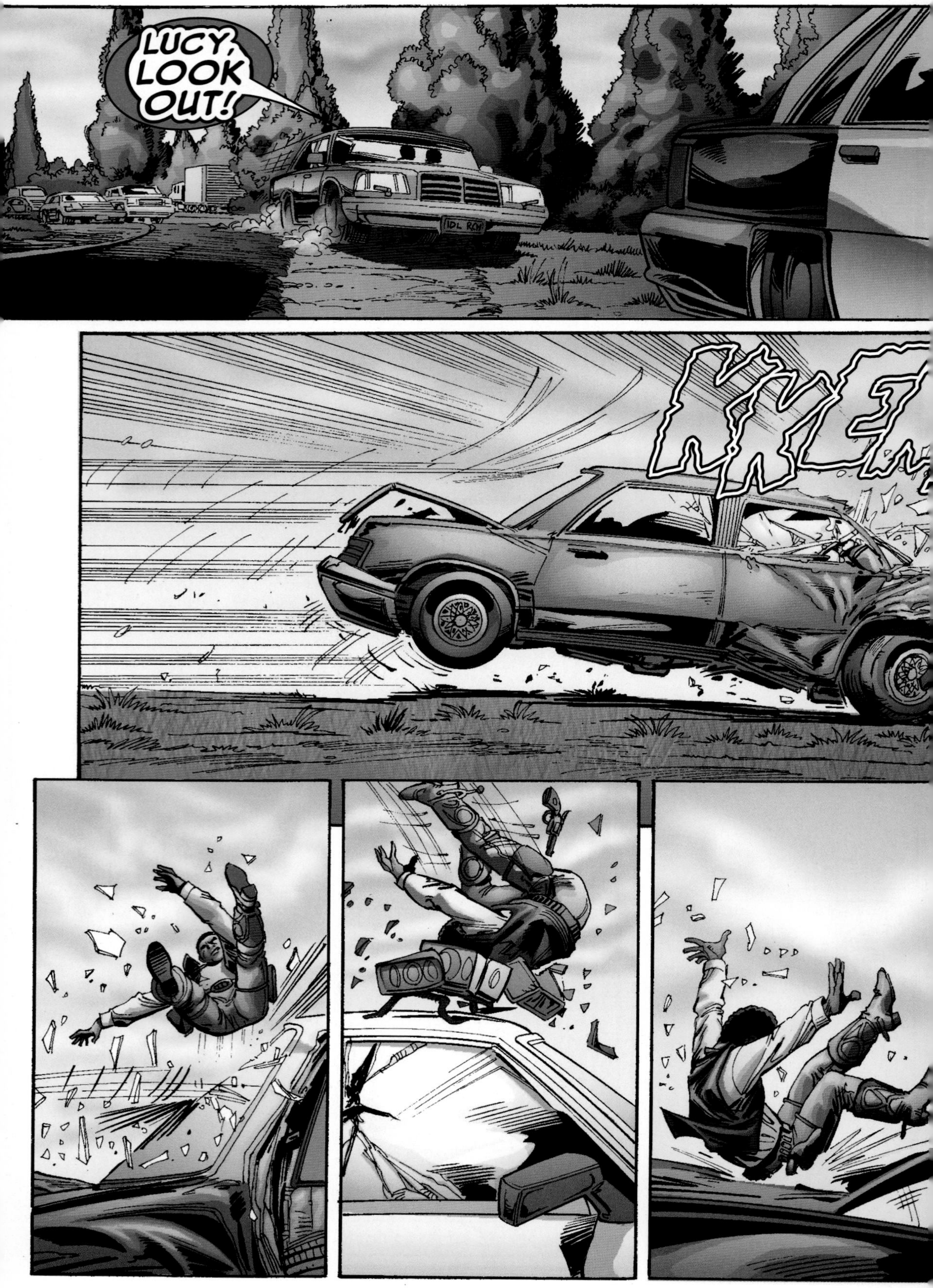
LUCY, LOOK OUT!

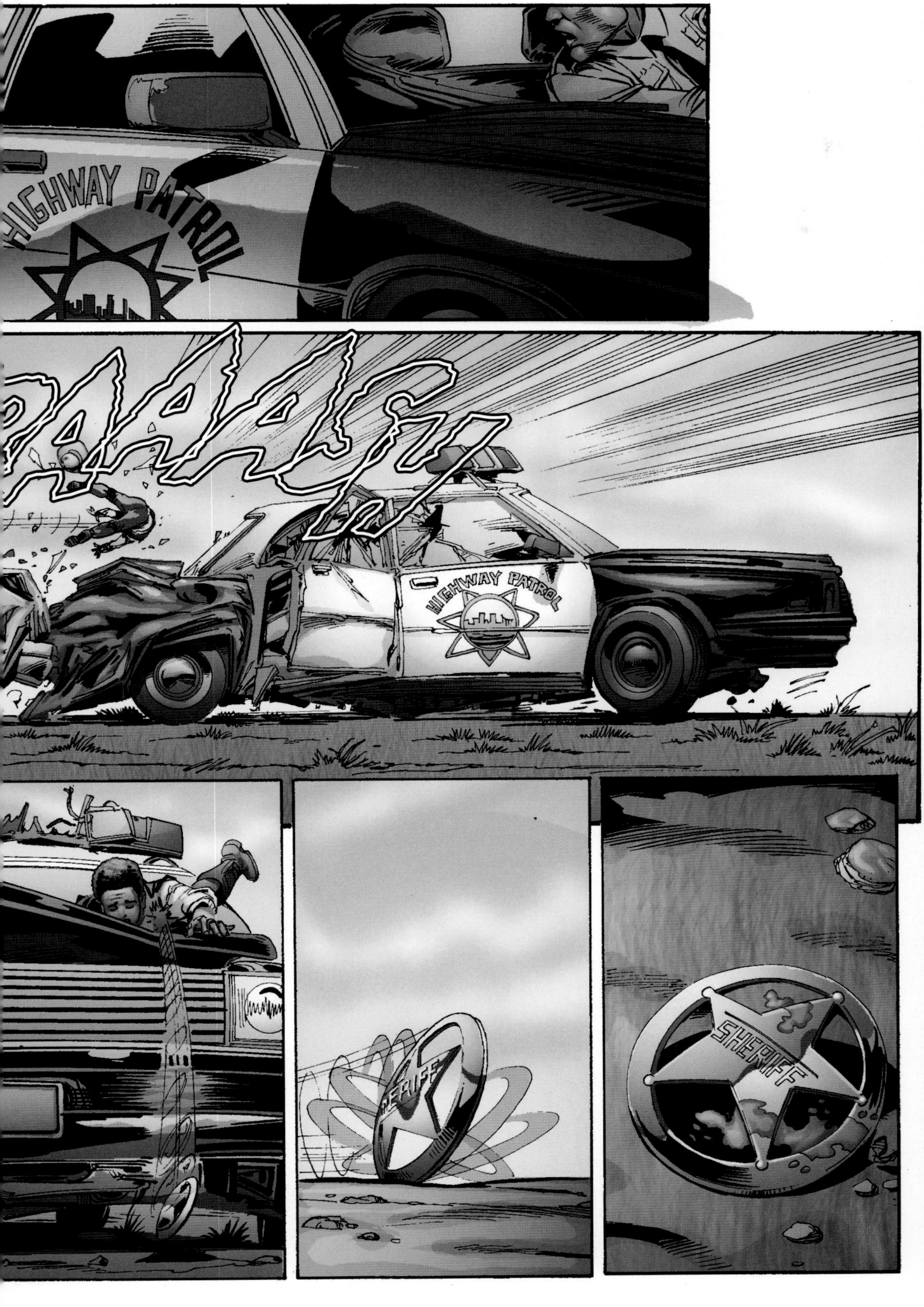
HIGHWAY PATROL
HIGHWAY PATROL
SHERIFF

"Nicole Austin Gray"

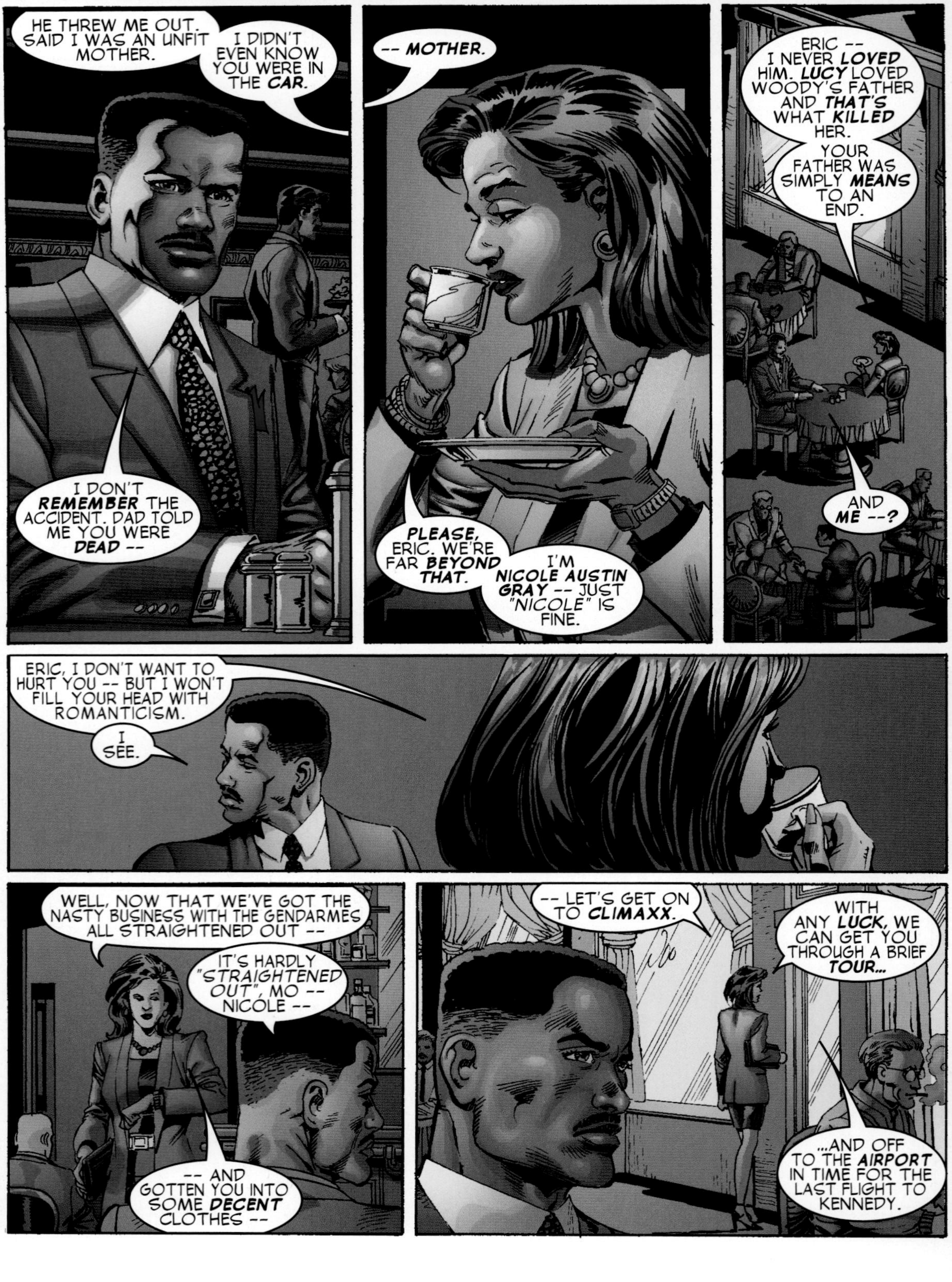
HE THREW ME OUT. SAID I WAS AN UNFIT MOTHER.
I DIDN'T EVEN KNOW YOU WERE IN THE CAR.
I DON'T REMEMBER THE ACCIDENT. DAD TOLD ME YOU WERE DEAD --
-- MOTHER.
PLEASE, ERIC. WE'RE FAR BEYOND THAT.
I'M NICOLE AUSTIN GRAY -- JUST "NICOLE" IS FINE.
ERIC -- I NEVER LOVED HIM. LUCY LOVED WOODY'S FATHER AND THAT'S WHAT KILLED HER.
YOUR FATHER WAS SIMPLY MEANS TO AN END.
AND ME --?
ERIC, I DON'T WANT TO HURT YOU -- BUT I WON'T FILL YOUR HEAD WITH ROMANTICISM.
I SEE.
WELL, NOW THAT WE'VE GOT THE NASTY BUSINESS WITH THE GENDARMES ALL STRAIGHTENED OUT --
IT'S HARDLY "STRAIGHTENED OUT", MO -- NICOLE --
-- AND GOTTEN YOU INTO SOME DECENT CLOTHES --
-- LET'S GET ON TO CLIMAXX.
WITH ANY LUCK, WE CAN GET YOU THROUGH A BRIEF TOUR...
...AND OFF TO THE AIRPORT IN TIME FOR THE LAST FLIGHT TO KENNEDY.

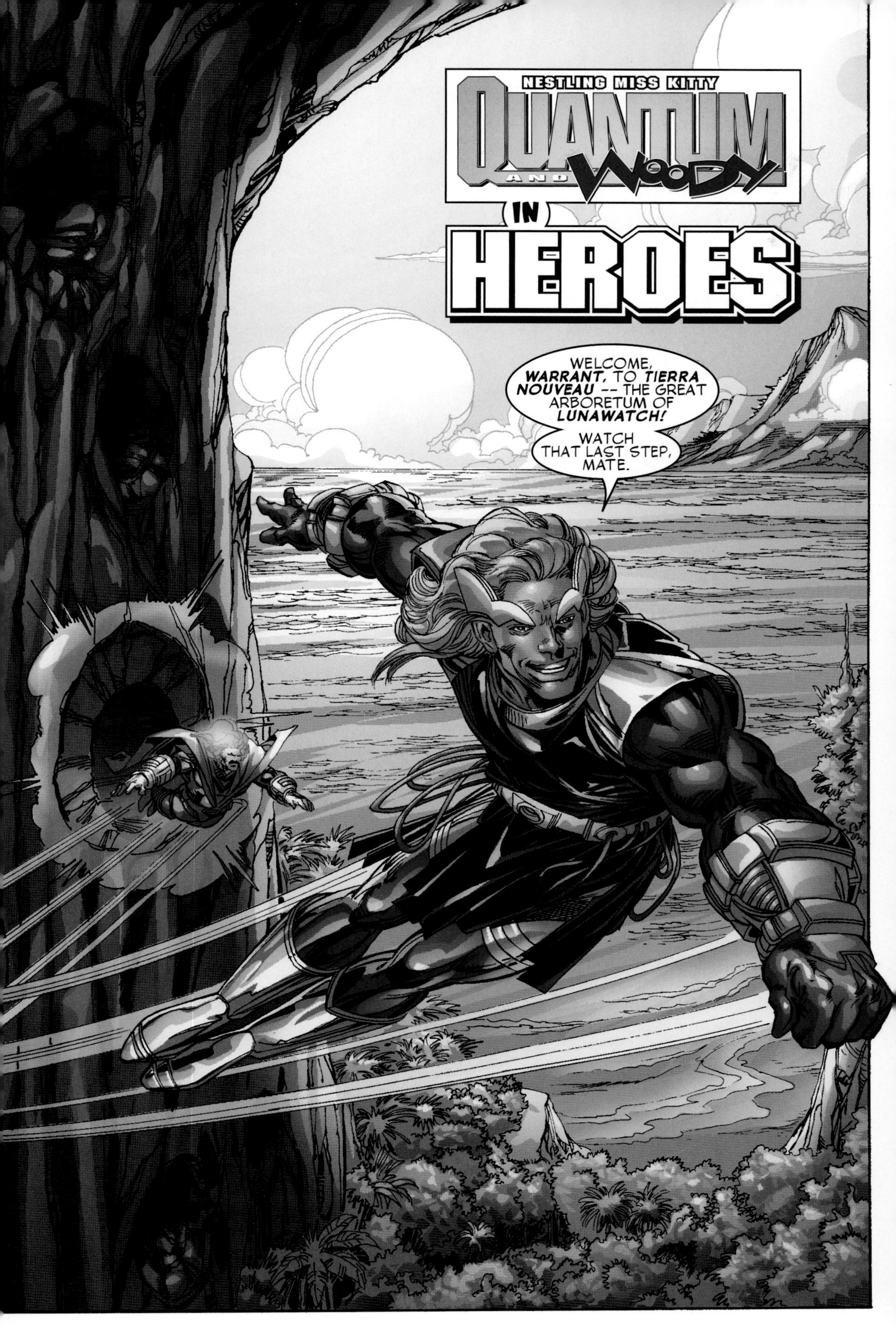

NESTLING MISS KITTY
QUANTUM AND WOODY
IN
HEROES
WELCOME, *WARRANT,* TO *TIERRA NOUVEAU* -- THE GREAT ARBORETUM OF *LUNAWATCH!*
WATCH THAT LAST STEP, MATE.

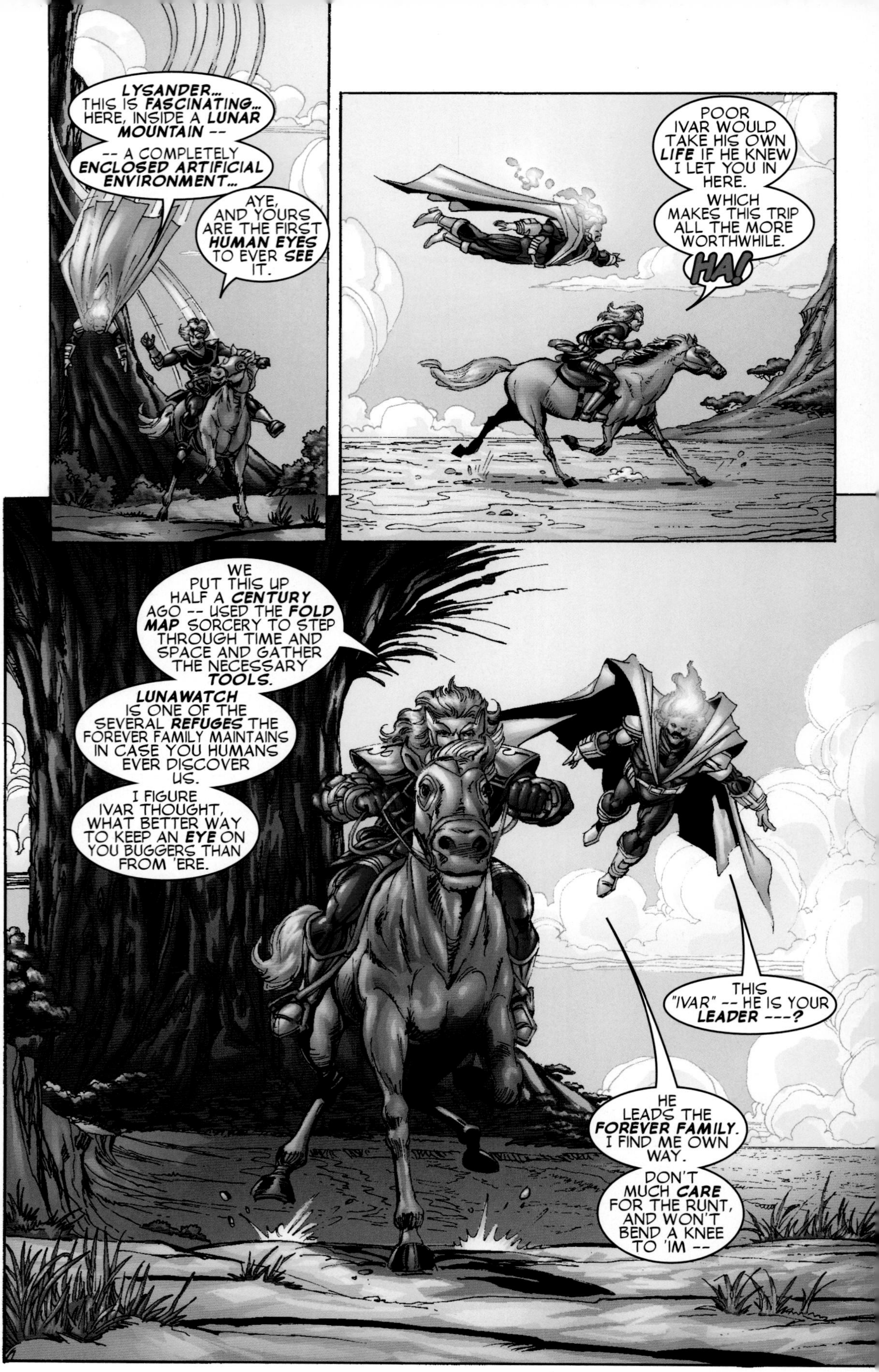
LYSANDER... THIS IS FASCINATING... HERE, INSIDE A LUNAR MOUNTAIN --
-- A COMPLETELY ENCLOSED ARTIFICIAL ENVIRONMENT...
AYE, AND YOURS ARE THE FIRST HUMAN EYES TO EVER SEE IT.
POOR IVAR WOULD TAKE HIS OWN LIFE IF HE KNEW I LET YOU IN HERE.
WHICH MAKES THIS TRIP ALL THE MORE WORTHWHILE.
HA!
WE PUT THIS UP HALF A CENTURY AGO -- USED THE FOLD MAP SORCERY TO STEP THROUGH TIME AND SPACE AND GATHER THE NECESSARY TOOLS.
LUNAWATCH IS ONE OF THE SEVERAL REFUGES THE FOREVER FAMILY MAINTAINS IN CASE YOU HUMANS EVER DISCOVER US.
I FIGURE IVAR THOUGHT, WHAT BETTER WAY TO KEEP AN EYE ON YOU BUGGERS THAN FROM 'ERE.
THIS "IVAR" -- HE IS YOUR LEADER ---?
HE LEADS THE FOREVER FAMILY. I FIND ME OWN WAY.
DON'T MUCH CARE FOR THE RUNT, AND WON'T BEND A KNEE TO 'IM --

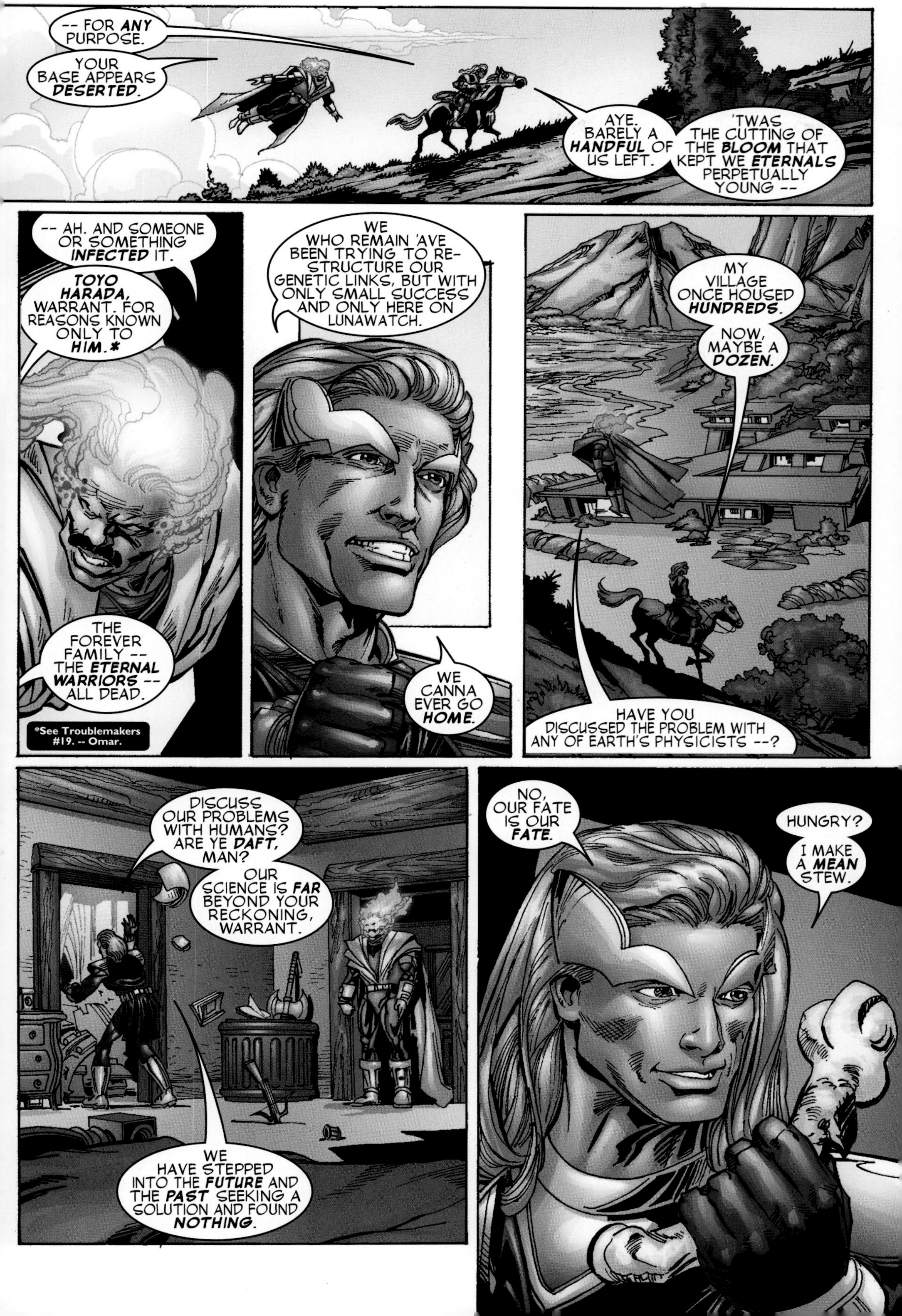

-- FOR ANY PURPOSE.
YOUR BASE APPEARS DESERTED.
AYE. BARELY A HANDFUL OF US LEFT.
'TWAS THE CUTTING OF THE BLOOM THAT KEPT WE ETERNALS PERPETUALLY YOUNG --
-- AH. AND SOMEONE OR SOMETHING INFECTED IT.
TOYO HARADA, WARRANT. FOR REASONS KNOWN ONLY TO HIM.*
THE FOREVER FAMILY -- THE ETERNAL WARRIORS -- ALL DEAD.
*See Troublemakers #19. -- Omar.
WE WHO REMAIN 'AVE BEEN TRYING TO RE-STRUCTURE OUR GENETIC LINKS, BUT WITH ONLY SMALL SUCCESS AND ONLY HERE ON LUNAWATCH.
WE CANNA EVER GO HOME.
MY VILLAGE ONCE HOUSED HUNDREDS.
NOW, MAYBE A DOZEN.
HAVE YOU DISCUSSED THE PROBLEM WITH ANY OF EARTH'S PHYSICISTS --?
DISCUSS OUR PROBLEMS WITH HUMANS? ARE YE DAFT, MAN?
OUR SCIENCE IS FAR BEYOND YOUR RECKONING, WARRANT.
WE HAVE STEPPED INTO THE FUTURE AND THE PAST SEEKING A SOLUTION AND FOUND NOTHING.
NO, OUR FATE IS OUR FATE.
HUNGRY?
I MAKE A MEAN STEW.

"The End (Part 1)"

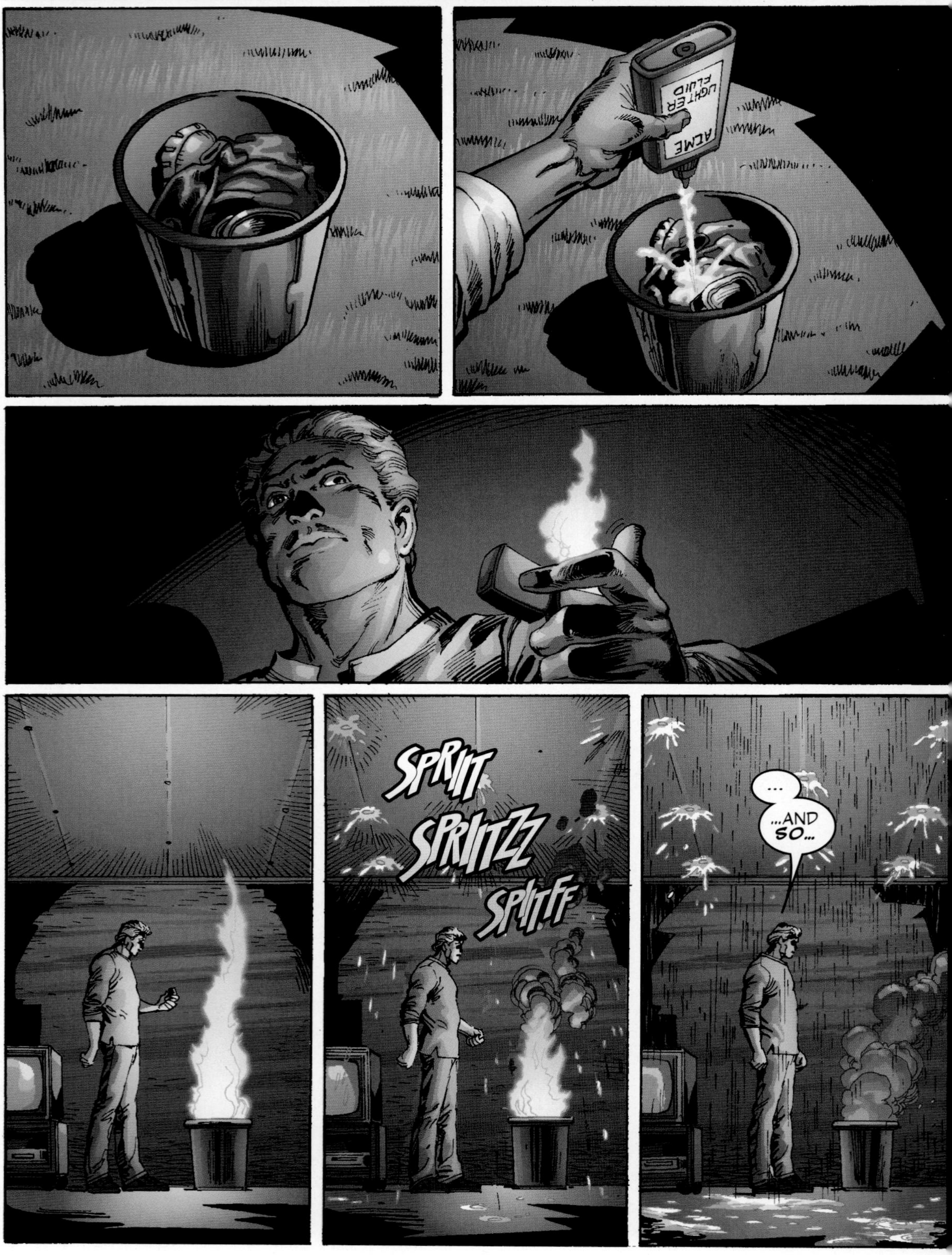
ACME
LIGHTER FLUID
SPRIIT
SPRIITZZ
SPIITFF
...
...AND SO...

"The End (Part 2)"

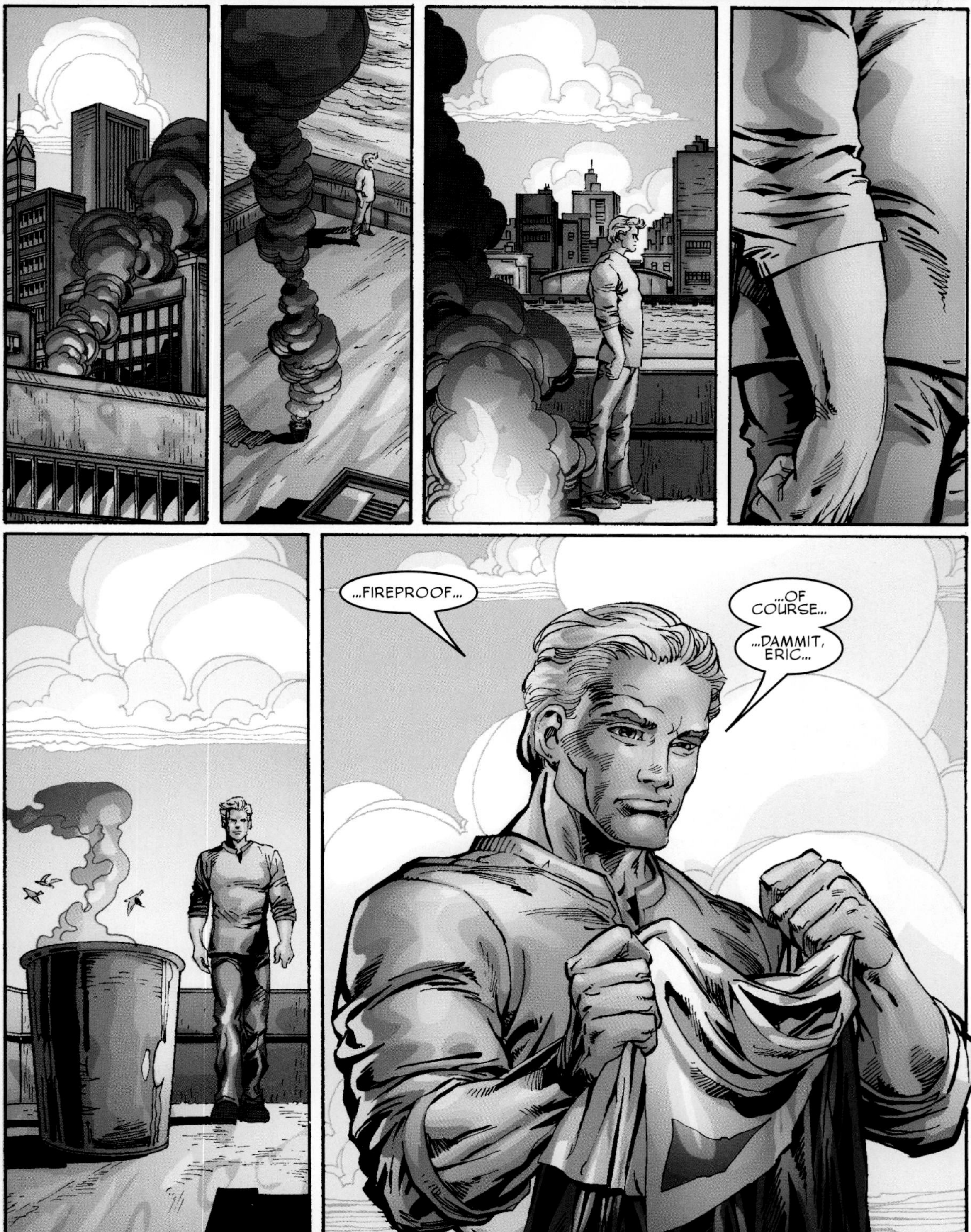
...FIREPROOF...
...OF COURSE...
...DAMMIT, ERIC...

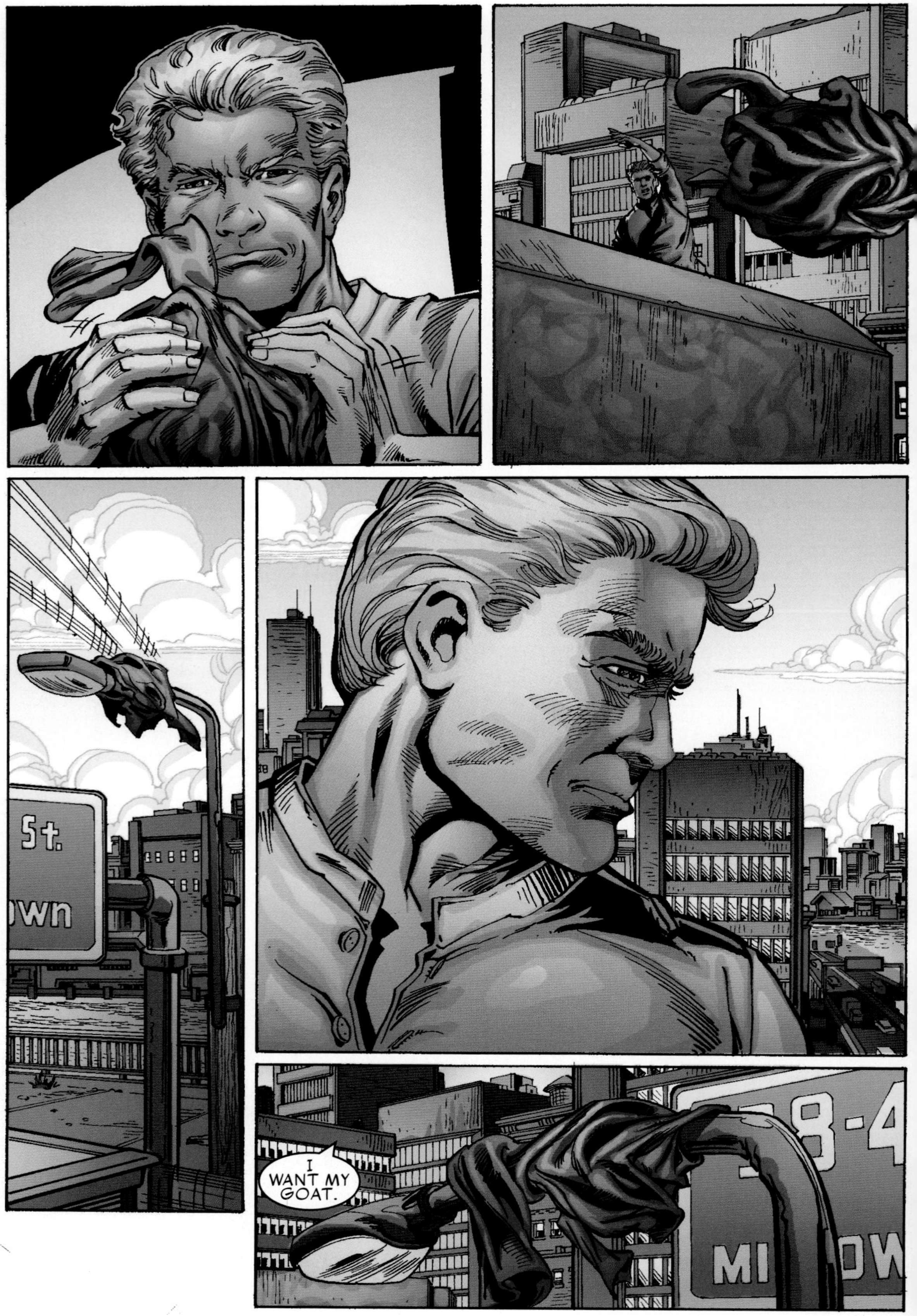
I WANT MY GOAT.

"Cats"

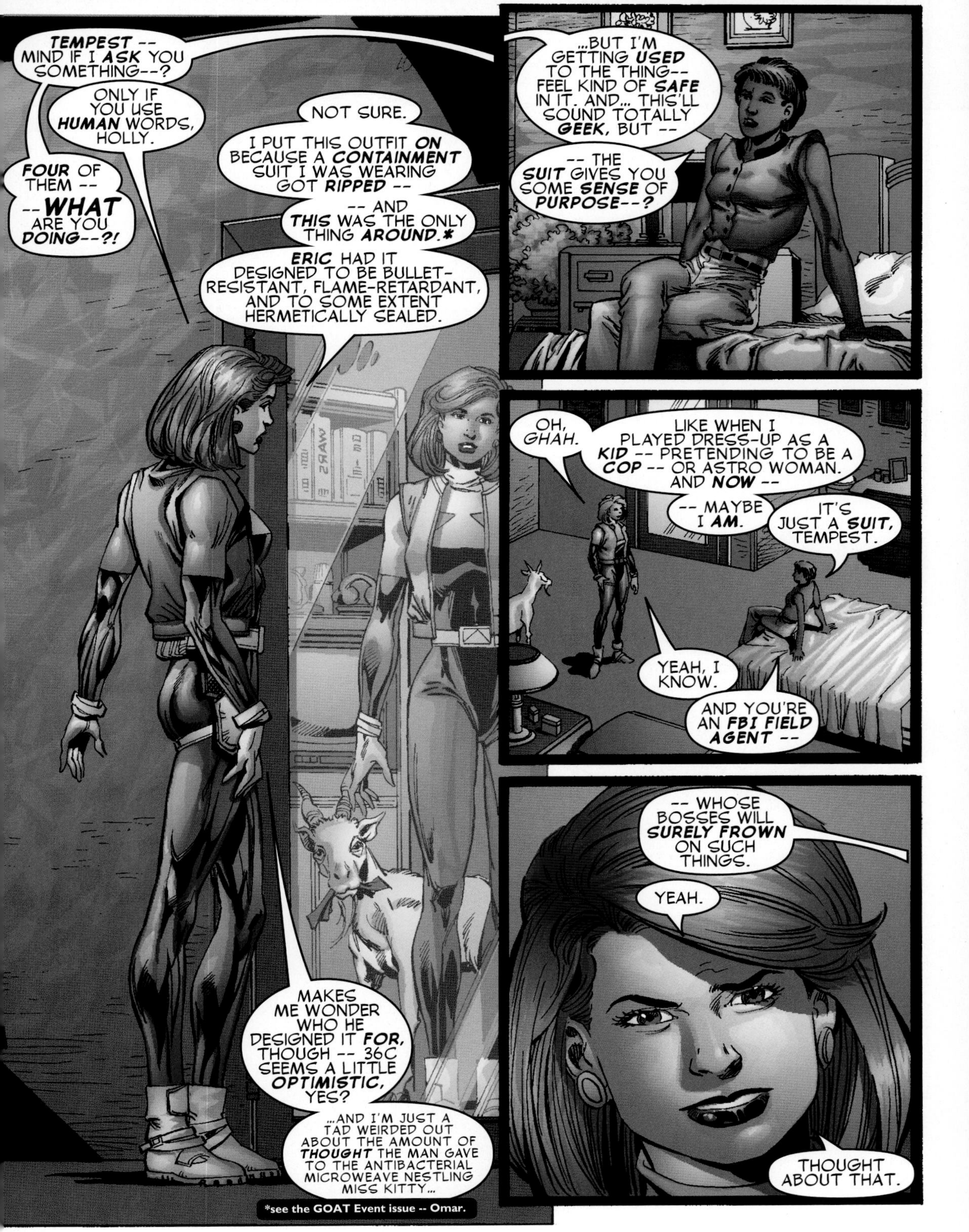

TEMPEST -- MIND IF I ASK YOU SOMETHING--?
ONLY IF YOU USE HUMAN WORDS, HOLLY.
FOUR OF THEM --
--WHAT ARE YOU DOING--?!
NOT SURE.
I PUT THIS OUTFIT ON BECAUSE A CONTAINMENT SUIT I WAS WEARING GOT RIPPED --
-- AND THIS WAS THE ONLY THING AROUND.*
ERIC HAD IT DESIGNED TO BE BULLET-RESISTANT, FLAME-RETARDANT, AND TO SOME EXTENT HERMETICALLY SEALED.
MAKES ME WONDER WHO HE DESIGNED IT FOR, THOUGH -- 36C SEEMS A LITTLE OPTIMISTIC, YES?
...AND I'M JUST A TAD WEIRDED OUT ABOUT THE AMOUNT OF THOUGHT THE MAN GAVE TO THE ANTIBACTERIAL MICROWEAVE NESTLING MISS KITTY...
*see the GOAT Event issue -- Omar.
...BUT I'M GETTING USED TO THE THING-- FEEL KIND OF SAFE IN IT. AND... THIS'LL SOUND TOTALLY GEEK, BUT --
-- THE SUIT GIVES YOU SOME SENSE OF PURPOSE--?
OH, GHAH.
LIKE WHEN I PLAYED DRESS-UP AS A KID -- PRETENDING TO BE A COP -- OR ASTRO WOMAN. AND NOW --
-- MAYBE I AM.
IT'S JUST A SUIT, TEMPEST.
YEAH, I KNOW.
AND YOU'RE AN FBI FIELD AGENT --
-- WHOSE BOSSES WILL SURELY FROWN ON SUCH THINGS.
YEAH.
THOUGHT ABOUT THAT.

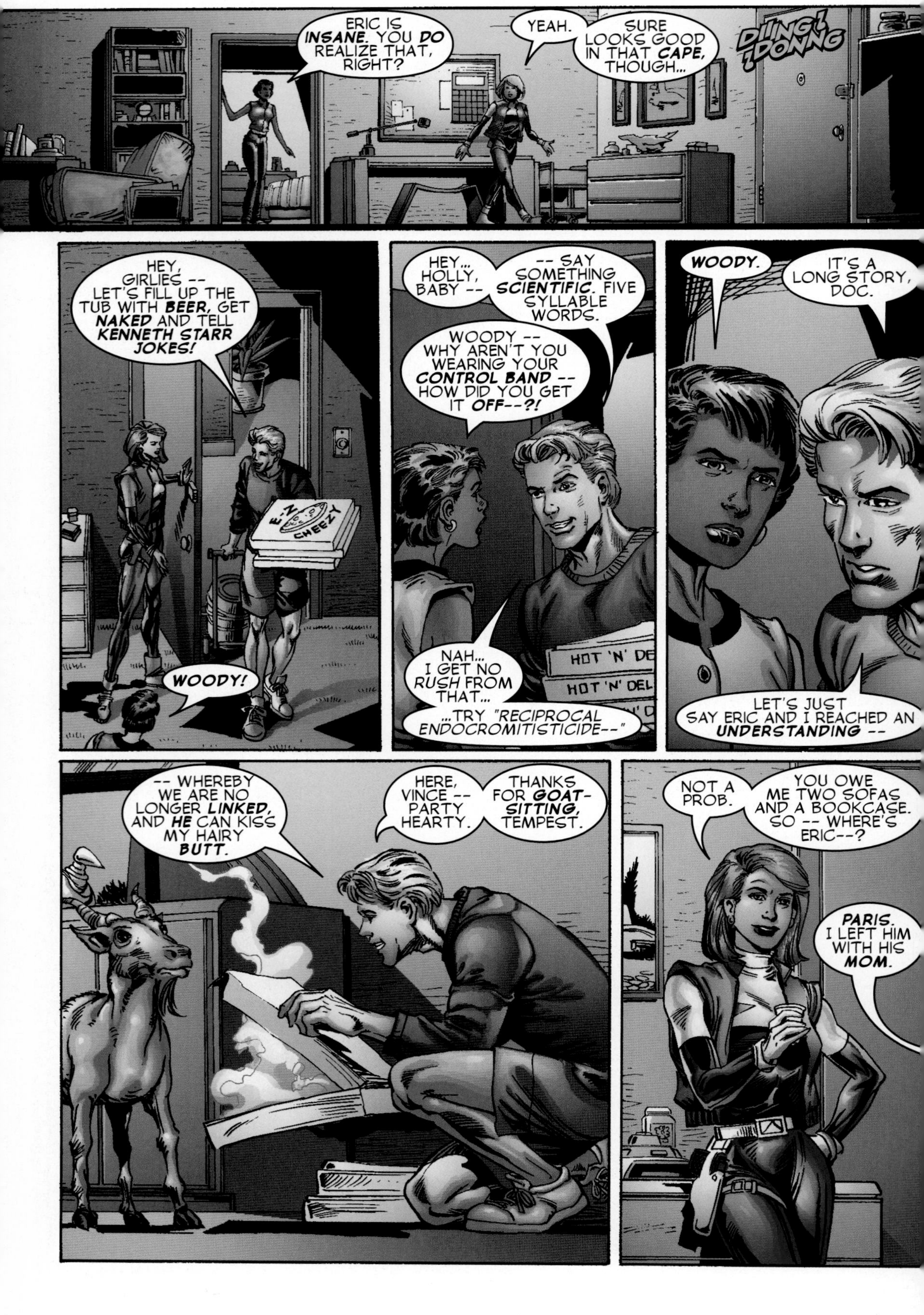

ERIC IS **INSANE**. YOU **DO** REALIZE THAT, RIGHT?
YEAH.
SURE LOOKS GOOD IN THAT **CAPE**, THOUGH...
DIING! DONNG
HEY, GIRLIES -- LET'S FILL UP THE TUB WITH **BEER**, GET **NAKED** AND TELL **KENNETH STARR JOKES!**
E-Z CHEEZY
WOODY!
HEY... HOLLY, BABY --
-- SAY SOMETHING **SCIENTIFIC**. FIVE SYLLABLE WORDS.
WOODY -- WHY AREN'T YOU WEARING YOUR **CONTROL BAND** -- HOW DID YOU GET IT **OFF**--?!
NAH... I GET NO *RUSH* FROM THAT...
...TRY *"RECIPROCAL ENDOCROMITISTICIDE--"*
HOT 'N' DE
HOT 'N' DEL
WOODY.
IT'S A LONG STORY, DOC.
LET'S JUST SAY ERIC AND I REACHED AN **UNDERSTANDING** --
-- WHEREBY WE ARE NO LONGER **LINKED**, AND **HE** CAN KISS MY HAIRY **BUTT**.
HERE, VINCE -- PARTY HEARTY.
THANKS FOR **GOAT-SITTING**, TEMPEST.
NOT A PROB.
YOU OWE ME TWO SOFAS AND A BOOKCASE. SO -- WHERE'S ERIC--?
PARIS. I LEFT HIM WITH HIS **MOM**.

"The Associate"

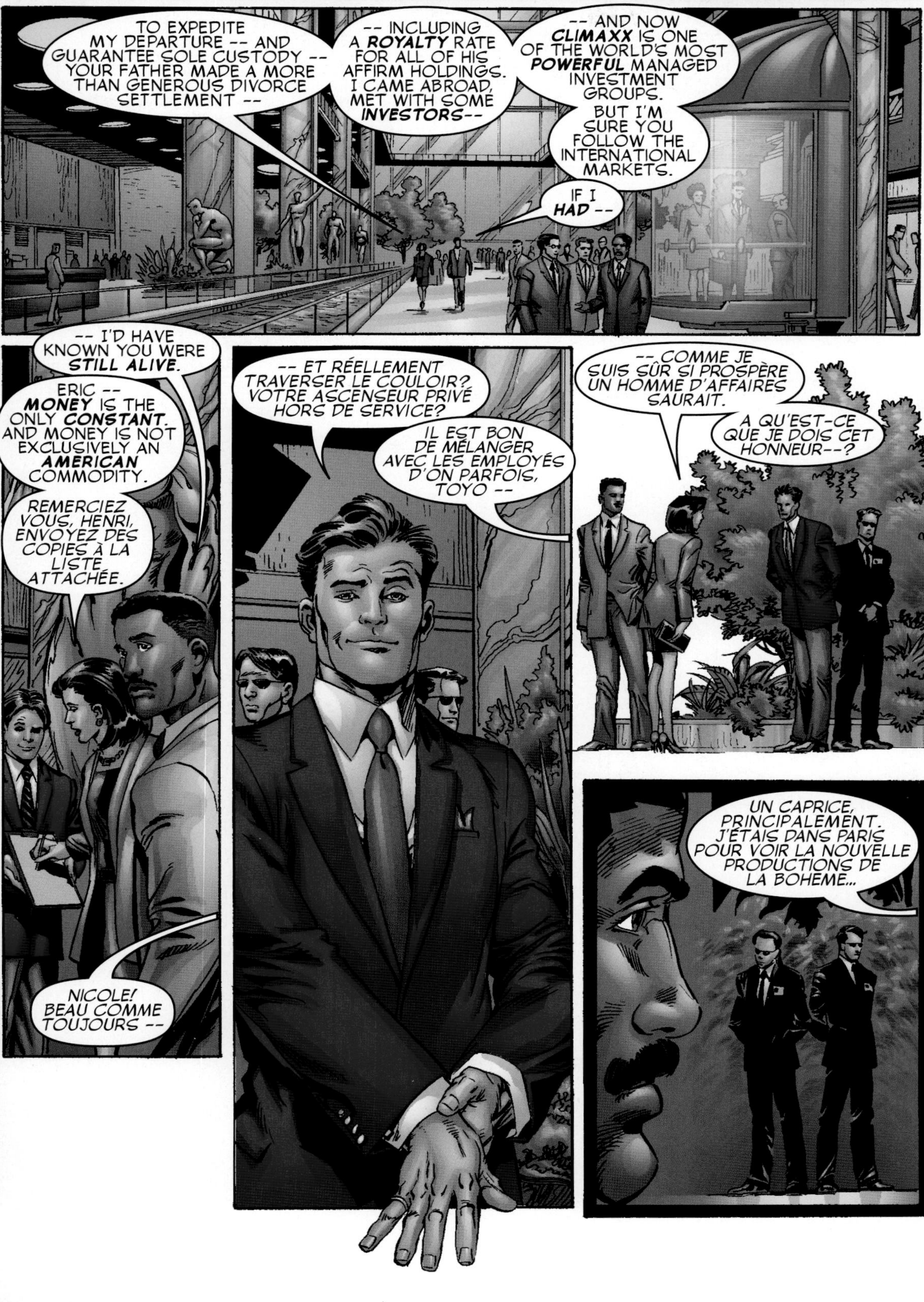
TO EXPEDITE MY DEPARTURE -- AND GUARANTEE SOLE CUSTODY -- YOUR FATHER MADE A MORE THAN GENEROUS DIVORCE SETTLEMENT --
-- INCLUDING A ROYALTY RATE FOR ALL OF HIS AFFIRM HOLDINGS. I CAME ABROAD, MET WITH SOME INVESTORS--
-- AND NOW CLIMAXX IS ONE OF THE WORLD'S MOST POWERFUL MANAGED INVESTMENT GROUPS.
BUT I'M SURE YOU FOLLOW THE INTERNATIONAL MARKETS.
IF I HAD --
-- I'D HAVE KNOWN YOU WERE STILL ALIVE.
ERIC -- MONEY IS THE ONLY CONSTANT. AND MONEY IS NOT EXCLUSIVELY AN AMERICAN COMMODITY.
REMERCIEZ VOUS, HENRI, ENVOYEZ DES COPIES À LA LISTE ATTACHÉE.
NICOLE! BEAU COMME TOUJOURS --
-- ET RÉELLEMENT TRAVERSER LE COULOIR? VOTRE ASCENSEUR PRIVÉ HORS DE SERVICE?
IL EST BON DE MÉLANGER AVEC LES EMPLOYÉS D'ON PARFOIS, TOYO --
-- COMME JE SUIS SÛR SI PROSPÈRE UN HOMME D'AFFAIRES SAURAIT.
A QU'EST-CE QUE JE DOIS CET HONNEUR--?
UN CAPRICE, PRINCIPALEMENT. J'ÉTAIS DANS PARIS POUR VOIR LA NOUVELLE PRODUCTIONS DE LA BOHEME...

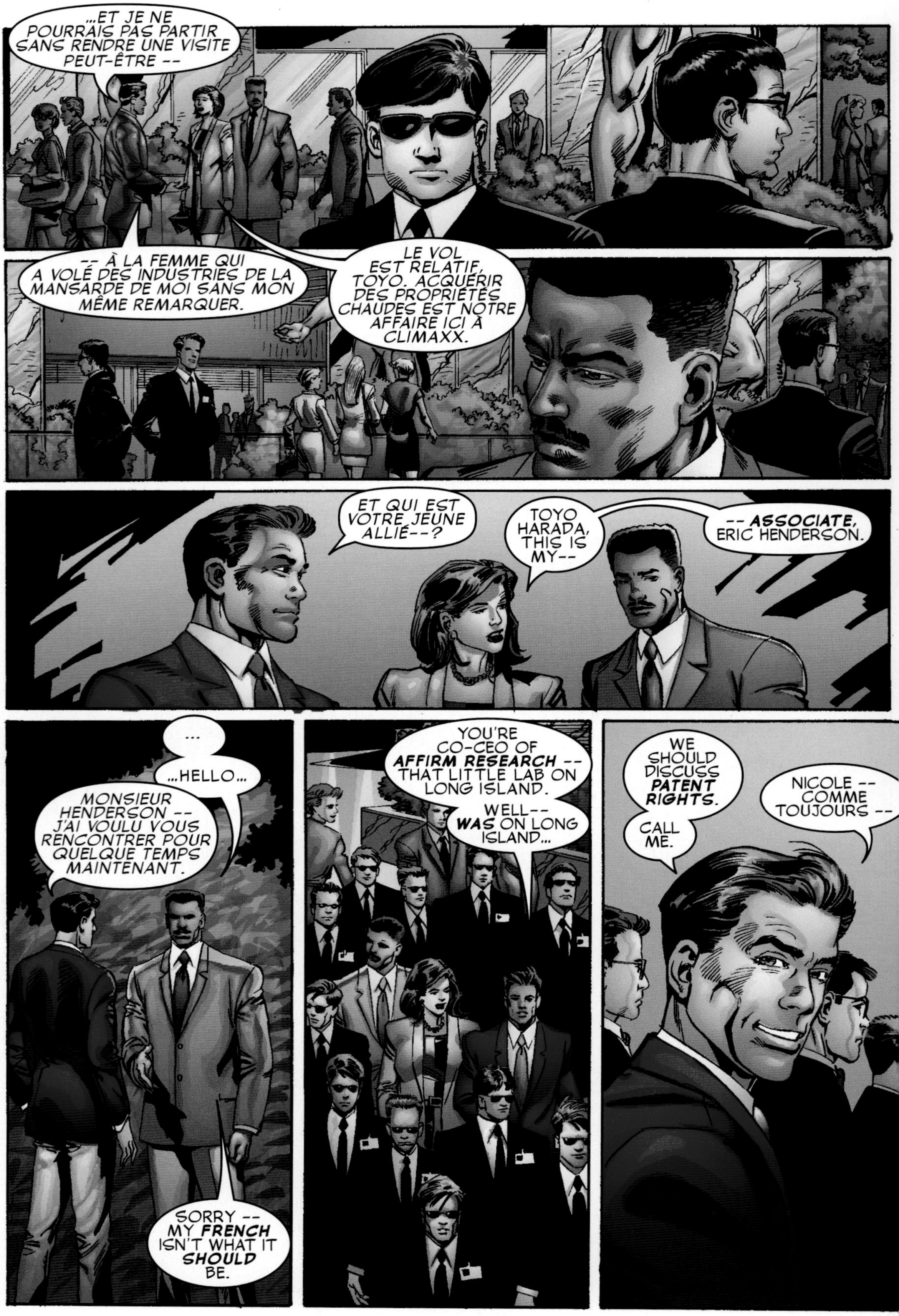
...ET JE NE POURRAIS PAS PARTIR SANS RENDRE UNE VISITE PEUT-ÊTRE --
-- À LA FEMME QUI A VOLÉ DES INDUSTRIES DE LA MANSARDE DE MOI SANS MON MÊME REMARQUER.
LE VOL EST RELATIF, TOYO. ACQUÉRIR DES PROPRIÉTÉS CHAUDES EST NOTRE AFFAIRE ICI À CLIMAXX.
ET QUI EST VOTRE JEUNE ALLIÉ--?
TOYO HARADA, THIS IS MY--
-- ASSOCIATE, ERIC HENDERSON.
...
...HELLO...
MONSIEUR HENDERSON -- J'AI VOULU VOUS RENCONTRER POUR QUELQUE TEMPS MAINTENANT.
SORRY -- MY FRENCH ISN'T WHAT IT SHOULD BE.
YOU'RE CO-CEO OF AFFIRM RESEARCH -- THAT LITTLE LAB ON LONG ISLAND.
WELL-- WAS ON LONG ISLAND...
WE SHOULD DISCUSS PATENT RIGHTS.
CALL ME.
NICOLE -- COMME TOUJOURS --

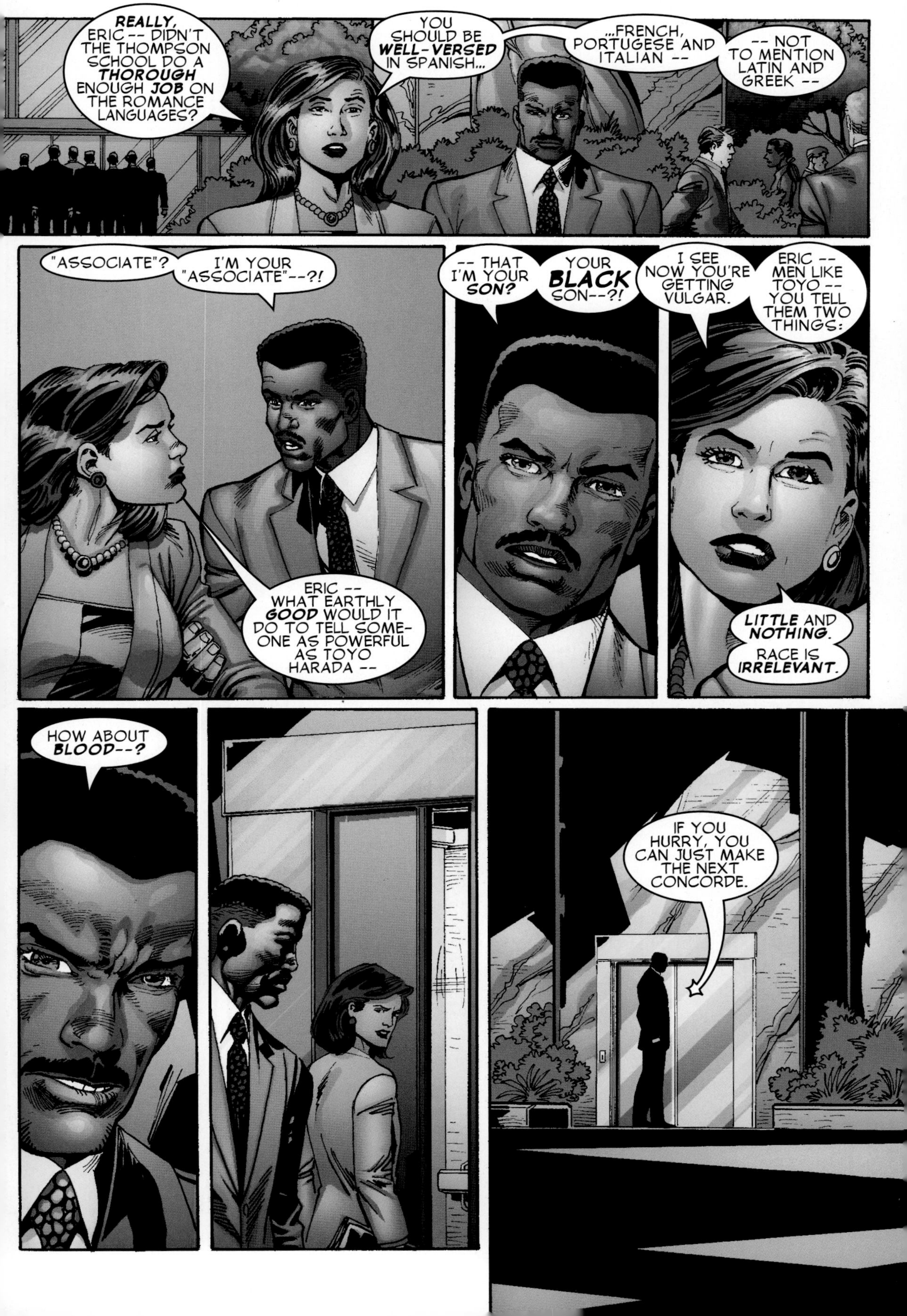
REALLY, ERIC -- DIDN'T THE THOMPSON SCHOOL DO A THOROUGH ENOUGH JOB ON THE ROMANCE LANGUAGES?
YOU SHOULD BE WELL-VERSED IN SPANISH...
...FRENCH, PORTUGESE AND ITALIAN --
-- NOT TO MENTION LATIN AND GREEK --
"ASSOCIATE"?
I'M YOUR "ASSOCIATE"--?!
ERIC -- WHAT EARTHLY GOOD WOULD IT DO TO TELL SOME-ONE AS POWERFUL AS TOYO HARADA --
-- THAT I'M YOUR SON?
YOUR BLACK SON--?!
I SEE NOW YOU'RE GETTING VULGAR.
ERIC -- MEN LIKE TOYO -- YOU TELL THEM TWO THINGS:
LITTLE AND NOTHING.
RACE IS IRRELEVANT.
HOW ABOUT BLOOD--?
IF YOU HURRY, YOU CAN JUST MAKE THE NEXT CONCORDE.

"Aye"

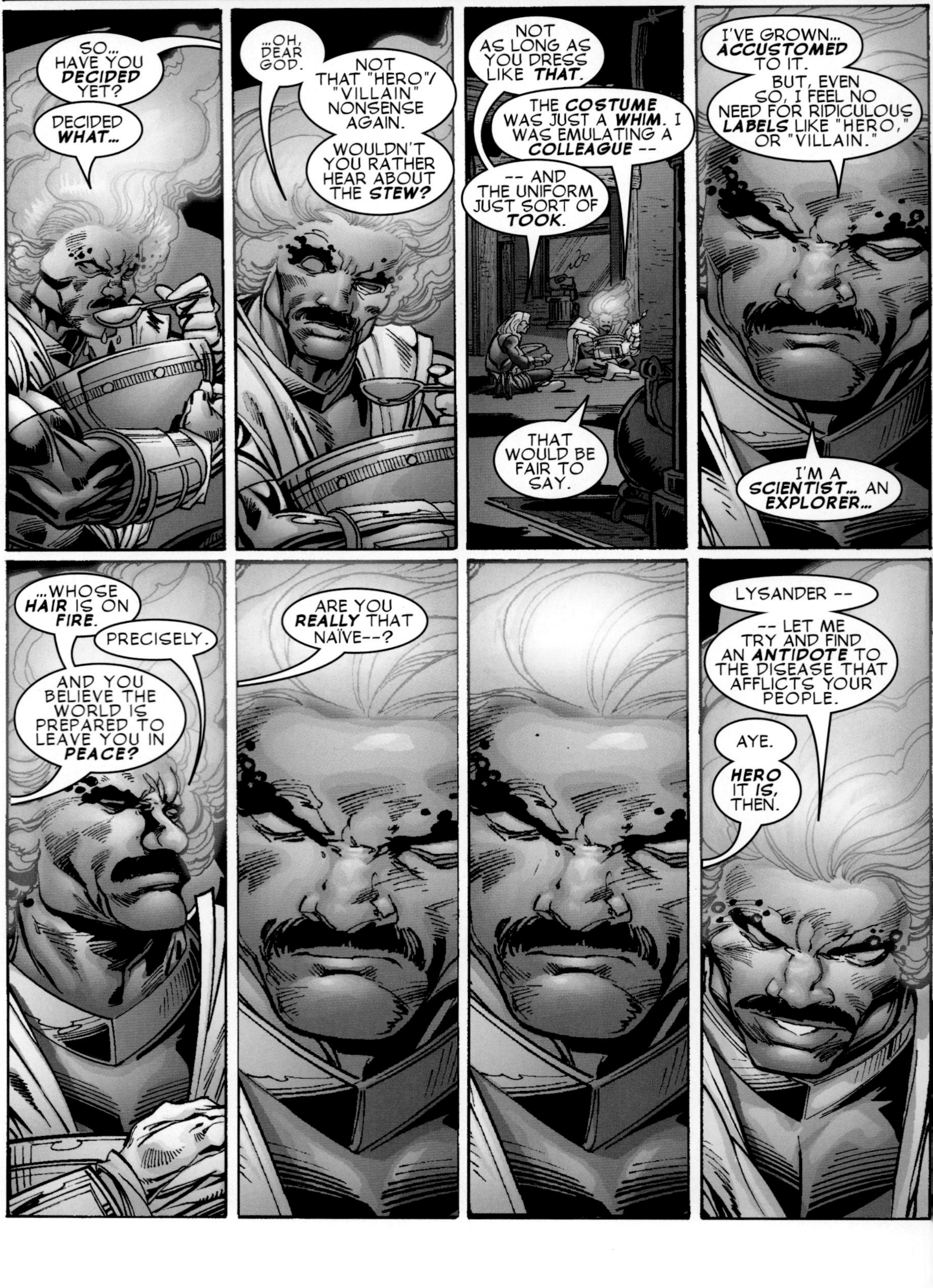
SO... HAVE YOU **DECIDED** YET?
DECIDED **WHAT...**
...OH, DEAR GOD.
NOT THAT "HERO"/ "VILLAIN" NONSENSE AGAIN.
WOULDN'T YOU RATHER HEAR ABOUT THE **STEW?**
NOT AS LONG AS YOU DRESS LIKE **THAT**.
THE **COSTUME** WAS JUST A **WHIM**. I WAS EMULATING A **COLLEAGUE** --
-- AND THE UNIFORM JUST SORT OF **TOOK**.
THAT WOULD BE FAIR TO SAY.
I'VE GROWN... **ACCUSTOMED** TO IT.
BUT, EVEN SO, I FEEL NO NEED FOR RIDICULOUS **LABELS** LIKE "HERO," OR "VILLAIN."
I'M A **SCIENTIST...** AN **EXPLORER...**
...WHOSE **HAIR** IS ON **FIRE**.
PRECISELY.
AND YOU BELIEVE THE WORLD IS PREPARED TO LEAVE YOU IN **PEACE?**
ARE YOU **REALLY** THAT NAÏVE--?
LYSANDER --
-- LET ME TRY AND FIND AN **ANTIDOTE** TO THE DISEASE THAT AFFLICTS YOUR PEOPLE.
AYE.
HERO IT **IS**, THEN.

"This Was Much Funnier When She Was Dead"

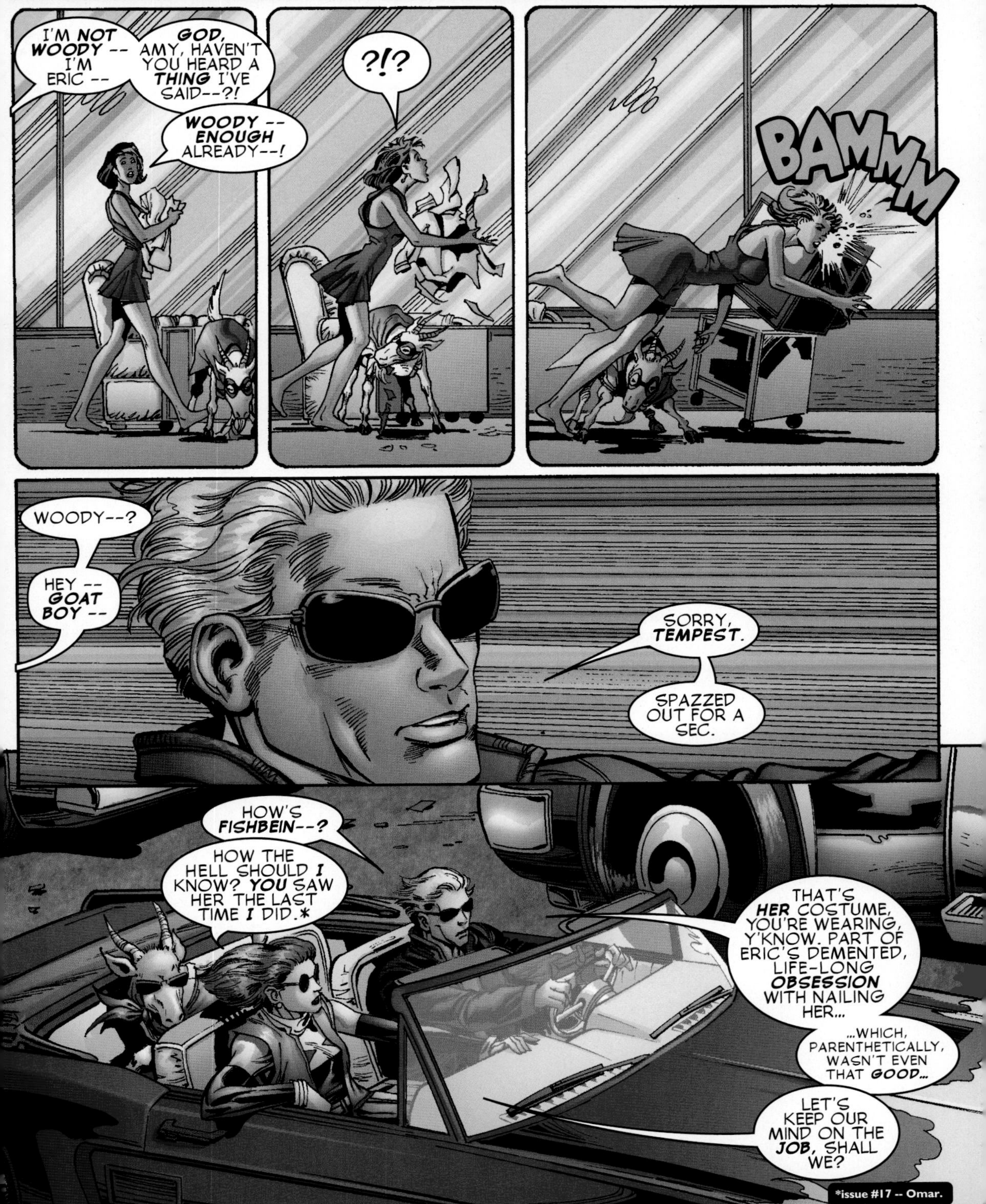
I'M NOT WOODY -- I'M ERIC --
GOD, AMY, HAVEN'T YOU HEARD A THING I'VE SAID--?!
WOODY -- ENOUGH ALREADY--!
?!?
BAMMM
WOODY--?
HEY -- GOAT BOY --
SORRY, TEMPEST.
SPAZZED OUT FOR A SEC.
HOW'S FISHBEIN--?
HOW THE HELL SHOULD I KNOW? YOU SAW HER THE LAST TIME I DID.*
THAT'S HER COSTUME, YOU'RE WEARING, Y'KNOW. PART OF ERIC'S DEMENTED, LIFE-LONG OBSESSION WITH NAILING HER...
...WHICH, PARENTHETICALLY, WASN'T EVEN THAT GOOD...
LET'S KEEP OUR MIND ON THE JOB, SHALL WE?
*issue #17 -- Omar.

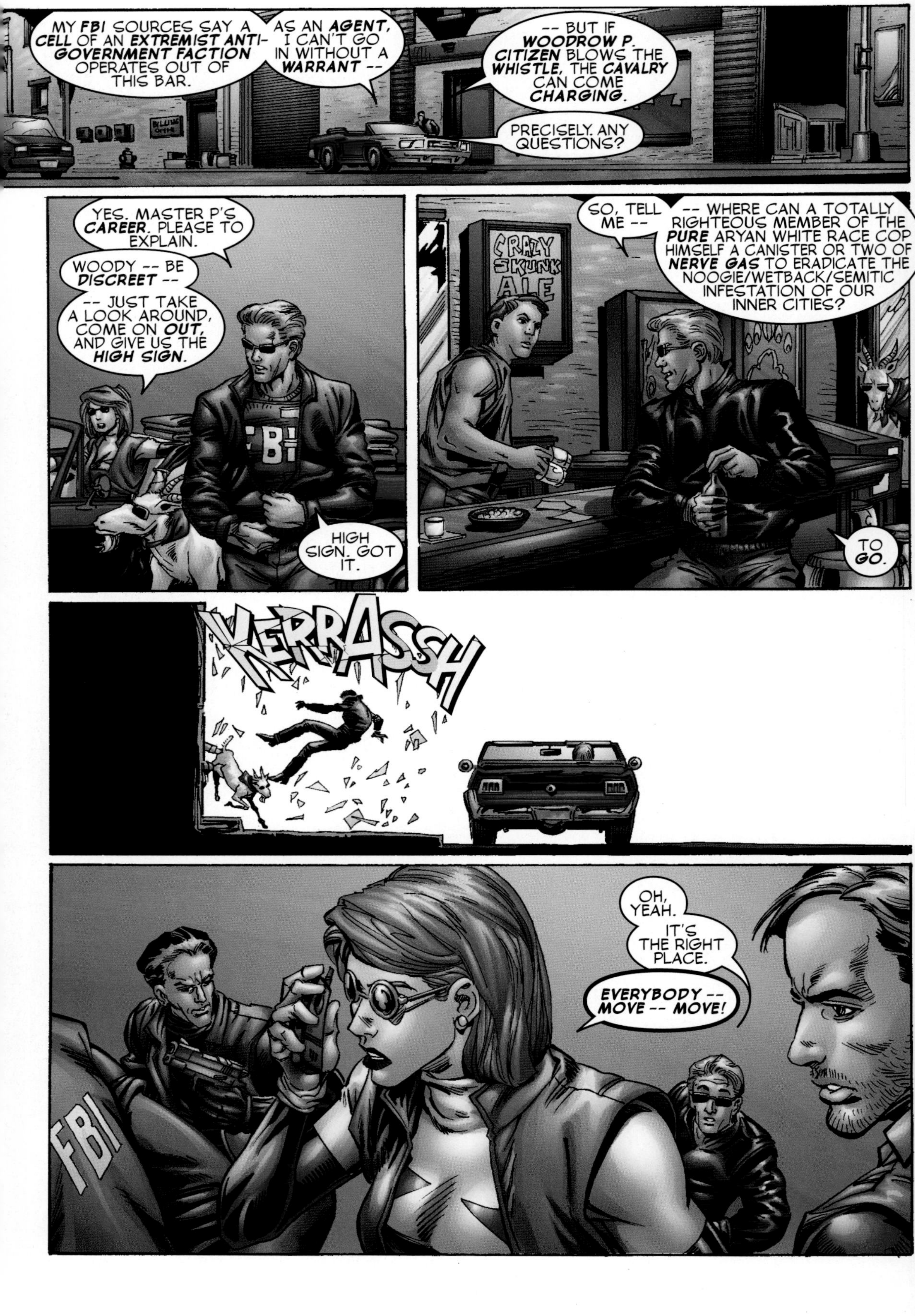

MY FBI SOURCES SAY A CELL OF AN EXTREMIST ANTI-GOVERNMENT FACTION OPERATES OUT OF THIS BAR.
AS AN AGENT, I CAN'T GO IN WITHOUT A WARRANT --
-- BUT IF WOODROW P. CITIZEN BLOWS THE WHISTLE, THE CAVALRY CAN COME CHARGING.
PRECISELY. ANY QUESTIONS?
YES. MASTER P'S CAREER. PLEASE TO EXPLAIN.
WOODY -- BE DISCREET --
-- JUST TAKE A LOOK AROUND, COME ON OUT, AND GIVE US THE HIGH SIGN.
HIGH SIGN. GOT IT.
CRAZY SKUNK ALE
SO, TELL ME --
-- WHERE CAN A TOTALLY RIGHTEOUS MEMBER OF THE PURE ARYAN WHITE RACE COP HIMSELF A CANISTER OR TWO OF NERVE GAS TO ERADICATE THE NOOGIE/WETBACK/SEMITIC INFESTATION OF OUR INNER CITIES?
TO GO.
KERRASSH
OH, YEAH.
IT'S THE RIGHT PLACE.
EVERYBODY -- MOVE -- MOVE!
FBI

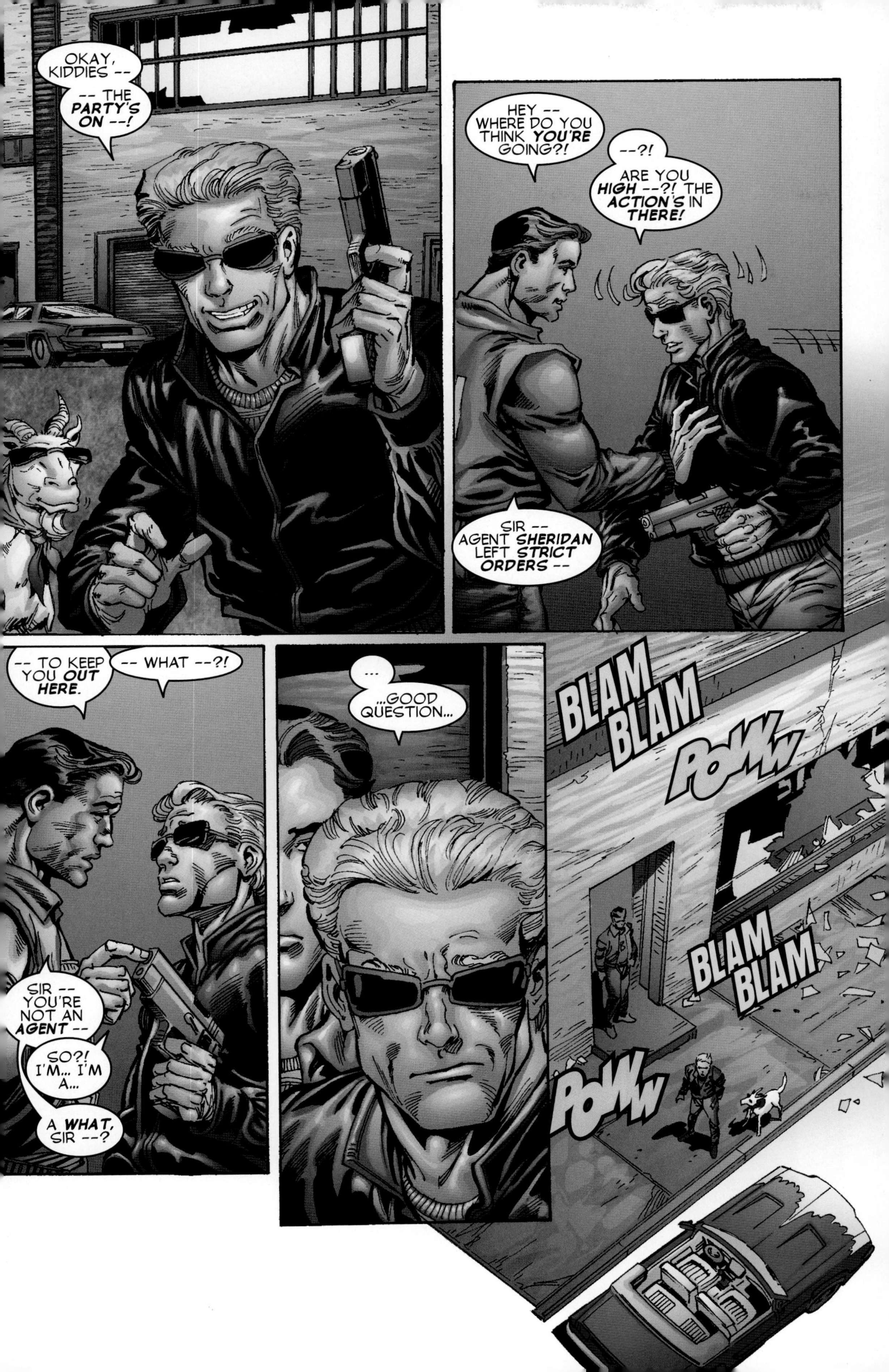
OKAY, KIDDIES --
-- THE PARTY'S ON --!
HEY -- WHERE DO YOU THINK YOU'RE GOING?!
--?!
ARE YOU HIGH --?! THE ACTION'S IN THERE!
SIR -- AGENT SHERIDAN LEFT STRICT ORDERS --
-- TO KEEP YOU OUT HERE.
-- WHAT --?!
SIR -- YOU'RE NOT AN AGENT --
SO?! I'M... I'M A...
A WHAT, SIR --?
...
...GOOD QUESTION...
BLAM BLAM
POWW
BLAM BLAM
POWW

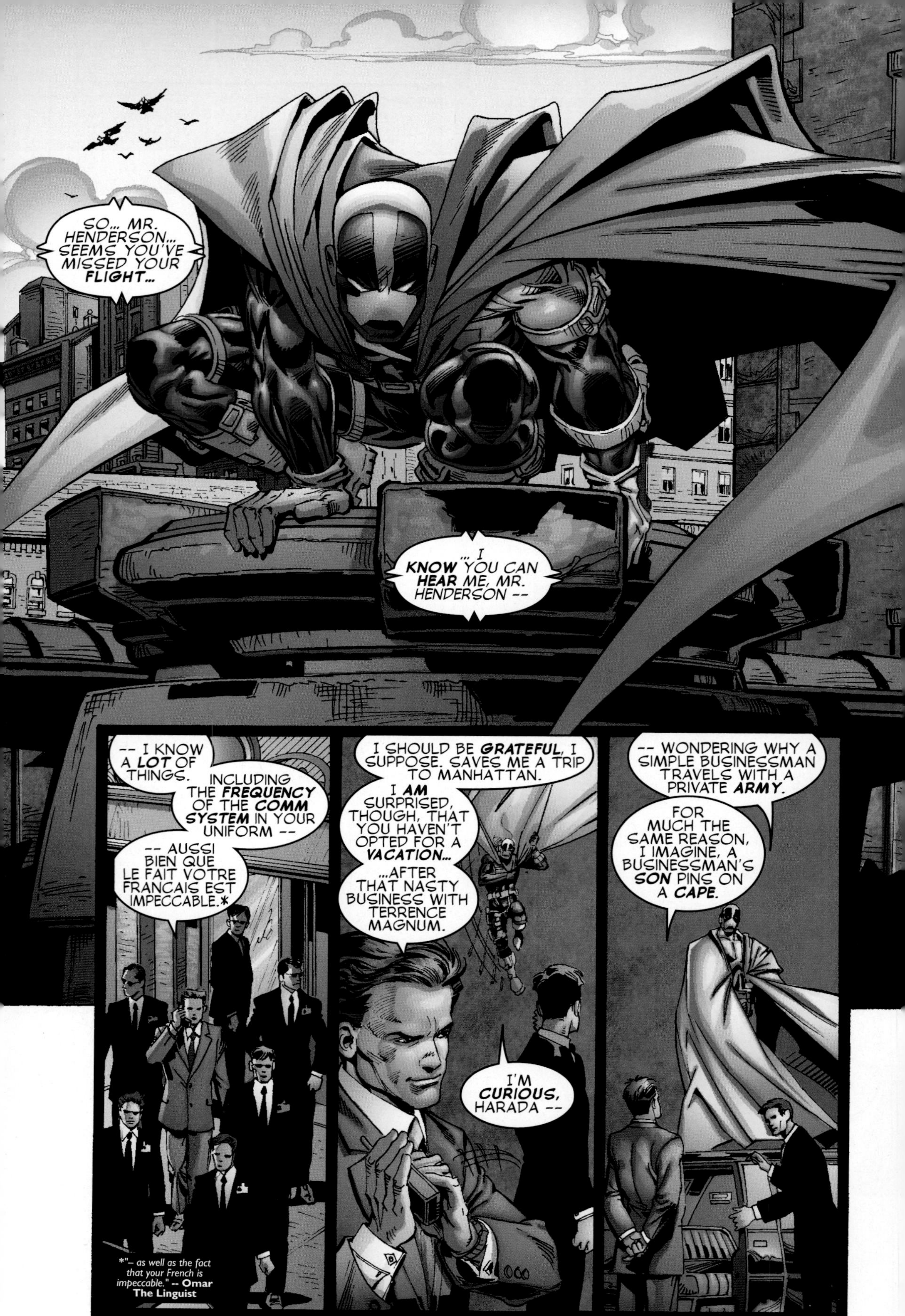
SO... MR. HENDERSON... SEEMS YOU'VE MISSED YOUR FLIGHT...
... I KNOW YOU CAN HEAR ME, MR. HENDERSON --
-- I KNOW A LOT OF THINGS.
INCLUDING THE FREQUENCY OF THE COMM SYSTEM IN YOUR UNIFORM --
-- AUSSI BIEN QUE LE FAIT VOTRE FRANCAIS EST IMPECCABLE.*
*"-- as well as the fact that your French is impeccable." -- Omar The Linguist
I SHOULD BE GRATEFUL, I SUPPOSE. SAVES ME A TRIP TO MANHATTAN.
I AM SURPRISED, THOUGH, THAT YOU HAVEN'T OPTED FOR A VACATION...
...AFTER THAT NASTY BUSINESS WITH TERRENCE MAGNUM.
I'M CURIOUS, HARADA --
-- WONDERING WHY A SIMPLE BUSINESSMAN TRAVELS WITH A PRIVATE ARMY.
FOR MUCH THE SAME REASON, I IMAGINE, A BUSINESSMAN'S SON PINS ON A CAPE.

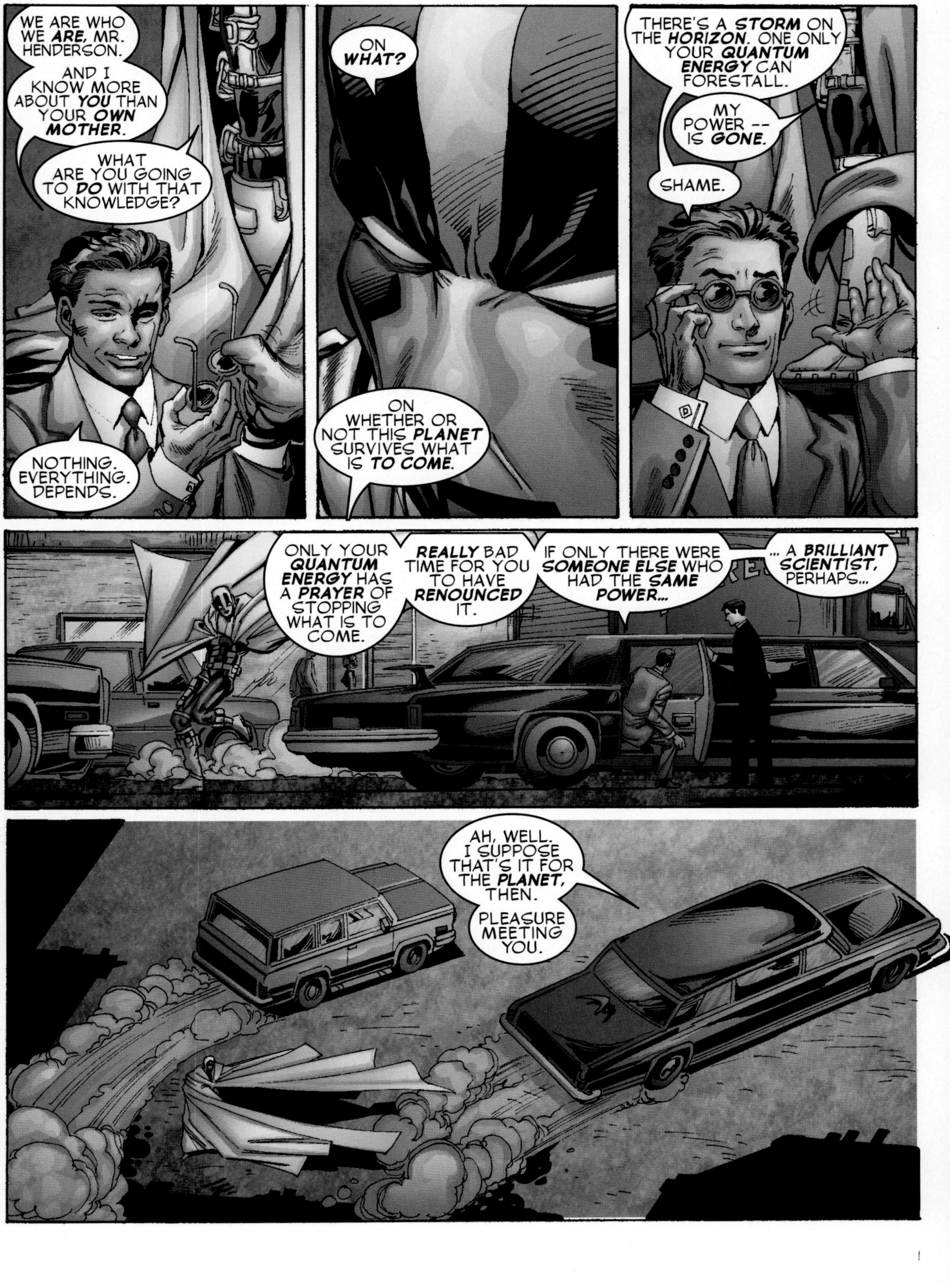
WE ARE WHO WE ARE, MR. HENDERSON.
AND I KNOW MORE ABOUT YOU THAN YOUR OWN MOTHER.
WHAT ARE YOU GOING TO DO WITH THAT KNOWLEDGE?
NOTHING. EVERYTHING. DEPENDS.
ON WHAT?
ON WHETHER OR NOT THIS PLANET SURVIVES WHAT IS TO COME.
THERE'S A STORM ON THE HORIZON. ONE ONLY YOUR QUANTUM ENERGY CAN FORESTALL.
MY POWER -- IS GONE.
SHAME.
ONLY YOUR QUANTUM ENERGY HAS A PRAYER OF STOPPING WHAT IS TO COME.
REALLY BAD TIME FOR YOU TO HAVE RENOUNCED IT.
IF ONLY THERE WERE SOMEONE ELSE WHO HAD THE SAME POWER...
... A BRILLIANT SCIENTIST, PERHAPS...
AH, WELL. I SUPPOSE THAT'S IT FOR THE PLANET, THEN.
PLEASURE MEETING YOU.

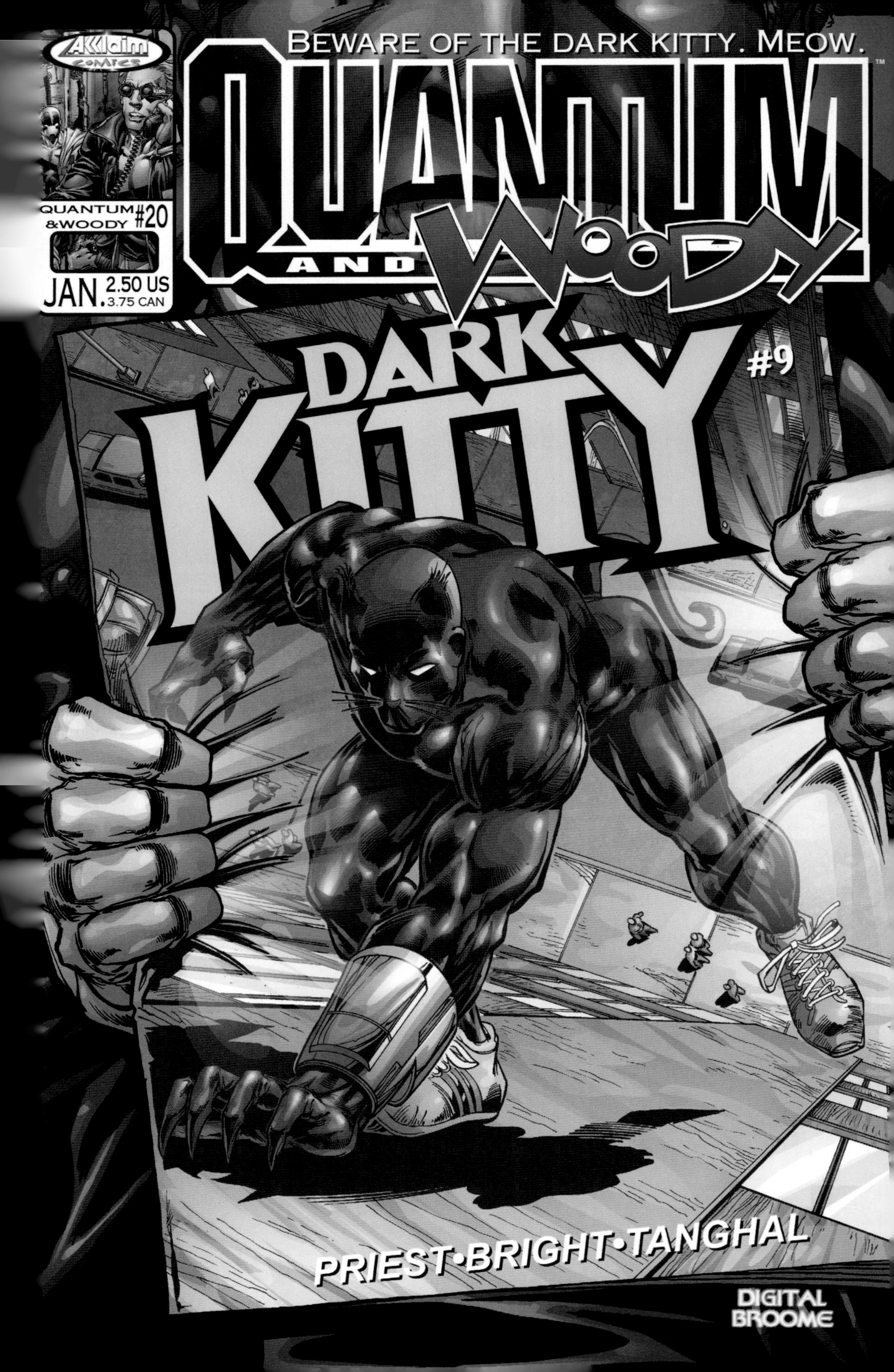
Acclaim Comics
QUANTUM & WOODY #20
JAN. 2.50 US 3.75 CAN
BEWARE OF THE DARK KITTY. MEOW.
QUANTUM AND WOODY
DARK KITTY #9
PRIEST•BRIGHT•TANGHAL
DIGITAL BROOME

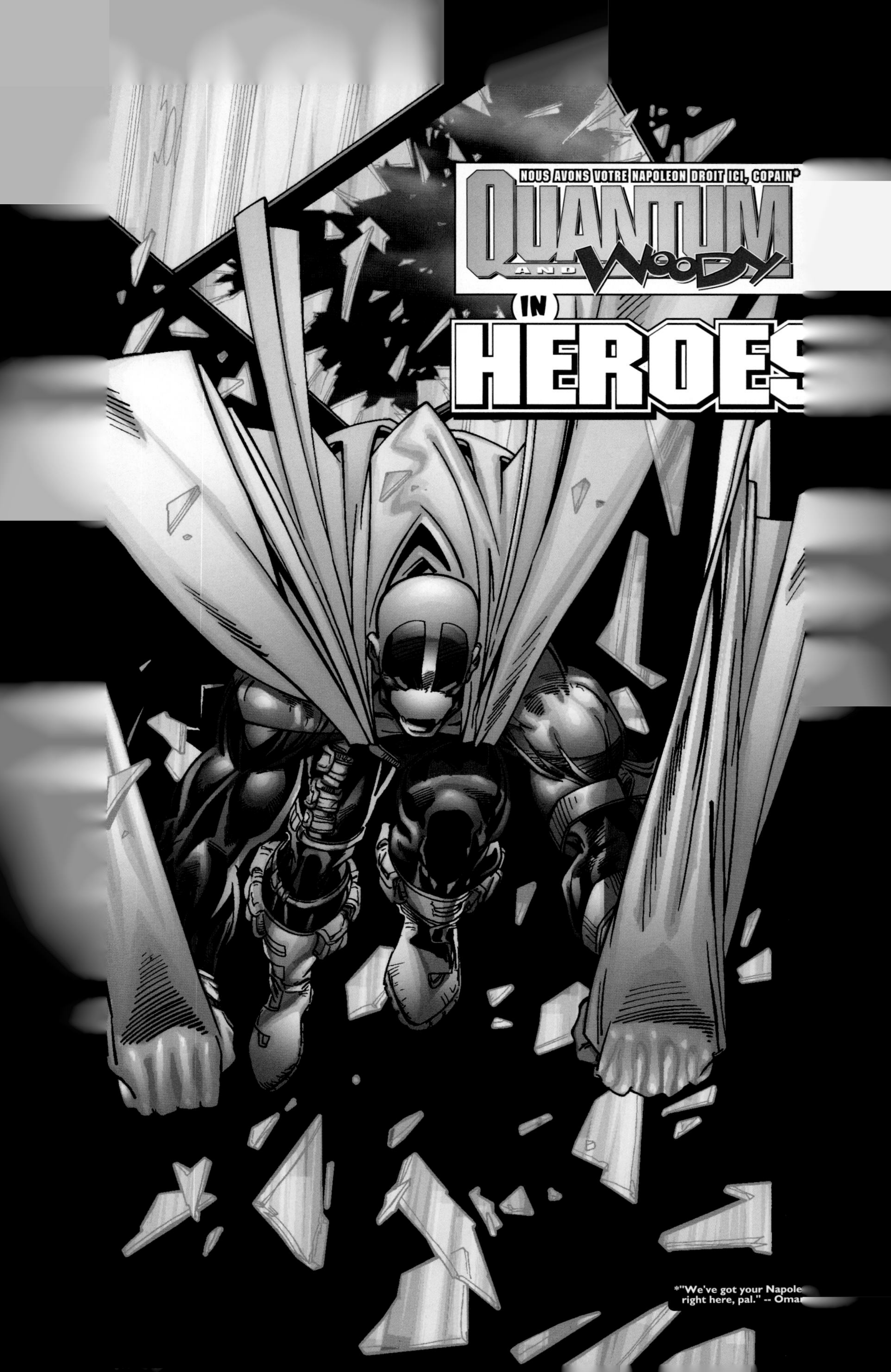
NOUS AVONS VOTRE NAPOLEON DROIT ICI, COPAIN*
QUANTUM AND WOODY
IN
HEROES
*"We've got your Napole
right here, pal." -- Omar

"'Jean' Is Pronounced "Szhon.' Beyond That, You're On Your Own"

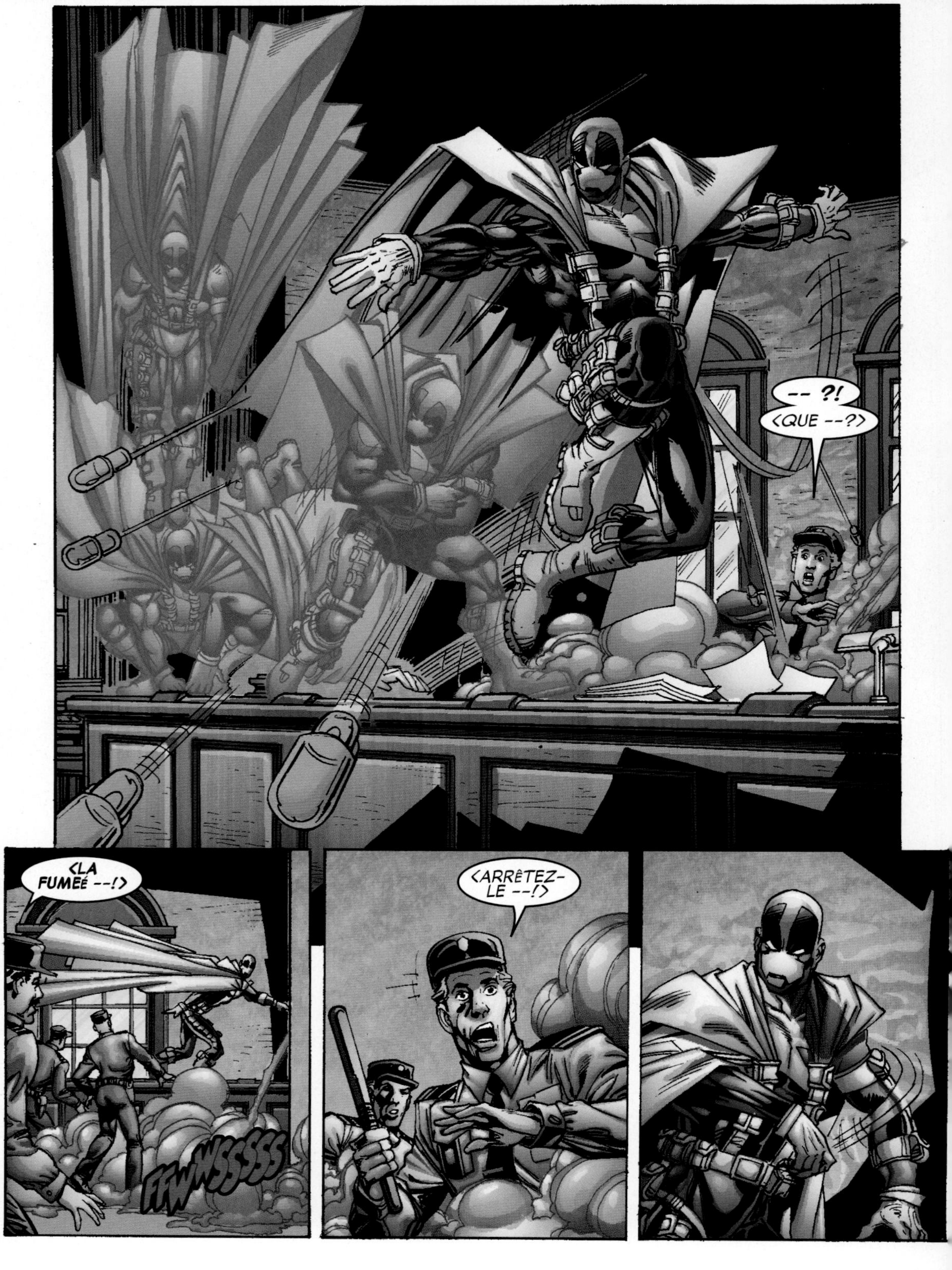
-- ?!
<QUE --?>
<LA FUMEÉ --!>
FFWSSSSS
<ARRÊTEZ-LE --!>

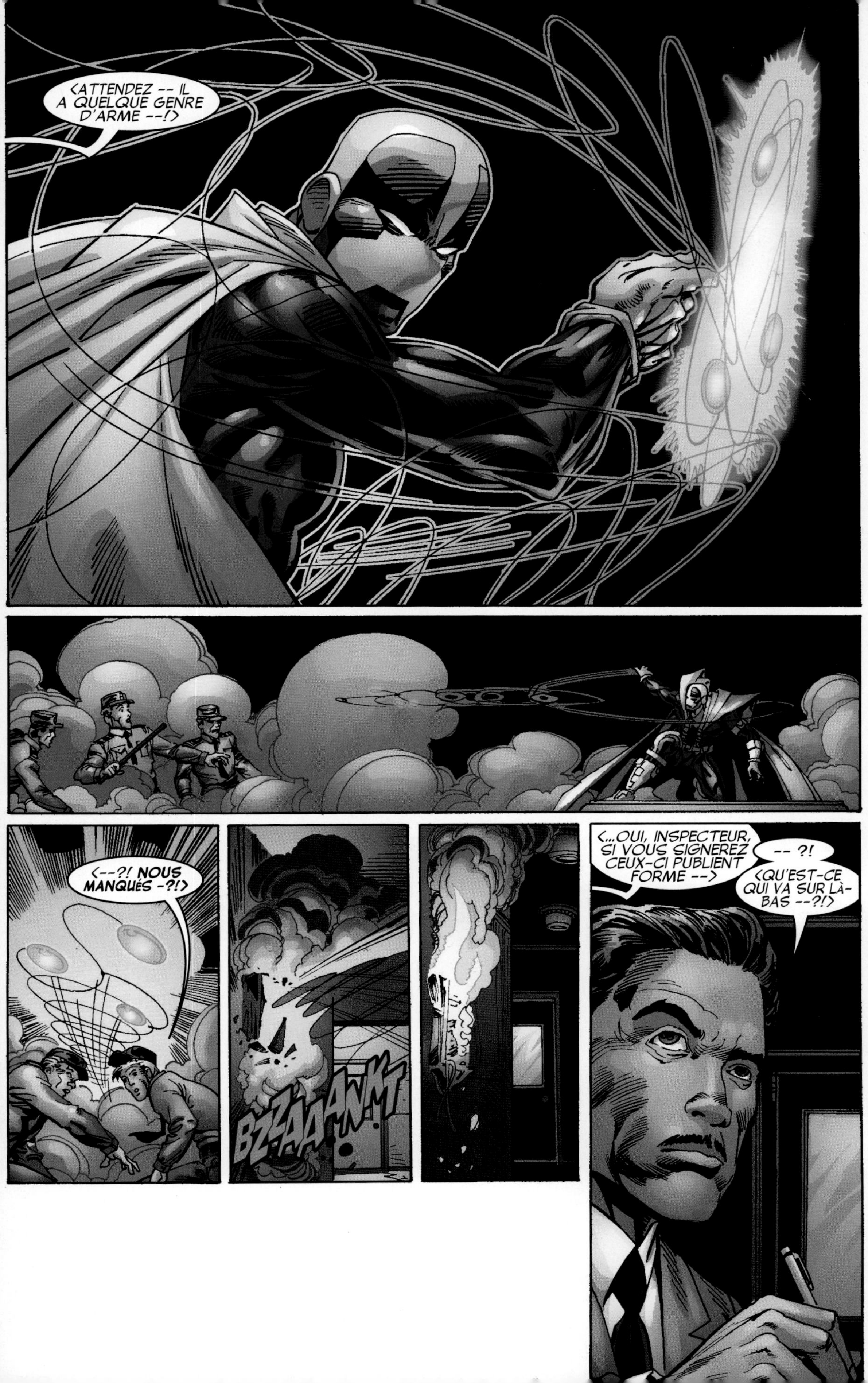
<ATTENDEZ -- IL A QUELQUE GENRE D'ARME --!>
<--?! NOUS MANQUÉS -?!>
BZZAAANKT
<...OUI, INSPECTEUR, SI VOUS SIGNEREZ CEUX-CI PUBLIENT FORME -->
-- ?!
<QU'EST-CE QUI VA SUR LÀ-BAS --?!>

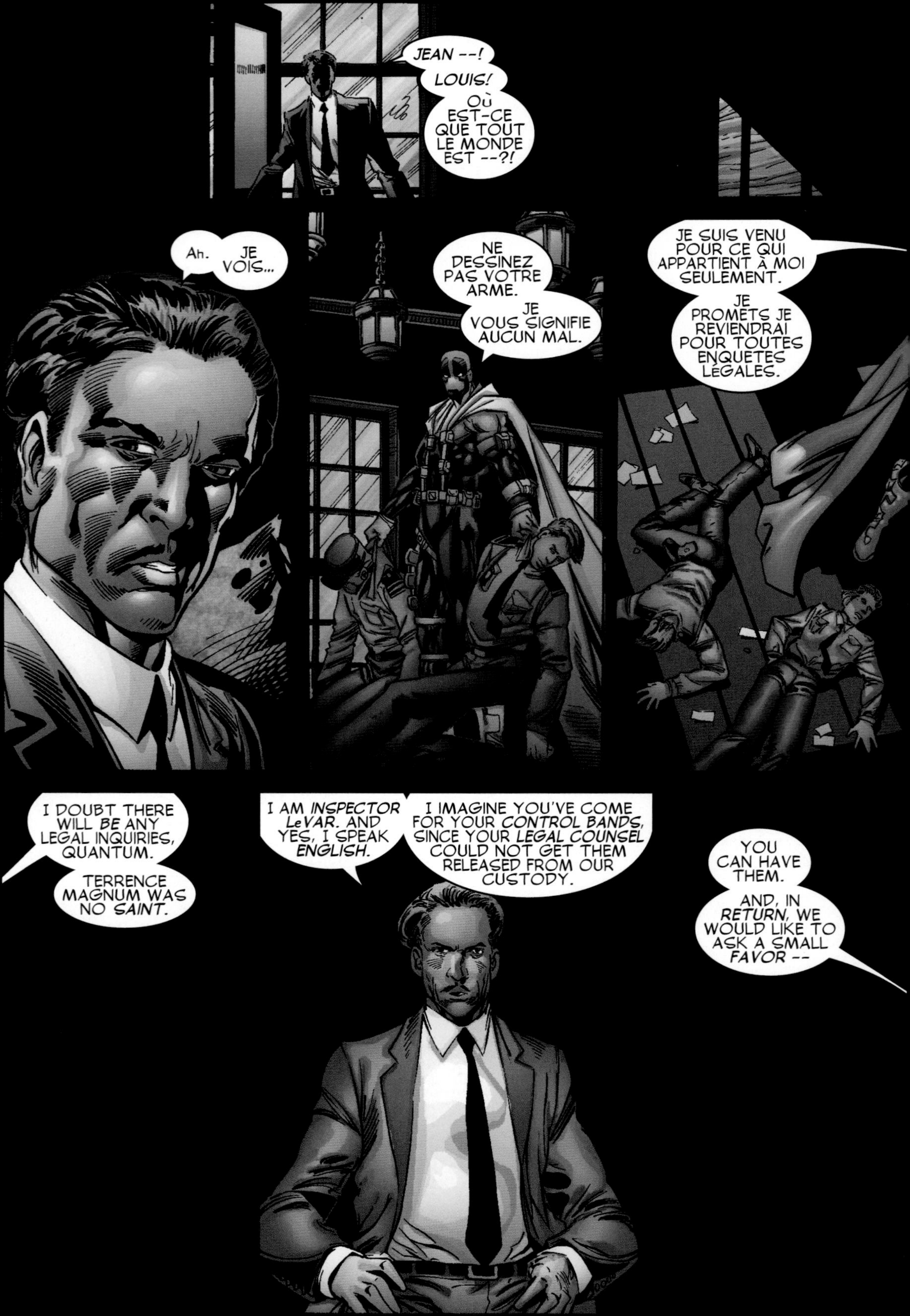
JEAN --!
LOUIS!
Où EST-CE QUE TOUT LE MONDE EST --?!
Ah. JE VOIS...
NE DESSINEZ PAS VOTRE ARME.
JE VOUS SIGNIFIE AUCUN MAL.
JE SUIS VENU POUR CE QUI APPARTIENT À MOI SEULEMENT.
JE PROMETS JE REVIENDRAI POUR TOUTES ENQUETES LÉGALES.
I DOUBT THERE WILL BE ANY LEGAL INQUIRIES, QUANTUM.
TERRENCE MAGNUM WAS NO SAINT.
I AM INSPECTOR LeVAR. AND YES, I SPEAK ENGLISH.
I IMAGINE YOU'VE COME FOR YOUR CONTROL BANDS, SINCE YOUR LEGAL COUNSEL COULD NOT GET THEM RELEASED FROM OUR CUSTODY.
YOU CAN HAVE THEM.
AND, IN RETURN, WE WOULD LIKE TO ASK A SMALL FAVOR --

"Le Quantum"

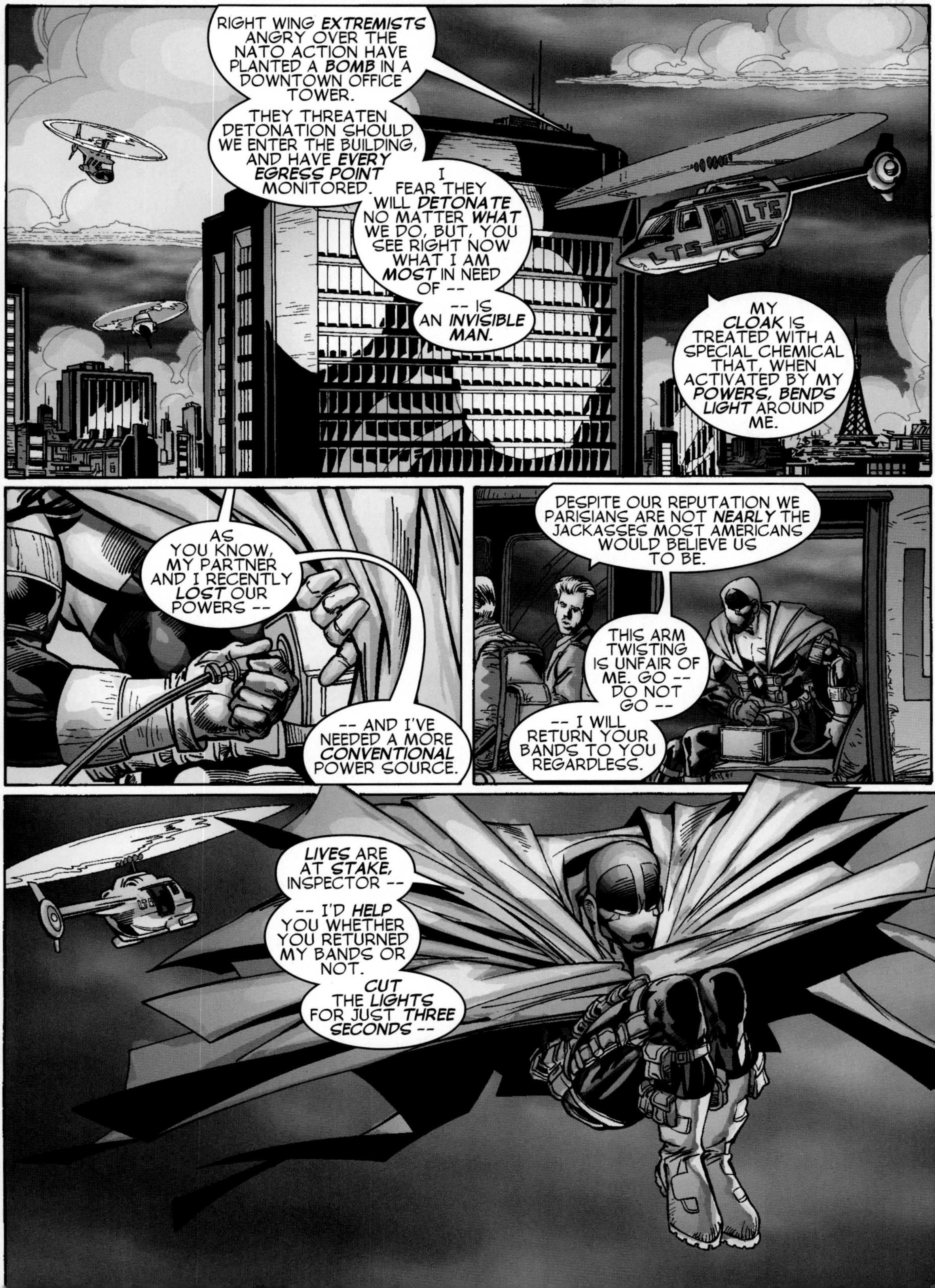
RIGHT WING EXTREMISTS ANGRY OVER THE NATO ACTION HAVE PLANTED A BOMB IN A DOWNTOWN OFFICE TOWER.
THEY THREATEN DETONATION SHOULD WE ENTER THE BUILDING, AND HAVE EVERY EGRESS POINT MONITORED.
I FEAR THEY WILL DETONATE NO MATTER WHAT WE DO, BUT, YOU SEE RIGHT NOW WHAT I AM MOST IN NEED OF --
-- IS AN INVISIBLE MAN.
LTS
MY CLOAK IS TREATED WITH A SPECIAL CHEMICAL THAT, WHEN ACTIVATED BY MY POWERS, BENDS LIGHT AROUND ME.
AS YOU KNOW, MY PARTNER AND I RECENTLY LOST OUR POWERS --
-- AND I'VE NEEDED A MORE CONVENTIONAL POWER SOURCE.
DESPITE OUR REPUTATION WE PARISIANS ARE NOT NEARLY THE JACKASSES MOST AMERICANS WOULD BELIEVE US TO BE.
THIS ARM TWISTING IS UNFAIR OF ME. GO -- DO NOT GO --
-- I WILL RETURN YOUR BANDS TO YOU REGARDLESS.
LIVES ARE AT STAKE, INSPECTOR --
-- I'D HELP YOU WHETHER YOU RETURNED MY BANDS OR NOT.
CUT THE LIGHTS FOR JUST THREE SECONDS --

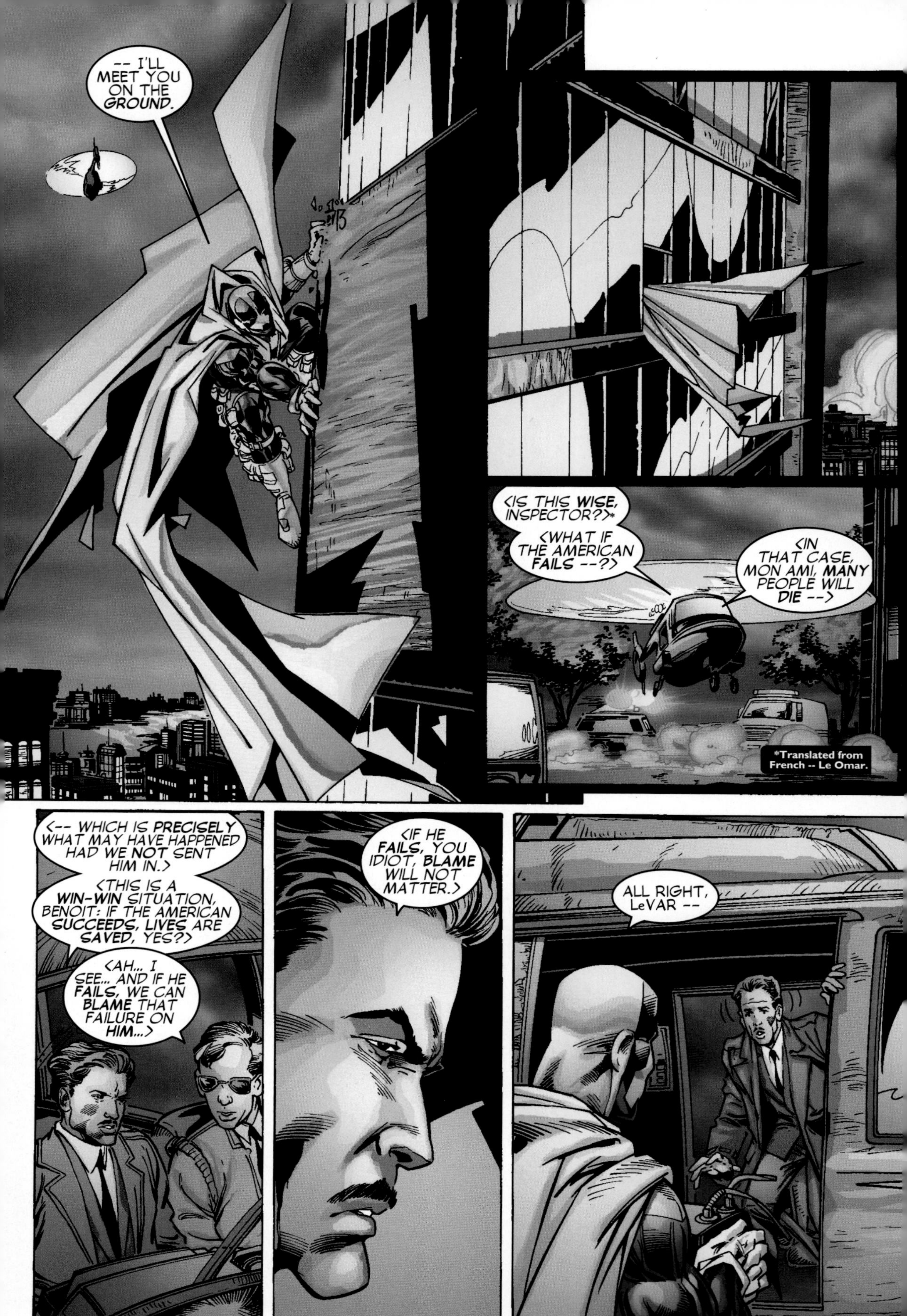
-- I'LL MEET YOU ON THE GROUND.
<IS THIS WISE, INSPECTOR?>*
<WHAT IF THE AMERICAN FAILS --?>
<IN THAT CASE, MON AMI, MANY PEOPLE WILL DIE -->
*Translated from French -- Le Omar.
<-- WHICH IS PRECISELY WHAT MAY HAVE HAPPENED HAD WE NOT SENT HIM IN.>
<THIS IS A WIN-WIN SITUATION, BENOIT: IF THE AMERICAN SUCCEEDS, LIVES ARE SAVED, YES?>
<AH... I SEE... AND IF HE FAILS, WE CAN BLAME THAT FAILURE ON HIM...>
<IF HE FAILS, YOU IDIOT, BLAME WILL NOT MATTER.>
ALL RIGHT, LeVAR --

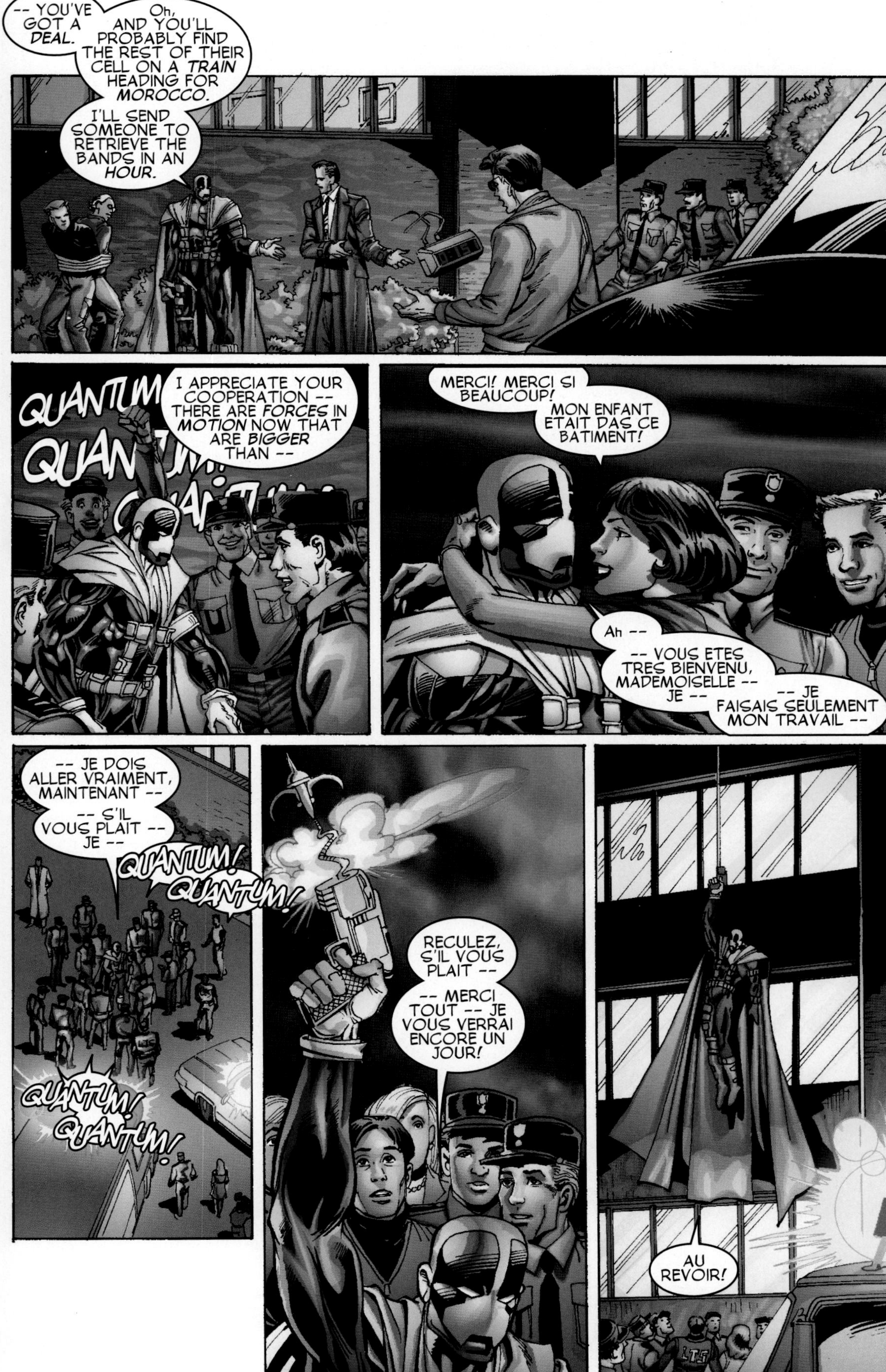
-- YOU'VE GOT A *DEAL*.
Oh, AND YOU'LL PROBABLY FIND THE REST OF THEIR CELL ON A *TRAIN* HEADING FOR *MOROCCO*.
I'LL SEND SOMEONE TO RETRIEVE THE BANDS IN AN *HOUR*.
QUANTUM!
I APPRECIATE YOUR COOPERATION -- THERE ARE *FORCES* IN *MOTION* NOW THAT ARE *BIGGER* THAN --
MERCI! MERCI SI BEAUCOUP!
MON ENFANT ETAIT DAS CE BATIMENT!
Ah --
-- VOUS ETES TRES BIENVENU, MADEMOISELLE -- JE --
-- JE FAISAIS SEULEMENT MON TRAVAIL --
-- JE DOIS ALLER VRAIMENT, MAINTENANT --
-- S'IL VOUS PLAIT -- JE --
QUANTUM! QUANTUM!
QUANTUM! QUANTUM!
RECULEZ, S'IL VOUS PLAIT --
-- MERCI TOUT -- JE VOUS VERRAI ENCORE UN JOUR!
AU REVOIR!

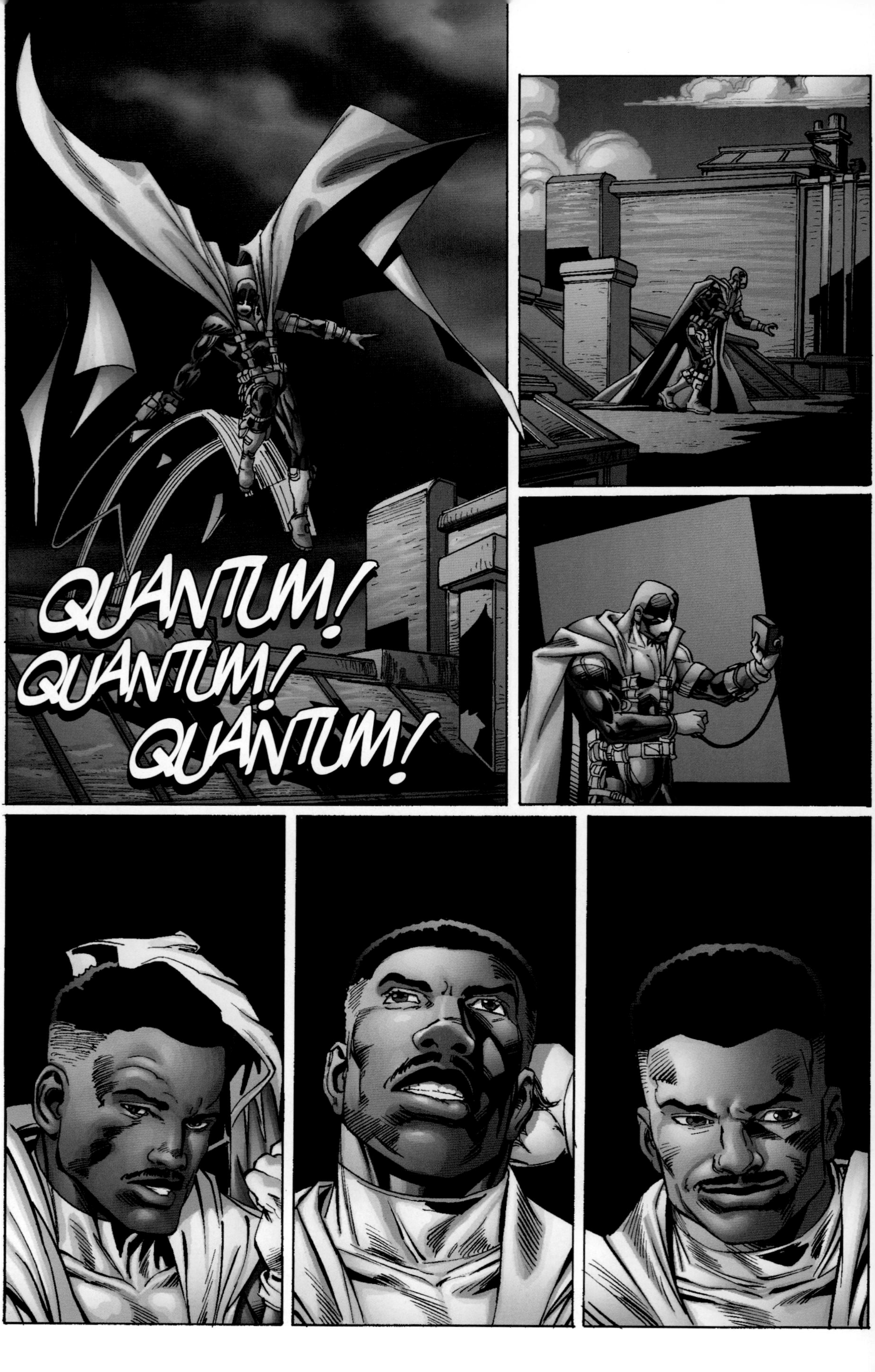
QUANTUM!
QUANTUM!
QUANTUM!

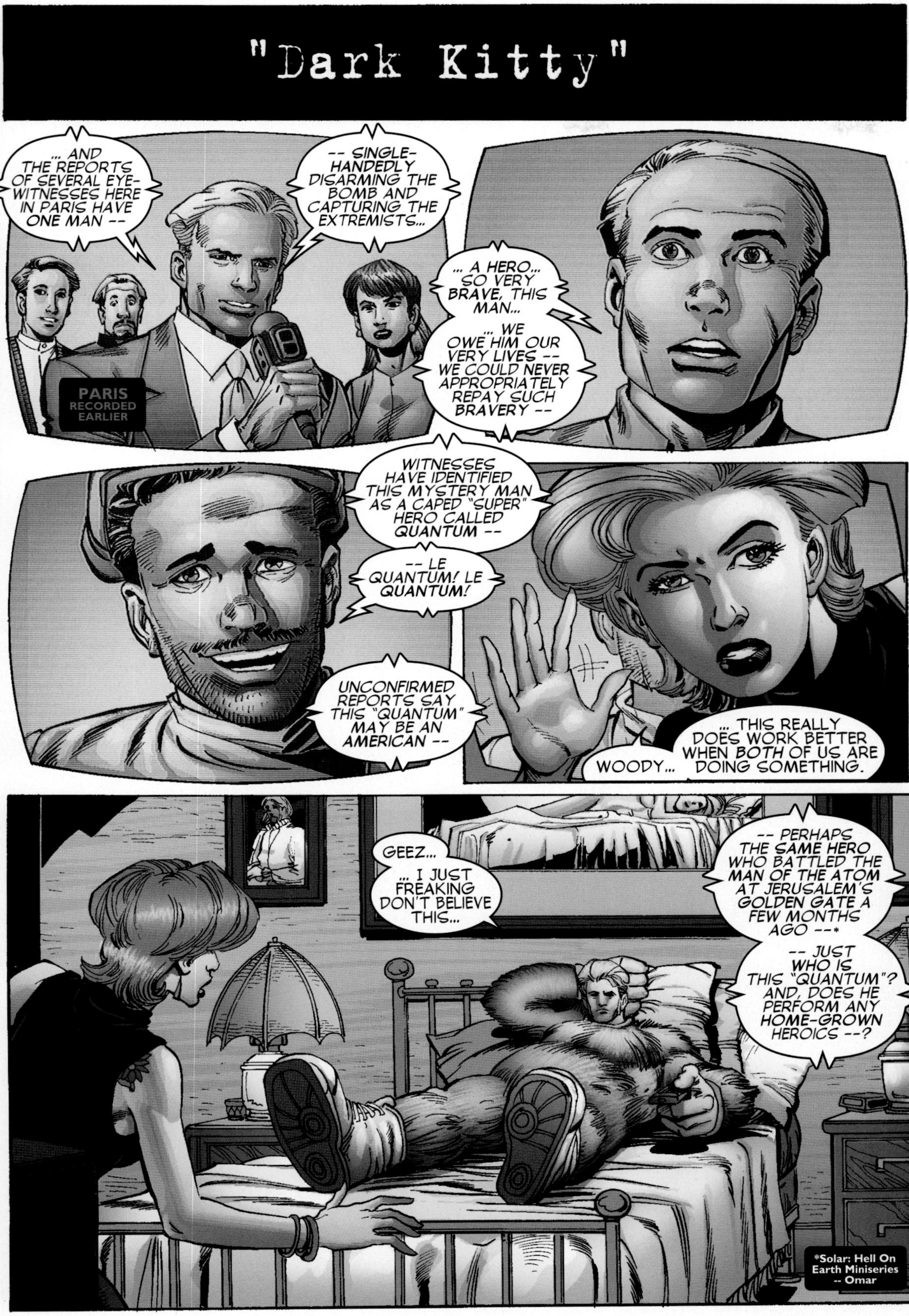
"Dark Kitty"
... AND THE REPORTS OF SEVERAL EYE-WITNESSES HERE IN PARIS HAVE ONE MAN --
-- SINGLE-HANDEDLY DISARMING THE BOMB AND CAPTURING THE EXTREMISTS...
PARIS RECORDED EARLIER
... A HERO... SO VERY BRAVE, THIS MAN...
... WE OWE HIM OUR VERY LIVES -- WE COULD NEVER APPROPRIATELY REPAY SUCH BRAVERY --
WITNESSES HAVE IDENTIFIED THIS MYSTERY MAN AS A CAPED "SUPER" HERO CALLED QUANTUM --
-- LE QUANTUM! LE QUANTUM!
UNCONFIRMED REPORTS SAY THIS "QUANTUM" MAY BE AN AMERICAN --
WOODY...
... THIS REALLY DOES WORK BETTER WHEN BOTH OF US ARE DOING SOMETHING.
GEEZ...
... I JUST FREAKING DON'T BELIEVE THIS...
-- PERHAPS THE SAME HERO WHO BATTLED THE MAN OF THE ATOM AT JERUSALEM'S GOLDEN GATE A FEW MONTHS AGO --*
-- JUST WHO IS THIS "QUANTUM"? AND, DOES HE PERFORM ANY HOME-GROWN HEROICS --?
*Solar: Hell On Earth Miniseries -- Omar

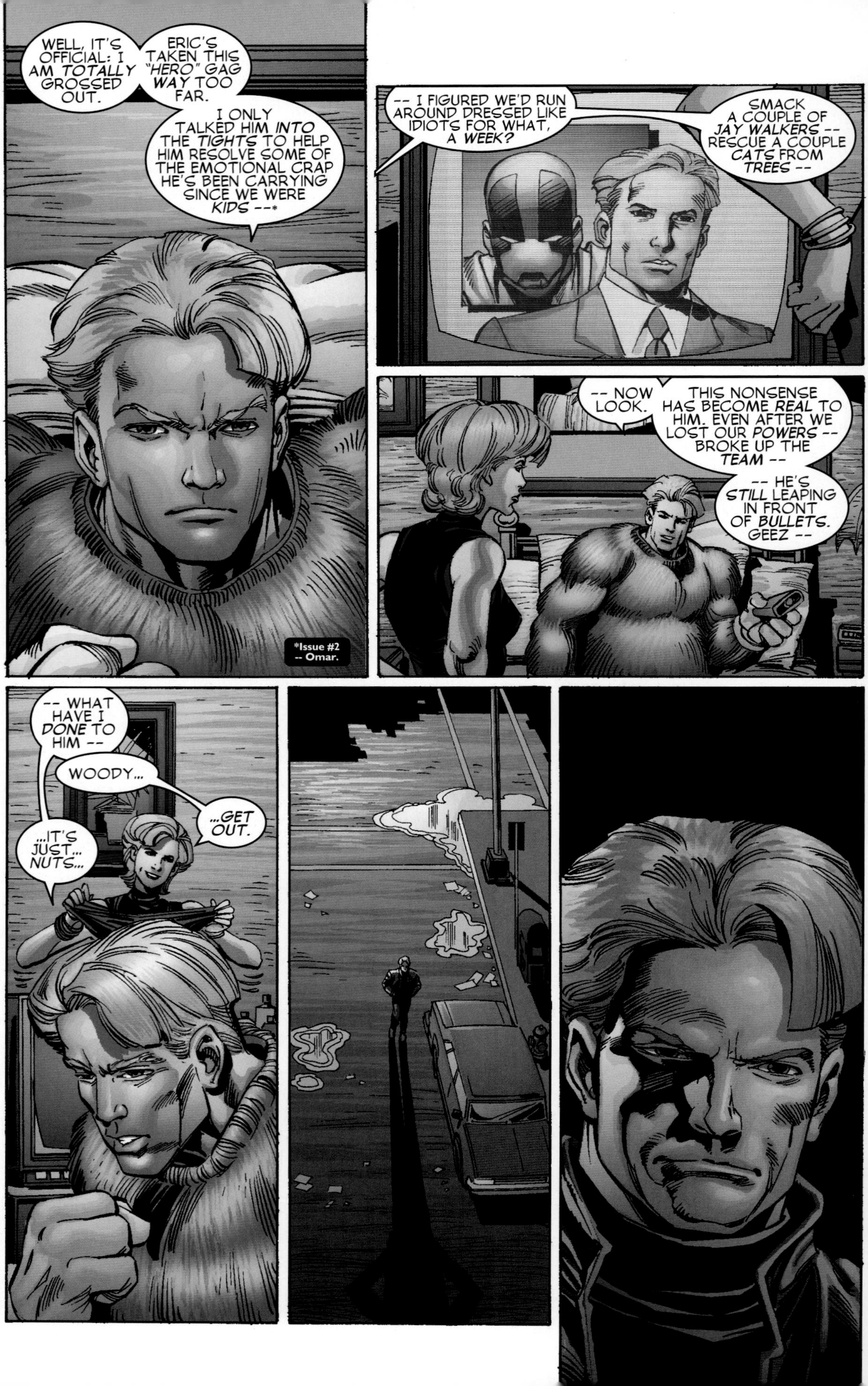
WELL, IT'S OFFICIAL: I AM TOTALLY GROSSED OUT.
ERIC'S TAKEN THIS "HERO" GAG WAY TOO FAR.
I ONLY TALKED HIM INTO THE TIGHTS TO HELP HIM RESOLVE SOME OF THE EMOTIONAL CRAP HE'S BEEN CARRYING SINCE WE WERE KIDS --*
*Issue #2 -- Omar.
-- I FIGURED WE'D RUN AROUND DRESSED LIKE IDIOTS FOR WHAT, A WEEK?
SMACK A COUPLE OF JAY WALKERS -- RESCUE A COUPLE CATS FROM TREES --
-- NOW LOOK.
THIS NONSENSE HAS BECOME REAL TO HIM. EVEN AFTER WE LOST OUR POWERS -- BROKE UP THE TEAM --
-- HE'S STILL LEAPING IN FRONT OF BULLETS. GEEZ --
-- WHAT HAVE I DONE TO HIM --
WOODY...
...GET OUT.
...IT'S JUST... NUTS...

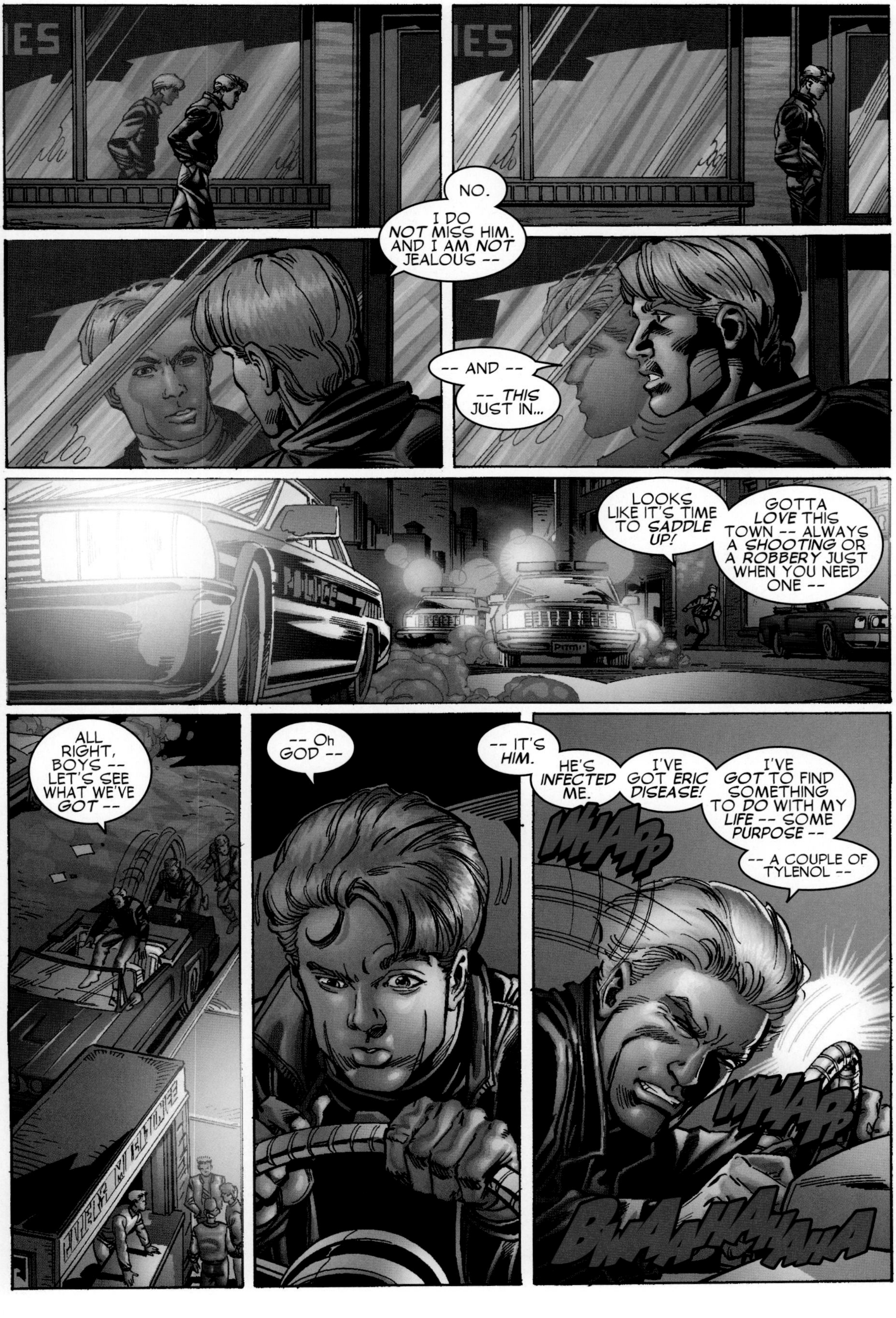
NO.
I DO NOT MISS HIM. AND I AM NOT JEALOUS --
-- AND --
-- THIS JUST IN...
LOOKS LIKE IT'S TIME TO SADDLE UP!
GOTTA LOVE THIS TOWN -- ALWAYS A SHOOTING OR A ROBBERY JUST WHEN YOU NEED ONE --
ALL RIGHT, BOYS -- LET'S SEE WHAT WE'VE GOT --
-- Oh GOD --
-- IT'S HIM.
HE'S INFECTED ME.
I'VE GOT ERIC DISEASE!
I'VE GOT TO FIND SOMETHING TO DO WITH MY LIFE -- SOME PURPOSE --
-- A COUPLE OF TYLENOL --
WHARP
WHARP
BWAAHAHAHAHA

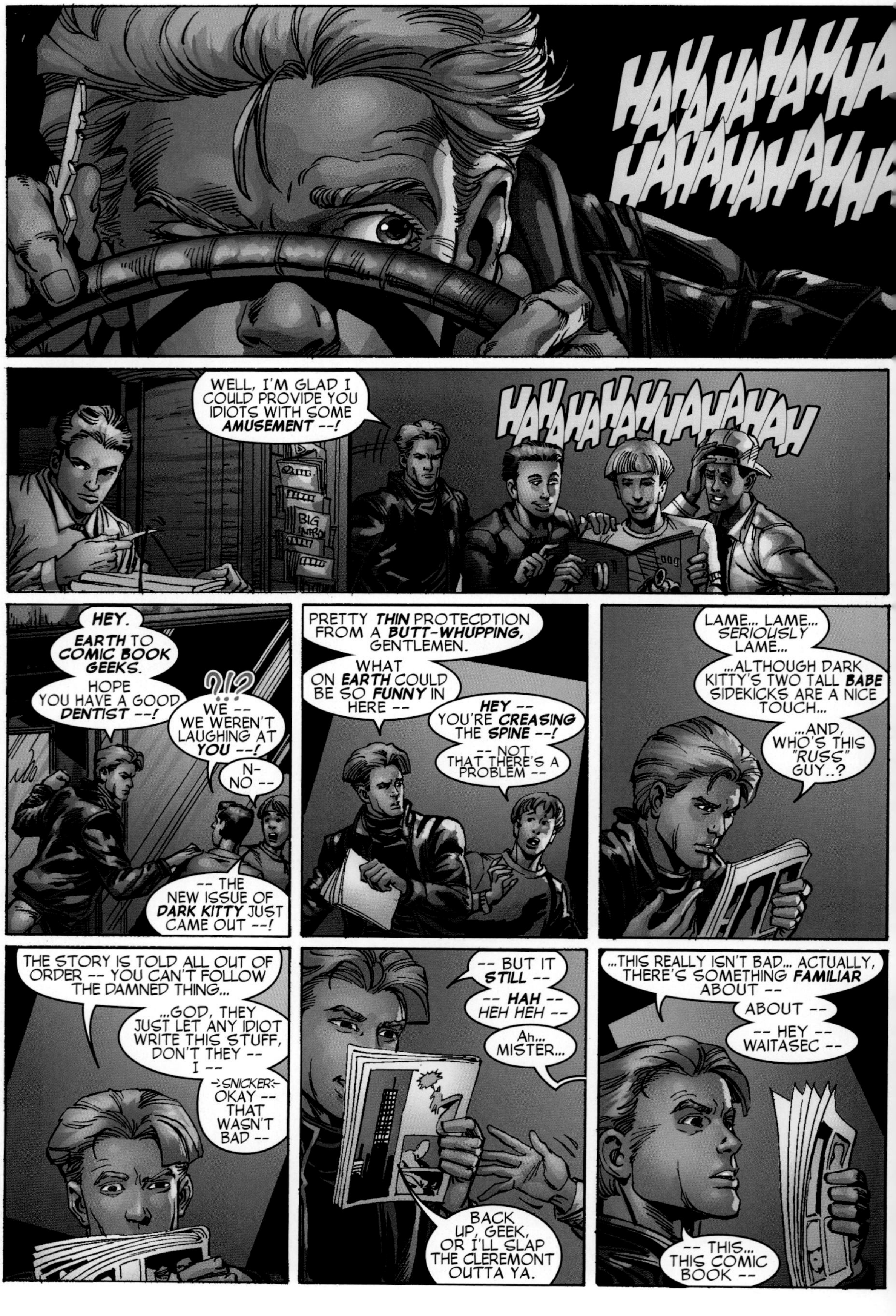
HAHAHAHAHAHAHA
HAHAHAHAHAHAHA
WELL, I'M GLAD I COULD PROVIDE YOU IDIOTS WITH SOME AMUSEMENT --!
HAHAHAHAHAHAHAHAH
BIG INTRO
HEY. EARTH TO COMIC BOOK GEEKS.
HOPE YOU HAVE A GOOD DENTIST --!
?!?
WE -- WE WEREN'T LAUGHING AT YOU --!
N- NO --
-- THE NEW ISSUE OF DARK KITTY JUST CAME OUT --!
PRETTY THIN PROTECDTION FROM A BUTT-WHUPPING, GENTLEMEN.
WHAT ON EARTH COULD BE SO FUNNY IN HERE --
HEY -- YOU'RE CREASING THE SPINE --!
-- NOT THAT THERE'S A PROBLEM --
LAME... LAME... SERIOUSLY LAME...
...ALTHOUGH DARK KITTY'S TWO TALL BABE SIDEKICKS ARE A NICE TOUCH...
...AND, WHO'S THIS "RUSS" GUY..?
THE STORY IS TOLD ALL OUT OF ORDER -- YOU CAN'T FOLLOW THE DAMNED THING...
...GOD, THEY JUST LET ANY IDIOT WRITE THIS STUFF, DON'T THEY -- I --
SNICKER
OKAY -- THAT WASN'T BAD --
-- BUT IT STILL --
-- HAH -- HEH HEH --
Ah... MISTER...
BACK UP, GEEK, OR I'LL SLAP THE CLEREMONT OUTTA YA.
...THIS REALLY ISN'T BAD... ACTUALLY, THERE'S SOMETHING FAMILIAR ABOUT --
ABOUT --
-- HEY -- WAITASEC --
-- THIS... THIS COMIC BOOK --

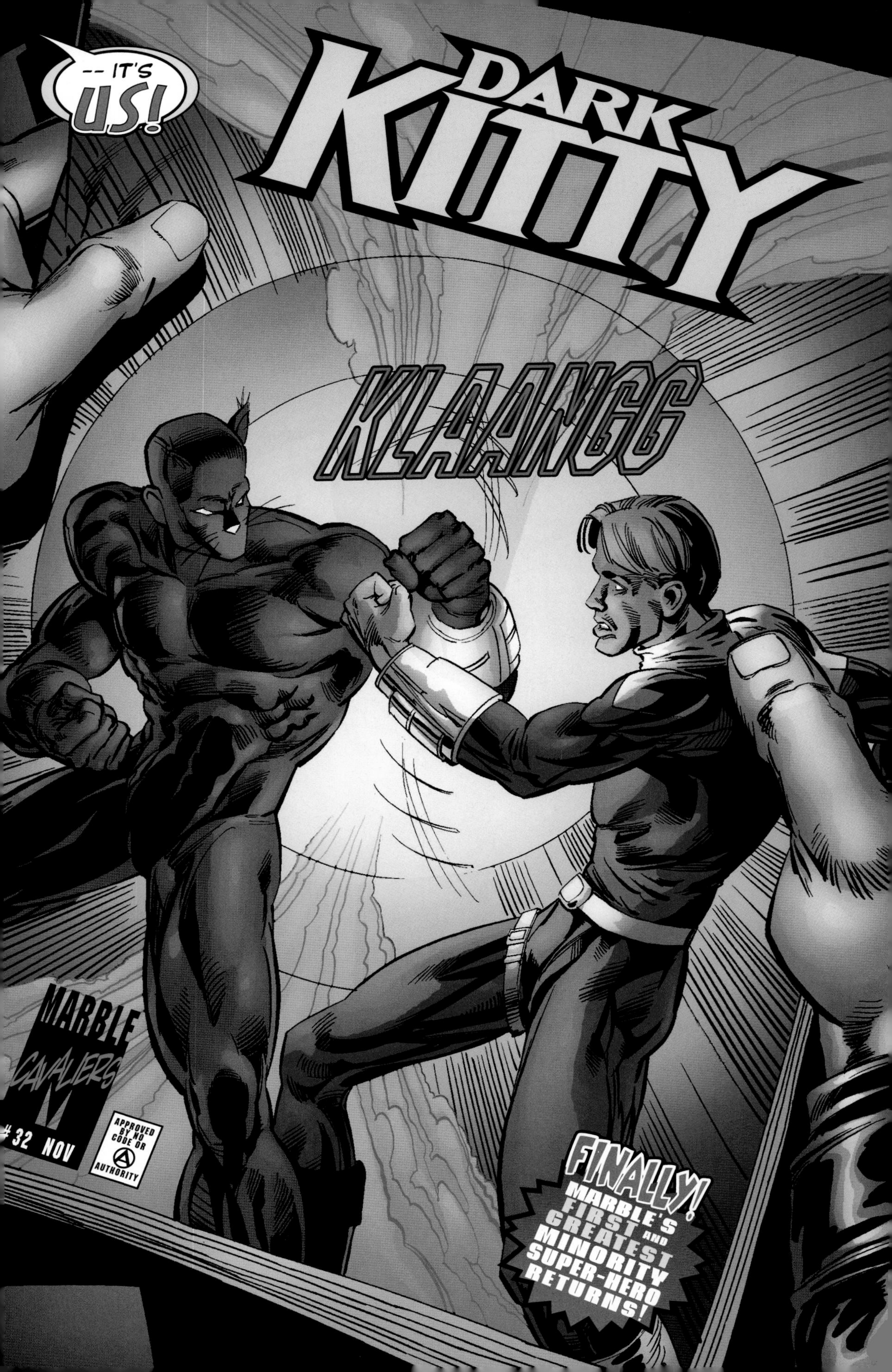
-- IT'S U.S.!
DARK KITTY
KLAANGG
MARBLE CAVALIERS
32 NOV
APPROVED BY NO CODE OR AUTHORITY
FINALLY! MARBLE'S FIRST AND GREATEST MINORITY SUPER-HERO RETURNS!

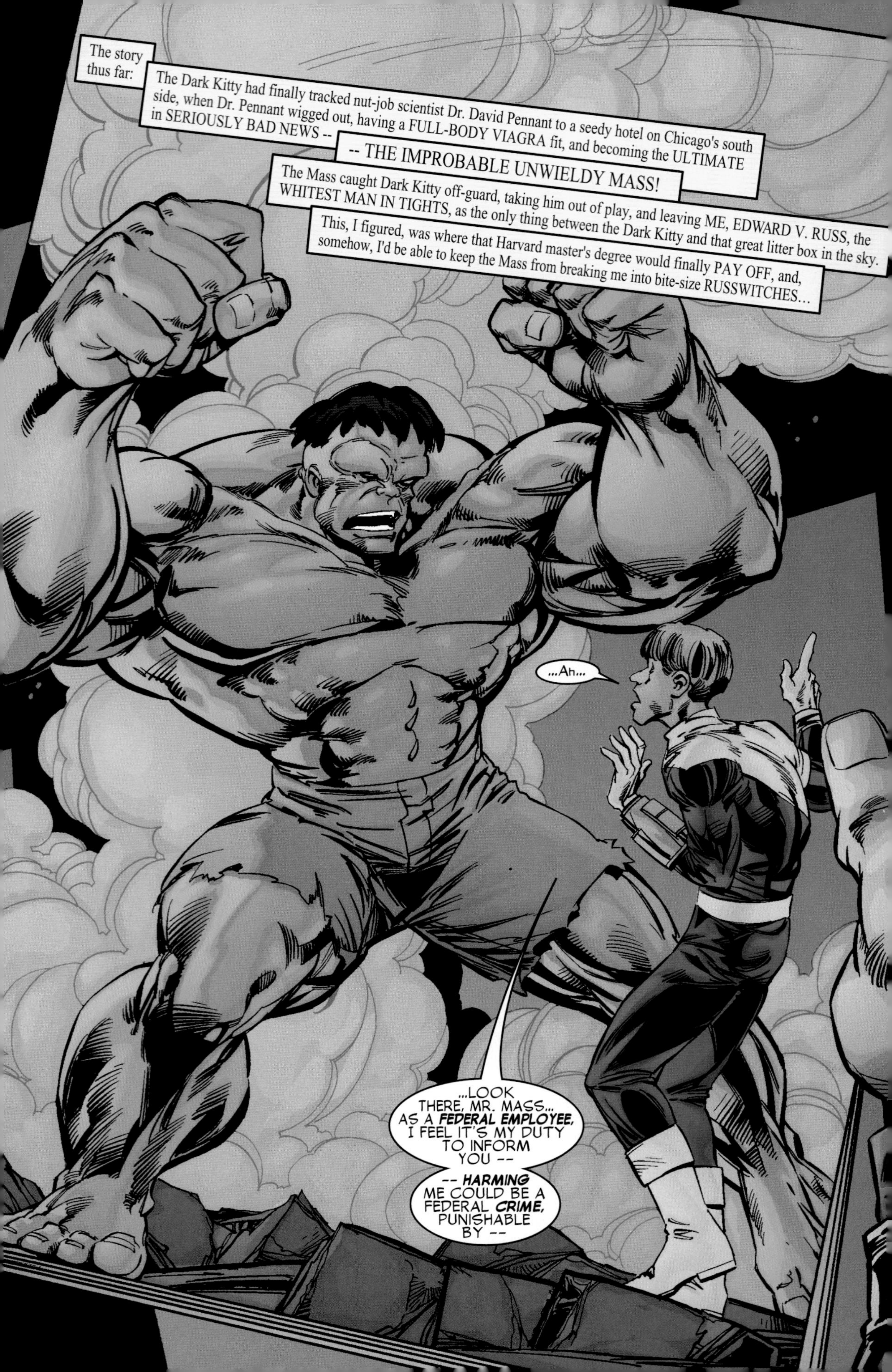
The story thus far:
The Dark Kitty had finally tracked nut-job scientist Dr. David Pennant to a seedy hotel on Chicago's south side, when Dr. Pennant wigged out, having a FULL-BODY VIAGRA fit, and becoming the ULTIMATE in SERIOUSLY BAD NEWS --
-- THE IMPROBABLE UNWIELDY MASS!
The Mass caught Dark Kitty off-guard, taking him out of play, and leaving ME, EDWARD V. RUSS, the WHITEST MAN IN TIGHTS, as the only thing between the Dark Kitty and that great litter box in the sky.
This, I figured, was where that Harvard master's degree would finally PAY OFF, and, somehow, I'd be able to keep the Mass from breaking me into bite-size RUSSWITCHES…
...Ah...
...LOOK THERE, MR. MASS... AS A FEDERAL EMPLOYEE, I FEEL IT'S MY DUTY TO INFORM YOU --
-- HARMING ME COULD BE A FEDERAL CRIME, PUNISHABLE BY --

CATFIGHT

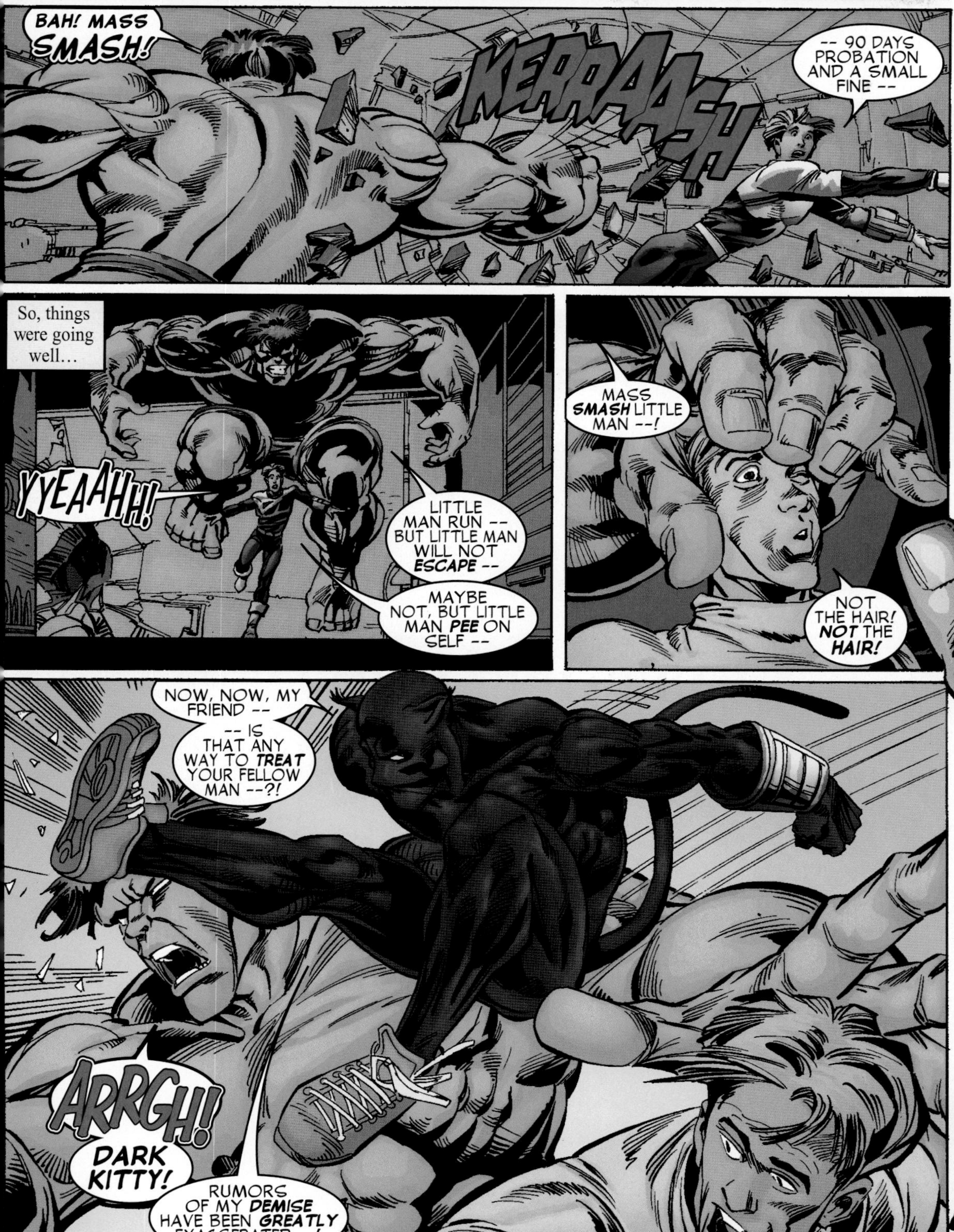
BAH! MASS SMASH!
KERRAASH
-- 90 DAYS PROBATION AND A SMALL FINE --
So, things were going well…
YYEAAHH!
LITTLE MAN RUN -- BUT LITTLE MAN WILL NOT ESCAPE --
MAYBE NOT, BUT LITTLE MAN PEE ON SELF --
MASS SMASH LITTLE MAN --!
NOT THE HAIR! NOT THE HAIR!
NOW, NOW, MY FRIEND --
-- IS THAT ANY WAY TO TREAT YOUR FELLOW MAN --?!
ARRGH! DARK KITTY!
RUMORS OF MY DEMISE HAVE BEEN GREATLY EXAGGERATED --!

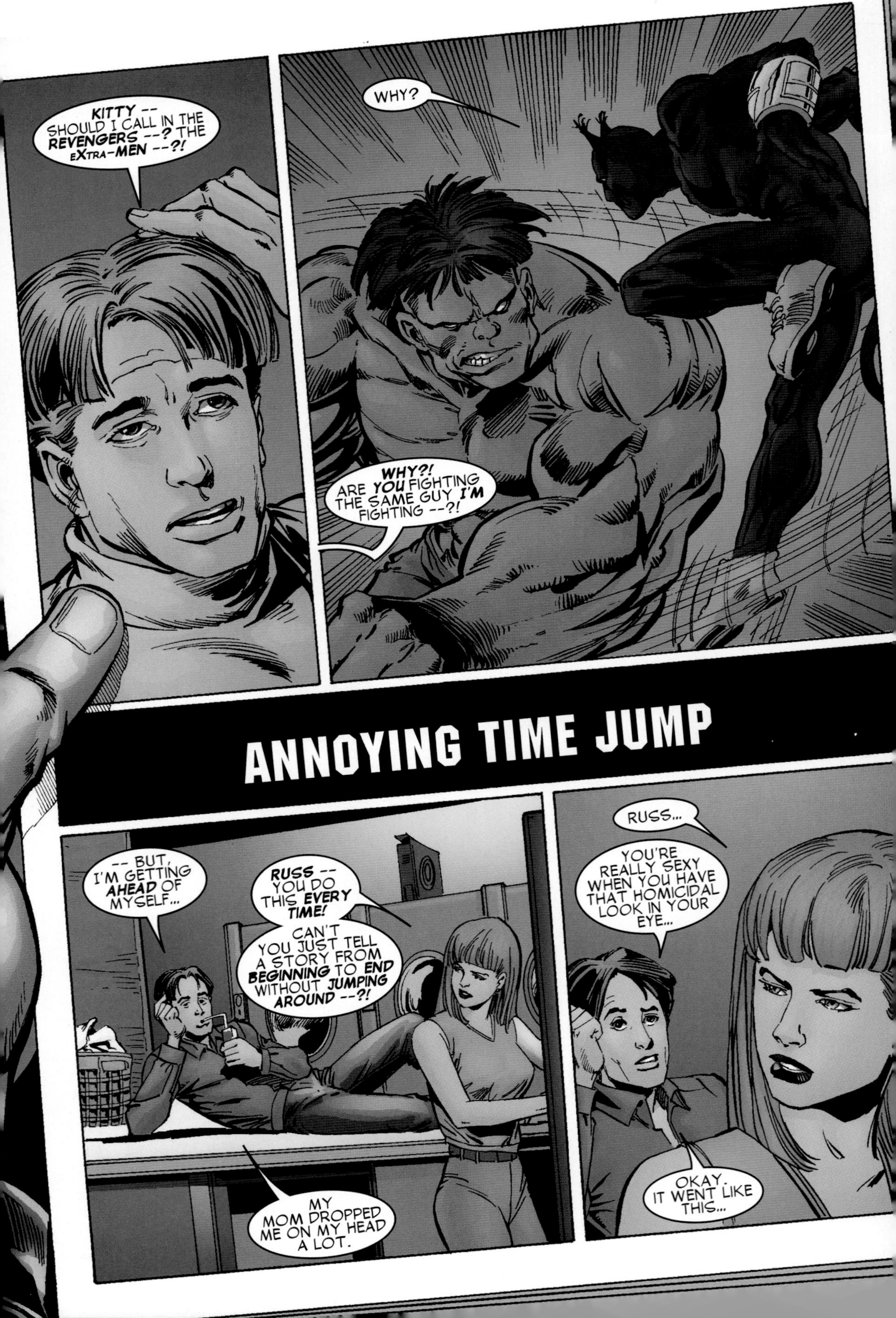
KITTY -- SHOULD I CALL IN THE REVENGERS --? THE EXTRA-MEN --?!
WHY?
WHY?! ARE YOU FIGHTING THE SAME GUY I'M FIGHTING --?!
ANNOYING TIME JUMP
-- BUT, I'M GETTING AHEAD OF MYSELF...
RUSS -- YOU DO THIS EVERY TIME!
CAN'T YOU JUST TELL A STORY FROM BEGINNING TO END WITHOUT JUMPING AROUND --?!
MY MOM DROPPED ME ON MY HEAD A LOT.
RUSS...
YOU'RE REALLY SEXY WHEN YOU HAVE THAT HOMICIDAL LOOK IN YOUR EYE...
OKAY. IT WENT LIKE THIS...

TECHNIQUE MASKING A LACK OF PLOT

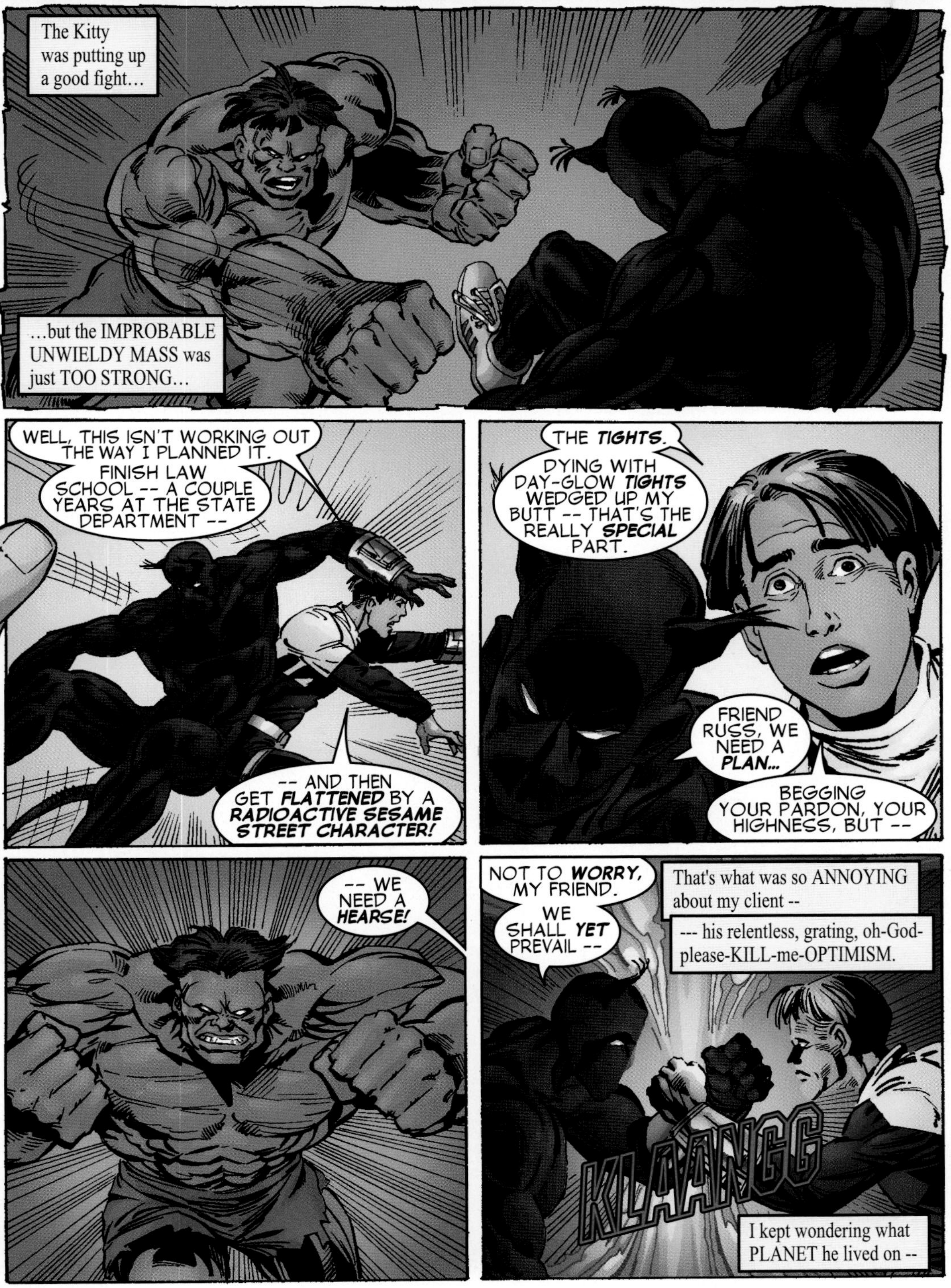

The Kitty was putting up a good fight…
…but the IMPROBABLE UNWIELDY MASS was just TOO STRONG…
WELL, THIS ISN'T WORKING OUT THE WAY I PLANNED IT.
FINISH LAW SCHOOL -- A COUPLE YEARS AT THE STATE DEPARTMENT --
-- AND THEN GET **FLATTENED** BY A ***RADIOACTIVE SESAME STREET CHARACTER!***
THE ***TIGHTS***.
DYING WITH DAY-GLOW ***TIGHTS*** WEDGED UP MY BUTT -- THAT'S THE REALLY ***SPECIAL*** PART.
FRIEND RUSS, WE NEED A ***PLAN...***
BEGGING YOUR PARDON, YOUR HIGHNESS, BUT --
-- WE NEED A ***HEARSE!***
NOT TO ***WORRY,*** MY FRIEND.
WE SHALL ***YET*** PREVAIL --
That's what was so ANNOYING about my client --
--- his relentless, grating, oh-God-please-KILL-me-OPTIMISM.
KLAANGG
I kept wondering what PLANET he lived on --

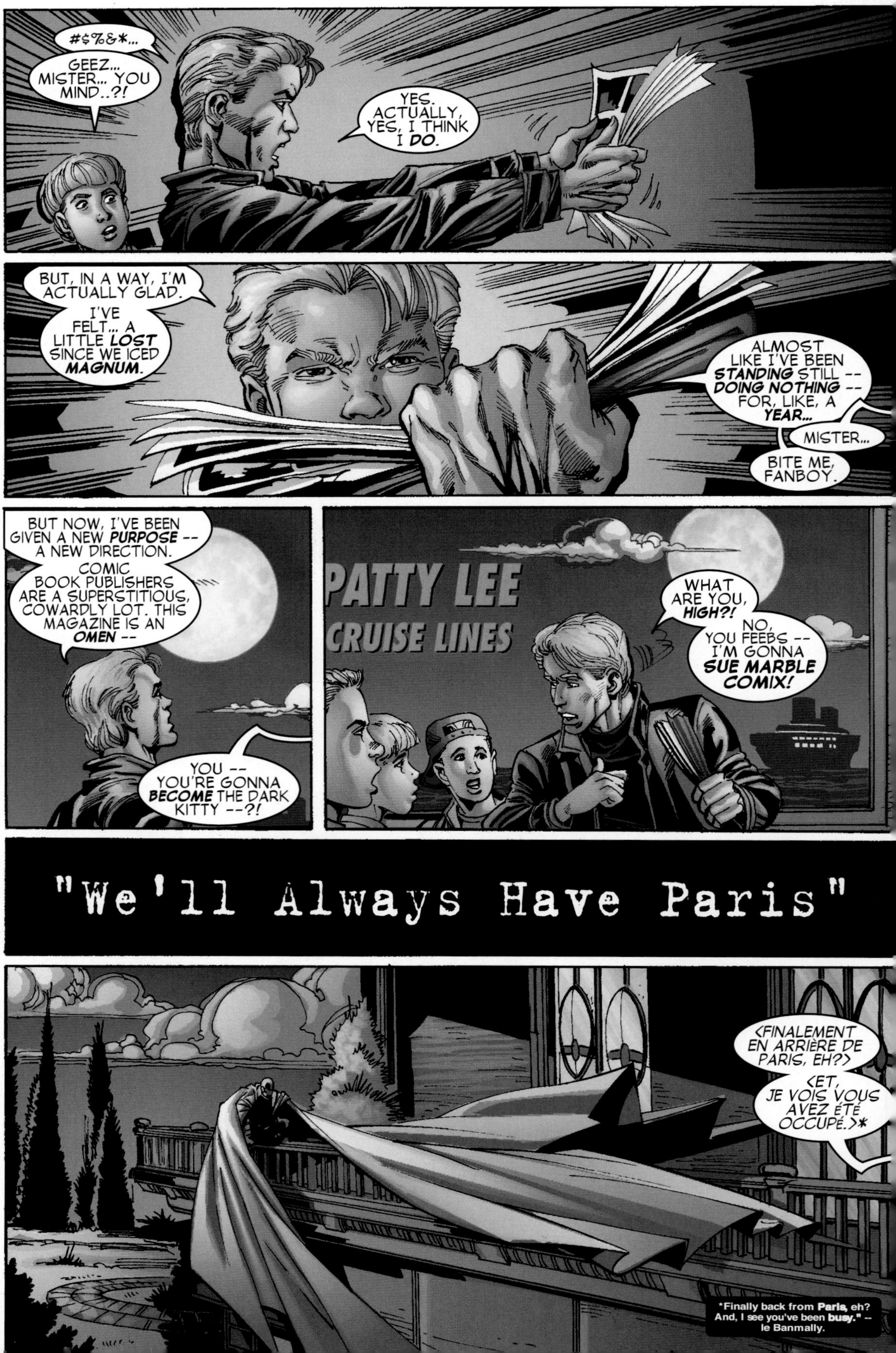
#$%&*...
GEEZ... MISTER... YOU MIND..?!
YES. ACTUALLY, YES, I THINK I DO.
BUT, IN A WAY, I'M ACTUALLY GLAD.
I'VE FELT... A LITTLE LOST SINCE WE ICED MAGNUM.
ALMOST LIKE I'VE BEEN STANDING STILL -- DOING NOTHING -- FOR, LIKE, A YEAR...
MISTER...
BITE ME, FANBOY.
BUT NOW, I'VE BEEN GIVEN A NEW PURPOSE -- A NEW DIRECTION.
COMIC BOOK PUBLISHERS ARE A SUPERSTITIOUS, COWARDLY LOT. THIS MAGAZINE IS AN OMEN --
YOU -- YOU'RE GONNA BECOME THE DARK KITTY --?!
PATTY LEE CRUISE LINES
WHAT ARE YOU, HIGH?!
NO, YOU FEEBS -- I'M GONNA SUE MARBLE COMIX!
"We'll Always Have Paris"
<FINALEMENT EN ARRIÈRE DE PARIS, EH?>
<ET, JE VOIS VOUS AVEZ ÉTÉ OCCUPÉ.>*
*Finally back from Paris, eh? And, I see you've been busy." -- le Banmally.

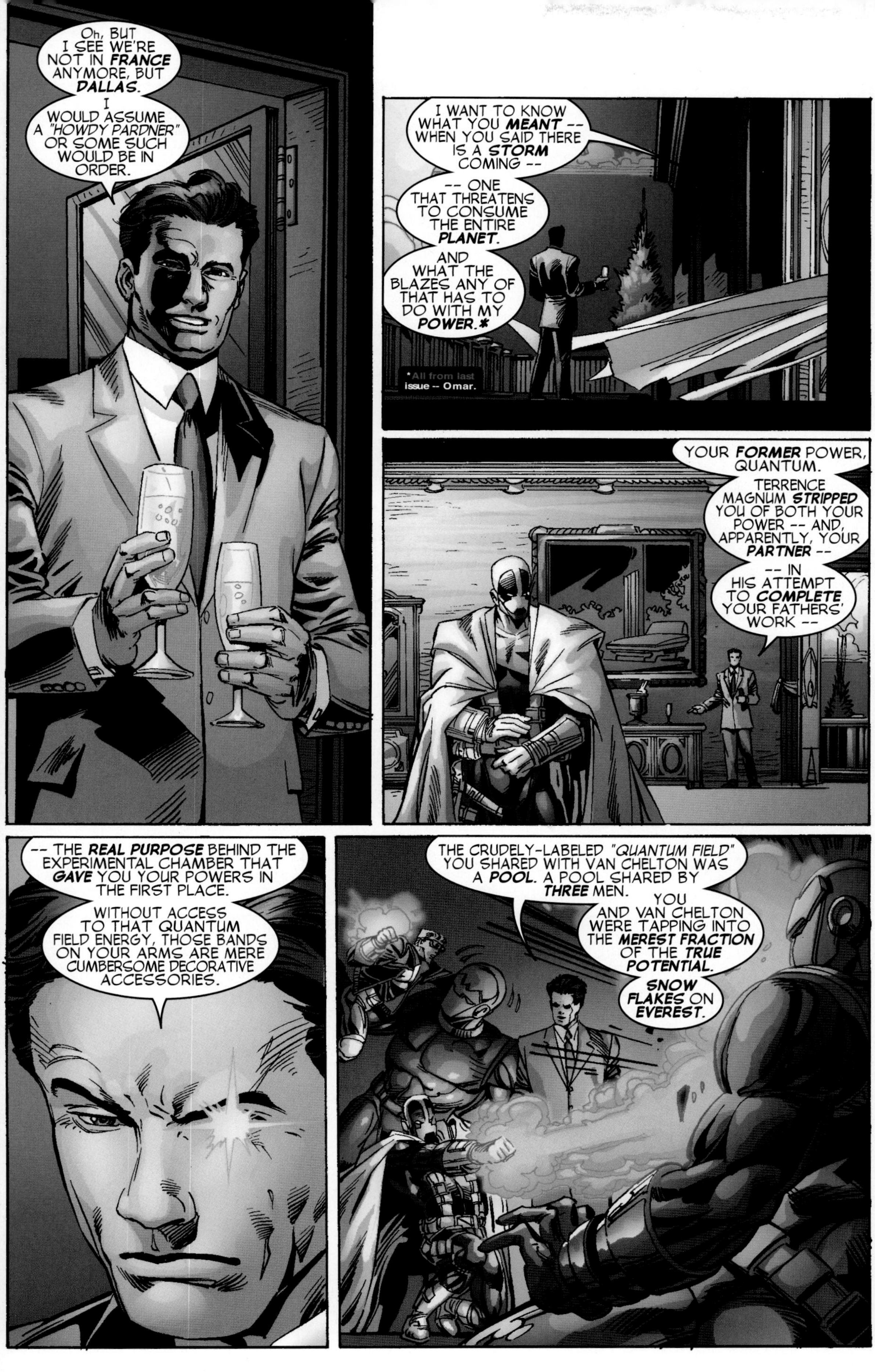
Oh, BUT I SEE WE'RE NOT IN FRANCE ANYMORE, BUT DALLAS.
I WOULD ASSUME A "HOWDY PARDNER" OR SOME SUCH WOULD BE IN ORDER.
I WANT TO KNOW WHAT YOU MEANT -- WHEN YOU SAID THERE IS A STORM COMING --
-- ONE THAT THREATENS TO CONSUME THE ENTIRE PLANET.
AND WHAT THE BLAZES ANY OF THAT HAS TO DO WITH MY POWER.*
*All from last issue -- Omar.
YOUR FORMER POWER, QUANTUM.
TERRENCE MAGNUM STRIPPED YOU OF BOTH YOUR POWER -- AND, APPARENTLY, YOUR PARTNER --
-- IN HIS ATTEMPT TO COMPLETE YOUR FATHERS' WORK --
-- THE REAL PURPOSE BEHIND THE EXPERIMENTAL CHAMBER THAT GAVE YOU YOUR POWERS IN THE FIRST PLACE.
WITHOUT ACCESS TO THAT QUANTUM FIELD ENERGY, THOSE BANDS ON YOUR ARMS ARE MERE CUMBERSOME DECORATIVE ACCESSORIES.
THE CRUDELY-LABELED "QUANTUM FIELD" YOU SHARED WITH VAN CHELTON WAS A POOL. A POOL SHARED BY THREE MEN.
YOU AND VAN CHELTON WERE TAPPING INTO THE MEREST FRACTION OF THE TRUE POTENTIAL.
SNOW FLAKES ON EVEREST.

YOU MISS IT. ADMIT IT. THE TASTE OF THE PARANORMAL -- THE GOD POWER IN YOUR HANDS.

POWER NOW OWNED BY ONE. BY A MAN YOU'VE NEVER TRUSTED --

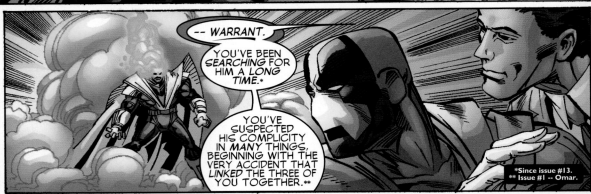

-- WARRANT. YOU'VE BEEN SEARCHING FOR HIM A LONG TIME.*

YOU'VE SUSPECTED HIS COMPLICITY IN MANY THINGS, BEGINNING WITH THE VERY ACCIDENT THAT LINKED THE THREE OF YOU TOGETHER.**

*Since issue #13.
** Issue #1 -- Omar.

IS HE HERO OR VILLAIN? BRILLIANT SCIENTIST OR MAD SCHEMER?

IS HE RESPONSIBLE FOR YOUR FATHER'S DEATH --?

SO MANY QUESTIONS, QUANTUM.

I'M WELL AWARE OF YOUR PARANORMAL TELEKINETIC ABILITIES, HARADA.

IMPRESSED AS I AM BY THE THEATRICS, I'D MUCH PREFER YOU STOPPED CIRCLING AND GOT ON WITH IT.

TO COMBAT WHAT IS TO COME WILL REQUIRE ALL OF THE POWER YOU THREE SHARED.

WHICH MEANS DR. WARRANT WILL NEED TO BECOME MY ALLY...THE FATE OF THE WORLD LEFT IN HIS HANDS.

THAT IS, OF COURSE, UNLESS YOU'D CARE TO MAKE ME A DEAL...

YOU'RE FINISHED, WARRANT. YOU'LL NEVER WIN.

WE SHALL SEE...

"Gone Fission"

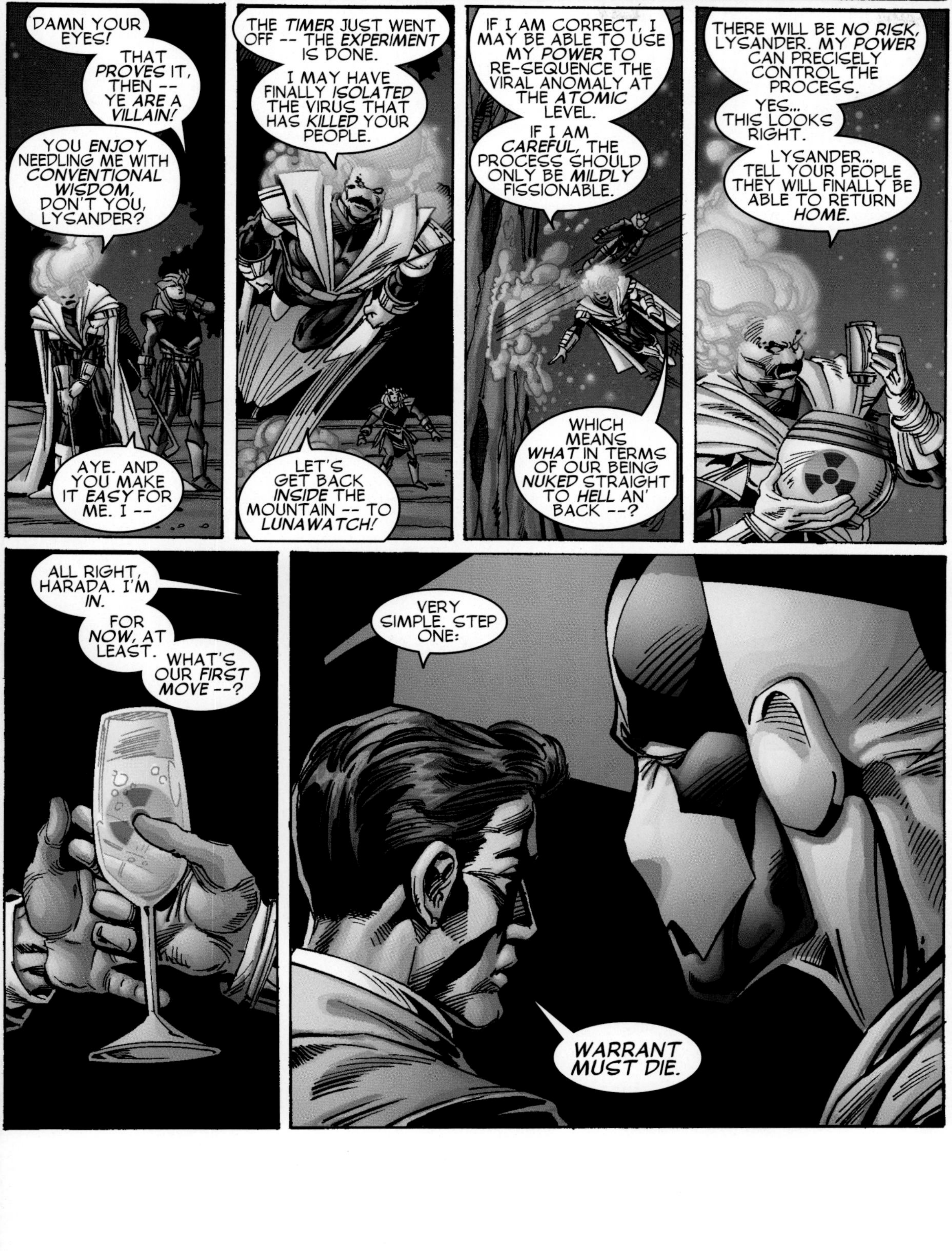
DAMN YOUR EYES!
THAT PROVES IT, THEN -- YE ARE A VILLAIN!
YOU ENJOY NEEDLING ME WITH CONVENTIONAL WISDOM, DON'T YOU, LYSANDER?
AYE. AND YOU MAKE IT EASY FOR ME. I --
THE TIMER JUST WENT OFF -- THE EXPERIMENT IS DONE.
I MAY HAVE FINALLY ISOLATED THE VIRUS THAT HAS KILLED YOUR PEOPLE.
LET'S GET BACK INSIDE THE MOUNTAIN -- TO LUNAWATCH!
IF I AM CORRECT, I MAY BE ABLE TO USE MY POWER TO RE-SEQUENCE THE VIRAL ANOMALY AT THE ATOMIC LEVEL.
IF I AM CAREFUL, THE PROCESS SHOULD ONLY BE MILDLY FISSIONABLE.
WHICH MEANS WHAT IN TERMS OF OUR BEING NUKED STRAIGHT TO HELL AN' BACK --?
THERE WILL BE NO RISK, LYSANDER. MY POWER CAN PRECISELY CONTROL THE PROCESS.
YES... THIS LOOKS RIGHT.
LYSANDER... TELL YOUR PEOPLE THEY WILL FINALLY BE ABLE TO RETURN HOME.
ALL RIGHT, HARADA. I'M IN.
FOR NOW, AT LEAST.
WHAT'S OUR FIRST MOVE --?
VERY SIMPLE. STEP ONE:
WARRANT MUST DIE.

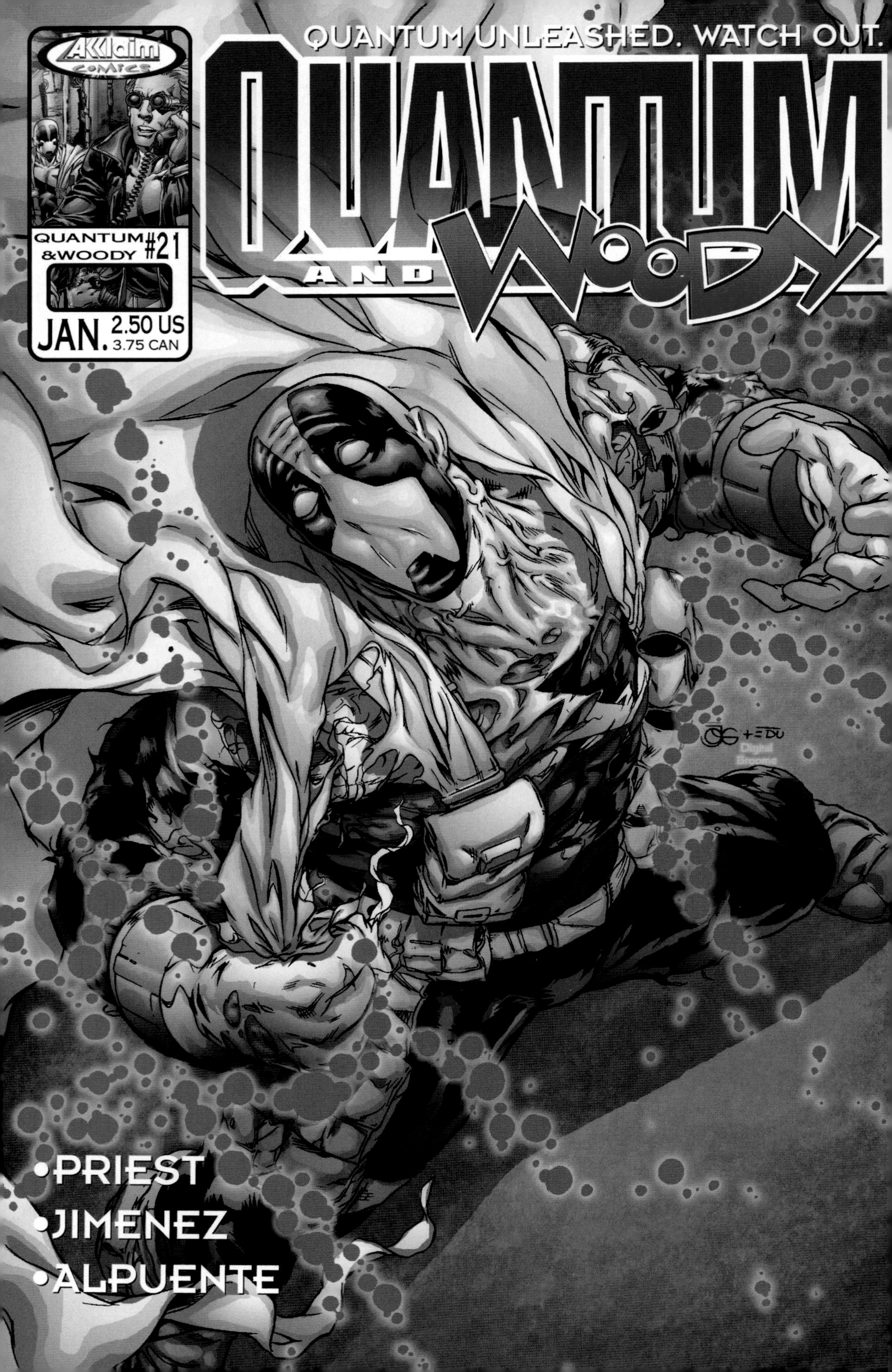
Acclaim Comics
QUANTUM UNLEASHED. WATCH OUT.
QUANTUM AND WOODY
QUANTUM &WOODY #21
JAN. 2.50 US 3.75 CAN
•PRIEST
•JIMENEZ
•ALPUENTE

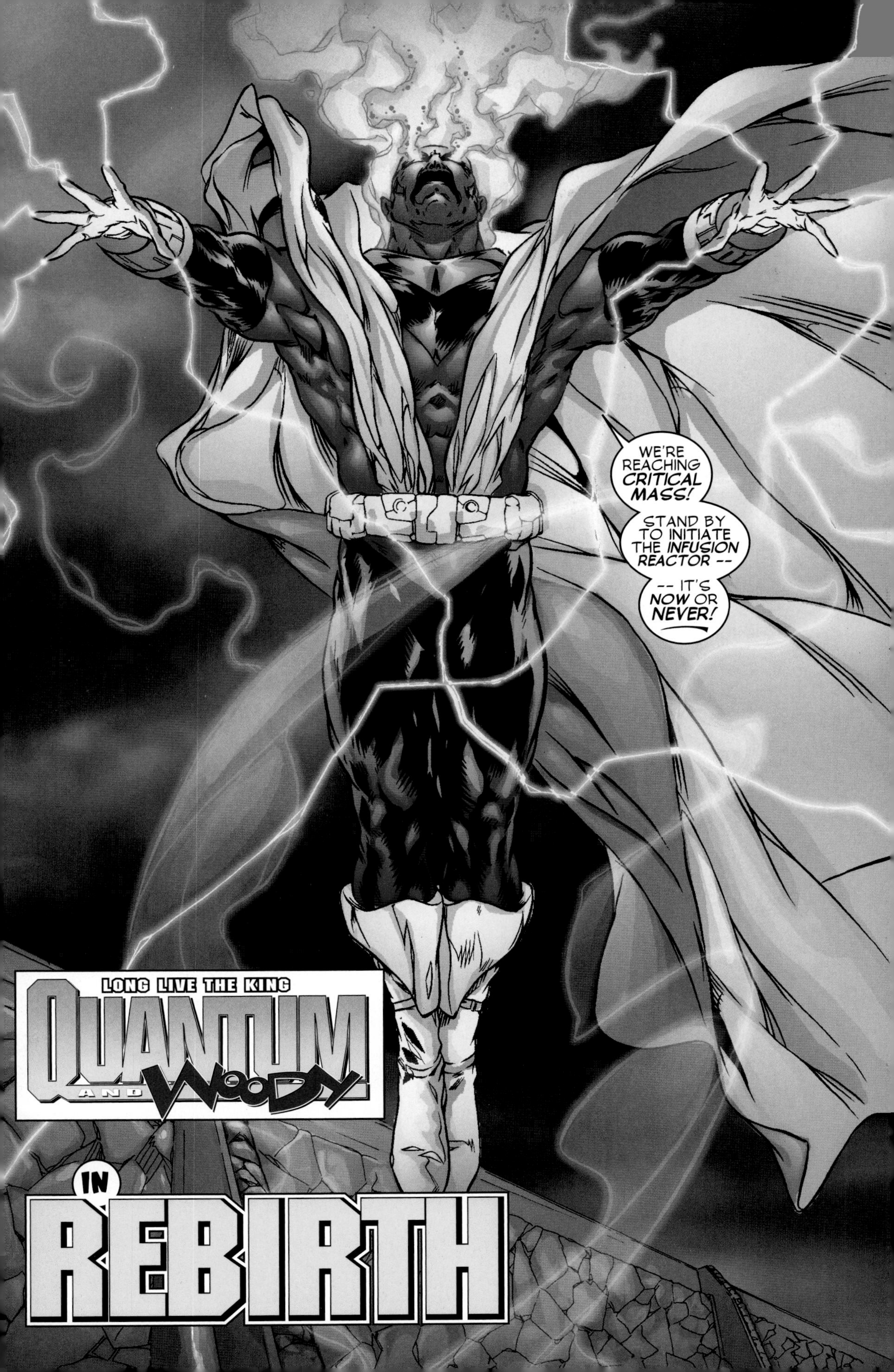
WE'RE REACHING CRITICAL MASS!
STAND BY TO INITIATE THE INFUSION REACTOR --
-- IT'S NOW OR NEVER!
LONG LIVE THE KING
QUANTUM AND WOODY
IN
REBIRTH

"Ducks"

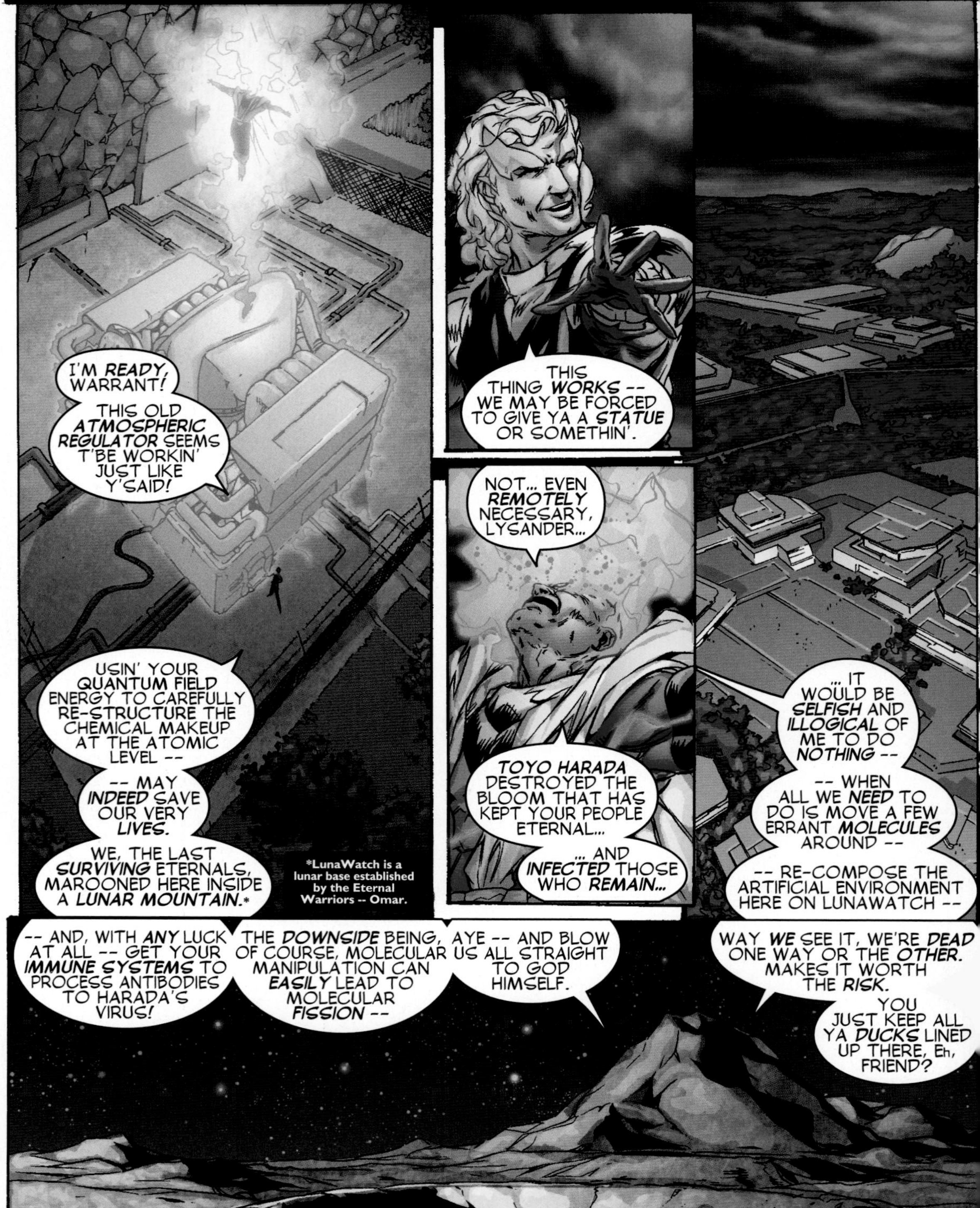
I'M *READY*, WARRANT!
THIS OLD *ATMOSPHERIC REGULATOR* SEEMS T'BE WORKIN' JUST LIKE Y'SAID!
THIS THING *WORKS* -- WE MAY BE FORCED TO GIVE YA A *STATUE* OR SOMETHIN'.
NOT... EVEN *REMOTELY* NECESSARY, LYSANDER...
USIN' YOUR *QUANTUM FIELD* ENERGY TO CAREFULLY RE-STRUCTURE THE CHEMICAL MAKEUP AT THE ATOMIC LEVEL --
-- MAY *INDEED* SAVE OUR VERY *LIVES.*
WE, THE LAST *SURVIVING* ETERNALS, MAROONED HERE INSIDE A *LUNAR MOUNTAIN.**
*LunaWatch is a lunar base established by the Eternal Warriors -- Omar.
TOYO HARADA DESTROYED THE BLOOM THAT HAS KEPT YOUR PEOPLE ETERNAL...
... AND *INFECTED* THOSE WHO *REMAIN...*
... IT WOULD BE *SELFISH* AND *ILLOGICAL* OF ME TO DO *NOTHING* --
-- WHEN ALL WE *NEED* TO DO IS MOVE A FEW ERRANT *MOLECULES* AROUND --
-- RE-COMPOSE THE ARTIFICIAL ENVIRONMENT HERE ON LUNAWATCH --
-- AND, WITH *ANY* LUCK AT ALL -- GET YOUR *IMMUNE SYSTEMS* TO PROCESS ANTIBODIES TO HARADA'S VIRUS!
THE *DOWNSIDE* BEING, OF COURSE, MOLECULAR MANIPULATION CAN *EASILY* LEAD TO MOLECULAR *FISSION* --
AYE -- AND BLOW US ALL STRAIGHT TO GOD HIMSELF.
WAY *WE* SEE IT, WE'RE *DEAD* ONE WAY OR THE *OTHER.* MAKES IT WORTH THE *RISK.*
YOU JUST KEEP ALL YA *DUCKS* LINED UP THERE, Eh, FRIEND?

"The Last Temptation Of Quantum"

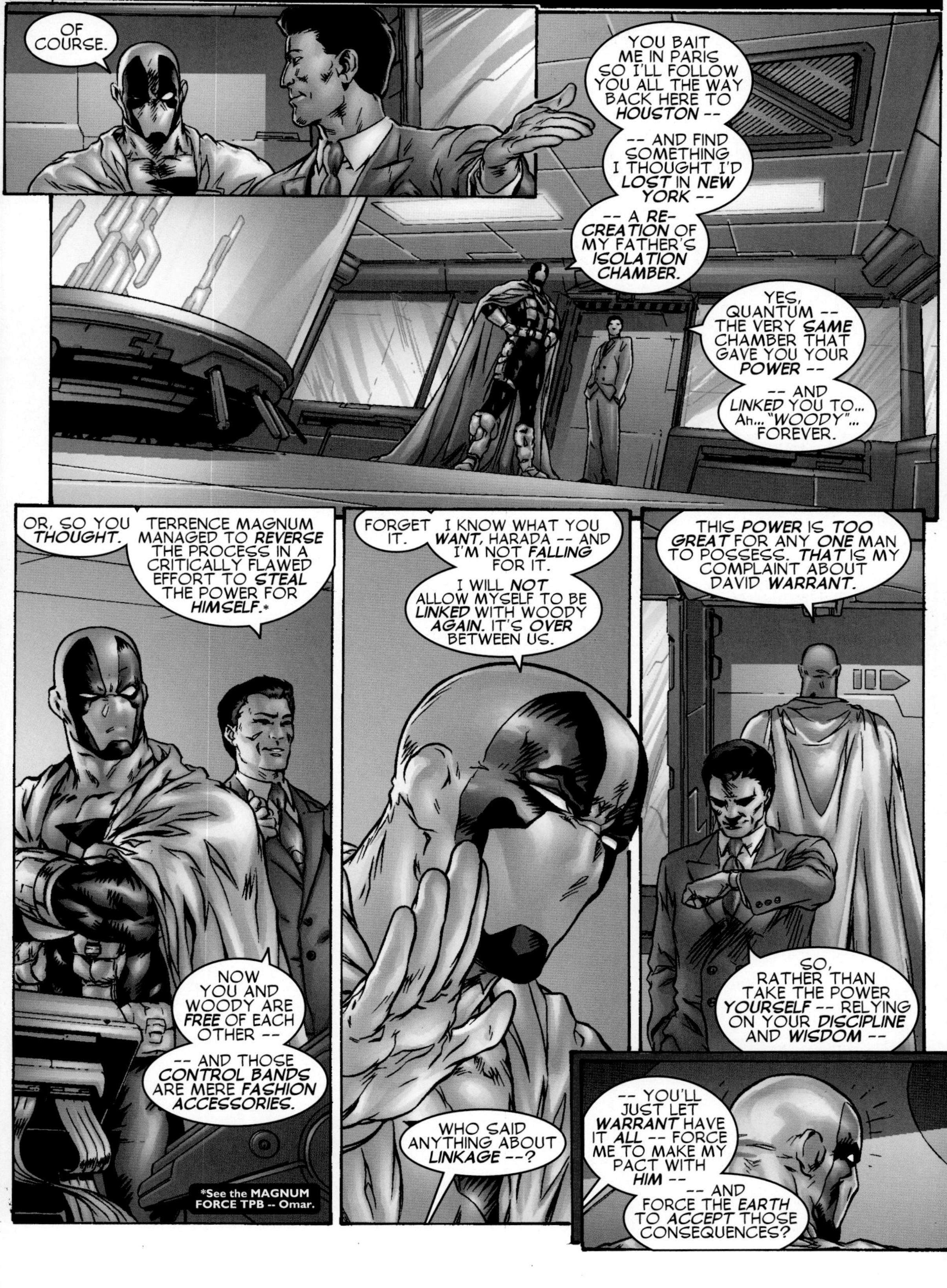

OF COURSE.
YOU BAIT ME IN PARIS SO I'LL FOLLOW YOU ALL THE WAY BACK HERE TO HOUSTON --
-- AND FIND SOMETHING I THOUGHT I'D LOST IN NEW YORK --
-- A RE-CREATION OF MY FATHER'S ISOLATION CHAMBER.
YES, QUANTUM -- THE VERY SAME CHAMBER THAT GAVE YOU YOUR POWER --
-- AND LINKED YOU TO... Ah... "WOODY"... FOREVER.
OR, SO YOU THOUGHT.
TERRENCE MAGNUM MANAGED TO REVERSE THE PROCESS IN A CRITICALLY FLAWED EFFORT TO STEAL THE POWER FOR HIMSELF.*
NOW YOU AND WOODY ARE FREE OF EACH OTHER --
-- AND THOSE CONTROL BANDS ARE MERE FASHION ACCESSORIES.
*See the MAGNUM FORCE TPB -- Omar.
FORGET IT.
I KNOW WHAT YOU WANT, HARADA -- AND I'M NOT FALLING FOR IT.
I WILL NOT ALLOW MYSELF TO BE LINKED WITH WOODY AGAIN. IT'S OVER BETWEEN US.
WHO SAID ANYTHING ABOUT LINKAGE --?
THIS POWER IS TOO GREAT FOR ANY ONE MAN TO POSSESS. THAT IS MY COMPLAINT ABOUT DAVID WARRANT.
SO, RATHER THAN TAKE THE POWER YOURSELF -- RELYING ON YOUR DISCIPLINE AND WISDOM --
-- YOU'LL JUST LET WARRANT HAVE IT ALL -- FORCE ME TO MAKE MY PACT WITH HIM --
-- AND FORCE THE EARTH TO ACCEPT THOSE CONSEQUENCES?

"Long Live The King"

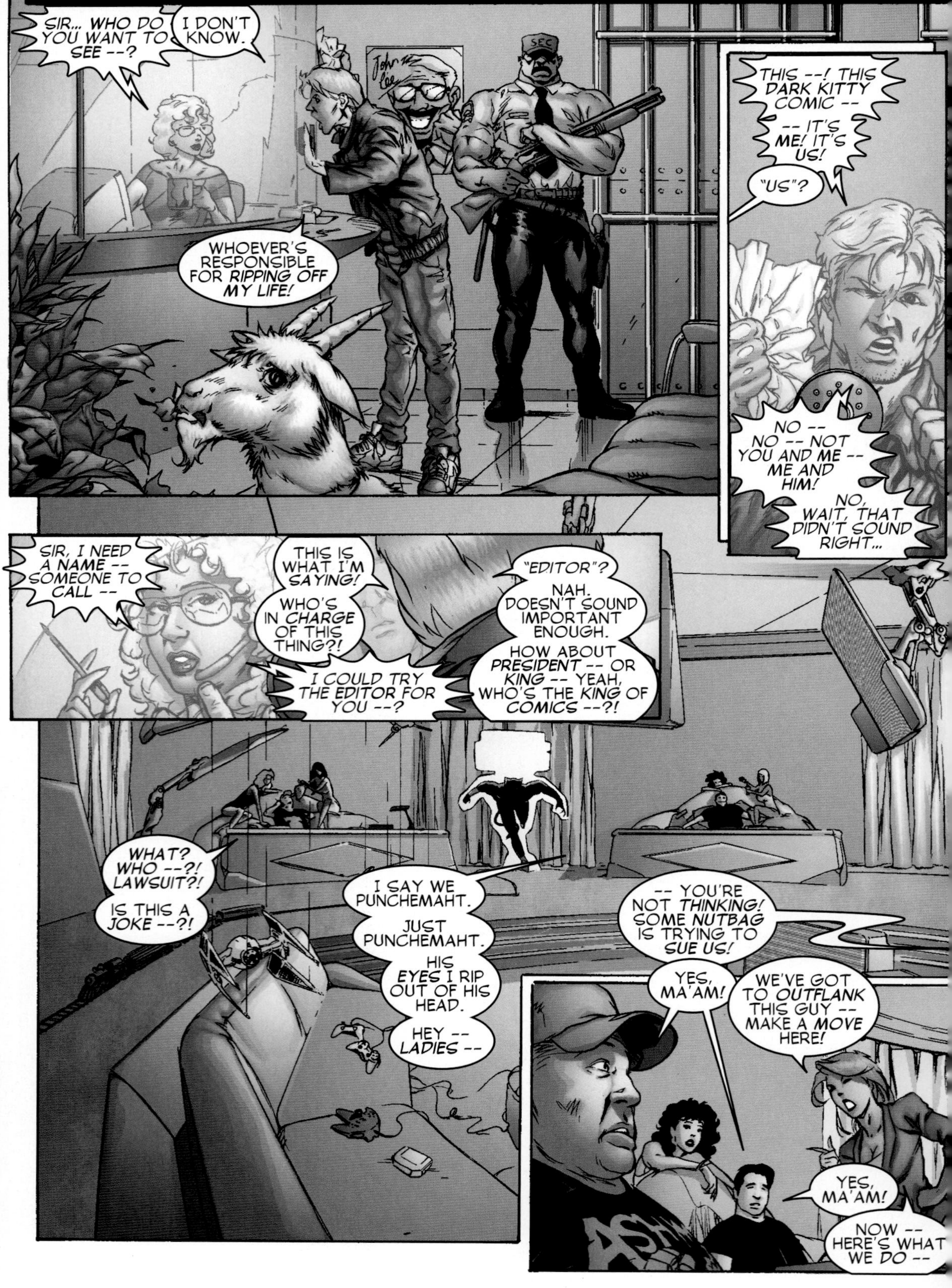

SIR... WHO DO YOU WANT TO SEE --?
I DON'T KNOW.
WHOEVER'S RESPONSIBLE FOR RIPPING OFF MY LIFE!
THIS --! THIS DARK KITTY COMIC --
-- IT'S ME! IT'S US!
"US"?
NO -- NO -- NOT YOU AND ME -- ME AND HIM!
NO, WAIT, THAT DIDN'T SOUND RIGHT...
SIR, I NEED A NAME -- SOMEONE TO CALL --
THIS IS WHAT I'M SAYING!
WHO'S IN CHARGE OF THIS THING?!
I COULD TRY THE EDITOR FOR YOU --?
"EDITOR"?
NAH. DOESN'T SOUND IMPORTANT ENOUGH.
HOW ABOUT PRESIDENT -- OR KING -- YEAH, WHO'S THE KING OF COMICS --?!
WHAT? WHO --?! LAWSUIT?!
IS THIS A JOKE --?!
I SAY WE PUNCHEMAHT.
JUST PUNCHEMAHT.
HIS EYES I RIP OUT OF HIS HEAD.
HEY -- LADIES --
-- YOU'RE NOT THINKING! SOME NUTBAG IS TRYING TO SUE US!
YES, MA'AM!
WE'VE GOT TO OUTFLANK THIS GUY -- MAKE A MOVE HERE!
YES, MA'AM!
NOW -- HERE'S WHAT WE DO --

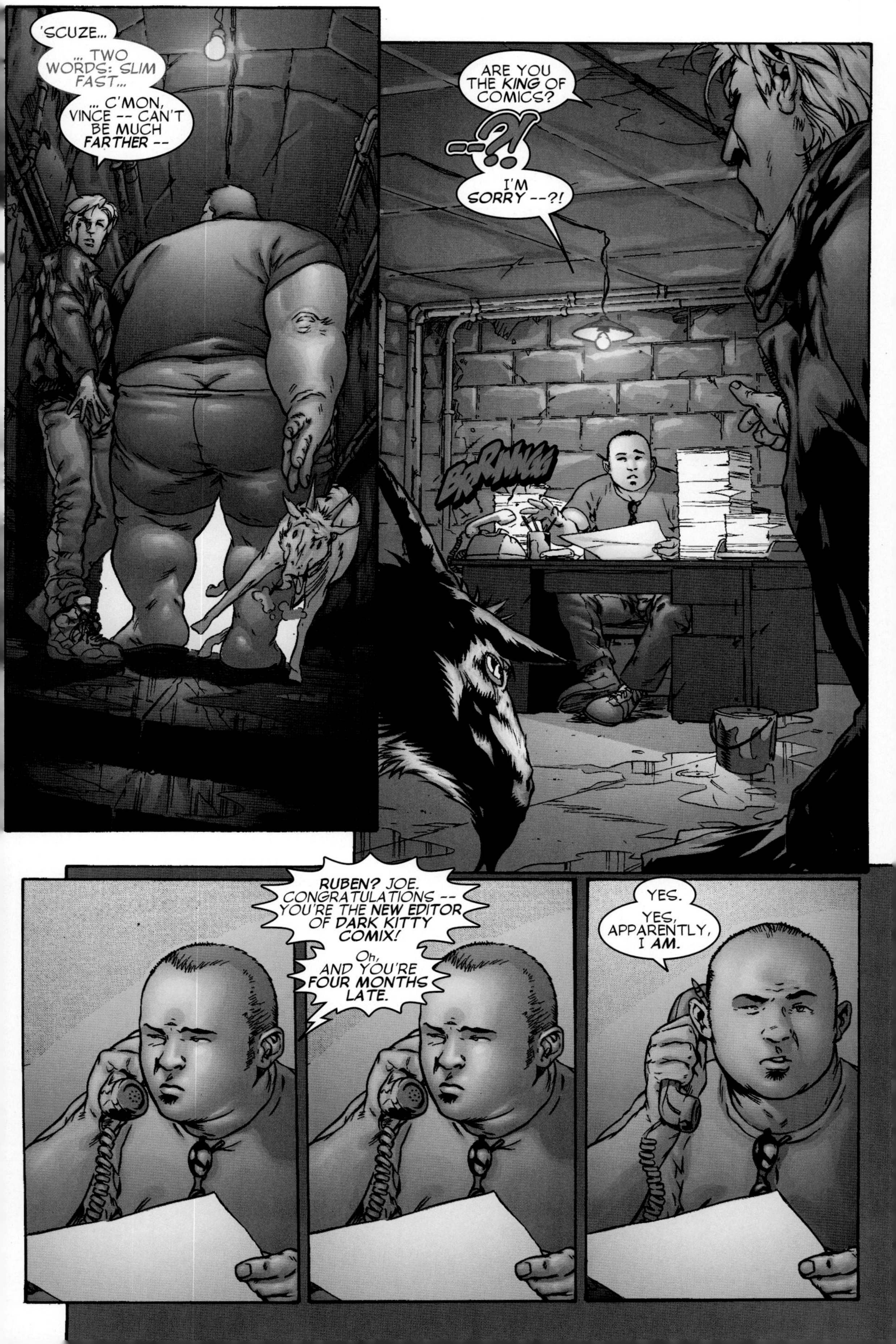
'SCUZE...
... TWO WORDS: SLIM FAST...
... C'MON, VINCE -- CAN'T BE MUCH FARTHER --
ARE YOU THE KING OF COMICS?
--?!
I'M SORRY --?!
BRRINNG
RUBEN? JOE. CONGRATULATIONS -- YOU'RE THE NEW EDITOR OF DARK KITTY COMIX!
Oh, AND YOU'RE FOUR MONTHS LATE.
YES.
YES, APPARENTLY, I AM.

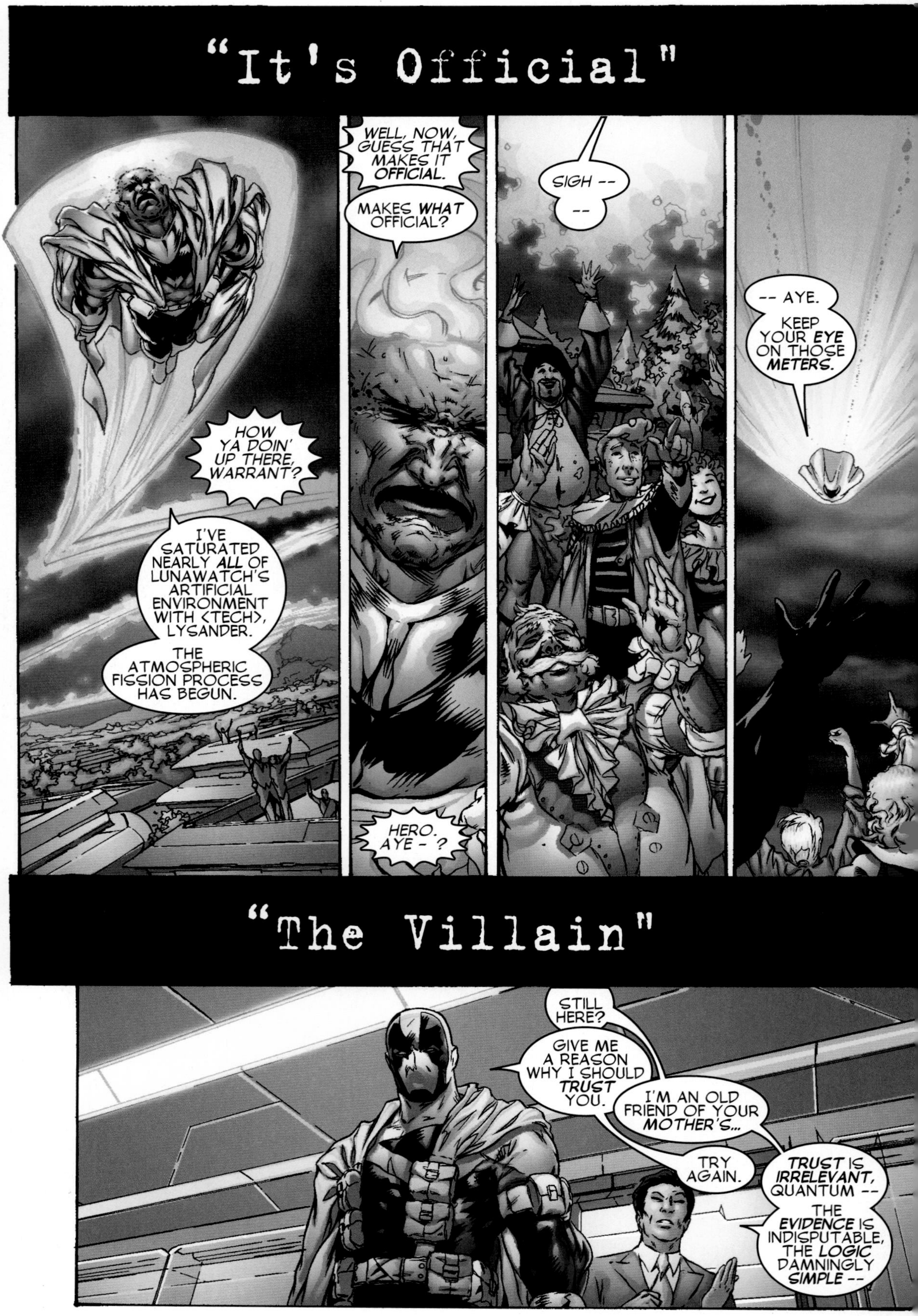
"It's Official"
HOW YA DOIN' UP THERE, WARRANT?
I'VE SATURATED NEARLY ALL OF LUNAWATCH'S ARTIFICIAL ENVIRONMENT WITH <TECH>, LYSANDER.
THE ATMOSPHERIC FISSION PROCESS HAS BEGUN.
WELL, NOW, GUESS THAT MAKES IT OFFICIAL.
MAKES WHAT OFFICIAL?
HERO. AYE - ?
SIGH --
--
-- AYE.
KEEP YOUR EYE ON THOSE METERS.
"The Villain"
STILL HERE?
GIVE ME A REASON WHY I SHOULD TRUST YOU.
I'M AN OLD FRIEND OF YOUR MOTHER'S...
TRY AGAIN.
TRUST IS IRRELEVANT, QUANTUM --
THE EVIDENCE IS INDISPUTABLE, THE LOGIC DAMNINGLY SIMPLE --

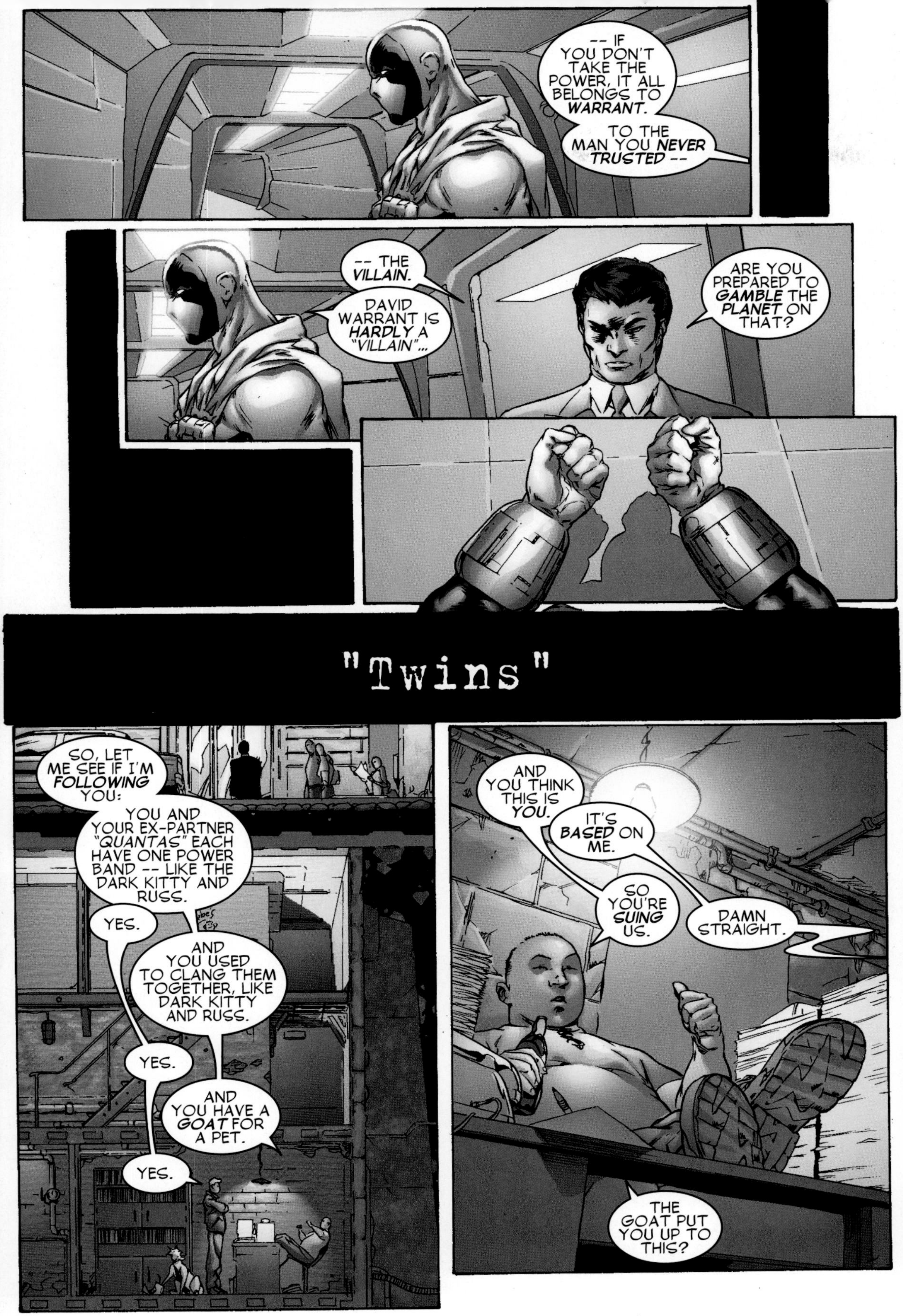
-- IF YOU DON'T TAKE THE POWER, IT ALL BELONGS TO *WARRANT*.
TO THE MAN YOU *NEVER TRUSTED* --
-- THE *VILLAIN*.
DAVID WARRANT IS *HARDLY* A "*VILLAIN*"...
ARE YOU PREPARED TO *GAMBLE* THE *PLANET* ON THAT?
"Twins"
SO, LET ME SEE IF I'M *FOLLOWING* YOU:
YOU AND YOUR EX-PARTNER "*QUANTAS*" EACH HAVE ONE POWER BAND -- LIKE THE DARK KITTY AND RUSS.
YES.
AND YOU USED TO CLANG THEM TOGETHER, LIKE DARK KITTY AND RUSS.
YES.
AND YOU HAVE A *GOAT* FOR A PET.
YES.
AND YOU THINK THIS IS *YOU*.
IT'S *BASED* ON ME.
SO YOU'RE *SUING* US.
DAMN STRAIGHT.
THE GOAT PUT YOU UP TO THIS?

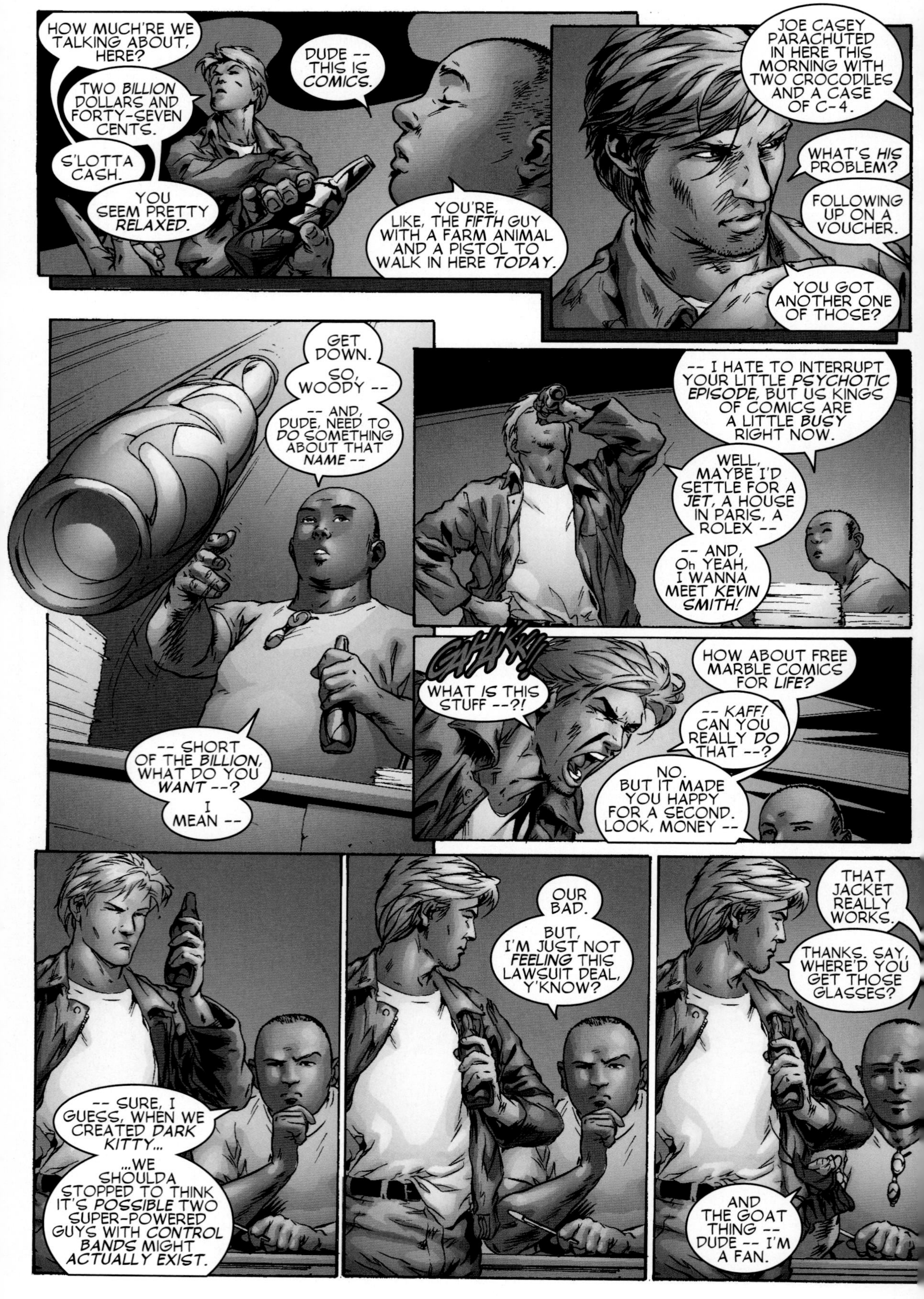
HOW MUCH'RE WE TALKING ABOUT, HERE?
TWO BILLION DOLLARS AND FORTY-SEVEN CENTS.
S'LOTTA CASH.
YOU SEEM PRETTY RELAXED.
DUDE -- THIS IS COMICS.
YOU'RE, LIKE, THE FIFTH GUY WITH A FARM ANIMAL AND A PISTOL TO WALK IN HERE TODAY.
JOE CASEY PARACHUTED IN HERE THIS MORNING WITH TWO CROCODILES AND A CASE OF C-4.
WHAT'S HIS PROBLEM?
FOLLOWING UP ON A VOUCHER.
YOU GOT ANOTHER ONE OF THOSE?
GET DOWN.
SO, WOODY --
-- AND, DUDE, NEED TO DO SOMETHING ABOUT THAT NAME --
-- SHORT OF THE BILLION, WHAT DO YOU WANT --?
I MEAN --
-- I HATE TO INTERRUPT YOUR LITTLE PSYCHOTIC EPISODE, BUT US KINGS OF COMICS ARE A LITTLE BUSY RIGHT NOW.
WELL, MAYBE I'D SETTLE FOR A JET, A HOUSE IN PARIS, A ROLEX --
-- AND, Oh YEAH, I WANNA MEET KEVIN SMITH!
GAHAKK!!
WHAT IS THIS STUFF --?!
HOW ABOUT FREE MARBLE COMICS FOR LIFE?
-- KAFF! CAN YOU REALLY DO THAT --?
NO. BUT IT MADE YOU HAPPY FOR A SECOND. LOOK, MONEY --
-- SURE, I GUESS, WHEN WE CREATED DARK KITTY...
...WE SHOULDA STOPPED TO THINK IT'S POSSIBLE TWO SUPER-POWERED GUYS WITH CONTROL BANDS MIGHT ACTUALLY EXIST.
OUR BAD.
BUT, I'M JUST NOT FEELING THIS LAWSUIT DEAL, Y'KNOW?
THAT JACKET REALLY WORKS.
THANKS. SAY, WHERE'D YOU GET THOSE GLASSES?
AND THE GOAT THING -- DUDE -- I'M A FAN.

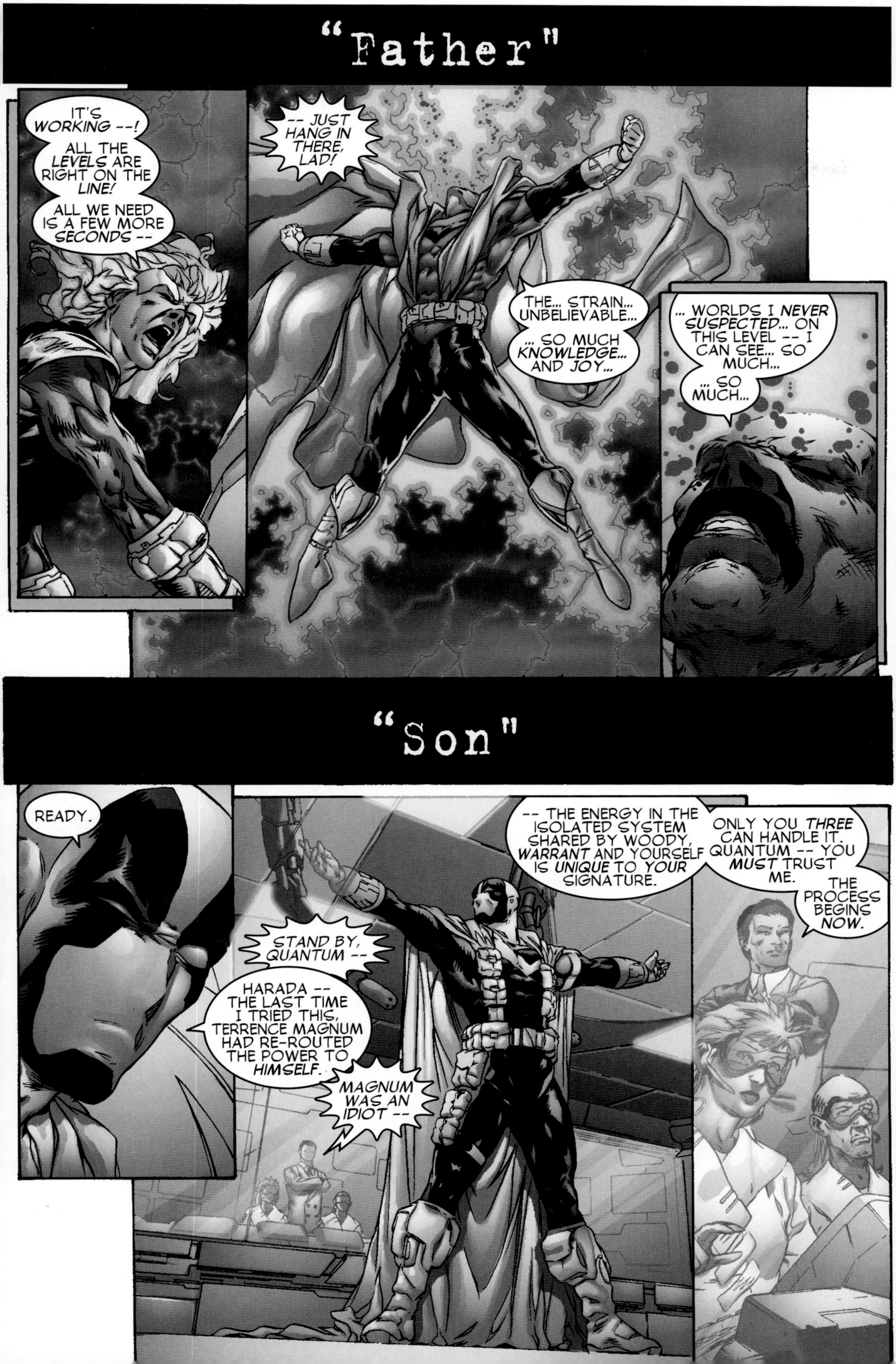
"Father"
IT'S WORKING --! ALL THE LEVELS ARE RIGHT ON THE LINE!
ALL WE NEED IS A FEW MORE SECONDS --
-- JUST HANG IN THERE, LAD!
THE... STRAIN... UNBELIEVABLE...
... SO MUCH KNOWLEDGE... AND JOY...
... WORLDS I NEVER SUSPECTED... ON THIS LEVEL -- I CAN SEE... SO MUCH...
... SO MUCH...
"Son"
READY.
STAND BY, QUANTUM --
HARADA -- THE LAST TIME I TRIED THIS, TERRENCE MAGNUM HAD RE-ROUTED THE POWER TO HIMSELF.
MAGNUM WAS AN IDIOT --
-- THE ENERGY IN THE ISOLATED SYSTEM SHARED BY WOODY, WARRANT AND YOURSELF IS UNIQUE TO YOUR SIGNATURE.
ONLY YOU THREE CAN HANDLE IT. QUANTUM -- YOU MUST TRUST ME.
THE PROCESS BEGINS NOW.

"Holy Goat"

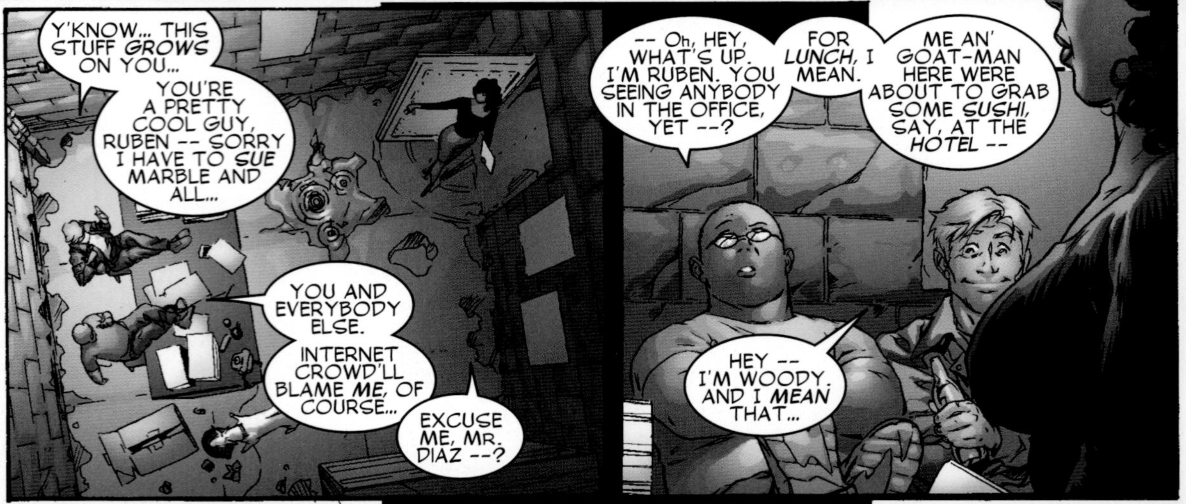
Y'KNOW... THIS STUFF GROWS ON YOU...
YOU'RE A PRETTY COOL GUY, RUBEN -- SORRY I HAVE TO SUE MARBLE AND ALL...
YOU AND EVERYBODY ELSE.
INTERNET CROWD'LL BLAME ME, OF COURSE...
EXCUSE ME, MR. DIAZ --?
-- OH, HEY, WHAT'S UP. I'M RUBEN. YOU SEEING ANYBODY IN THE OFFICE, YET --?
FOR LUNCH, I MEAN.
ME AN' GOAT-MAN HERE WERE ABOUT TO GRAB SOME SUSHI, SAY, AT THE HOTEL --
HEY -- I'M WOODY. AND I MEAN THAT...

"Unity"

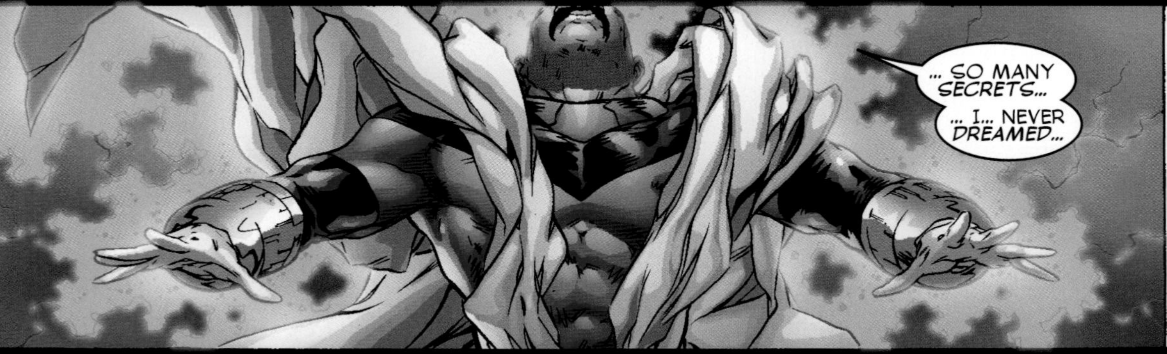
... SO MANY SECRETS...
... I... NEVER DREAMED...

"Trinity"

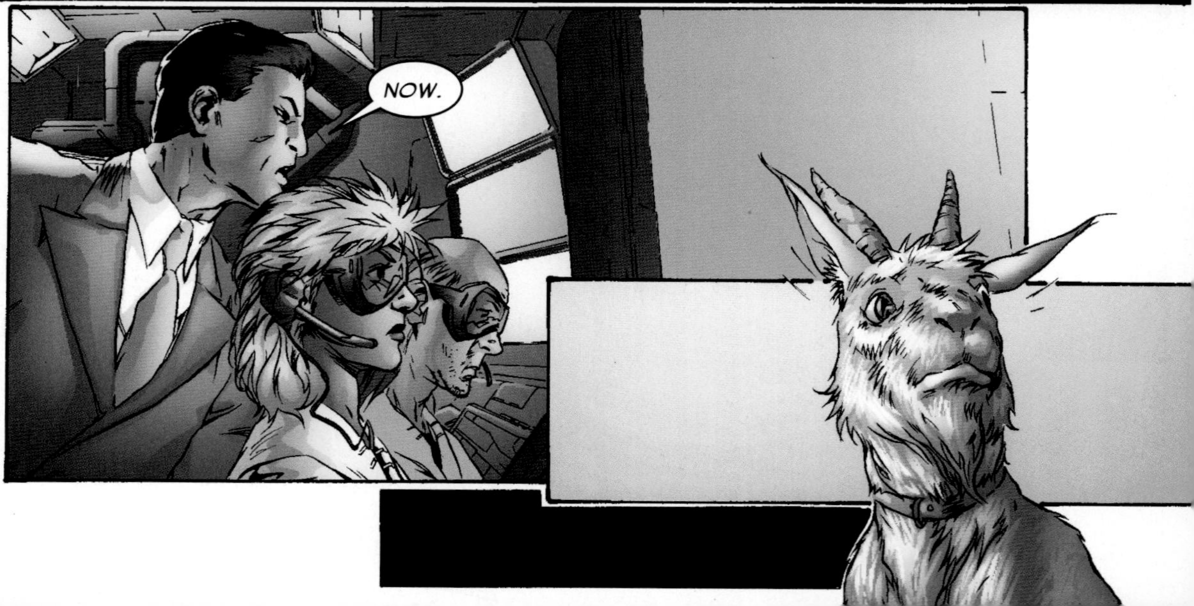
NOW.

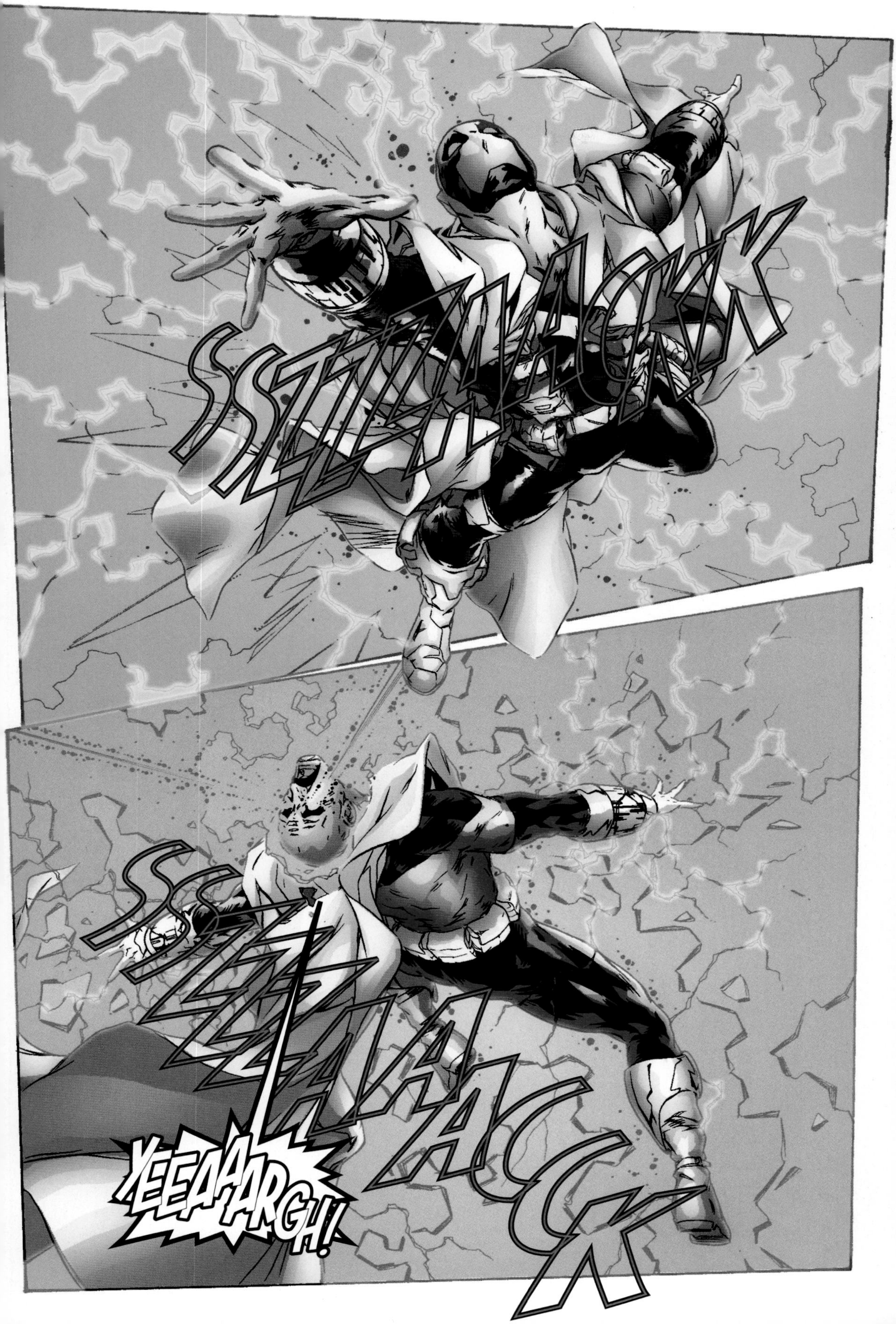
YEEAAARGH!

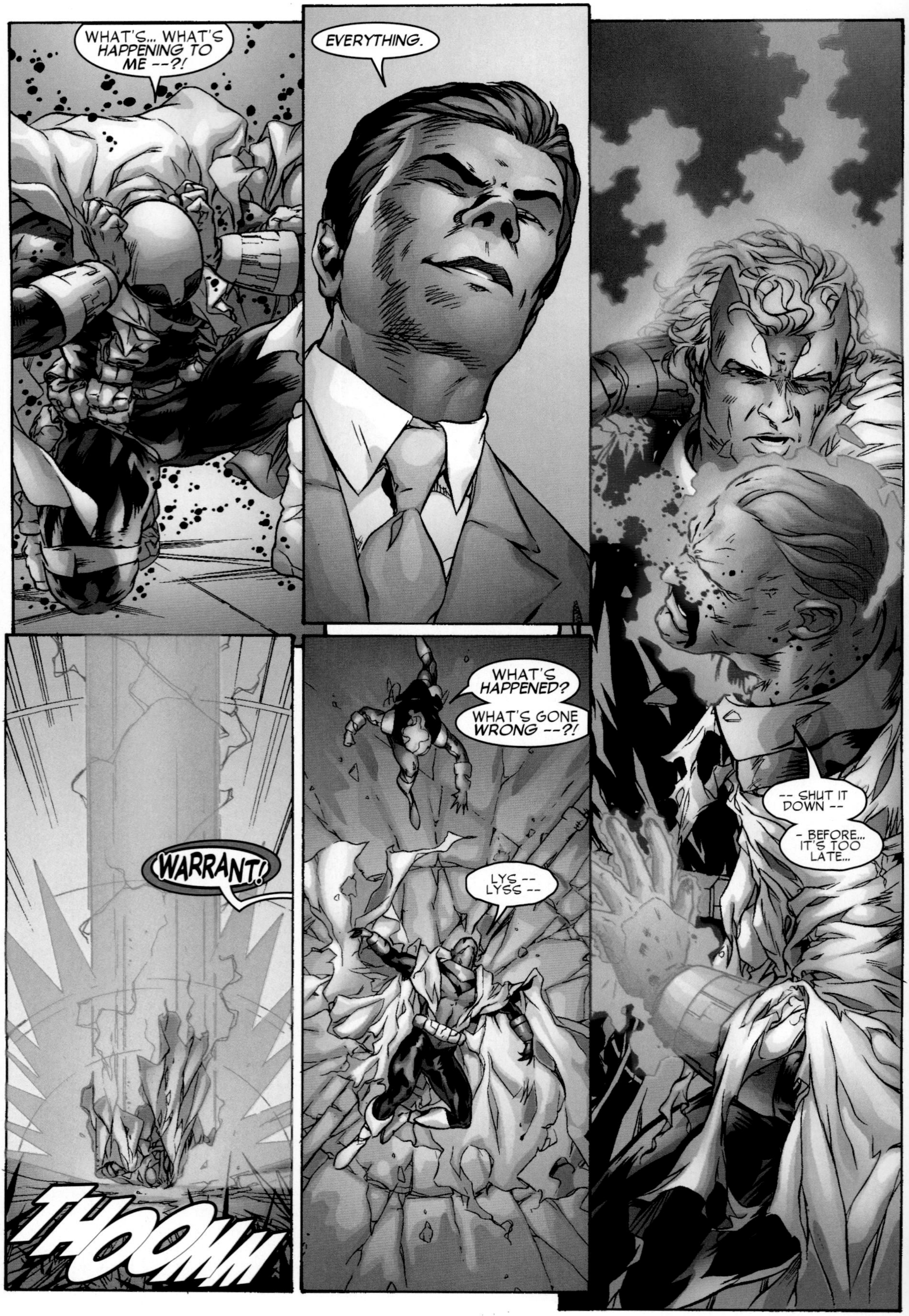

WHAT'S... WHAT'S HAPPENING TO ME --?!
EVERYTHING.
-- SHUT IT DOWN --
- BEFORE... IT'S TOO LATE...
WARRANT!
THOOMM
WHAT'S HAPPENED?
WHAT'S GONE WRONG --?!
LYS -- LYSS --

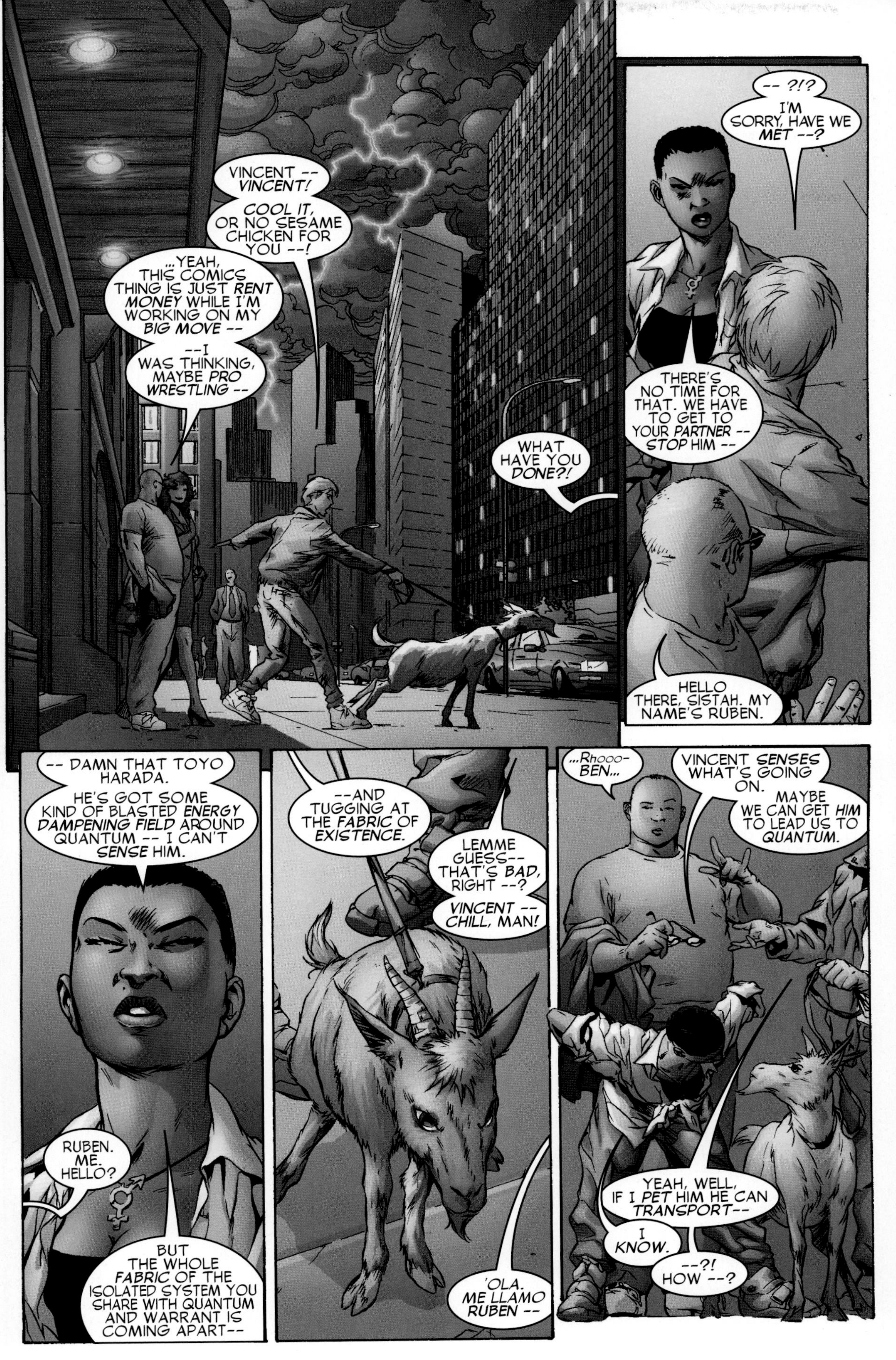
VINCENT -- VINCENT! COOL IT, OR NO SESAME CHICKEN FOR YOU --!
...YEAH, THIS COMICS THING IS JUST RENT MONEY WHILE I'M WORKING ON MY BIG MOVE --
--I WAS THINKING, MAYBE PRO WRESTLING --
WHAT HAVE YOU DONE?!
-- ?!?
I'M SORRY, HAVE WE MET --?
THERE'S NO TIME FOR THAT. WE HAVE TO GET TO YOUR PARTNER -- STOP HIM --
HELLO THERE, SISTAH. MY NAME'S RUBEN.
-- DAMN THAT TOYO HARADA.
HE'S GOT SOME KIND OF BLASTED ENERGY DAMPENING FIELD AROUND QUANTUM -- I CAN'T SENSE HIM.
RUBEN. ME. HELLO?
BUT THE WHOLE FABRIC OF THE ISOLATED SYSTEM YOU SHARE WITH QUANTUM AND WARRANT IS COMING APART--
--AND TUGGING AT THE FABRIC OF EXISTENCE.
LEMME GUESS-- THAT'S BAD, RIGHT --?
VINCENT -- CHILL, MAN!
'OLA. ME LLAMO RUBEN --
...RHOOO-BEN...
VINCENT SENSES WHAT'S GOING ON.
MAYBE WE CAN GET HIM TO LEAD US TO QUANTUM.
YEAH, WELL, IF I PET HIM HE CAN TRANSPORT--
I KNOW.
--?! HOW --?

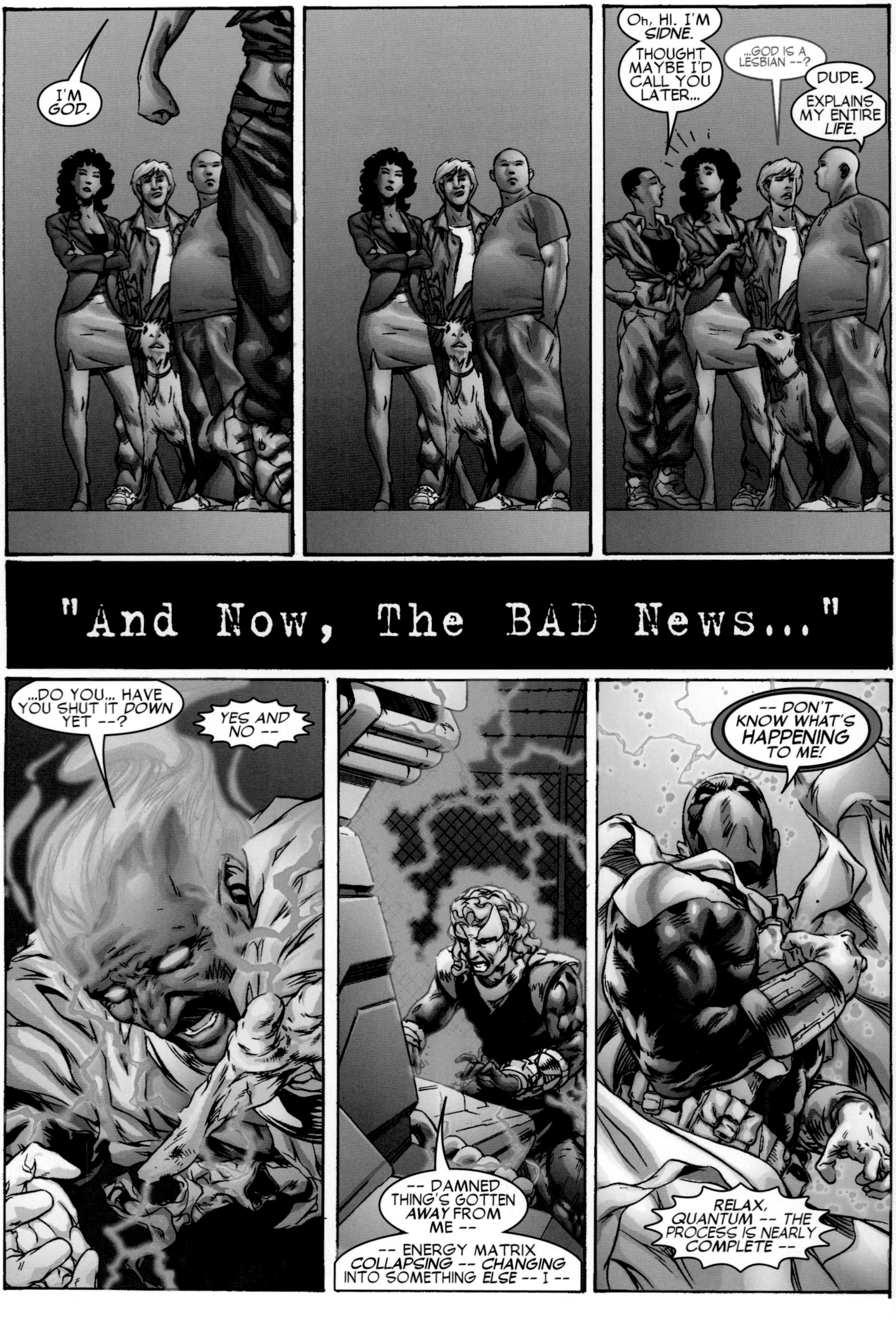
I'M GOD.
OH, HI. I'M SIDNE.
THOUGHT MAYBE I'D CALL YOU LATER...
...GOD IS A LESBIAN --?
DUDE.
EXPLAINS MY ENTIRE LIFE.
"And Now, The BAD News..."
...DO YOU... HAVE YOU SHUT IT DOWN YET --?
YES AND NO --
-- DAMNED THING'S GOTTEN AWAY FROM ME --
-- ENERGY MATRIX COLLAPSING -- CHANGING INTO SOMETHING ELSE -- I --
-- DON'T KNOW WHAT'S HAPPENING TO ME!
RELAX, QUANTUM -- THE PROCESS IS NEARLY COMPLETE --

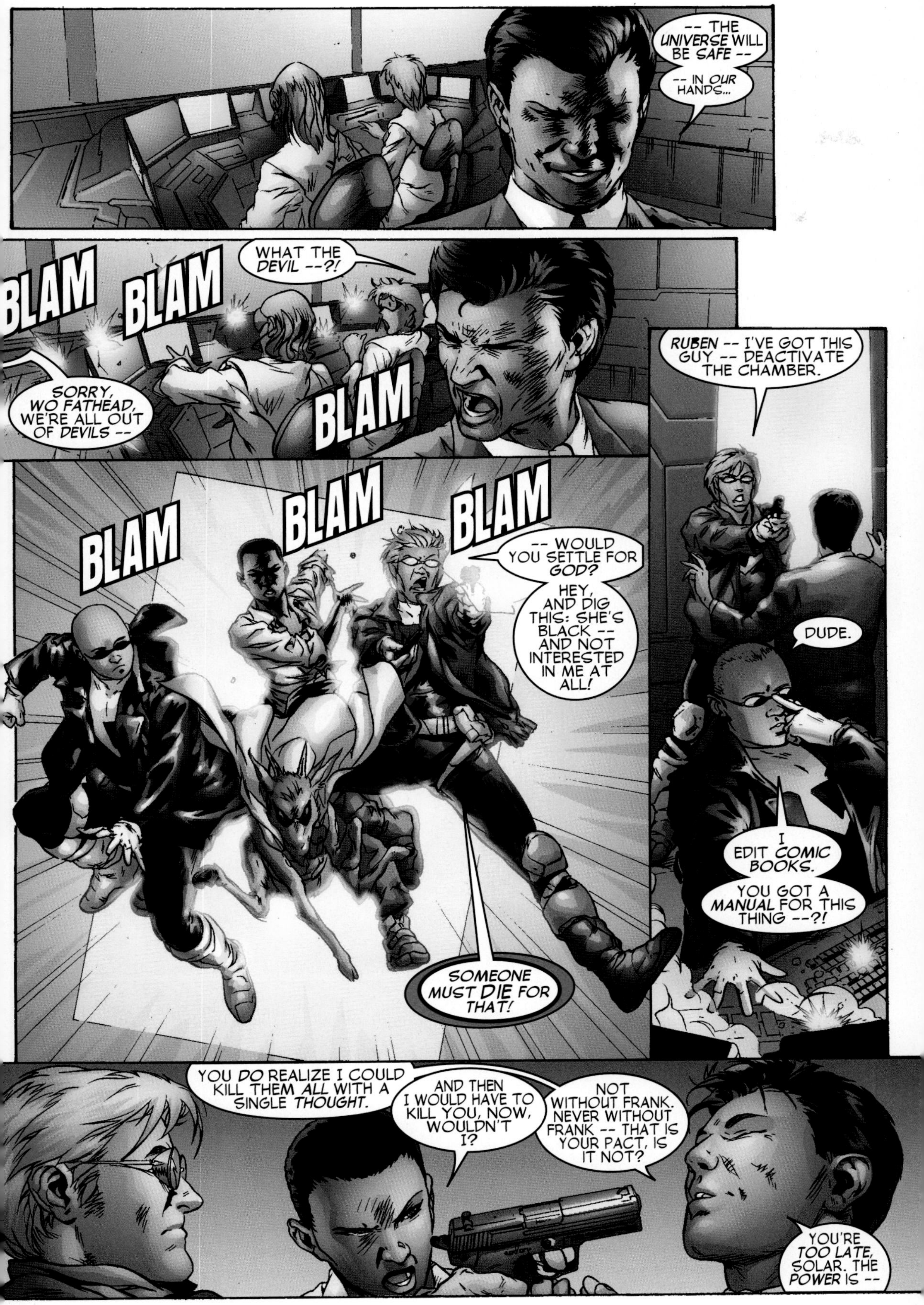

-- THE UNIVERSE WILL BE SAFE --
-- IN OUR HANDS...
BLAM
BLAM
WHAT THE DEVIL --?!
SORRY, WO FATHEAD, WE'RE ALL OUT OF DEVILS --
BLAM
RUBEN -- I'VE GOT THIS GUY -- DEACTIVATE THE CHAMBER.
BLAM
BLAM
BLAM
-- WOULD YOU SETTLE FOR GOD?
HEY, AND DIG THIS: SHE'S BLACK -- AND NOT INTERESTED IN ME AT ALL!
SOMEONE MUST DIE FOR THAT!
DUDE.
I EDIT COMIC BOOKS.
YOU GOT A MANUAL FOR THIS THING --?!
YOU DO REALIZE I COULD KILL THEM ALL WITH A SINGLE THOUGHT.
AND THEN I WOULD HAVE TO KILL YOU, NOW, WOULDN'T I?
NOT WITHOUT FRANK. NEVER WITHOUT FRANK -- THAT IS YOUR PACT, IS IT NOT?
YOU'RE TOO LATE, SOLAR. THE POWER IS --

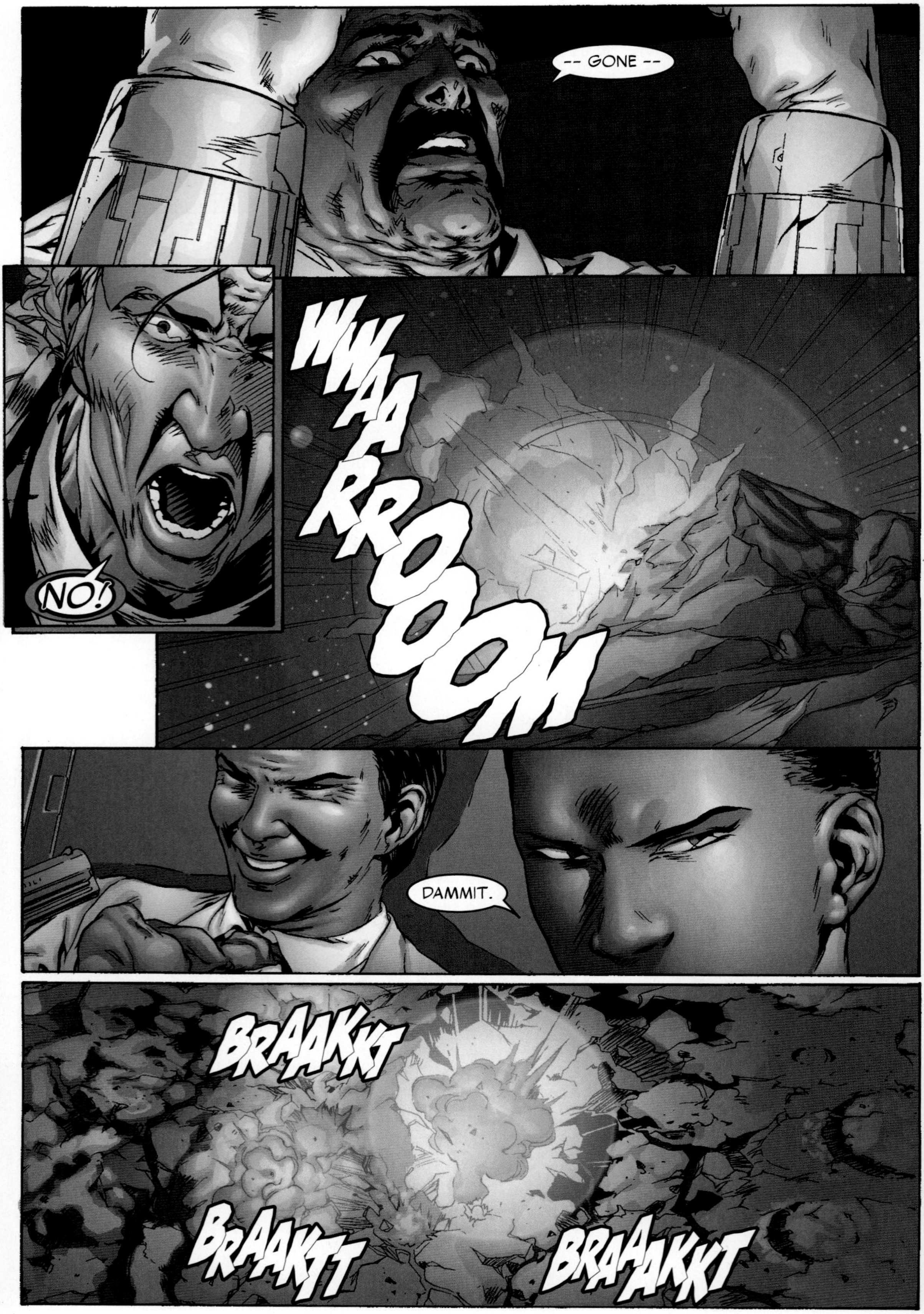
-- GONE --
NO!
WWAARRROOOOM
DAMMIT.
BRAAKKT
BRAAKTT
BRAAAKKKT

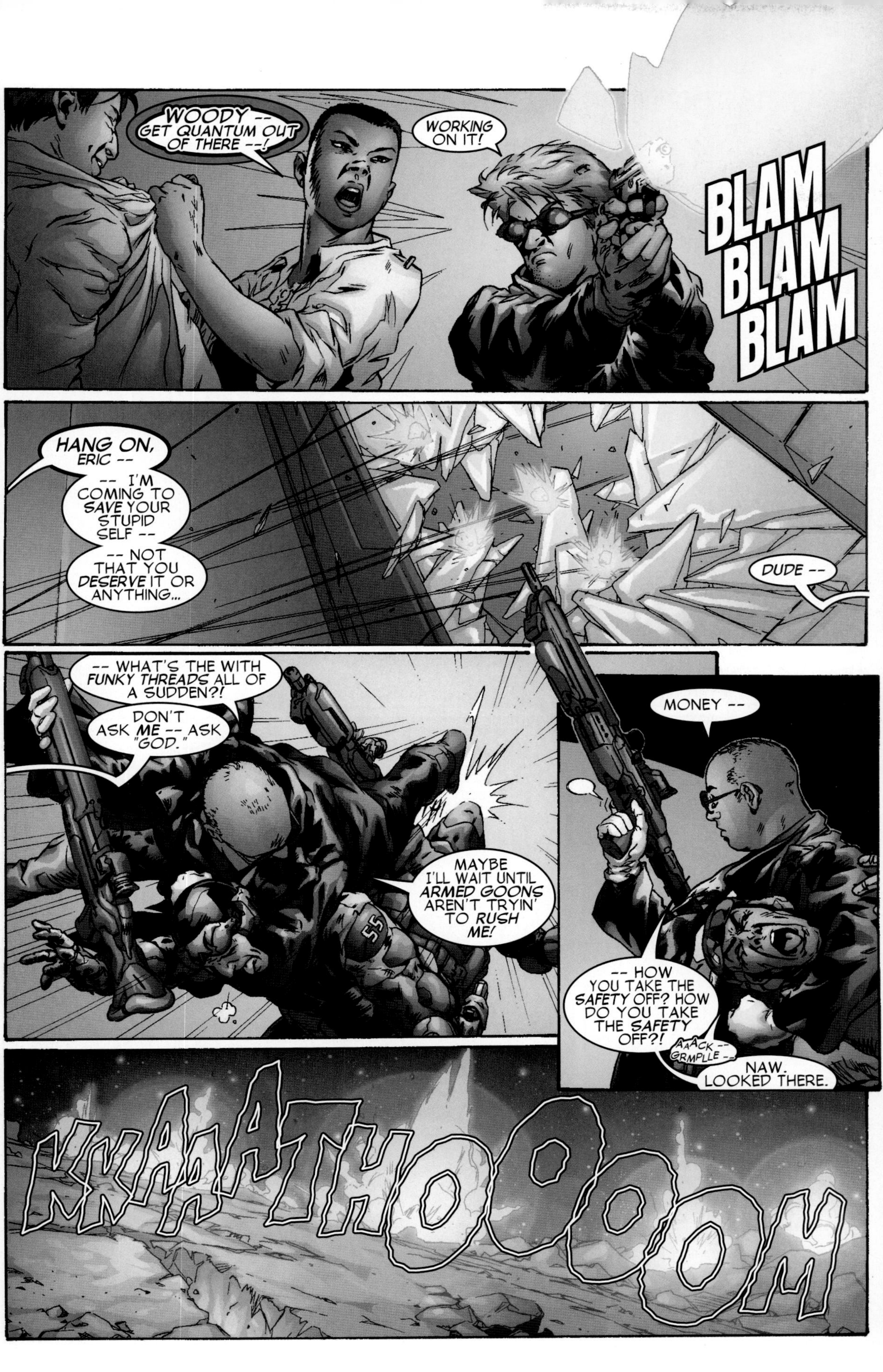
WOODY -- GET QUANTUM OUT OF THERE --!
WORKING ON IT!
BLAM BLAM BLAM
HANG ON, ERIC --
-- I'M COMING TO SAVE YOUR STUPID SELF --
-- NOT THAT YOU DESERVE IT OR ANYTHING...
DUDE --
-- WHAT'S THE WITH FUNKY THREADS ALL OF A SUDDEN?!
DON'T ASK ME -- ASK "GOD."
MAYBE I'LL WAIT UNTIL ARMED GOONS AREN'T TRYIN' TO RUSH ME!
MONEY --
-- HOW YOU TAKE THE SAFETY OFF? HOW DO YOU TAKE THE SAFETY OFF?!
AAACK -- GRMPLLE --
NAW. LOOKED THERE.
KKAAATHOOOOOM

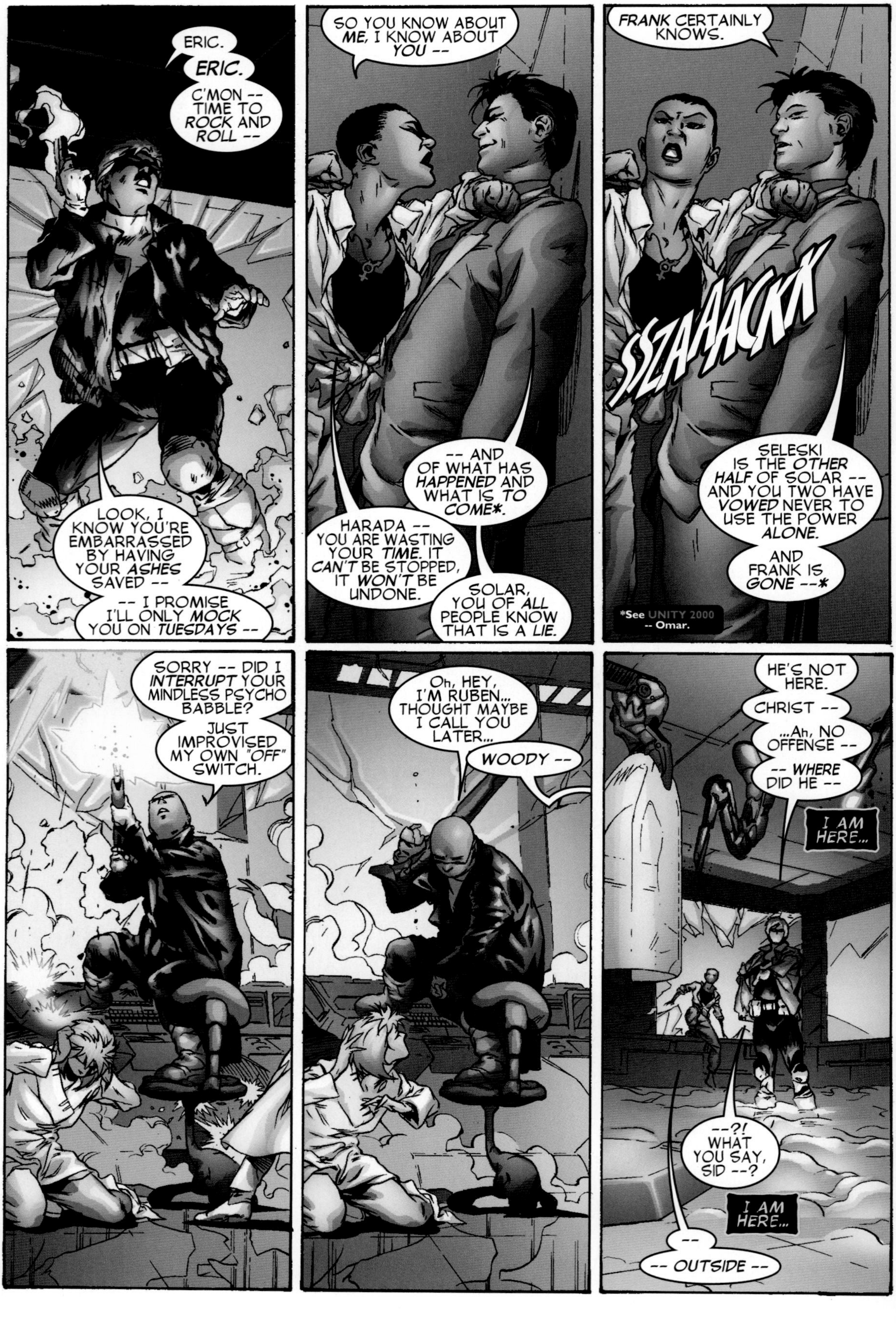
ERIC.
ERIC.
C'MON -- TIME TO ROCK AND ROLL --
LOOK, I KNOW YOU'RE EMBARRASSED BY HAVING YOUR ASHES SAVED --
-- I PROMISE I'LL ONLY MOCK YOU ON TUESDAYS --
SO YOU KNOW ABOUT ME, I KNOW ABOUT YOU --
-- AND OF WHAT HAS HAPPENED AND WHAT IS TO COME*.
HARADA -- YOU ARE WASTING YOUR TIME. IT CAN'T BE STOPPED, IT WON'T BE UNDONE.
SOLAR, YOU OF ALL PEOPLE KNOW THAT IS A LIE.
FRANK CERTAINLY KNOWS.
SSZAAACKK
SELESKI IS THE OTHER HALF OF SOLAR -- AND YOU TWO HAVE VOWED NEVER TO USE THE POWER ALONE.
AND FRANK IS GONE --*
*See UNITY 2000 -- Omar.
SORRY -- DID I INTERRUPT YOUR MINDLESS PSYCHO BABBLE?
JUST IMPROVISED MY OWN "OFF" SWITCH.
Oh, HEY, I'M RUBEN... THOUGHT MAYBE I CALL YOU LATER...
WOODY --
HE'S NOT HERE.
CHRIST --
...Ah, NO OFFENSE --
-- WHERE DID HE --
I AM HERE...
--?! WHAT YOU SAY, SID --?
I AM HERE...
--
-- OUTSIDE --

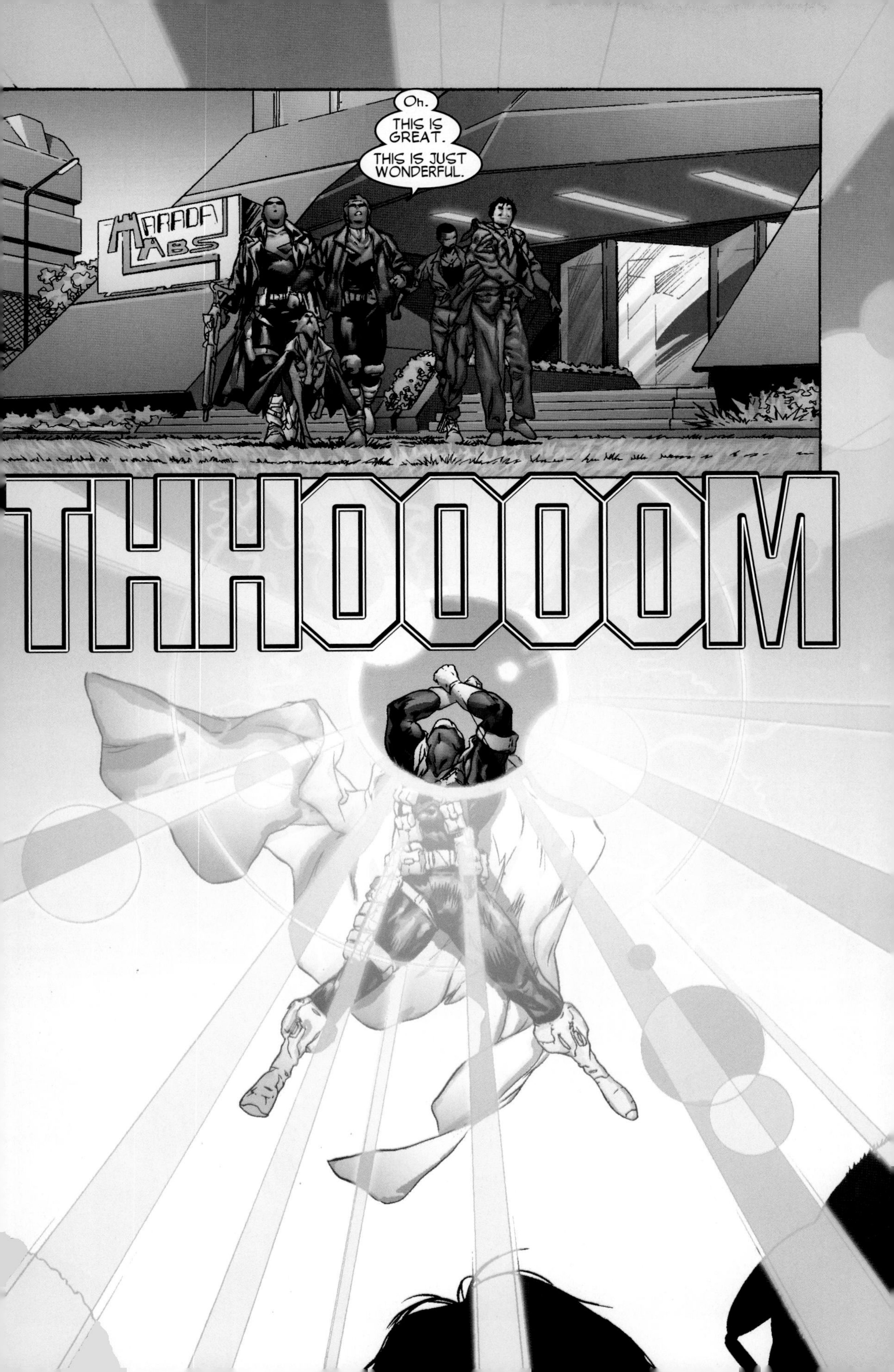

Oh.
THIS IS GREAT.
THIS IS JUST WONDERFUL.
THOOOOM

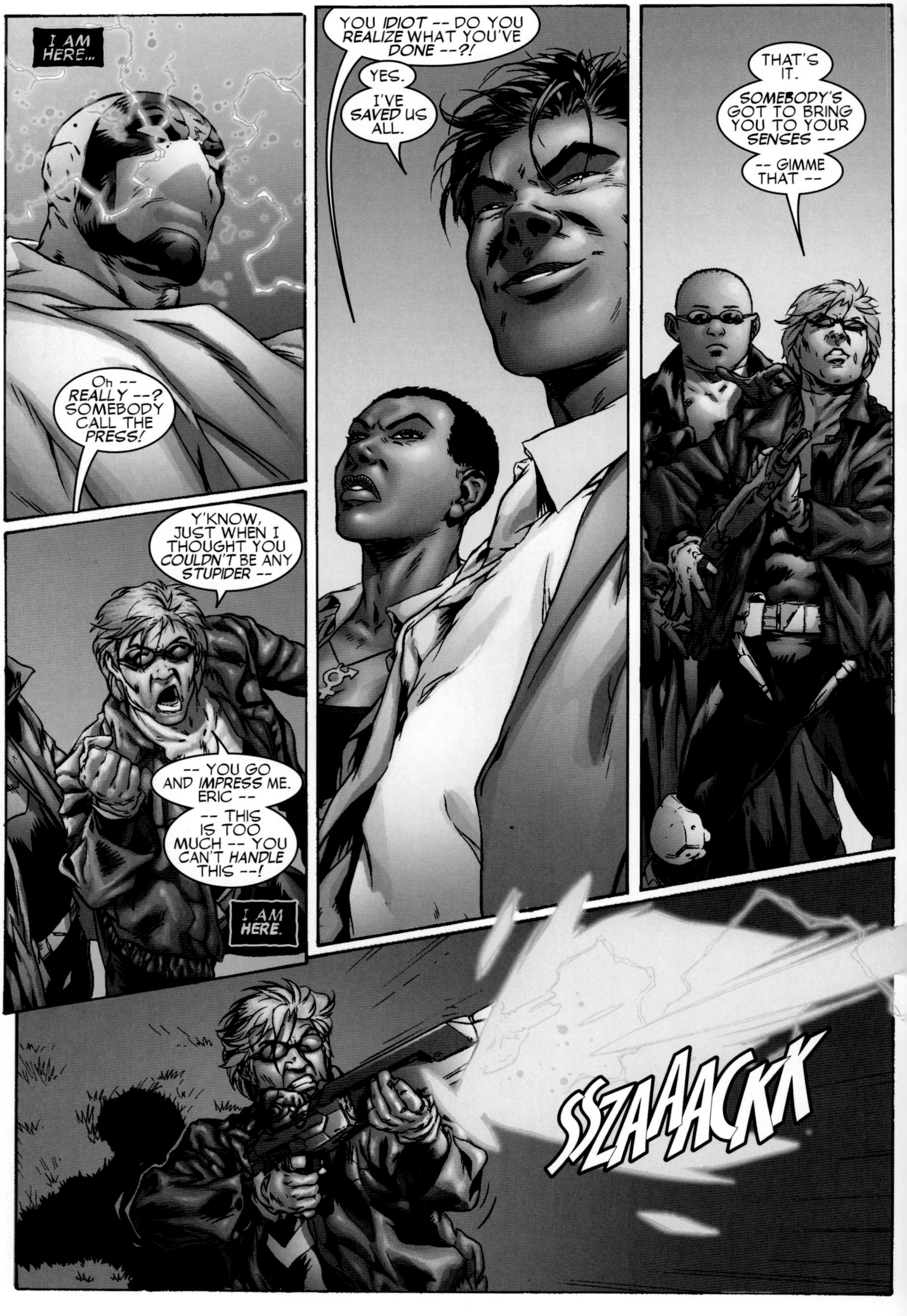
I AM HERE...
Oh -- REALLY --? SOMEBODY CALL THE PRESS!
YOU IDIOT -- DO YOU REALIZE WHAT YOU'VE DONE --?!
YES.
I'VE SAVED US ALL.
THAT'S IT.
SOMEBODY'S GOT TO BRING YOU TO YOUR SENSES --
-- GIMME THAT --
Y'KNOW, JUST WHEN I THOUGHT YOU COULDN'T BE ANY STUPIDER --
-- YOU GO AND IMPRESS ME. ERIC --
-- THIS IS TOO MUCH -- YOU CAN'T HANDLE THIS --!
I AM HERE.
SSZAAACKK

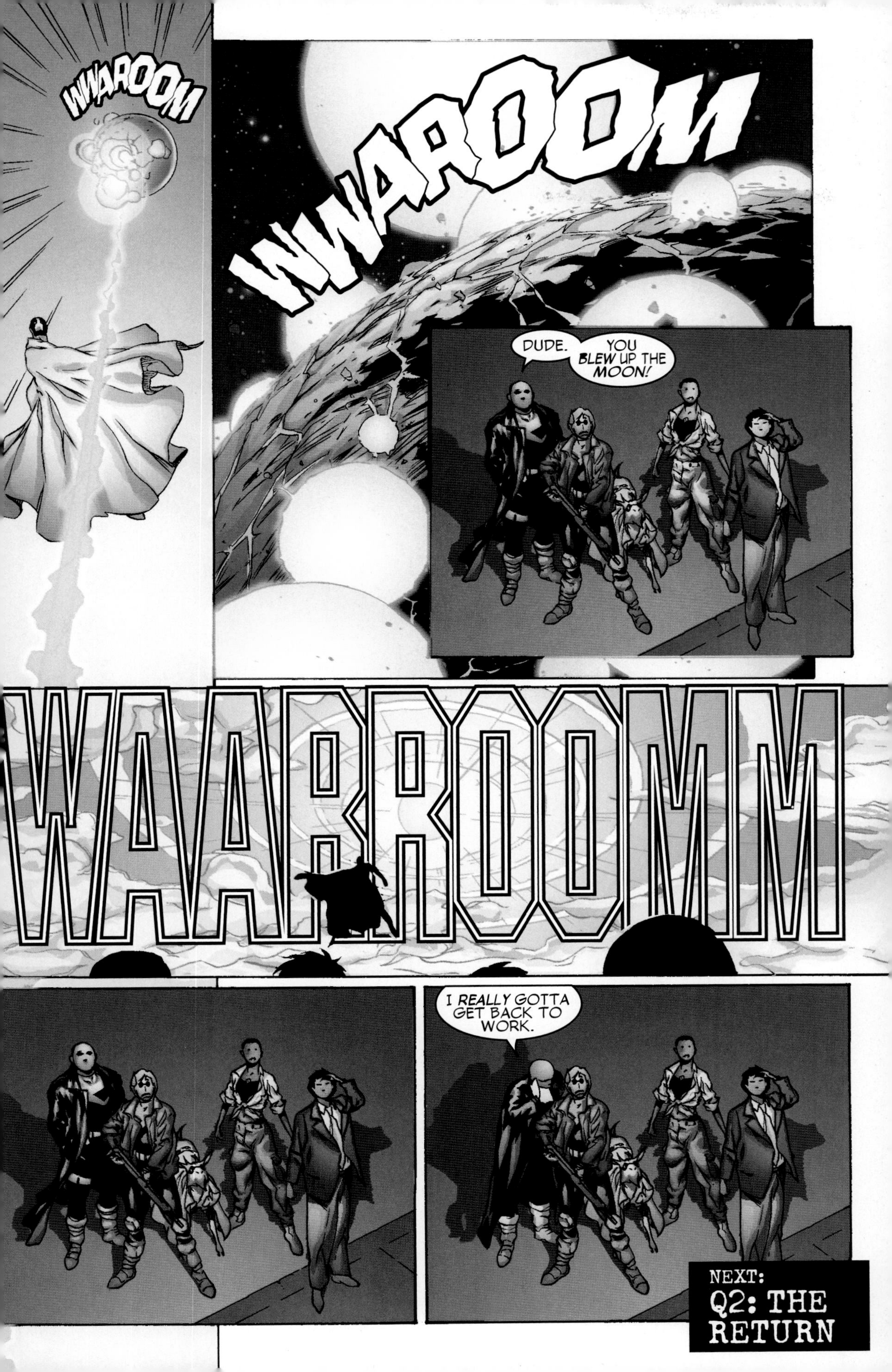
WWAROOM
WWAROOM
DUDE.
YOU BLEW UP THE MOON!
WAARROOMM
I REALLY GOTTA GET BACK TO WORK.
NEXT: Q2: THE RETURN

GALLERY

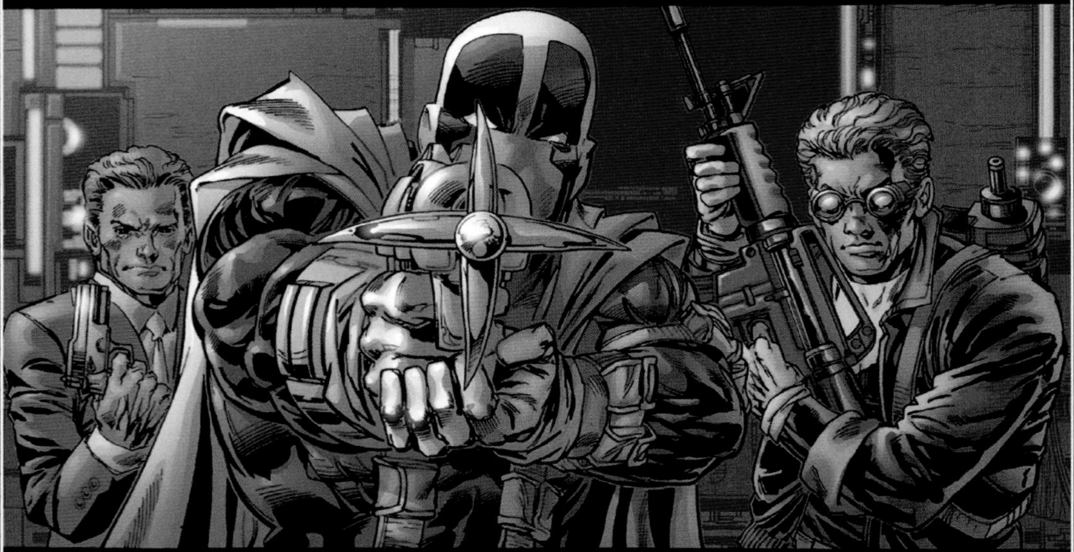

QUANTUM AND WOODY: MAGNUM FORCE
TRADE PAPERBACK COVER
Art by MD BRIGHT and GREG ADAMS
with DIGITAL BROOME

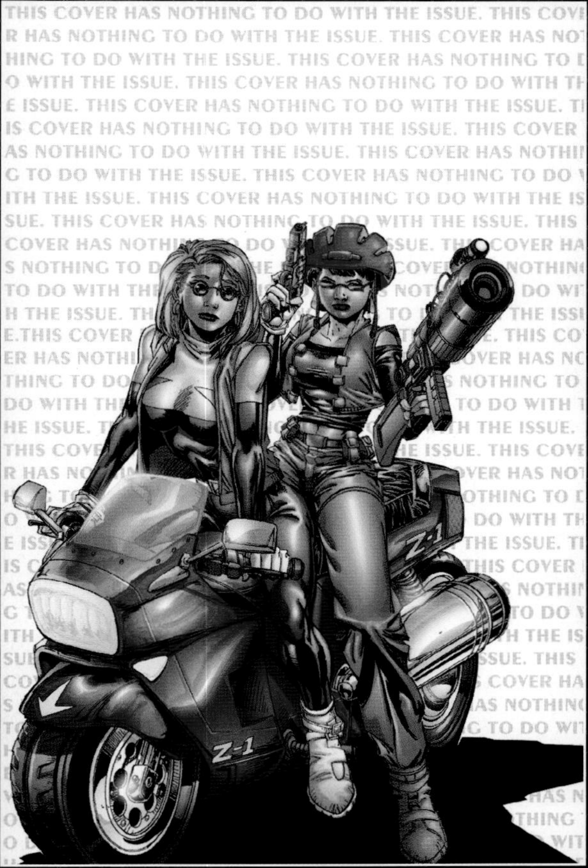
THIS COVER HAS NOTHING TO DO WITH THE ISSUE.
Z-1
Z-1

QUANTUM AND WOODY #22 (UNPUBLISHED) COVER
Art by MD BRIGHT and GREG ADAMS
with DIGITAL BROOME

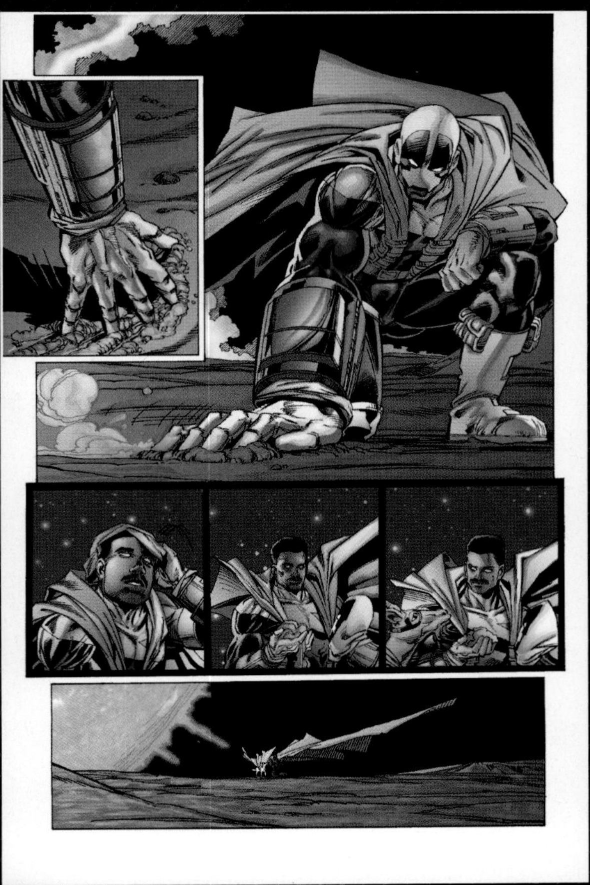

QUANTUM AND WOODY #22 (UNPUBLISHED) PAGE 4
By CHRISTOPHER PRIEST and MD BRIGHT
Inks by ROMEO TANGHAL
Color by DIGITAL BROOME

QUANTUM AND WOODY #22 (UNPUBLISHED) PAGES 2-3
By CHRISTOPHER PRIEST and MD BRIGHT
Inks by ROMEO TANGHAL
Color by DIGITAL BROOME

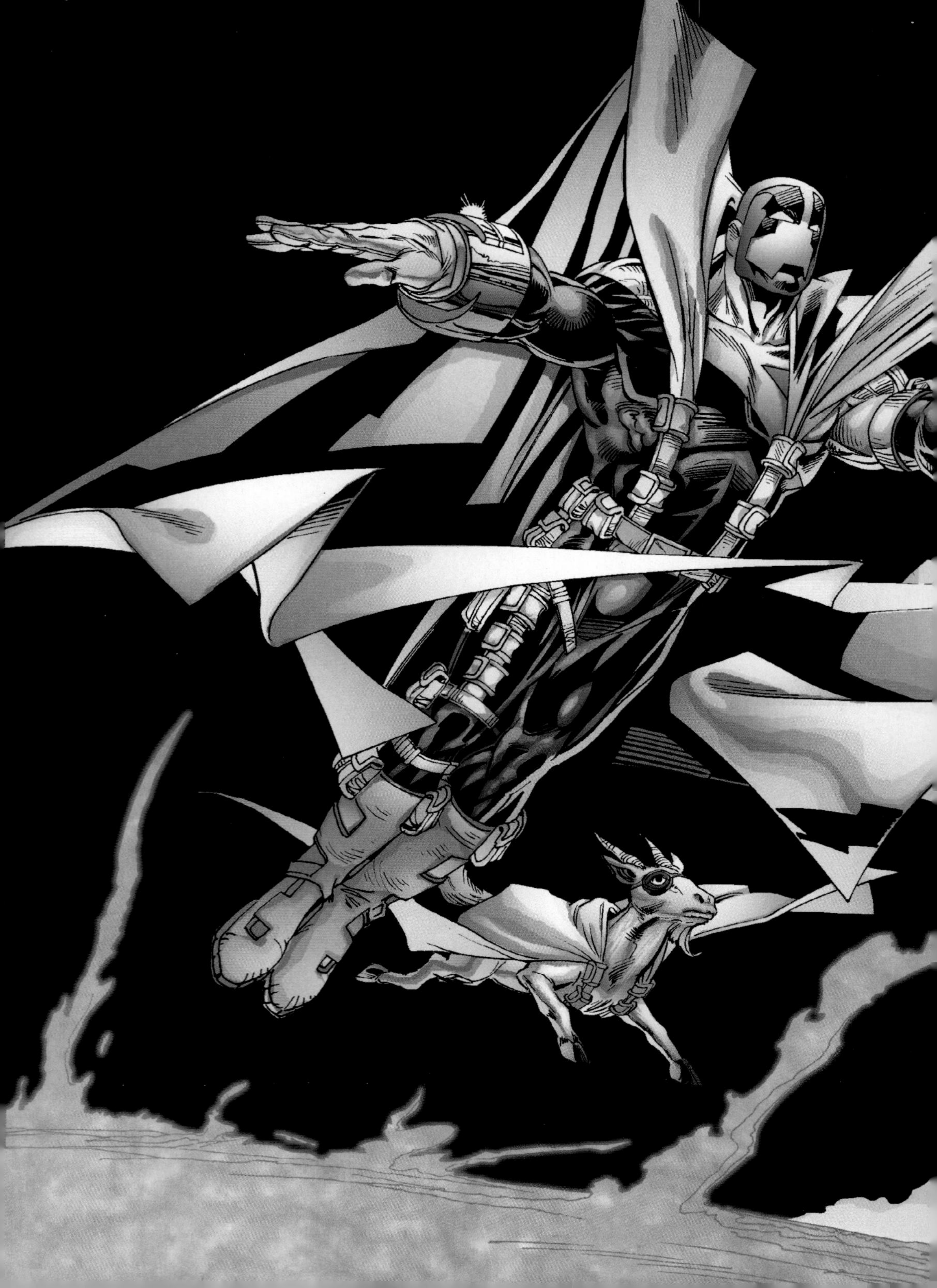

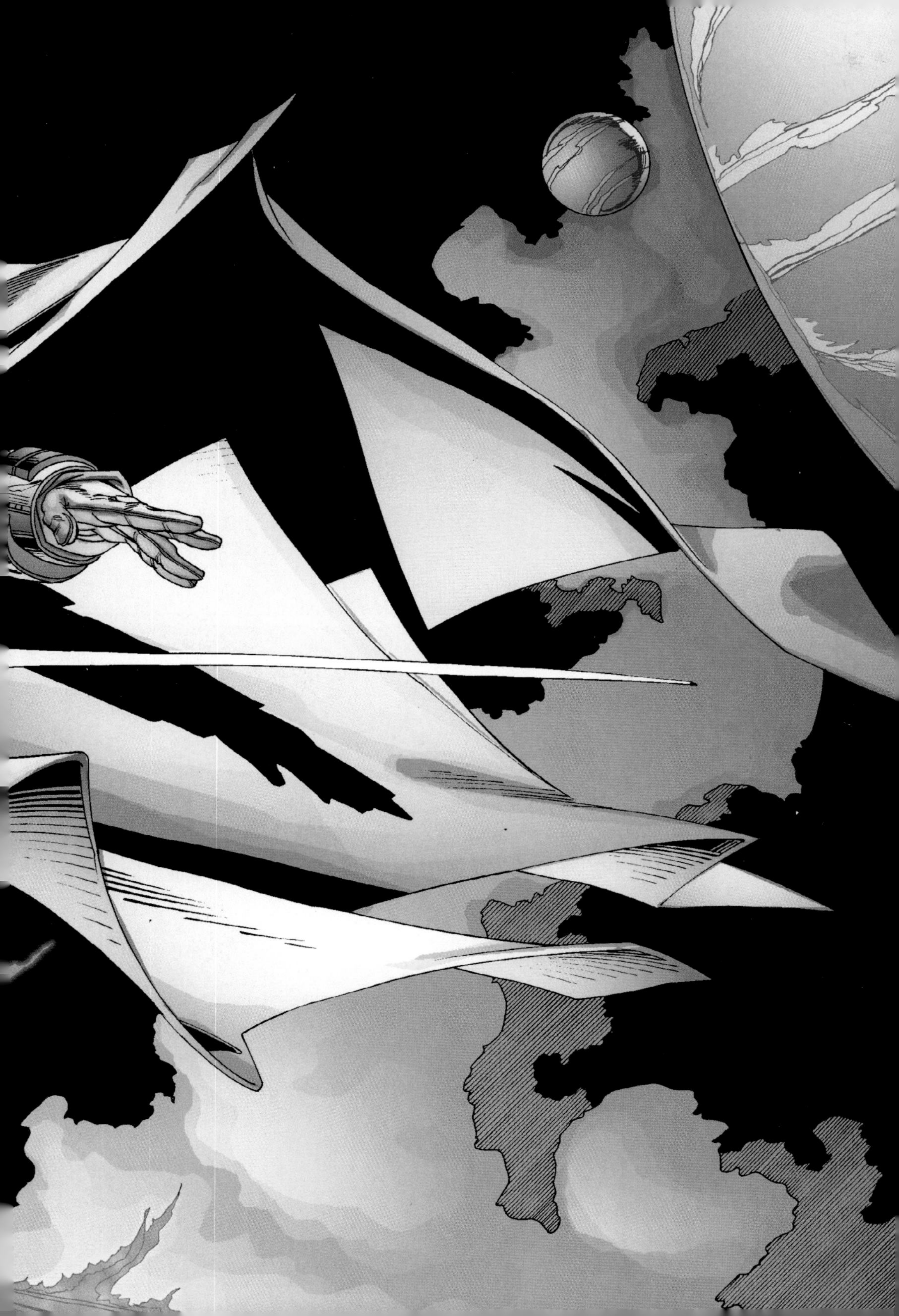

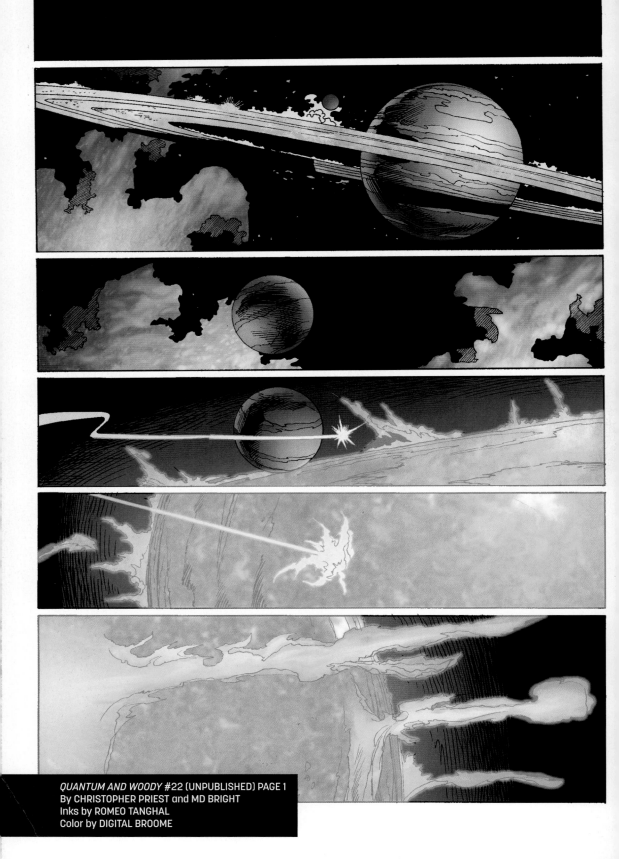

QUANTUM AND WOODY #22 (UNPUBLISHED) PAGE 1
By CHRISTOPHER PRIEST and MD BRIGHT
Inks by ROMEO TANGHAL
Color by DIGITAL BROOME

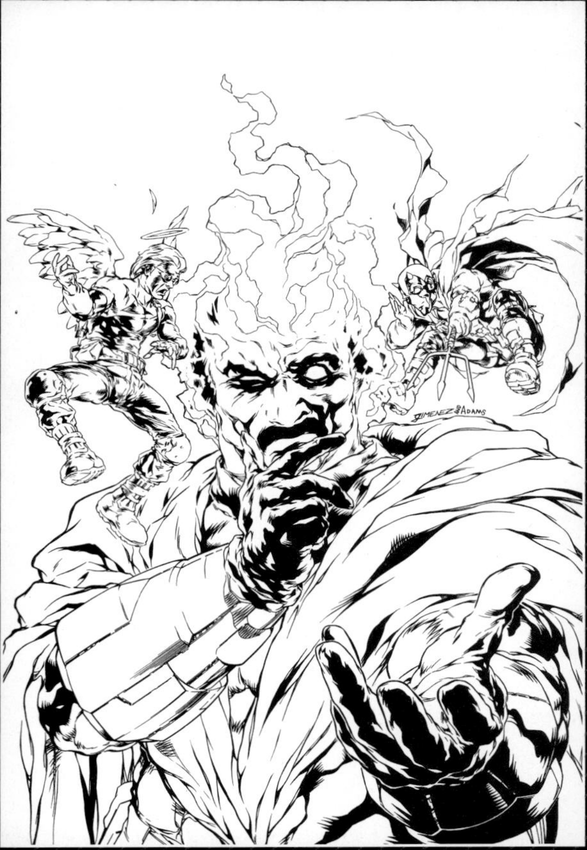
JIMENEZ ADAMS

QUANTUM AND WOODY #18 UNUSED COVER
Pencils by OSCAR JIMENEZ
Inks by GREG ADAMS

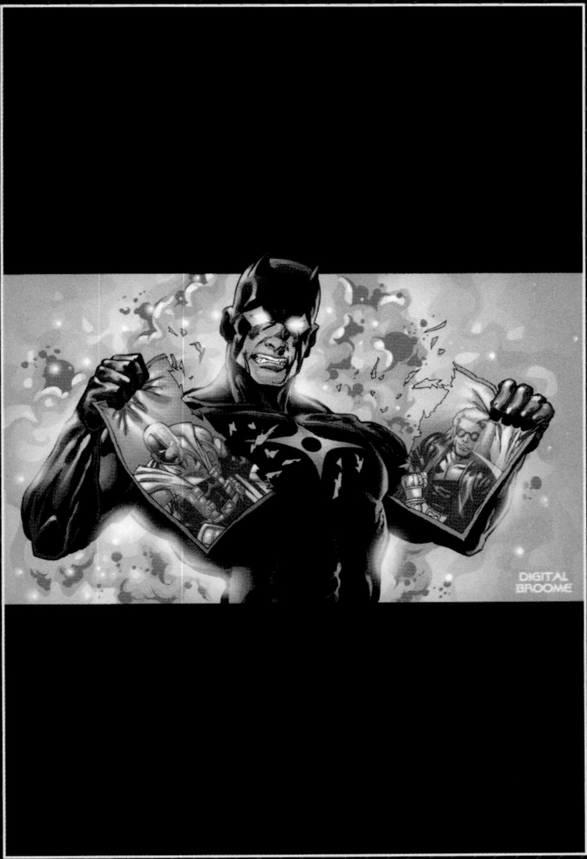
DIGITAL
BROOME

QUANTUM AND WOODY #33 COVER
(FROM NEXT-ISSUE BLURB IN #32)

Art by MD BRIGHT and GREG ADAMS
with DIGITAL BROOME

EXPLORE THE VALIANT UNIVERSE

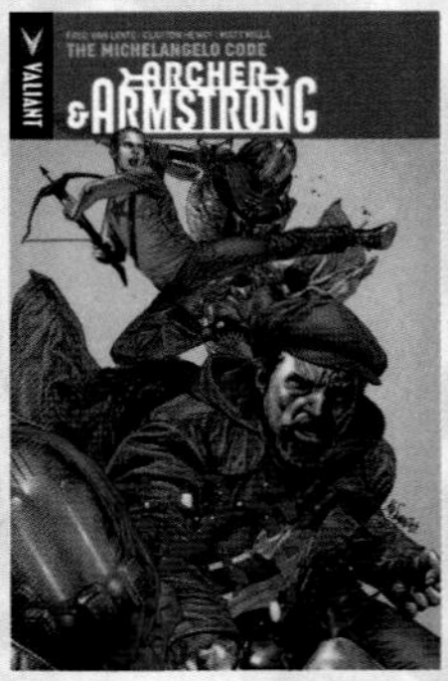
VALIANT
THE MICHELANGELO CODE
ARCHER & ARMSTRONG

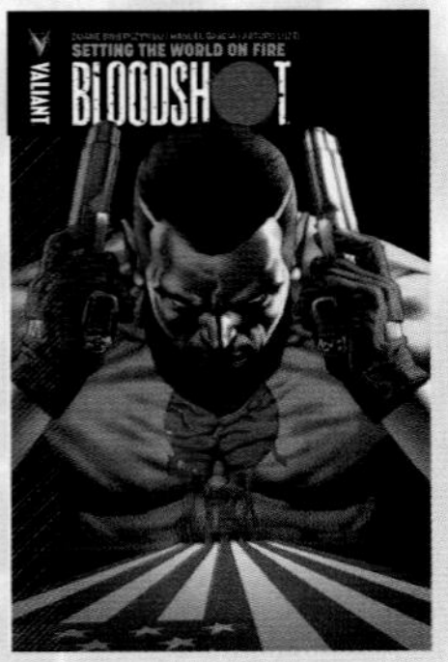
VALIANT
SETTING THE WORLD ON FIRE
BLOODSHOT

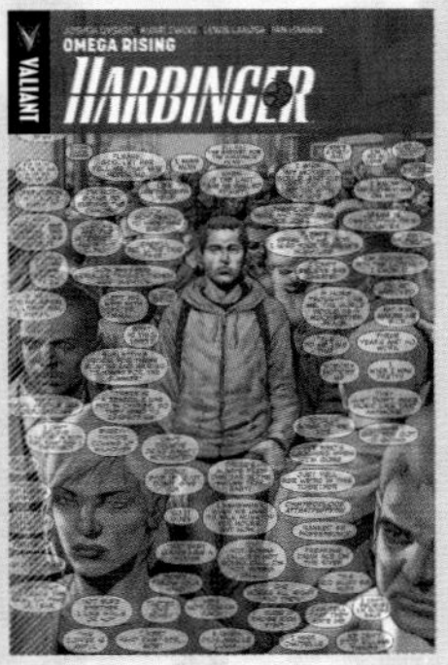
VALIANT
OMEGA RISING
HARBINGER

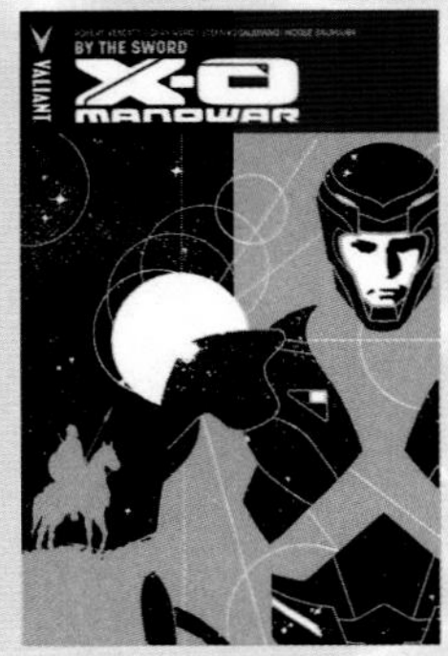
VALIANT
BY THE SWORD
X-O MANOWAR

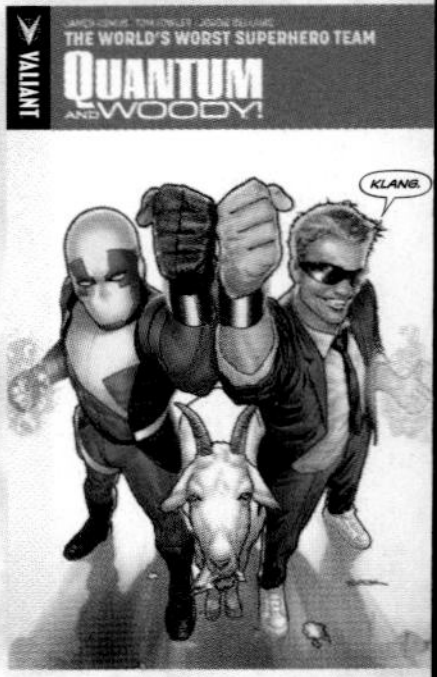
VALIANT
THE WORLD'S WORST SUPERHERO TEAM
QUANTUM AND WOODY!
KLANG.

ARCHER & ARMSTRONG

Volume 1: The Michelangelo Code
ISBN: 9780979640988

Volume 2: Wrath of the Eternal Warrior
ISBN: 9781939346049

Volume 3: Far Faraway
ISBN: 9781939346148

Volume 4: Sect Civil War
ISBN: 9781939346254

Volume 5: Mission: Improbable
ISBN: 9781939346353

Volume 6: American Wasteland
ISBN: 9781939346421

Volume 7: The One Percent and Other Tales
ISBN: 9781939346537

ARMOR HUNTERS

Armor Hunters
ISBN: 9781939346452

Armor Hunters: Bloodshot
ISBN: 9781939346469

Armor Hunters: Harbinger
ISBN: 9781939346506

Unity Vol. 3: Armor Hunters
ISBN: 9781939346445

X-O Manowar Vol. 7: Armor Hunters
ISBN: 9781939346476

BLOODSHOT

Volume 1: Setting the World on Fire
ISBN: 9780979640964

Volume 2: The Rise and the Fall
ISBN: 9781939346032

Volume 3: Harbinger Wars
ISBN: 9781939346124

Volume 4: H.A.R.D. Corps
ISBN: 9781939346193

Volume 5: Get Some!
ISBN: 9781939346315

Volume 6: The Glitch and Other Tales
ISBN: 9781939346711

BLOODSHOT REBORN

Volume 1: Colorado
ISBN: 9781939346674

DEAD DROP

Dead Drop
ISBN: 9781939346858

THE DEATH-DEFYING DOCTOR MIRAGE

The Death-Defying Dr. Mirage
ISBN: 9781939346490

THE DELINQUENTS

The Delinquents
ISBN: 9781939346513

DIVINITY

DIVINITY
ISBN: 9781939346766

ETERNAL WARRIOR

Volume 1: Sword of the Wild
ISBN: 9781939346209

Volume 2: Eternal Emperor
ISBN: 9781939346292

Volume 3: Days of Steel
ISBN: 9781939346742

HARBINGER

Volume 1: Omega Rising
ISBN: 9780979640957

Volume 2: Renegades
ISBN: 9781939346025

Volume 3: Harbinger Wars
ISBN: 9781939346117

Volume 4: Perfect Day
ISBN: 9781939346155

Volume 5: Death of a Renegade
ISBN: 9781939346339

Volume 6: Omegas
ISBN: 9781939346384

HARBINGER WARS

Harbinger Wars
ISBN: 9781939346094

Bloodshot Vol. 3: Harbinger Wars
ISBN: 9781939346124

Harbinger Vol. 3: Harbinger Wars
ISBN: 9781939346117

EXPLORE THE VALIANT UNIVERSE

IMPERIUM

Volume 1: Collecting Monsters
ISBN: 9781939346759

NINJAK

Volume 1: Weaponeer
ISBN: 9781939346667

QUANTUM AND WOODY!

Volume 1: The World's Worst Superhero Team
ISBN: 9781939346186

Volume 2: In Security
ISBN: 9781939346230

Volume 3: Crooked Pasts, Present Tense
ISBN: 9781939346391

Volume 4: Quantum and Woody Must Die!
ISBN: 9781939346629

Volume 1: Klang
ISBN: 9781939346780

Volume 2: Switch
ISBN: 9781939346803

Volume 3: And So...
ISBN: 9781939346865

RAI

Volume 1: Welcome to New Japan
ISBN: 9781939346414

Volume 2: Battle for New Japan
ISBN: 9781939346612

Volume 3: The Orphan
ISBN: 9781939346841

SHADOWMAN

Volume 1: Birth Rites
ISBN: 9781939346001

Volume 2: Darque Reckoning
ISBN: 9781939346056

Volume 3: Deadside Blues
ISBN: 9781939346162

Volume 4: Fear, Blood, And Shadows
ISBN: 9781939346278

Volume 5: End Times
ISBN: 9781939346377

Ivar, Timewalker

Volume 1: Making History
ISBN: 9781939346636

UNITY

Volume 1: To Kill a King
ISBN: 9781939346261

Volume 2: Trapped by Webnet
ISBN: 9781939346346

Volume 3: Armor Hunters
ISBN: 9781939346445

UNITY (Continued)

Volume 4: The United
ISBN: 9781939346544

Volume 5: Homefront
ISBN: 9781939346797

THE VALIANT

The Valiant
ISBN: 9781939346605

VALIANT ZEROES AND ORIGINS

Valiant: Zeroes and Origins
ISBN: 9781939346582

X-O MANOWAR

Volume 1: By the Sword
ISBN: 9780979640940

Volume 2: Enter Ninjak
ISBN: 9780979640995

Volume 3: Planet Death
ISBN: 9781939346087

Volume 4: Homecoming
ISBN: 9781939346179

Volume 5: At War With Unity
ISBN: 9781939346247

Volume 6: Prelude to Armor Hunters
ISBN: 9781939346407

Volume 7: Armor Hunters
ISBN: 9781939346476

Volume 8: Enter: Armorines
ISBN: 9781939346551

Volume 9: Dead Hand
ISBN: 9781939346650

EXPLORE THE VALIANT UNIVERSE

VALIANT
HARBINGER
DELUXE EDITION 2

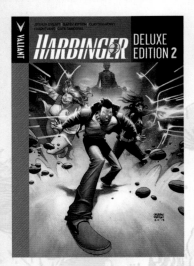

OMNIBUSES

Archer & Armstrong: The Complete Classic Omnibus
ISBN: 9781939346872
Collecting ARCHER & ARMSTRONG (1992) #0-26, ETERNAL WARRIOR (1992) #25 along with ARCHER & ARMSTRONG: THE FORMATION OF THE SECT.

Quantum and Woody: The Complete Classic Omnibus
ISBN: 9781939346360
Collecting QUANTUM AND WOODY (1997) #0, 1-21 and #32, THE GOAT: H.A.E.D.U.S. #1, and X-O MANOWAR (1996) #16

X-O Manowar Classic Omnibus Vol. 1
ISBN: 9781939346308
Collecting X-O MANOWAR (1992) #0-30, ARMORINES #0, X-O DATABASE #1, as well as material from SECRETS OF THE VALIANT UNIVERSE #1

DELUXE EDITIONS

Archer & Armstrong Deluxe Edition Book 1
ISBN: 9781939346223
Collecting ARCHER & ARMSTRONG #0-13

VALIANT
ARMOR HUNTERS
DELUXE EDITION

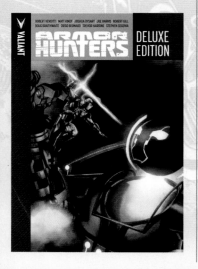

Armor Hunters Deluxe Edition
ISBN: 9781939346728
Collecting ARMOR HUNTERS #1-4, ARMOR HUNTERS: AFTERMATH #1, ARMOR HUNTERS: BLOODSHOT #1-3, ARMOR HUNTERS: HARBINGER #1-3, UNITY #8-11 and X-O MANOWAR #23-29

Bloodshot Deluxe Edition Book 1
ISBN: 9781939346216
Collecting BLOODSHOT #1-13

Harbinger Deluxe Edition Book 1
ISBN: 9781939346131
Collecting HARBINGER #0-14

Harbinger Deluxe Edition Book 2
ISBN: 9781939346773
Collecting HARBINGER #15-25, HARBINGER: OMEGAS #1-3, and HARBINGER: BLEEDING MONK #0

Harbinger Wars Deluxe Edition
ISBN: 9781939346322
Collecting HARBINGER WARS #1-4, HARBINGER #11-14, and BLOODSHOT #10-13

Quantum and Woody Deluxe Edition Book 1
ISBN: 9781939346681
Collecting QUANTUM AND WOODY #1-12 and QUANTUM AND WOODY: THE GOAT #0

Quantum and Woody by Priest & Bright Vol. 4: The Return
ISBN: 9781939346568
Collecting Q2: THE RETURN OF QUANTUM AND WOODY #1-5

Shadowman Deluxe Edition Book 1
ISBN: 9781939346438
Collecting SHADOWMAN #0-10

Unity Deluxe Edition Book 1
ISBN: 9781939346575
Collecting UNITY #0-14

X-O Manowar Deluxe Edition Book 1
ISBN: 9781939346100
Collecting X-O MANOWAR #1-14

X-O Manowar Deluxe Edition Book 2
ISBN: 9781939346520
Collecting X-O MANOWAR #15-22, and UNITY #1-4

VALIANT
JIM SHOOTER | DAVID LAPHAM
CHILDREN OF THE EIGHTH DAY
HARBINGER
VALIANT MASTERS

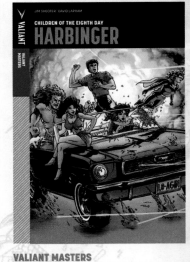

VALIANT MASTERS

Bloodshot Vol. 1 - Blood of the Machine
ISBN: 9780979640933

H.A.R.D. Corps Vol. 1 - Search and Destroy
ISBN: 9781939346285

Harbinger Vol. 1 - Children of the Eighth Day
ISBN: 9781939346483

Ninjak Vol. 1 - Black Water
ISBN: 9780979640971

Rai Vol. 1 - From Honor to Strength
ISBN: 9781939346070

Shadowman Vol. 1 - Spirits Within
ISBN: 9781939346018

VALIANT
KEVIN VANHOOK | DON PERLIN
BLOOD OF THE MACHINE
BLOODSHOT
VALIANT MASTERS

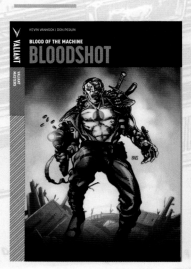

VALIANT

QUANTUM AND WOODY

BY PRIEST & BRIGHT

VOLUME FOUR: THE RETURN

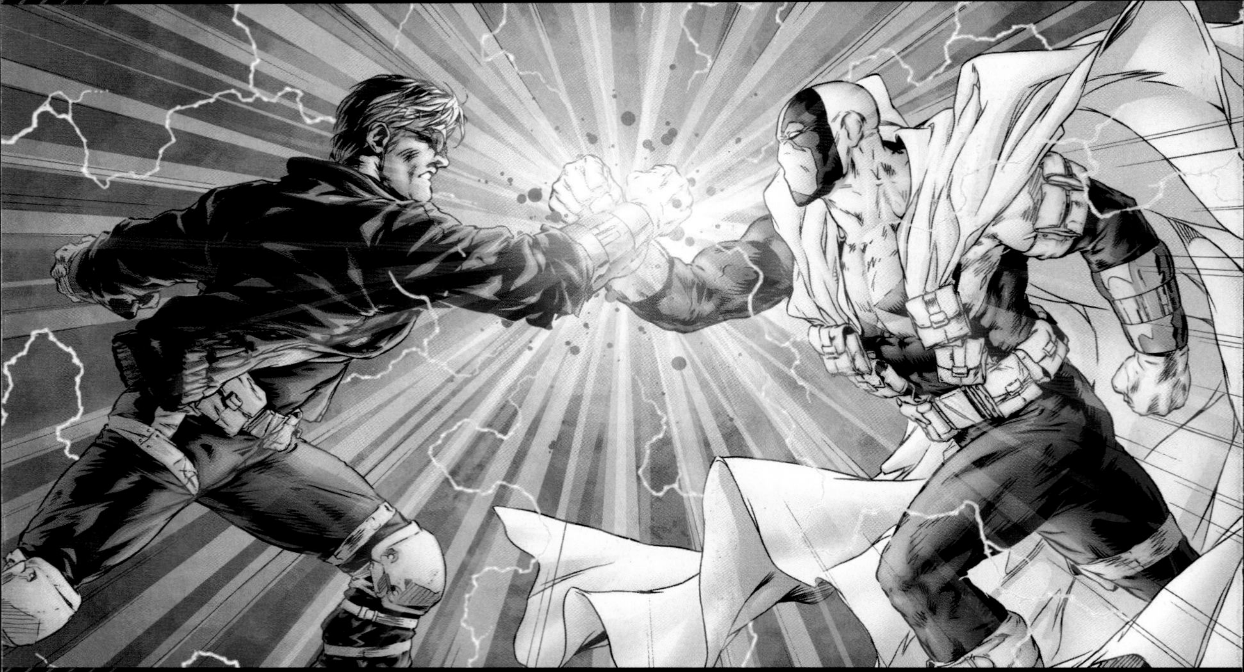

THE MOST DEMANDED RETURN IN COMICS IS FINALLY HERE! THE ORIGINAL QUANTUM AND WOODY ARE BACK! LEGENDARY CREATORS CHRISTOPHER PRIEST (*BLACK PANTHER*) AND MD BRIGHT (*IRON MAN*) RETURN TO ONE OF THE MOST ACCLAIMED SERIES OF THE MODERN ERA!

Whatever happened to the world's worst superhero team? Twenty years past their prime, the unlikely crime-fighting duo known as Quantum and Woody (not a couple) have long since parted ways...until a middle-aged Quantum suddenly reappears with a brand-new teenage partner. Now Woody is out to break up the all-new, all-different Quantum and Woody and put an end to Quantum's recklessness...just as Quantum takes on a life-or-death personal mission for national security. Can these former friends set aside their differences...and their age...and their numerous health difficulties...to join forces one last time without driving each other crazy?

Collecting Q2: THE RETURN OF QUANTUM AND WOODY #1-5 in trade paperback as a perfect companion to the QUANTUM AND WOODY BY PRIEST & BRIGHT collections!

TRADE PAPERBACK
978-1-68215-109-9

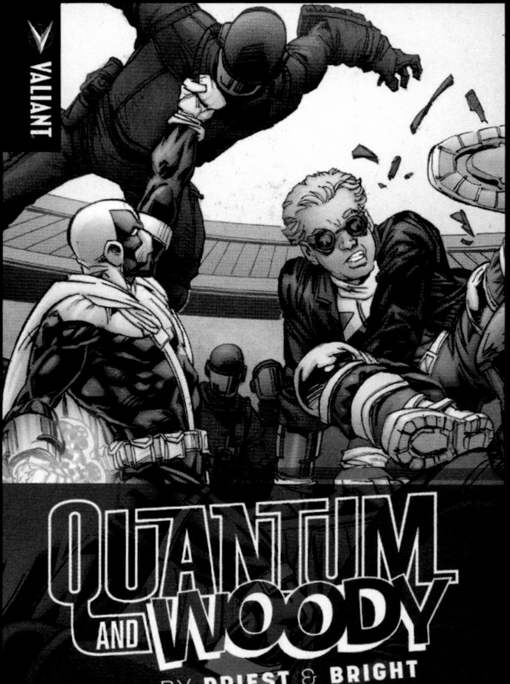
VALIANT
QUANTUM AND WOODY
BY PRIEST & BRIGHT
VOL 4: THE RETURN